Economics, Politics and Budgets:
The Political Economy of Fiscal Consolidations in Europe

Economics, Politics and Budgets

The Political Economy of Fiscal Consolidations in Europe

Carlos Mulas-Granados

palgrave
macmillan

Softcover reprint of the hardcover 1st edition 2006

First published 2006 by
PALGRAVE MACMILLAN
Houndmills, Basingstoke, Hampshire RG21 6XS and
175 Fifth Avenue, New York, N.Y. 10010
Companies and representatives throughout the world.

PALGRAVE MACMILLAN is the global academic imprint of the Palgrave Macmillan division of St. Martin's Press, LLC and of Palgrave Macmillan Ltd. Macmillan® is a registered trademark in the United States, United Kingdom and other countries. Palgrave is a registered trademark in the European Union and other countries.

ISBN 978-1-349-54783-8 ISBN 978-0-230-50163-8 (eBook)
DOI 10.1007/978-0-230-50163-8

A catalogue record for this book is available from the British Library.

Library of Congress Cataloging-in-Publication Data
Mulas-Granados, Carlos.
Economics, politics and budgets : the political economy of fiscal consolidations in Europe / by Carlos Mulas-Granados.
p. cm.
Includes bibliographical references and index.
ISBN 978-1-4039-9942-9 (cloth)
1. Europe – Economic conditions – 21st century. 2. Europe – Economic policy. 3. Fiscal policy – Europe. I. Title.
HC240.M757 2005
336.3'094'09051—dc22 2005049571

10 9 8 7 6 5 4 3 2 1
15 14 13 12 11 10 09 08 07 06

Transferred to Digital Printing in 2014

Contents

List of Tables

List of Figures

List of Abbreviations

DG ECFIN	Directorate General for Economic and Financial Affairs
EC	European Commission
EMU	European Monetary Union
EU	European Union
EU-11	Group of 11 EU member states adopting the euro at Stage 3 of EMU in 1999
EU-15	Group of 15 EU member states before accession of 10 new member states in 2004
FEDEA	Fundación de Estudios de Economía Aplicada
IMF	International Monetary Fund
PCABB	Primary Cyclically Adjusted Budget Balance
OECD	Organisation for Economic Co-operation and Development
SGP	Stability and Growth Pact

Acknowledgements

In the limited space of this preface, it is very difficult to express all my gratitude to the academic institutions, colleagues, friends and family that have helped me in many different ways to finish this book. Nevertheless, there are some who deserve here a special mention for their crucial role in all this process.

First of all, I have to thank the five sponsors that have financed different parts of the required research for this book over these years. In Spain, the Juan March Foundation, La Caixa Foundation and the Caja Madrid Foundation deserve all my gratitude. The Social Science Research Council in the United States and the Cambridge European Trust in the United Kingdom also provided me with crucial financial assistance in the final stages of this work.

Intellectual motivation, specialized help and encouraging critiques are as important as financial assistance for the success of any research project. This is especially true in this case, since this book has benefited from the help, comments, suggestions and criticisms of leading scholars and professionals from around the world. In this respect, I owe much to Carles Boix, J.Mª Maravall, J.R. Montero, Magdalena Nebreda and Andrew Richards for their help during my period at the Center for Advanced Studies in the Social Sciences of the Juan March Institute; Michael Gilligan, Robert Mundell, Roberto Perotti, Adam Przeworski, Joseph Stiglitz and Kenneth Waltz for their help during my period at Columbia University; Marco Buti, Elena Flores, Carlos Martínez-Mongay, Luis Planas and Pedro Solbes, for their help during my period at the European Commission; Emanuele Baldacci, Benedict Clements and Sanjeev Gupta, Teresa Ter-Minassian and Erwin Trongson for their help during my period at the International Monetary Fund; Javier Casares Marco Celantani, J.J. Dolado, J.M. González-Páramo, J.A. Herce, A. L. Lopez-Roa, Carmela Martín, Rafael Muro, Jesús Ruíz-Huerta and Juan Urrutia for their help during my periods at Carlos III and at Complutense Universities; and Toke Aidt, Gernot Doppelhoffer, Sean Holly and, Melvyn Weeks for their help during my period at the University of Cambridge.

There are other colleagues and friends who have helped me with their ideas, their comments, their example, their advice or their friendship throughout these years. For differing reasons this has been the case with Alberto Alesina, Joaquín Almunia, Irene Arias, Úrsula Castro, J.M. Eguiagaray, Anthony Giddens, Enrique Guerrero, Stathis Kalyvas, Merit Janow Peter Katzenstein, Pablo Lledó, Reyes Maroto, Wolfgang Merkel, Ignacio Sánchez-Cuenca, Andre Sopir, Alex Segura-Ubiergo, Rolf Strauch, Ignacio Torreblanca and Fernando Vallespín. A special mention should also go to Miguel Sebastian and the members of the Spanish Prime Minister's Economic Bureau.

In the process of shaping the final version of the manuscript into the present book, the work by Keith Povey and the flexibility of my editor at Palgrave, Katie Button, also deserve my gratitude.

My last word goes to those closest to me. In addition to all the guidance, help and support that I have received along these years from the persons and institutions mentioned above, it is fair to recognize that the strength, the self-confidence and the intellectual ambition that one needs to confront the daunting task of writing a book, always find their roots in the very close circle formed by the family. For their constant support, and the safety net of love and comprehension that they have always represented for me, the highest of my love and gratitude goes to Carlos, Isabel and Jaime. For the constant demonstration of the power of will, the greatness of wisdom, the courage of freedom, and above all for her unconditional love, this book is dedicated to my wife Irene.

CARLOS MULAS-GRANADOS

1
Introduction

> 'Provided that the Maastricht criteria are kept to, there remains very little leeway for single nations to "go it alone" in their fiscal policy.'
>
> Rees, 2000: 167

Since the early 1990s, it has become usual to affirm that economic policy in western capitalist democracies is so constrained by external factors that domestic economic and political forces no longer play a role in the process of economic policy formulation.

In a globalizing world, where capital moves freely in international markets looking for the best rates of return, and where trade liberalization advances through different regional and international agreements, sound monetary and fiscal policies to increase competitiveness and attract investors are a 'must', and this makes 'go-it-alone' approaches to economic policy-making difficult, if not impossible.

These constraints are even more significant for those advanced economies that joined the European Monetary Union (EMU), where monetary policy is already in the hands of the European Central Bank, and fiscal policy is constrained by the Maastricht convergence criteria and the Stability and Growth Pact.

Nevertheless, this study argues that even within this very restrictive context, national governments have still found ways to formulate differentiated fiscal policies during this period. In spite of this very constrained framework, the formulation of crucial economic policies such as fiscal policy is still heavily influenced by domestic economic, institutional and political factors. It is undeniable that, by the end of the 1990s, there was a generalized convergence of budget balances across Europe. The fiscal consolidation[1] effort required to pass the 'Maastricht exam' was such that the average budget deficit for the whole European Union was reduced by five percentage points (from 6 per cent to 1 per cent of European GDP) between 1993 and 1999, while the debt-to-GDP ratio was reduced from a maximum level of 72 per cent in 1996 to 64 per cent in 2000. Some countries made tremendous improvements in order to qualify for the third phase of EMU. For example, in only four years – from 1993 to 1997 – Sweden reduced its public deficit by 11.4 percentage points of GDP, Finland by 7.1 points, Italy by 6.8 points, and the United Kingdom by 6 points. The Greek effort, with a reduction of 9.2 percentage points, was not enough to qualify with the rest of candidates in 1999, and Greece had to wait until 2001 to join EMU.[2] Finally, the initial objective in all EU member states was to achieve close to balanced budgets between 2002 and 2003.[3]

However, convergence in fiscal outcomes does not mean convergence in fiscal policies. Not every country chose the same means to achieve the common objective. In fact, this generalized trend towards balanced budgets in Europe during the 1990s suddenly turns into remarkable divergence if one considers the timing and the ways in which every country decided to reach the 3 per cent limit. Whereas some countries like Spain, Austria and France waited until 1995 to reduce their deficits rapidly, others, like Greece, Sweden and the Netherlands, maintained their consolidations throughout the 1990s. These different choices in the strength, the timing, and the duration of fiscal adjustments diverge still further when one considers the composition of these adjustments. Portugal increased its expenditures and, in order to consolidate its budget, it increased its revenues even more. Greece, Belgium, France and the United Kingdom also increased their revenues, but they reduced their primary expenditures by a relatively smaller amount. Italy, Finland, and Sweden followed a similar strategy, but placed more emphasis on reductions in primary expenditures. And, finally, Denmark, Germany, Spain, Ireland, and the Netherlands decided to reduce both their public revenues and their public expenditures.[4]

Because this 'fiscal divergence' is very paradoxical in the process of European economic convergence, this book will address the following questions:

- Why were fiscal adjustments launched in the first place? And what made them last?
- What is the explanation of the finding that different countries chose different strategies of fiscal adjustment in terms of budgetary composition, when they apparently faced similar constraints, and aimed at fulfilling the same objectives, in the run-up to EMU?
- And, finally, what were the economic and political consequences of choosing one or another type of fiscal adjustment strategy?

There exists an abundant literature on fiscal policy from which partial responses and interesting hypothesis can be drawn to answer these questions.

In the 1960s the public choice school identified a deficit bias in the fiscal policy decision-making process (Buchanan, 1960), caused by the tendency that policy-makers exhibit to try and benefit their own constituencies through the allocation of additional resources.[5] Two decades later, a growing number of scholars highlighted the correlation between electoral cycles and economic cycles. The political business cycle approach holds that politicians use fiscal policy to stimulate the economy before the election, because reduced unemployment and increased economic output substantially increases the probabilities of being re-elected.[6] More recently, scholars have concentrated on a variety of issues related to fiscal policy such as the effects of electoral systems and fiscal institutions on fiscal policies[7] and the importance of ideology to influence some components of the budget.[8]

These political economy approaches have assisted traditional economics in explaining such paradoxical facts as the permanent accumulation of debt since the mid-1970s in western economies,[9] and the marked bias towards running pro-cyclical fiscal policies (instead of using deficits to smooth the cycle in times of recession). Besides the mentioned lines of research, until now the specialized literature on fiscal adjustments has focused primarily on the non-Keynesian effects of certain types of fiscal consolidations,[10] and on the importance of certain type of adjustments for the likelihood of their success.[11]

However, to date none of these works has explained why during episodes of fiscal consolidation, similar countries, aiming at achieving a balanced budget, would pursue different strategies of fiscal adjustment. Quite surprisingly, among the vast literature on the political economy of fiscal policies, nobody has yet studied the political and economic determinants of fiscal adjustments. That is, either scholars have studied the politico-institutional determinants of deficits and debt accumulation, or they have studied the effects of correcting these deviations via fiscal consolidations. But there is no study that explains the step in between. A step about the characteristics of fiscal adjustments: their timing, their duration, their composition and their political and economic consequences.

This study combines a comprehensive theoretical framework and an exhaustive empirical analysis with recent data from the countries of the European Union, to explain which economic and political factors influence policy-makers' decisions regarding any strategy of fiscal adjustment, and what are the consequences of those crucial decisions.

The book limits its analysis to the former EU-15 member states between 1960 and 2000, and therefore does not include any of the countries that joined the EU in 2004. There are three basic reasons for this: (1) the ten new member states joined the EU after the last year of the statistical series covered by this study; (2) these countries joined the market economy during the 1990s and therefore do not have comparable data on public finances previous to that date; and (3) none of them has yet joined the EMU and adopted the euro: only very lately have their fiscal consolidations aimed at fulfilling this goal.[12]

The rest of this chapter will summarize the most important concepts and arguments of this book. First, it will provide the reader with the definition of fiscal adjustment used in this book, and, secondly, it will elaborate on the different economic and political factors that affect the design and implementation of any fiscal adjustment strategy, regarding its timing, its duration,[13] and its composition. Following this, the chapter will turn to introduce the main concepts relative to the possible economic and political consequences that different adjustment strategies may bring about. And, finally, this introduction will finish with a summary of the book's argument and a detailed description of the book's structure.

1.1 Strategies of fiscal adjustment

A public deficit exists when total public revenues are insufficient to pay for total public expenditures. This difference is covered annually by borrowing money, and this constitutes the public debt, which will produce some interest payments that the government has to repay in the following year.

If the process of debt accumulation does not stop and the fiscal policy stance shows a persistent structural deficit, the probability of launching a fiscal adjustment increases dramatically. The probability that a fiscal consolidation will start is even higher in those years when the international economy has been doing badly and the domestic economy is starting to improve (Von Hagen, Hallett and Strauch, 2001).

Once the decision to launch a fiscal adjustment has been taken, any group of measures aimed at reducing the public deficit constitutes a fiscal adjustment strategy. Strategies of fiscal adjustment can vary in their duration and their composition. These are the three dimensions that the first part of this study will explore more in depth, because every government willing to consolidate its budget has to decide: (1) when to launch the adjustment; (2) how long the adjustment episode is going to last; and (3) what items of the budget will be affected by this adjustment effort.

The duration of fiscal consolidations is important because if they are too short and very strong, they can start a recession in situations in which the private sector does not compensate quickly enough for the decrease in public demand which is brought about by the fiscal contraction, while if they are slow and sustained, they can have very negative political consequences for the government which implements these measures. In addition, the duration of fiscal consolidations is closely related to their composition, because, according to the finding of some economists, those adjustments that rely mostly on cuts in the government wage bill and in public transfers are likely to last longer (and thus to be successful), than those which rely on increased revenues and reduced public investment (Alesina and Perotti, 1996b).

Any government willing to reduce the public deficit has a set of five adjustment strategies from which to choose. It can: (1) increase revenues more than it increases expenditures; (2) increase revenues and freeze expenditures;

(3) increase revenues and reduce expenditures; (4) freeze revenues and reduce expenditures; or (5) reduce revenues less than it reduces expenditures. Basically, consolidations that rely on the first two strategies of adjustment can be termed revenue-based adjustments, and those based on the last two strategies, can be termed expenditure-based adjustments. A final option is somewhat in between, and this is why it can be termed a mixed strategy. For example, the European Commission considered that Austria, Belgium, Denmark, the Netherlands, and Spain had all implemented mixed strategies to qualify for EMU, because they relied first on revenue-based compositions, and then turned to expenditure-based approaches, when it became clear that the initial strategy would not be enough to meet the criteria (EC, 2000b: 11).

1.2 Economic and political factors influencing the adoption of different adjustment strategies

Because in all European countries the cabinet is the government body that takes the lead in the design and implementation of every aspect related to the timing, the duration and the composition of fiscal adjustments, the first part of this book focuses on the economic and political factors that influence the cabinet when it is taking these decisions.

On the one hand, there are important economic factors that affect fiscal policy choices, and that therefore constrain the cabinet's decisions. In particular, the economic cycle, the unemployment rate, and the accumulated level of debt exert extremely significant pressures on fiscal policies.

But, on the other hand, there are also important political factors that affect fiscal policy decisions. If politics is generally defined as the decision over 'who gets what, when, and how' (Laswell, 1936: 19), it is clear that fiscal policy and the choice of consolidation strategies have a lot to do with politics. When episodes of fiscal adjustment are analysed by political economists, normally the effect of interest payments and the cycle are discounted, and the resulting cyclically adjusted primary budget balance becomes the object of study. If this balance improves from one year to another, then this year can be considered as a year in which a discretionary fiscal adjustment has begun. These types of episodes require a strong commitment from the government and are the result of a planned decision and not an unintended outcome. And this is why political factors are so important to understand what makes the cabinet finally choose one among the set of available adjustment strategies.

Economic factors

Economic cycle and unemployment rate

The economic cycle affects the public budget through automatic stabilizers: when there is a recession, tax revenues decrease, and unemployment benefits raise the level of public expenditure. In very generous welfare systems the effect of the unemployment rate on the budget is very strong: when the unemployment rate is growing, the increase in the amount of public resources devoted to unemployment benefits makes it more difficult to launch a fiscal adjustment based on spending cuts. Given these effects, it is very likely that governments take into account the economic cycle when deciding about the timing of the consolidation. For example, balanced budgets are easier to achieve when the economy is growing, because this automatically means more revenues and less expenditures. In fact, the group of countries that met the Maastricht deficit criteria would have been considerably smaller, if the second half of the nineties had not been one of remarkable economic growth in Europe.

The economic environment is also important in determining the likelihood of starting a fiscal consolidation. As demonstrated by Von Hagen, Hallett and Strauch (2001: 12): 'a persistently weak international environment strengthens the pressure on governments to enter a consolidation experiment'. The combination of the effects of the domestic economic cycle and the surrounding economic conditions indicates that fiscal consolidations are more likely to start when the domestic economy is doing well relative to those of its neighbours.

Prices and monetary conditions

Growing prices can be the result of different disequilibria, from excess of demand and wage rigidities in the labour market to malpractice in the way of financing public deficits by printing money. In all cases, tight monetary policy in the form of higher interest rates is the primarily tool used to control inflation. But fiscal policy is also a relevant instrument since taxes increase prices and public outlays tend to boost economic activity, creating temporary excesses of demand. Therefore, when prices are high, there is an increased probability of starting a fiscal consolidation. But when prices are under control as a result of a tight monetary policy the probability of starting a fiscal consolidation the following year diminishes.

Debt accumulation

The third economic constraint that governments face when deciding the composition of the budget and the strategy of fiscal adjustment, is the accumulated level of debt. The higher it is, the higher the share of public expenditures that has to be dedicated to interest payments generated by that debt. This is known as the 'snow-ball effect', and it can seriously diminish the alternatives available to governments. In this respect, if we subtract the effect of cycle and interest payments on the budget balance, the remaining structural balance is also very important in predicting the likelihood of fiscal adjustments to start and survive. The higher and more persistent the structural deficit in a country, the more difficult it will be for that country to change this tendency and to generate structural surpluses to avoid defaulting on the debt. In these situations the probability of entering episodes of fiscal consolidation increases significantly.

Political factors

Fragmentation of decision-making

The first among the political factors influencing fiscal policy formulation, and the one which has been most extensively studied in the literature of fiscal adjustments, is the fragmentation of decision-making. The idea is that fragmentation in decision-making is negative for expenditure control, because each group in the majority will push for expenditure on its preferred policy areas, but it will only internalize a part of the costs and distortions of the associated increase in revenues needed to equilibrate the budget (Weingast, Shepsle and Johnson, 1981). Therefore, the larger the number of actors with a voice in the fiscal decision-making process, the stronger the pressure for more expenditures, and thus the larger the deviation from the optimal fiscal policy. For example, coalition governments or big cabinets (with many spending ministries) would be less likely to undertake a fiscal adjustment, and, if forced to do so, it is likely that it will be short and revenue-based, in order to maintain their shares in public expenditures. Spending limits, and institutional configurations that guarantee 'strong' finance ministers with veto powers, can in theory help to counteract the cabinet's fragmentation problems that large coalitions and many spending ministers could generate.[14]

Proximity of elections

The second element that is very important for any cabinet to consider is the electoral calendar, especially the distance between the moment at which they take important decisions and the date at which the next elections will be held. Because politicians want to be re-elected, they will try to implement different fiscal policies that may affect the voters' decision, such as reducing taxes and increasing transfers before elections. They can also affect this decision by boosting economic activity through a fiscal expansion during the election year, or in cases where they are sure that they will be defeated at the polls, they could even try to constrain the available fiscal choices to the new incoming cabinet, in order to increase the probabilities of returning very soon to office.[15]

Ideology of the party in government

Finally, cabinets are composed of politicians that belong to political parties. And political parties do not only formulate policies to win government,[16] but win the government to formulate policies that are beneficial to their constituencies, and that, overall, are usually consistent with their understanding of how economics work, and what is the best way to achieve their preferred objectives.

In the realm of economic policy-making, social democratic governments, driven by their stronger preference for equality,[17] have traditionally been associated with the stronger intervention of the public sector in the economy, not only to provide public goods, but also attempting to reallocate resources, redistribute income, and compensate for socially inequitable market outcomes.[18] On the other hand, conservative governments are convinced that in order to improve the general well-being of the whole society, it is more important to increase the overall level of economic output, than to argue about how this output is distributed. This conviction makes them relatively more concerned about economic efficiency than about equality, and thus conservative governments have been traditionally associated with a lower level of state intervention in the economy.

Applying this characterization to the cabinet's decision on the composition of the budget, and the strategy of fiscal adjustment, one would expect left-wing governments to be associated with higher average levels of public expenditures on public consumption, social transfers, public investment, and the government wage bill to pay for an extensive public administration. To finance all of these expenditures, and also driven by this preference for redistribution, one would also expect left-wing governments to tax in an increasingly progressive manner. Higher public expenditures financed by higher public revenues do not mean that left-wing governments should run deficits more frequently than right-wing ones. A stronger state presence in the economy does not initially have to be associated with unbalanced budgets.

In a positivist understanding of science it should be possible to decide in an empirical manner if all of these economic and political factors did in fact have any effect on the choice of fiscal policies and adjustment strategies in Europe. Although theories cannot be refuted by means of empirical testing, the explanatory power of competing hypotheses can be discerned.[19]

This is the aim of this book, combining statistical analysis of the determinants of the timing, the duration and the composition of fiscal policies and adjustment strategies, and historical analysis of the decisions taken by economic and political actors during episodes of fiscal consolidation. However, this book does not only analyse the factors affecting the decision to launch a fiscal consolidation and the duration and composition of these episodes. In its final chapters, it also has a thorough examination of the economic and political consequences attached to these fiscal adjustment decisions, since the strategic choice in terms of duration and composition of the consolidation episode has considerable effects on economic growth and income distribution.

The combined analysis of the causes and the consequences of fiscal adjustment strategies gives this book a circular structure, aiming to provide the reader with a clear explanation of the fiscal policy-making process in all its dimensions: from its design, based on expected outcomes and collateral interests and pressures, to its implementation and its actual consequences.

1.3 Economic and political consequences of adopting different adjustment strategies

The macroeconomic consequences of fiscal adjustments are intimately related to both the demand-side and supply-side effects of fiscal policy.

Demand-side effects on growth

The natural place to start a consideration of demand-side effects of fiscal policy is the Keynesian model that assumes price rigidity and slack in productive capacity so that output is determined by aggregate demand. In this model, fiscal adjustments based on tax increases or spending cuts reduce the aggregate demand, and thus precipitate a recession. This straight conclusion was subsequently contested when extensions of the simple model allowed for price flexibility, and for crowding-out through induced changes in interest rates and exchange rates.

Non-Keynesian demand-side effects of fiscal policy emerge from new classical models that address one of the main shortcomings of the Keynesian approach, namely its lack of microeconomic foundations. In these new models fiscal adjustments can have expansionary effects on economic activities, mainly through the crowding-in of private consumption and investment when these rational agents perceive that fiscal adjustments are likely to be permanent. In this respect, there is very recent empirical evidence pointing towards the fact that in situations of fiscal stress, if the first measures of fiscal adjustment are very strong, private agents interpret them as a signal of a credible commitment towards a permanent reduction of the budget deficit. Under such circumstances, risk premia diminish, and fiscal multipliers could turn negative, resulting in expansionary fiscal adjustments (Giavazzi and Pagano, 1990).

Another way of achieving expansionary fiscal consolidations is to decisively reduce the most rigid items of the budget (such as transfers and the wage bill), because this will be seen by private agents as a signal of the government's commitment to balance the budget (Alesina and Perotti, 1997a).

Supply-side effects on growth

Supply-side effects of fiscal policy are generally classified as the long-term effects that fiscal policies can have on ameliorating the productive capacity of the economy and improving its productivity. In this respect, it is reasonable to expect that fiscal adjustments that rely on tax increases on labour will affect the supply of labour, and those relying on capital taxes will affect saving and investment decisions.

The sign of the impact that taxes may have on the supply of labour and capital, and thus on growth, is an empirical issue about which clear-cut conclusions are yet to be provided (Blundell and MacCurdy, 1999).

For example, Alesina and Perotti (1997a) affirm that increases in labour income taxes can have a significant negative supply-side effect in unionized, imperfectly competitive labour markets where before-tax wages, and hence labour costs increase to reflect higher taxes.

On the spending side, public investment in public goods and other goods with positive externalities can lead to positive long-term supply-side effects and growth. In this respect, the positive effect on growth of models where the government invests in both physical and human capital is well known (Murphy, Schleifer, and Vishny, 1989; Lucas, 1988). These models have been enthusiastically embraced by social democratic governments since the failure of the Keynesian approach to economic policy management in the 1970s.

Income distribution

Most budget deficits in Europe have arisen as the result of excessive public outlays provided by generous welfare states aimed at redistributing income and developing a safety net that assists citizens in contingencies such as sickness or unemployment. Given that the source of budgetary imbalances is closely related to welfare policies, it is reasonable to expect that one of the most important economic consequences of fiscal consolidations is increases in income inequality. Surprisingly, despite its importance, only Ford (1998) and Smeeding (2000) have referred directly to this consequence, but their studies lack a systematic analysis of the empirical evidence for EU countries. Part of the problem comes from the lack of good data sources on income distribution. But through the simple incorporation to the empirical study of economic consequences of the well-known Gini coefficient (available for most EU countries), the book provides very significant new conclusions in this area.

Electoral costs

Equally important as the economic consequences that fiscal adjustments can have is the question of the political consequences that these policies can bring about for those governments implementing them.

Any particular policy can have many different political consequences. These range from gains/losses in public support, to confrontation with other parties in the governing coalition, or internal confrontation between cabinets and their supporting parties or unions. But whatever the political costs or benefits of fiscal adjustments, the most important test for any policymaker comes at election time.

If politicians tend to avoid fiscal adjustments during election years this is because they assume that voters dislike the tax increases or the spending cuts associated with consolidations. However, the only study to date to have addressed empirically the question of the political consequences of fiscal adjustments in advanced democracies affirms that 'governments do not seem to be punished at the ballot box for engaging in fiscal adjustments' (Alesina, Perotti and Tavares, 1998). However, if this conclusion were correct, why then would politicians relate decisions on fiscal adjustments to the proximity of elections? Are they misinterpreting voters' preferences? The final chapter of this book will empirically examine the same issue through a redefinition of the dependent variable, and will demonstrate that the probability of re-election does indeed decrease when expenditure-based fiscal adjustments occur.

The political cost of launching a fiscal consolidation can only be avoided if the results in terms of economic growth and employment creation arrive on time before the election takes place, or if the government convinces the electorate that these positive effects will come in the medium term. This argument of assuming that a hard sacrifice today will yield abundant economic benefits tomorrow was used across Europe in the 1990s to encourage the public opinion of different countries to accept and support the economic efforts required by the Maastricht criteria. As a result of this policy, the introduction of fiscal adjustments has stopped being associated with bad electoral results in Europe during the 1990s.

1.4 Five questions and hypotheses: a summary of the book's argument

This book is, therefore, motivated by five clear questions and five related hypotheses that no previous study has jointly formulated and tested in a comprehensive manner. These questions deal with:

- the *timing* of fiscal adjustments: why and when are fiscal adjustments launched by governments in the first place?
- the *duration* of adjustment episodes: what makes fiscal consolidations last?
- the *composition* of fiscal adjustments: what factors explain why different countries implement different consolidation strategies in terms budgetary composition, in a generalized process of deficit reduction?
- the *economic consequences* of fiscal adjustments: what is the macroeconomic impact of alternative consolidation strategies in terms of growth and equality?
- the *political consequences* of fiscal adjustments: what is the electoral impact of cutting the budget deficit?

Based on the political economy literature of fiscal policy briefly introduced in this chapter, this book develops and tests five related hypotheses to answer these initial questions:

The fiscal stress hypothesis Fiscal adjustments tend to start sooner when the country's public finances are in a situation of fiscal stress and when the relative cyclical position of the economy is positive;

The debt burden hypothesis Fiscal adjustments tend to last longer when the debt burden is high, when there is a strong government in place, and when elections are not imminent;
The partisanship hypothesis Fiscal adjustments tend to rely on revenue increases rather than on spending cuts when there is a social democratic majority in the government and/or when the cabinet is fragmented. The opposite applies for conservative governments and/or cohesive cabinets;
The economic trade-off hypothesis Expenditure-based fiscal adjustments can have, under certain accompanying conditions, a positive impact on economic growth but at the expense of growing income inequality;
The fiscal voting hypothesis Fiscal adjustments diminish the probabilities of prime minister re-election.

In order to test these five hypotheses, three types of economic factors and three types of political factors are repeatedly used in the rest of the book. These sets of factors are expected to affect the different dimensions of every fiscal adjustment strategy (in terms of timing, duration and composition); three aspects which are, in turn, expected to explain the economic and political consequences that these adjustments bring about.

In a circular conception of the fiscal decision-making process, this book asserts that these likely economic and political consequences feed back the fiscal adjustment decision made by rational forward-looking politicians, and as such affect the whole process.

Summing up, the main arguments and findings that the reader can find in this book are the following:

1. Contrary to the common book understanding and the apparent convergence of fiscal policies, this study argues that differentiated fiscal policies are still possible, because the convergence of budgetary balances still allows for divergence in budget sizes and composition. Despite the Maastricht criteria, the limits set by the Stability and Growth Pact, and the attentive monitoring of the European Commission, national governments still have the possibility to pursue different strategies of fiscal adjustment, in terms of both their duration and their composition.
2. What this book argues is that domestic economic and political factors affecting the cabinet are crucial to understand those different choices, regarding the timing, the duration, and the composition of these strategies of fiscal adjustment pursued by EU member states since the 1970s.
   a. The accumulated level of debt, the cyclical stance, the degree of fragmentation in decision-making, and the proximity of elections are more important factors in explaining why some consolidation episodes started sooner than later, and why some lasted longer than others.
   b. The ideology of the party in government is central to determining whether or not a country choses a revenue-based strategy of adjustment,

or an expenditure-based one. Even during the 1990s, when the 'Maastricht exam' forced strong consolidations across Europe, leftist governments prioritized their preferences, and increased direct taxes to finance increases in public consumption and public investments, demonstrating very clearly the current social democratic commitment to supply-side policies of physical and human capital formation.[20] The comparison between the Spanish expenditure-based adjustment in the period 1996–2000 and the Portuguese revenue-based consolidation in the period 1995–1999 offers a very interesting illustration of the effect that partisanship has on the choice of adjustment strategy. Similar case studies for the UK, Italy, France and Germany provide the reader with recent historical evidence of the influence of decision-making fragmentation and elections on fiscal policy decisions.

3. Finally, the book argues that the economic and political consequences that these adjustments bring about are equally as important as the fiscal policy strategies.
   a. Results show that while expenditure-based adjustments that rely on cuts in transfers and public wages tend to last longer and have been expansionary during the 1990s, they also tend to generate more income inequality. On the contrary, revenue-based adjustments have been less successful in terms of economic growth, but have performed considerably better in terms of income inequality.
   b. In addition to these economic consequences, results also show that the probability of re-election decreases during episodes of fiscal adjustment, but increases with economic growth and lower income inequality. This tendency has only been reversed during the 1990s, when the public campaigns of the European Commission and national governments highlighting the future economic benefits of the single currency, seem to have transformed the traditional aversion of European citizens towards expenditure-based adjustments.

1.5 The structure of the study

This book is structured as follows:

Chapter 2 provides the theoretical framework for the study. It dedicates its first section to developing a very simple explanation of what exactly constitutes fiscal policy, and how it plays a crucial role in affecting the aggregate demand of the economy in the short and medium run, and the aggregate supply in the long run. Readers with some economic background can skip this section and concentrate on the second section, which is dedicated to a review of the record of fiscal policy outcomes in the European Union over the last thirty years. This section is very important because it presents abundant evidence of variation in fiscal policies and strategies of fiscal adjustment. In order to discuss what could be the economic and political determinants of that observed variation, the last two sections of the chapter offer an extensive review of different theoretical and empirical works that have directly or indirectly addressed what factors could explain different fiscal policies and fiscal adjustments. Because traditional economic explanations are insufficient to answer why different countries decide to pursue different strategies of adjustment, three political factors affecting the cabinet that has to take the final decision on the adjustment strategy are presented. The chapter discusses the theoretical reasons why economic variables such as the economic cycle, monetary conditions, and the accumulated level of debt should by complemented by some others, such as the fragmentation of decision-making, the proximity of elections, and the ideology of the party in government, in order to explore the determinants of fiscal adjustment strategies. The chapter closes by presenting the five hypotheses that will be tested throughout the book.

Once the nature of fiscal policy has been clarified and possible explanatory factors of its variation have been presented, Chapter 3 starts by defining what could be considered a fiscal adjustment episode, and how strategies to consolidate the budget can vary in terms of their timing, duration and composition. The chapter then splits into the timing and the duration analysis of fiscal adjustments.

The analysis of the timing involves estimating the probability of starting a fiscal consolidation in any given year, dependent on a set of economic and political factors. Results from this analysis show that the probability of starting fiscal adjustments increases when the economy is doing well relative to other European economies, when the debt-to-GDP ratio is high, when monetary policy has been eased in previous years, when government coalitions and cabinets are small, and when elections have just passed.

The rest of the chapter is dedicated to a detailed duration analysis of fiscal consolidation experiences in the 15 EU member states, between 1960 and 2000. Results from the non-parametric and the parametric analysis show that accumulated duration, cabinet fragmentation and the accumulated level of debt are very important economic and political factors in understanding why some consolidations lasted longer than others. But the most important results from this analysis are those presented in the last section, where a sensitivity test is performed, which shows how duration of stronger consolidations is explained much better by politico-institutional factors than by economic ones. This suggests that if strong fiscal adjustments are to last longer, they require not only the proper initial and accompanying conditions but also a very firm political commitment, which is more easily achieved if the cabinet is not fragmented, if it is ideologically homogeneous and if elections are not too close. Otherwise, the probability of a rapid end to strong consolidation episodes increases dramatically.

Finally, the first part of this book ends in Chapter 4 with an extensive analysis of the determinants of the third dimension of fiscal adjustment strategies (besides timing and duration): that is, the composition of the budget.

After explaining the importance of the budget's composition in terms of its consequences for economic growth and income distribution, this chapter deals with two related questions. First, it tries to determine the economic and political factors that affect the composition of the budget in general, both during years of fiscal expansion and during years of fiscal adjustment. And secondly, it addresses the question of whether this group of factors also affect the composition of the budget, but only during episodes of fiscal adjustment. Because in the second section of this chapter the ideology of the party in government proves to be a crucial variable in explaining the budget's composition in general (and especially during the second half of the 1990s), the third section focuses on trying to answer if ideology is also influential in explaining the choice of adjustment composition.

The empirical evidence presented in that section shows that leftist governments try to affect the supply side of the economy consuming and investing relatively more than rightist governments. This preference is so strong that it is maintained even during episodes of fiscal adjustment, when typically public investment and public consumption are either frozen or reduced, and they have maintained this strategy during the 1990s – even at the cost of cuts in transfers and subsidies.

This study does not only maintain that domestic economic and political variables decisively affect strategies of fiscal adjustment in terms of their timing, their duration, and their composition, but the results from the first four chapters present very convincing evidence that, even under the strongest pressures for further convergence of fiscal outcomes at the European level, governments have found the way to implement their different approaches to fiscal policies at sub-aggregate levels.

If the first part of the book was characterized by the constant presentation of stylised arguments and facts (e.g. economic variables are better predictors of the timing and duration of fiscal adjustments, but political variables are better predictors of their composition), the second part starts by answering some of the most difficult questions that arise from the previous conclusions.

The first group of questions raised in view of the results of the first part of the book, would mainly take the following form: if domestic political factors decisively influence the formulation of fiscal adjustment strategies, why did European countries tie their own hands in the first place by establishing the Maastricht convergence criteria? An extension of this question would be: why did social democratic parties, which are traditionally associated with economic management within national boundaries, embrace monetary union so enthusiastically?

The answer to these questions in terms of foreign policy interests forms the first part of Chapter 5 and opens the ground for another set of questions that basically try to test if the conclusions that arise from the statistical analysis of Chapters 3 and 4 still hold in the face of concrete case studies. These case studies form the basis for the second part of chapter 5. In that section, the experiences in the 1990s of Portugal, Spain, the UK, Italy, France and Germany are analysed and compared from different perspectives. Portugal and Spain are chosen as paradigmatic examples of the opposite effects that the ideology of the party in government has on the formulation of fiscal adjustment strategies. By contrast, the UK and Italy exemplify the capacity that fragmentation of decision-making has on distorting the traditional effect of a cabinet's ideology. And, finally, France and Germany are compared as two different cases where the proximity of elections had a dramatic effect on their approaches to fiscal adjustments throughout the whole convergence process.

The analysis of the political economy of different fiscal adjustment strategies, in terms of their timing, their duration, and their composition, can be complemented with illustrative case studies, but the analysis lacks definitive consistency if the consequences of these different economic policy choices bring about are not also analysed.

This analysis is the aim of the final two chapters of this book. Chapter 6 analyses the economic consequences of different adjustment strategies, and Chapter 7 deals with the political consequences.

Chapter 6 starts by reviewing thoroughly the theoretical effects of fiscal adjustments in terms of growth (both demand-side and supply-side effects) and equality, and concludes by providing empirical evidence that expenditure-based adjustments can have non-Keynesian expansionary effects, if they are accompanied by a previous currency devaluation and if the country was in a difficult fiscal position. However, these types of adjustment strategies have high costs in terms of increased income inequality.

Finally, Chapter 7 confirms that the electorate tends to punish those governments that implement expenditure-based adjustments, but reward them if they perform well in terms of economic growth and reduced income inequality. This aversion to expenditure-based adjustments was weakened during the 1990s, mostly as a consequence of the multiplicity of official campaigns in favour of the single currency. The results from Chapter 7 confirm that politicians are rational when they plan the timing, the duration and the composition of their adjustment strategies, assuming that the electorate will punish them if the adjustment has been made through spending cuts, unless these cuts have generated visible economic growth before elections arrive, in order to compensate for the initial disappointment of voters. In this respect, the choice of adjustment strategy is a matter of the preferences of the party in government. Some governments will be willing to implement expenditure-based adjustments if they believe that this would trigger a 'crowding in' of the private sector in the economy that would expand the economy in time to win the re-election. By contrast, other governments will be willing to implement revenue-based adjustment strategies (even if this could imply more modest achievements in terms of economic growth) because in exchange they will obtain better results in terms of income distribution.

2
Economics, Politics and Fiscal Policy

> 'A crude distinction between economics and politics would be that economics is concerned with expanding the pie while politics is about distributing it.'
>
> Alesina and Rodrik, 1994: 465

Any analysis of the use that governments make of fiscal policies would lack clarity if it were not understood in the broader context of economic policy-making. One cannot start discussing the variation of fiscal policy and fiscal adjustment strategies along time and among different European countries, without first outlining the main characteristics of this macroeconomic tool. The purpose of this chapter is to provide the reader with the general framework in which fiscal policies in general, and fiscal adjustments in particular, have to be understood. In the first section, fiscal policy will be placed in the broader context of macroeconomic policy as one of the most important policy instruments available to governments that want to intervene in the economy. The second section, once the nature of fiscal policies has been understood, will present empirical evidence on the strong variation of fiscal outcomes during the last forty years in the European Union. Once the macroeconomics of fiscal policy have been understood, and after a first consideration of the history of fiscal policies has been presented, I will then elaborate on different hypotheses that could explain the observed variability in fiscal policy outcomes, and strategies of fiscal adjustment. Section three of this chapter will present economic determinants of fiscal policies, section four will discuss the political factors and section five will group them in five hypotheses within a circular theoretical framework. Finally, the conclusion will summarize the main arguments of the chapter.

2.1 Governments and economic policy

Traditionally, governments have seen how to predict and how to smooth economic fluctuations, how to increase employment and how to reduce inflation, as the main economic problems that affect citizens in the short run. They have also been concerned to increase the production capacity of the whole economy, as the only source of economic prosperity in the long run.

Aggregate supply and demand: monetary and fiscal policies

To summarize very simply how the economy works, let me start with the *aggregate supply* of goods and services in the economy – that is, the total level of production in the economy.

Once firms' managers have invested their money in their enterprises, and have hired their workers at given wages, if the prices for the products they sell in the market increase, they will be willing to produce more. At the economy-wide level, the aggregate supply is simply the sum of quantities supplied by each of the firms in the economy at a given price level. At low levels of output, there is excess capacity in the economy, with under-utilized workers and machines. A slight increase in the price level would then elicit a very large increase in output. As production increases, and the economy reaches higher levels of output, machines and workers are working at close to their capacities, and it is hard to produce much more output. The marginal cost of producing an extra unit may be very large, and it takes an enormous increase in the price level to elicit even a small increase in output. If the economy eventually reaches full capacity, all workers and machines would be occupied in full production, and to increase output even further would require the addition of more labour and more machines, or a more productive use of their capacity. At this point the short-run problem of output production would have become a long-run problem of making new investments in buildings, machines, human capital and research. Only through additional investment will it be possible to move one step further the *production possibilities frontier* of the economy in question.

On the other hand, if all those products are to be sold in the market, there have to be other households (C), other firms (I), and governments (G), at home or abroad (X, M), willing to buy them. The *aggregate demand* can then be defined as the sum of all individual demands of these groups of consumers for the available output in the economy. If the wages of consumers are constant, the higher the level of prices of the goods and services supplied, the less the quantities of that output that consumers will be willing to buy.

Economic theory states that the product market is in equilibrium at the intersection of the aggregate supply and the aggregate demand; or, in other words, the market is in equilibrium when the willingness to produce and sell a given amount at a given price coincide with the willingness to buy and consume the same amount at the same price. Equilibrium requires then that total output (Y) equals aggregate demand, which in turn consists of consumption (C), investment (I), government spending (G), and the difference between what is exported to other economies and what is imported from those economies.

$$Y=C+I+G+(X-M) \quad (2.1)$$

In this framework, employment is a function of total output. Governments willing to increase employment will attempt to increase total output. And they can only do so by increasing aggregate supply or aggregate demand.

As can be seen in Figure 2.1, expanding the aggregate demand or the aggregate supply does not have the same effects. The former increases output at the cost of increasing prices, while the latter increases output but decreases prices.

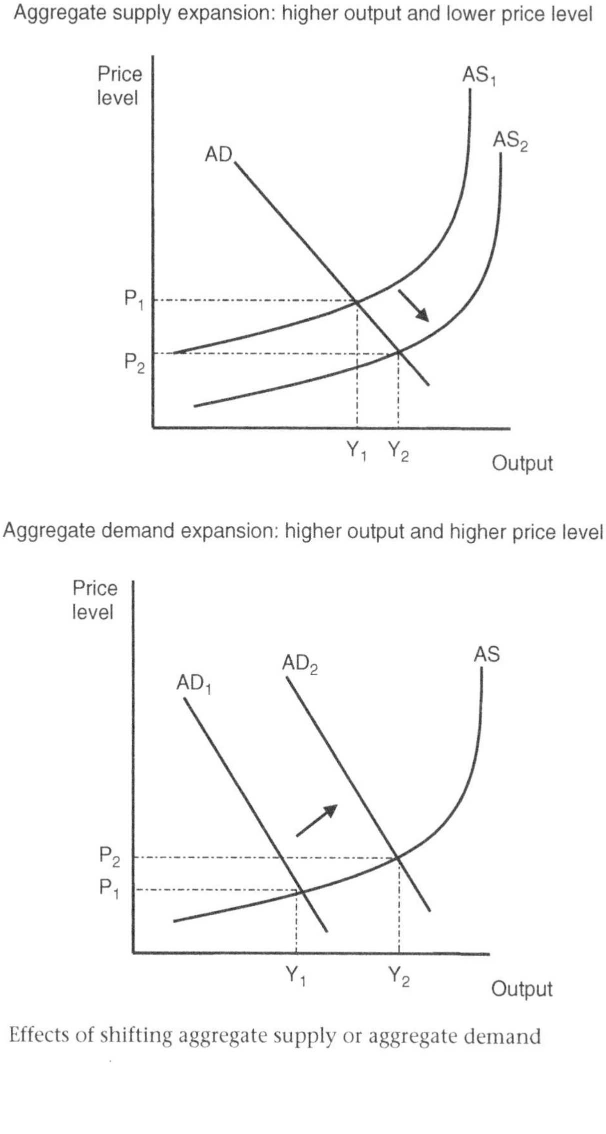

Figure 2.1 Effects of shifting aggregate supply or aggregate demand

The problem for governments is that they can directly affect aggregate demand (increasing government spending, for example), but they can only induce increases in aggregate supply. The only way in which governments could induce increases in the aggregate supply, would be, for example, by easing the conditions met by investors and entrepreneurs (reducing the taxes they pay, educating the labour force they use to make it more productive, etc.).[1] But the ultimate decision to increase the aggregate supply is an investors' decision, and is beyond the scope of government.

Thus, because changing the economic conditions faced by entrepreneurs to stimulate aggregate supply takes time, and its effects are uncertain because they are mediated by firms' decisions, governments that are willing to increase output to reduce unemployment have traditionally tended to manage aggregate demand.

A government firmly committed to smooth the economic cycle and to intervene in the economy by managing the aggregate demand, has two economic policy tools: on the one hand, the government can increase the supply of money in the economy by reducing interest rates (monetary policy). This will reduce the incentive for savers to have their money in the bank, and it will induce them to use it in alternative ways (buying houses, cars or televisions). This increase in demand will increase prices because of the temporary shortage of the products. But these higher prices will stimulate production by firms that will need to hire more workers. At the end, this policy will increase total output and prices, and it will also increase employment.

On the other hand, governments which are willing to expand the aggregate demand can increase public spending in different goods and services produced by the private sector. This will increase demand and will have the previously described effect of increases in output and employment (see Figure 2.2). In addition, governments can decide to lower income taxes, which will increase the disposable income held by consumers and will induce them to demand new products; or they can also decide to lower corporate taxes, increasing the share of profits kept by producers, that in part will be consumed by producers, and in part will be invested in new production.

In this very simple Keynesian framework, monetary expansion and both types of budgetary policies (government spending and tax cuts) will increase aggregate demand, and this will have a further positive effect on total output and total employment.[2]

The management of public expenditures and public revenues to influence aggregate demand and then the total economy, in the way described in the previous paragraph, constitutes what is known as fiscal policy.

If the government decides to cut taxes and/or to increase expenditures, we say that this government is undertaking a fiscal expansion. If it increases taxes and/or reduces public expenditures, we say that it is undertaking a fiscal adjustment. Fiscal policy in general, and the motivations and characteristics behind fiscal adjustments, in particular, are the subject of this book.

Aggregate demand expansion higher output and higher price level

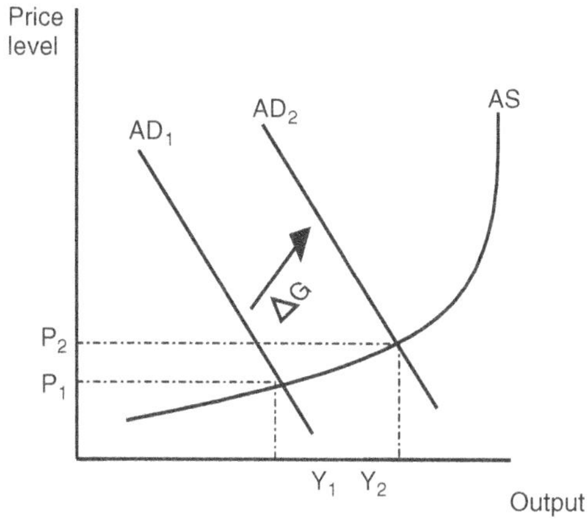

Comment: Public spending rises, a *fiscal expansion* takes place, and as a result of the new equilibrium between IS-LM, there is an *expansion of aggregate demand*, that rises the level of output and level of prices

Fiscal expansion: higher output and higher interest rate

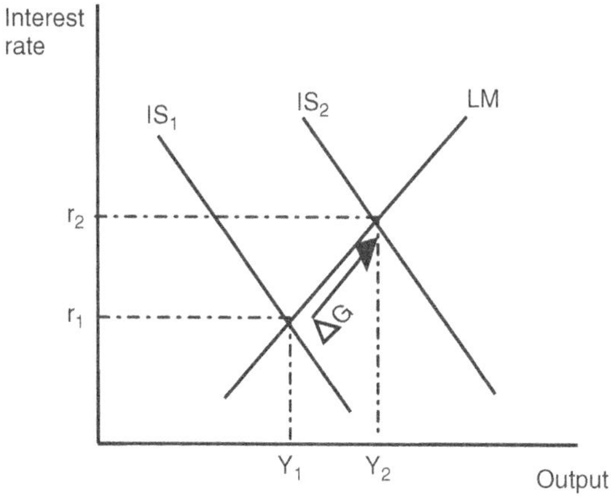

Comment: Public spending rises, and the new equilibrium between the goods and services market (IS) and the money market (LM), takes place at a higher level of output and interest rate

Figure 2.2 Effects of fiscal policy on aggregate demand

In fact, almost every action that a government takes is related to the budget. For example, if the government wants to change the structure of the labour market, it can basically do so by fostering the employment of youngsters and women (for example), through tax cuts to firms that employ these specific groups. Similarly, if the government wants to increase the growth potential of the economy, it has to invest in infrastructure, new technologies, formation of workers and younger generations. These policies, which are typically described as labour-market policies, imply an increase in public expenditures (financed by tax/debt increases), and finally constitute a fiscal policy which also has short-run effects on the demand side of the economy.

Interventionists and non-interventionists

Whether or not governments should intervene in the economy using the monetary and fiscal policies available to them has been a topic of strong debates among economists and politicians throughout the twentieth century.

The debate is extensive and very rich, but, in essence, it can be said that there are economists who reject government intervention in the economy (non-interventionists), and those who support this intervention (interventionists). Basically, these two positions reflect different views about how beneficial or pernicious the government's intervention can be, based on different interpretations of the sources of economic fluctuations,[3] and the capability of the government to solve them.

Those who think that economic fluctuations arise from exogenous shocks in the economy, mainly on the supply side through changes in technology, and those who think that shocks in aggregate demand are caused by misguided monetary policies, are opposed to government intervention in the economy. Monetarists and neoclassical economists hold the view that the market will provide the best possible solution to any change in the economic environment, thus impairing the effectiveness of policy instruments. Based on rational expectations, they believe that private actions in the medium run will offset any governmental intervention in the economy. By assuming that the Phillips curve (the curve that relates inflation and unemployment) is vertical, they affirm that any attempt by the government to stimulate the economy, will only increase the price level, and receiving no benefits. According to their view, if impediments on the full functioning of the market are eliminated, actual output will tend to potential output, and the economy will progressively reach its natural rate of employment. At that point, the most the government might be able to do is to reduce the unemployment rate below the natural rate for a short period of time. But the cost in terms of increased inflation will be so large that the best choice is not to intervene in the economy.

On the other hand, there are economists who maintain the view that economic fluctuations are inherent to the capitalist system and reflect the normal process of the investment–production cycle.[4] These economists, together with Keynesian economists, who see economic slowdowns as resulting from insufficient aggregate demand, think that government policies can positively influence economic growth. They do not believe that the market economy is always able to absorb and respond to shocks, so that full employment is maintained. For them, even under conditions of rational expectations, some government policies can have large effects, because wages and prices are not as flexible as neoclassical economists affirm. These rigidities cause market failures that can be solved by government intervention. But, according to this view, even if the functioning of markets was perfectly efficient, the government would still have a role to play in providing public goods,[5] in affecting the decisions of consumers and firms through tax policies, investment credits, and welfare spending. Governments may be willing to affect market mechanisms to correct for some imbalances among productive sectors of the economy, or most importantly to affect the distribution of income.

According to Notermans (2000), the general prevalence of one or the other type of approach to economic policy allows us to identify three economic regimes. Until the 1920s, the liberal regime of the Gold Standard with a pure floating exchange rate system was purely non-interventionist. This gave way to a progressively regulated economy from the 1930s onwards, and especially from the 1950s until the mid-1970s. These two first decades of the postwar period witnessed the golden age of Keynesian interventionist economics. However, following the oil shock of the mid-1970s and the subsequent stagflation period, economic policy formulation turned again to be under full neoclassical non-interventionist dominance, the position which prevails today.

The current situation in the European Union is one of mixed Keynesian and neoclassical intervention. The complete liberalization of capital markets in 1992, and the completion of the Internal Market with full free mobility of goods, services, people and capital, is a triumph of neoclassical postulates in line with their non-interventionist preferences. The process of making central banks independent, which has been occurring since the mid-1980s, giving them full capacity to set annual objectives for the rate of growth of the money supply, and to intervene in the exchange rate markets to maintain the parity of national currencies with respect to the central ECU parity in the European Monetary System, was nothing but the victory of the 'rules vs discretion' postulates of monetarists, and constitutes another important example of that triumph.

With the completion of the European Monetary Union and the Single Currency in 1999, monetary policies have become supranational and managed by the European Central Bank, while fiscal policies remain in the hands of national governments. As the well-known Mundell–Fleming model describes, in contexts such that which currently exists in Europe, where exchange rates are totally fixed, and where there exists full capital mobility, fiscal policy is totally effective (Mundell, 1962). This is why, although the debate between interventionists and non-interventionists is far from resolved, under the current situation, this debate is totally focused on fiscal policy.

In the current situation, European governments that have joined the single currency and who would be willing to affect the economy only have access to fiscal policies. But although the number of tools available for intervention has been dramatically reduced (because the supranationalized monetary policy and the Stability Pact place nominal restrictions on budget deficits), it does not mean that fewer or less important things can still be done. Fiscal policy alone can still guarantee that governments will keep playing their three main economic roles: the reallocation of resources, the stabilization of the economy, and the redistribution of income. In addition, fiscal policy is still fully responsible for increasing or decreasing the size of the public sector in the economy, for smoothing or accentuating the effects of economic recessions, and for implementing long-run policies oriented towards increasing the growth potential of the economy.

2.2 Fiscal policies in the European Union, 1970–2000

The truth is that the previously described disparity of opinions about the role that the public sector has to play and the degree of intervention that the government must have in the economy, seem to have run in parallel to a wide disparity in the fiscal policies undertaken by different EU countries over the past thirty years. Nevertheless, when one considers the general record of fiscal outcomes in the last decades, it is possible to draw a general picture of fiscal policy developments for the whole European Union (EU-15).

As can be observed in Figure 2.3, fiscal policy since the mid-1970s was characterized by a tremendous increase in the level of public expenditures. Public expenditures of general government in the European Union rose from 35 per cent of European GDP in 1970 to a peak of 53 per cent in 1993, basically due to the expansion of public consumption and social transfers, associated with the welfare state. In 2000, they declined to about 46 per cent of GDP. But this means that the size of the European public sector was, at the end of the century, still 13 percentage points of GDP higher than in the US and 20 percentage points of GDP higher than in Japan.

This general picture in the composition of public expenditures in the European Union becomes more complex when variation in the composition of public expenditures is disaggregated by member states (Figure 2.4).

In the last thirty years, some countries – such as the Netherlands, Portugal, Belgium and France – increased their public consumption expenditures by around ten percentage points of GDP, while other countries – like Germany, Ireland or the UK – increased them by only between one and three percentage points. Variation in transfer expenditures is also very significant, with

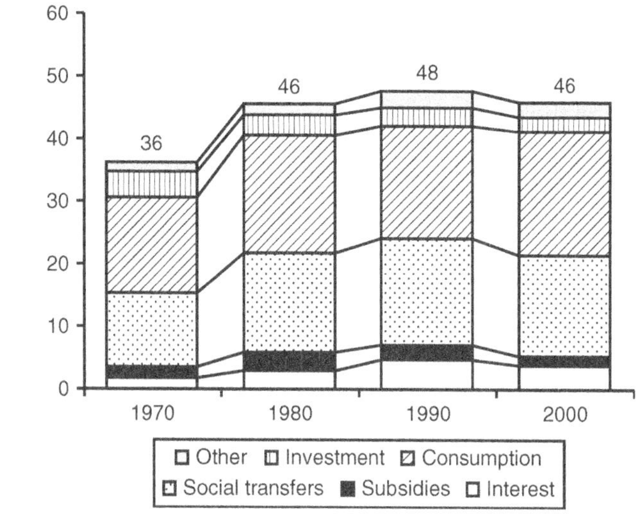

Figure 2.3 The structure of public spending in the EU-15, 1970–2000 (per cent GDP)
Source: EC (2000b).

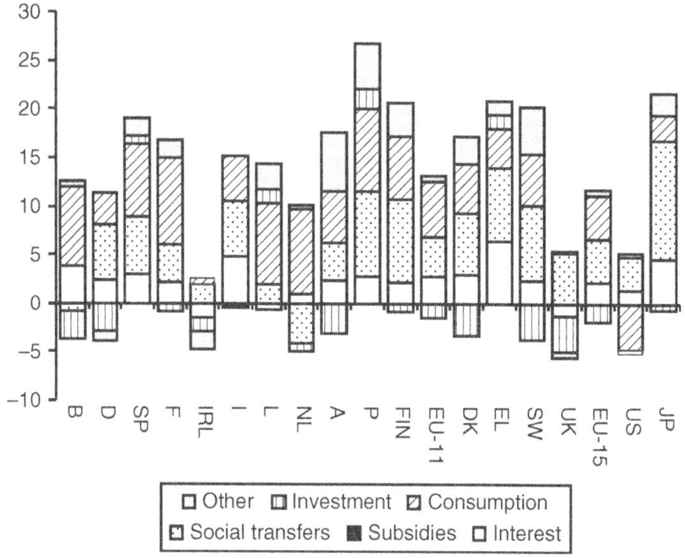

Figure 2.4 Changes in the components of government spending, 1970–2000 (per cent GDP)
Source: EC (2000b).

countries such as Greece, Portugal, Sweden and Finland having increased their transfers around eight percentage points, while others, like Luxembourg, Ireland or France, only increased these expenditures by three percentage points of GDP.

Finally, as most European economies in the past three decades reached very high levels of development, the share of GDP dedicated to public investment has generally fallen. In the period from 1970 to 2000, only Spain, Greece, Portugal, the UK and Luxembourg increased their share of GDP dedicated to public investment.

In order to finance the strong growth in public expenditure, public revenues in the EU grew from 35 per cent in 1970 to a peak of 46 per cent in 2000. The increase was based on higher taxes on labour. Both direct taxes and social contributions increased by 3 percentage points of GDP. By contrast, indirect taxes fell by 6 percentage points over this period (Figure 2.5).

Nevertheless, the increase in public revenues did not run parallel to the increase in public expenditures, and it became increasingly difficult to balance the budget. As a consequence, large and persistent deficits arose, which had to be financed through issuing debt.

This general behaviour of fiscal policies around Europe meant that public deficits in the EU remained above 3 per cent from 1975 onwards. Public deficit reached its maximum in 1993 after the 1992–93 recession, reaching

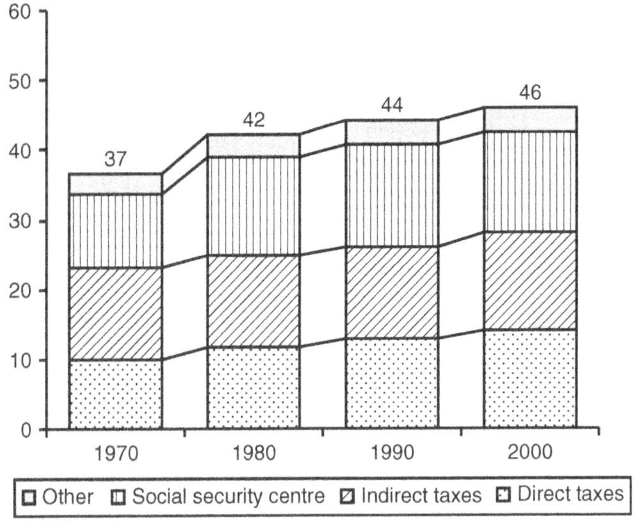

Figure 2.5 The structure of government resources in the EU-15, 1970–2000 (per cent GDP)

Source: EC (2000b).

6 per cent of GDP. These persistent deficits led to a rapidly increasing government debt, which jumped from 30 per cent of GDP in the 1970s to a maximum of 72 per cent in 1996. Public debt in the EU still remains at an average of 64 per cent of GDP (with Belgium, Greece and Italy over 100 per cent). Under such an unsustainable path, the Maastricht convergence criteria forced a strong fiscal consolidation in the European Union, which achieved a deficit reduction of 5 percentage points between 1993 and 1999 (Figure 2.6).

Despite the previous general picture, fiscal policies in the EU have varied significantly between member states. In the last decades, some countries decided to dedicate very large shares of their GDP to the public provision of goods and services and the welfare state, while others preferred to limit the presence of the public sector in the economy.

The variation in fiscal developments among different European countries that is illustrated by Table 2.1 was also translated into a remarkable variation in the timing, length and composition of fiscal adjustment episodes. At different moments in time, countries found that their fiscal imbalances were unsustainable in the medium and long run.

A policy consisting of a determined attempt to correct those imbalances and approximate public revenues and public expenditures constitutes a fiscal adjustment. But fiscal adjustments can vary in their timing, their duration, and their composition, as will be explained in detail in Chapter 3.

For example, during the fiscal adjustment episodes that occurred in Europe in the mid-1990s, some countries chose to reduce their budget deficit gradually through successive short fiscal consolidations (like Finland or the Netherlands), while others preferred to pursue fewer but longer adjustments (like Greece or Ireland).

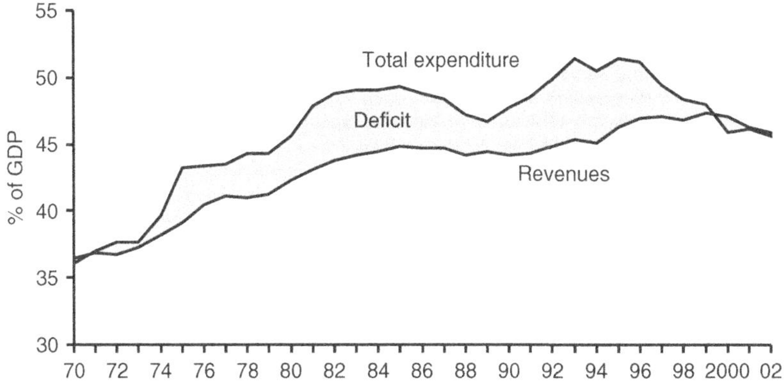

Figure 2.6 General government expenditures, revenues, and borrowing in the EU, 1970–2002

Source: EC (2000b).

Table 2.1 Average public revenues, expenditures, deficit and debt, 1970–2000 (per cent GDP)

	Public revenues	*Public expenditures*	*Public deficit/surplus*	*Public debt*
Austria	45.7	48.3	−2.17	45.24
Belgium	47.3	53.0	−2.55	100.14
Denmark	52.6	52.9	−0.50	46.85
Finland	46.1	44.7	1.90	23.84
France	45.8	48.0	−1.98	37.16
Germany	44.5	46.6	−2.05	39.37
Greece	30.3	37.3	−6.26	61.74
Ireland	35.7	44.4	−5.26	74.39
Italy	38.5	46.7	−8.10	82.40
Luxembourg	45.5	44.6	2.43	9.04
Netherlands	48.1	47.9	−2.76	62.50
Portugal	32.3	36.6	−4.33	50.83
Spain	32.7	35.4	−2.90	35.95
Sweden	56.5	58.0	−0.75	49.98
UK	39.0	41.6	−2.40	53.94
EU-15	42.7	45.7	−2.53	51.67

Source: Own elaboration.

Table 2.2 Frequency, duration and composition of fiscal adjustments in the EU, 1970–2000

		Number of episodes	*Total years*
Austria	1992–93; 1995–98	2	5
Belgium	1977–78; 1982–85; **1987–88**; 1993–98	4	13
Denmark	**1983–87**; 1992–93; 1996–97; 1999–00	4	10
Finland	**1971–72**; 1975–77; 1981–82; 1984–85; 1988–89; 1995–96; **1998–99**	7	15
France	1976–77; **1980–81**; 1996–98	3	7
Germany	**1982–83**; 1989–90	2	4
Greece	1974–75; 1982–83; 1986–88; 1991–92; **1994–2000**	4	16
Ireland	1976–77; **1983–85**; **1991–95**; **1996–99**	4	13
Italy	**1976–78**; 1983–84; 1991–94; **1997–2000**	4	13
Luxembourg	1977–78; **1982–86**; 1996–97	3	9
Netherlands	1972–73; 1977–78; 1985–86; 1988–89; 1991–94; **1996–97**; 1999–2000	7	16
Portugal	1969–70; **1982–84**; **1986–87**; 1992–93; 1995–98	5	12
Spain	1992–93; **1996–2000**	2	7
Sweden	1976–77; **1983–84**; 1986–90; **1996–99**	4	12
UK	**1969–70**; 1976–78; 1980–82; 1988–89; **1996–2000**	5	15

Notes:

1. Expenditure-based episodes of fiscal adjustment in bold.
2. For the purpose of this table, fiscal adjustment years are those in which the cyclically adjusted budget balance increased by more than 1per cent of adjusted GDP from the previous year. In Chapter 3, a discussion on the definition of periods of fiscal adjustments will be presented.

Source: Own elaboration.

The comparison between Greece and Germany shows this variation very clearly. While Greece was involved in short but recurring fiscal adjustment strategies for 16 of the last 30 years, over the same period Germany has involved in consolidation episodes for only 4 years.

Those episodes of fiscal adjustment not only varied in the strength and duration of the consolidation strategy, but they also varied considerably in the composition of the adjustment. Table 2.2 is also very illuminating in this respect. For example, between 1970 and 2000, countries such as Ireland showed a clear preference for expenditure-based fiscal adjustments, while others such as Austria only underwent revenue-based consolidations.

More recently, in the run-up to EMU, this variation in the composition of fiscal adjustment strategies was not only maintained, but even increased.[6]

Table 2.3 Composition of fiscal adjustments in the EU, 1990–2000

				Change in structural primary spending		
Period	*Change in structural balance*	*Change in structural revenue*	*Total*	*Change in capital spending*	*Change in current primary spending*	*Change in interest payments*
Revenue-based retrenchment						
FR 1995–97	3.3	2.6	−0.9	−0.1	−0.8	0.2
GR 1990–98	11.8	11.1	−1.0	0.8	−1.8	0.3
IRL 1990–94	2.3	3.0	2.5	0.6	1.9	−1.8
I 1991–97	9.4	6.4	−3.1	−1.0	−2.1	0.0
P 1992–96	3.6	7.4	6.1	0.9	5.2	−2.3
Expenditure-based retrenchment						
DK 1996–99	5.2	0.6	−2.9	−0.3	−2.6	−1.7
FIN 1993–99	4.0	−4.6	−9.5	−0.7	−8.8	1.0
SW 1994–98	10.9	3.0	−7.5	−0.1	−7.4	−0.4
UK 1994–98	6.6	4.2	−2.8	−0.5	−2.3	0.5
'Switching strategy'						
A –1st phase 1995–96	1.3	2.3	0.8	−0.4	1.2	0.2
–2nd phase 1997	2.2	−0.4	−2.3	−0.9	−1.4	−0.4
B –1st phase 1992–93	1.7	2.9	0.5	0.2	0.3	0.7
–2nd phase 1994–96	3.6	1.4	−0.2	0.1	−0.2	−1.9
DK –1st phase 1992–93	1.4	3.3	1.3	0.1	1.1	0.6
–2nd phase 1994–97	1.7	1.5	−0.7	−0.8	0.0	0.4
NL –1st phase 1991–93	4.3	4.2	−0.4	0.0	−0.4	0.2
–2nd phase 1994–97	1.7	−4.5	−5.4	0.9	−6.4	−0.8
SP –1st phrase 1992–93	−0.3	3.9	2.8	−0.6	3.5	1.3
P –2nd phase 1994–97	3.5	−1.4	−4.6	−1.0	−3.6	−0.2
EU-11 –1st phase 1992–93	0.7	3.1	1.8	−0.2	2.0	0.6
–2nd phase 1994–97	3.1	0.7	−2.0	−0.4	−1.6	−0.4

Source: EC (2000b).

As shown in Table 2.3, while some member states decided to follow revenue-based strategies (France, Greece, or Italy), others attempted to pursue expenditure-based consolidation strategies (Denmark, Sweden, or Finland). Expenditure-based strategies of adjustment also varied in the degree of current and capital expenditures that were cut. Finally, a group of countries (Austria, Belgium, and the Netherlands) switched their strategies in the middle of the fiscal consolidation episode, in view of the relatively low success of their initial strategy.

This change in the consolidation strategy typically meant the introduction of additional spending cuts once the sole reliance on revenue increases had proved insufficient to achieve the overall fiscal target.

It must also be pointed out that in all cases classified by the European Commission in Table 2.3 as 'mixed strategy cases', the change in the consolidation strategy occurred immediately after a general election had taken place (either to re-elect the government or to appoint a new cabinet).

2.3 The economics of fiscal policies and fiscal adjustments

The above variation in fiscal policies in general, and in the size, the timing, the duration and the composition of fiscal adjustment episodes in particular, can be explained according to many different perspectives.

The literature in the field is vast but does not offer specific answers to these questions. Since this book poses new questions, it has to generate new hypotheses to arrive at new answers. Nevertheless, the set of five hypotheses mentioned in the Introduction will be made explicit in section 2.5 and tested in Chapters 3, 4, 6 and 7 of this book. These hypotheses find their roots in the economic and political literature of public finance. Accordingly, the next two sections of this chapter will review a group of potential explanatory factors from the economics and political science literature and will relate them to fiscal policy and fiscal consolidations.

Economic cycle and unemployment rate

Both the theory and data show that the economic cycle affects the budget both on the revenue side and on the expenditure side. If the economy is booming, firms will be increasing their profits, and public income will increase via growing tax revenues. In that situation, more employment will be created and the state will see its unemployment subsidies charges reduced. The effect of an economic downturn will be exactly the opposite, and that is why fiscal adjustments tend to take place when the economy is doing well, and rarely take place during recessions.

But the output gap (the difference between the actual output and the potential output) is not only important for the timing of fiscal adjustments. It can also have a crucial effect on determining the duration and the composition of adjustment episodes. According to Von Hagen, Hallett and Strauch (2001), a large output gap increases the likelihood of fiscal adjustments being started, but reduces the likelihood of the consolidation being long-lasting. In addition, if bad economic initial conditions coincide with high debt-to-GDP ratios, the likelihood of the adjustment being expenditure-based increases.

Nevertheless, it is important to note at this point that this effect of the economic cycle on the budget deficit through automatic stabilizers is very important in European countries because they have very well-developed welfare systems and also because tax revenues from direct taxation constitute their biggest source of public revenues. But this is not the case everywhere. For example, in less developed countries the effect of the economic cycle at home is not an important factor affecting public revenues, because these countries obtain most of their public resources from customs revenues, indirect taxation, and grants from multilateral organizations. Under such circumstances, the budgetary impact of the economic cycle is not even considered to be among the group of important explanatory variables of fiscal policies in those countries (Gupta, Clements, Baldacci, and Mulas-Granados, 2002).

Prices and monetary conditions

Fiscal policy and monetary policy are interrelated, and the policy mix between the two has a decisive influence upon the level of output, prices and interest rates in the economy. Imagine a situation in which the economy has been hit by an external shock in the prices of primary inputs that affects the final prices of most products in the economy. In such an inflationary scenario, the Central Bank would tend to tighten monetary policy, by increasing interest rates or by raising the level of the domestic currency, in order to prevent prices from spiralling out of control. Under such circumstances, there is empirical evidence (Mélitz, 1997) showing that fiscal policy tends to relax when monetary policy tightens. This can be for several reasons: to compensate the contraction effect on output by implementing a fiscal expansion, or just because high interest rates make new public debt more attractive for private investors and, thus, obtaining private financing of public works becomes easier for the government. Due to this 'compensation mechanism' between fiscal policy and monetary policy, there are some authors that maintain that monetary easing can induce governments to reduce budget deficits (Mélitz, 1997; Wyplosz, 1999). In fact, recent empirical evidence provided by Von Hagen, Hallett and Strauch (2001) support the mentioned hypothesis, according to which easing monetary policy in year t increases the likelihood of starting a fiscal consolidation in year $t + 1$.

But these authors have also provided evidence that points towards a weakening during the 1990s of the impact that these variables have traditionally had on fiscal policy: 'Instead, fiscal policy became [in the last decade] less responsive to economic and monetary policy circumstances, and thus may have been driven more strongly by efforts to achieve fiscal surpluses for other reasons, namely to fulfil the Maastricht criteria' (p. 59).

Debt accumulation

Finally, the effect of accumulated debt on fiscal adjustment strategies is also very important. This is even more the case, if during periods of economic expansion, budgetary surpluses are not used to reduce the accumulated level of debt. In such instances, the debt burden will increase up to a point at which the interest payments associated with the repayment of that growing debt will consume most of the share dedicated to public expenditure, in such a way that may finally end up rendering useless any governmental attempt to influence the economy through fiscal policy.[7]

The effect of economic shocks on the budget, and the subsequent generation of debt, was first modelled by Robert Barro in 1979. Barro's tax-smoothing theory of the government budget can be summarized as follows. Imagine that a government has a certain expenditure plan that is to be financed by distortionary taxes.[8] However, the government also wants to minimize the distortionary effect of those taxes, so it faces a situation in which it has to choose the optimal tax policy that enables it to finance the government's spending plans, at the same time as it minimizes the loss associated to its distortionary effect. The famous result of Barro's theory is that the optimal fiscal policy that minimizes tax distortions is a constant tax rate over time. This tax rate is then a function of the permanent level of spending, and the public debt can be explained as a 'distortion smoother' and a 'shock absorber' (Grilli, Masciandaro and Tabellini, 1991: 342).[9] Establishing this constant path, deficits generated during periods of decreasing revenues and growing expenditures (typical of adverse economic shocks), should be financed by issuing debt (Figure 2.7). This debt will be cancelled during times of better economic conditions, when budgetary surpluses will be generated.[10]

According to the theory's postulates, tax rates must not be changed when temporary shocks occur, but only when the permanent conditions in the economy change.

This economic theory presents very clearly the sources of public deficits and surpluses, as well as associating public debt generation with cyclical

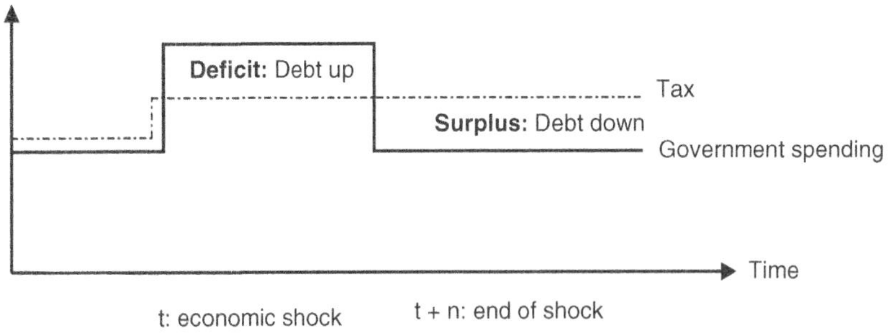

Figure 2.7 Tax-smoothing model

smoothing. It is important to note at this point that Barro's tax-smoothing theory borrows some important elements from alternative theories about optimal fiscal policies, such as the pro-cyclical and the counter-cyclical theories of fiscal policy.

The main difference between Barro's theory and the other two is the following: the pro-cyclical fiscal policy theory states that the optimal fiscal policy is the policy that maintains a balanced budget by adjusting public spending to the fluctuation of public revenues and the economic cycle; the counter-cyclical fiscal policy theory proposed by Keynes advocates increasing public spending during times of recession in order to spend out of the recession and return to a situation of economic growth when public revenues will be higher than public expenditures and new surpluses will be generated to repay the debt generated by the deficits created during the recession. In this respect, the new contribution made by Barro was to advocate a constant tax over time in a Keynesian framework of counter-cyclical fiscal policies.

This theory seems to provide a very convincing explanation for at least part of the observed variation in fiscal policies in Europe between 1960 and 2000. The tax-smoothing theory is very useful in explaining, for example, why after the oil shock of 1973 the debt-to-GDP ratios increased in all western economies. At that moment, the shock was interpreted as a temporary one, and deficits generated by the shock were financed issuing new debt. In addition, if periods of deficit, in Figure 2.7, are considered as episodes of fiscal expansion, and periods of surpluses are considered as episodes of fiscal adjustment, then the theory also provides an explanation for the economic determinants of fiscal adjustments.

But what this economic theory cannot explain is why after the 1980s, when it was already assumed by most economists that the shock had permanently affected the structure of the economy, debt continued to accumulate.[11] Nor can the theory explain why we observe in the last three decades wide variations in the levels of debt (in a range that goes from an average of 25 per cent of GDP in Finland, to over 100 per cent in Belgium[12]), in cases where those economies are closely interrelated, and had been impacted by economic cycles of very similar strength and timing.

This economic theory cannot explain why different countries present different composition of their revenues and expenditures, and why during episodes of fiscal adjustment some countries decide to increase taxes, while others decide to reduce expenditures.

Finally, it cannot account either for the persistent tendency to run pro-cyclical fiscal policies in the last 30 years. Instead of reducing government deficits during periods of economic growth, governments have been launching expansionary fiscal policies. This has impeded counter-cyclical smoothing, because in these circumstances governments have been forced to reduce deficits during economic recessions to prevent deficits and debt spiralling out of control. 'Fiscal policies have thereby amplified the effects of cyclical swings in a pro-cyclical way rather that having the desired stabilizing effect' (EC, 2001: 7). This pro-cyclical behaviour is especially illustrative of the rigidities of the budget, and it is an example of how political leaders find it easier to justify a fiscal adjustment during an economic downturn.

2.4 The politics of fiscal policies and fiscal adjustments

Given the previously mentioned limitations of economic theory to give a full account of the observed variation in fiscal policy, the introduction of political factors into the analysis of budgetary processes is intended to reach a deeper understanding of how these processes work by integrating domestic economic conditions and politico-institutional factors into the same framework.

The literature on the political economy of fiscal policy dates back to the nineteenth century with the Italian and Swedish schools of public finance (see Casares Ripol, 2002). In the past century, the work of Buchanan (1960) and Buchanan and Wagner (1976) connecting the inability of voters to understand the caveats of fiscal policy with the government's tendency to deviate from the optimal path revived the interest on the political determinants of fiscal policy.

Since the end of the 1980s, a substantial number of scholars started to study different institutional and political aspects which influence the fiscal decisions made by governments. Initially, all of these new politico-economic models of fiscal decision departed from the tax-smoothing framework described in the previous section, and tried to explain observed deviations in the smoothing behaviour as the result of institutional factors mediated by electoral constraints.[13] These new models varied substantially in the type of electoral system,[14] the degree of fiscal centralization,[15] and the budgetary laws[16] under which fiscal policy decisions were taken. But, in general, their most important contribution was to develop a new theoretical framework under which the effect of political factors on fiscal policy decisions could be empirically tested.[17]

This first wave of theoretical and empirical literature on the political determinants of 'deviated' fiscal policies served as the basis for a second wave of studies, during the second half of the 1990s, which aimed to ascertain what would be the economic and political effects of correcting those 'deviated' fiscal policies through strong fiscal adjustments. In terms of economic effects, the most relevant articles were those that presented the non-Keynesian effects of a certain type of fiscal consolidations,[18] and those that discussed the importance of the timing[19] and composition[20] of fiscal adjustments for the likelihood of their success. And regarding the possible political effects of undertaking a fiscal adjustment, the most important studies were those that surprisingly demonstrated that large consolidations do not necessarily have to be associated with electoral defeats.[21]

In trying to find what are the political and economic determinants that explain the variation observed in the timing, the duration, and the composition of fiscal adjustments in the EU, the last section of this chapter will elaborate the main hypotheses of the book based on the literature on the political and economic determinants that explain different fiscal policies (deviated or not). But, in this case, because this book is not about fiscal policies in general, but mainly focuses on fiscal adjustments, it will pay special attention to those factors directly affecting the cabinet when they are confronted with the politically difficult decision of launching a fiscal consolidation. Under this premise, only three groups of factors will be considered fully because they are the only ones that really affect any cabinet when it has to decide how to reduce the public deficit: (1) how many politicians have a voice in the decision; (2) when is the next election that may or may not punish these politicians for this decision; and (3) what is the ideological position of the politicians who take that decision.

Fragmentation of decision-making

Most studies dealing with the problem of public deficit creation and public deficit reduction have focused primarily on the idea that fragmentation in decision-making has negative implications for expenditure control. The reasoning behind this idea is the following: if a majority has to be formed to pass any legislation on the budget, and there are a lot of parties that need to be satisfied to count on their vote, then a balanced budget will be very difficult to achieve because each group in the majority will push for particular spending programmes, but it will only internalize a part of the costs and distortions of the associated increase in revenues needed to equilibrate the budget (Weingast, Shepsle and Johnson, 1981).

Therefore, the larger the number of actors with a voice in the fiscal decision-making process, the stronger the pressure for more expenditures, and thus the larger the deviation from the optimal fiscal policy. For example, coalition governments or big cabinets (with many spending ministries) would be less likely to undertake a fiscal adjustment.

Alesina and Drazen (1991) show in a war of attrition model how the distributional struggle among different interest groups delays the adoption of the efficient policy of balancing the budget.[22] They also show that the more polarized the groups are in a country, the group that concedes first bears a relatively higher burden, and then each group tries to hold out longer and stabilization is delayed. The predictions of this theoretical work have been confirmed by many empirical studies. Both Roubini and Sachs (1989a, 1989b) and Grilli, Masciandaro and Tabellini (1991) found that fragmented governments, defined in a scale called 'type of government' ranging from majority governments to minority coalitions, tended to be associated with larger public deficits.

Taking into account all of these previous considerations about the effects of fragmentation on fiscal policy, when the book proceeds in Chapters 3 and 4 with the analysis of the determinants of different fiscal adjustment strategies in the European Union, it will basically examine the effect of coalition size and cabinet size on fiscal adjustment strategies. This is so because, as already explained, the first part of this book focuses on the factors that affect fiscal decisions at the cabinet level. Thus, to consider the effect of electoral systems or the polarization of the electorate, will be nothing but analysing proxies instead of actual factors. If more proportional systems are more likely to generate coalition governments, then what is appropriate is to study the number of parties in the coalition and not an artificial classification of the type of electoral system or the type of government.

Therefore, in the context of fiscal adjustment episodes, one would expect large coalitions and big cabinets to be negatively correlated to the likelihood of starting a fiscal consolidation. And if forced to do so (in the context of the Maastricht process, for example), these fragmented governments would probably prefer to undertake the fastest adjustment possible, and through a revenue-based strategy of adjustment that leaves the level of expenditures unchanged. Note that coalition governments do not necessarily have to be associated with many spending ministers. Sometimes that is the case, but in other situations, as usually occurs in Italy, different parties agree to form a government as long as all parties' elites get a position in the cabinet, even if those are merely representative ministries and do not have spending powers.

This is so, because coalition governments are made of different parties representing different groups of the electorate that they want to satisfy. Satisfaction of those groups does not necessarily mean direct transfers of money (even though sometimes it is the case), but it will certainly imply the implementation of at least part of the policies contained in their electoral programmes. The higher the number of different policies to be implemented the higher the expenditures generated, and the higher the level of revenues that must be levied to finance those expenditures. In countries like Belgium, where the electorate is very fragmented (divided simultaneously by ideological, religious and nationalistic cleavages), and the proportionality of its electoral system tries to provide representation to all these groups, governments have been traditionally formed by more than three parties. The skyrocketing levels of their public debt reflects precisely, the historical tendency of these fragmented governments to spend more than they collect, and to finance the difference by issuing debt.

Proximity of elections

Elections can influence the government's decision on the budget in various ways.

First of all, if the government considers that it will be re-elected when the economy is growing and the unemployment rate is low, then it may be willing to initiate a fiscal expansion just before the election in order to increase the probability of being re-elected. This behaviour on the part of government will generate political business cycles.[23] But if this behaviour is never punished by the electorate, it will also generate progressively accumulating debt associated with each fiscal expansion previous to every election. This type of electoral influence on fiscal policy only holds under two assumptions: (1) there exists fiscal illusion among voters, according to which they overestimate the benefits of current expenditures and underestimate the future tax burden that will be needed to finance current expenditure;[24] and/or (2) voters are totally misinformed, and this is why it is difficult for them to fully understand the details of public budget's composition and its long-term impact. Thus politicians that give validity to these previous assumptions will be willing to cut taxes and increase public consumption and transfers before elections.

The second type of electoral effect on fiscal policies is related to the previous one, and has to do with the strategic use of debt by the incumbent government. For example, a conservative government which dislikes the provision of public goods, if it is certain that it is going to be substituted by a leftist spending government willing to expand the provision of public services, may find it strategically optimal to leave less money to spend by the incoming new cabinet. By leaving a significant level of debt, the conservative government would have 'tied the hands' of the leftist government, and would have obliged it to raise new taxes (which is unpopular) and/or not to comply with its electoral programme of expansion of public services (which will cause considerable disillusionment in its electorate). With this strategic use of the debt, the incumbent conservative government would have dramatically increased its probabilities of defeating the new leftist government in the next round of elections, and coming back into government.[25]

Taking the previous literature into consideration, one would expect the proximity of elections to decrease the probability that any type of government starts a fiscal consolidation. Or, if it is inside a fiscal adjustment episode, one would expect the proximity of elections to increase the probability that the adjustment effort ends, because it is very unpopular and reduces the probability of a government being re-elected. With respect to the composition of the fiscal adjustment, proximity of elections should be associated with a stronger preference among governments not to reduce the most popular items of the budget (like transfers and family allowances), and cutting instead other items if this is necessary for the fiscal adjustment to succeed.

Ideology of the party in government

Finally, the third political element that may have an effect in the formulation of fiscal policies and fiscal adjustment strategies is the ideology of the party in government.

By assuming that the ideology of cabinet members can influence their decision in relation to a fiscal adjustment strategy, this study is assuming that ideology of the party in government matters for economic policy-making. In taking this position, this book departs totally from Downs' assertion that policy-makers are only office-seekers, and also from Lindblom's assertion that economic policies tend to converge as the role of businesses in the economy gains importance.

The rejection of the Downsian view, according to which political parties 'formulate policies in order to win elections, rather than win elections in order to formulate policies' (Downs, 1957: 28), is based on two arguments. First, as spelled out by Przeworski and Sprague (1986), Alesina (1989) and Alesina and Rosenthal (1994) the prospect of new parties entering to fill any ideological gap left unoccupied, the threat of abstention by voters with strong ideological preferences, and the crucial role played by party activists in controlling the degree of ideologization of their candidate, are three factors[26] that contribute decisively to generating centrifugal pressures in two-party systems. And secondly, if the left benefits electorally from pursuing interventionist economic policies that alleviate the situation of the workers and the poor, and the right benefits from being more supportive of market forces,[27] one could expect that those parties keep pursuing differentiated economic policies, because this behaviour will simultaneously satisfy their policy preferences and their goal of re-election.

Together with the Downsian argument that centripetal competition to win the median voter means the end of partisan politics, most advocates of the 'unique economic policy' thesis have argued that increasing globalization offers a new exit possibility to investors threatened by taxing leftist governments. The argument is based on that made by Charles Lindblom (1977) according to which, because governments depend upon good macroeconomic performance to be re-elected, and this good performance depends in turn on the investment made by capitalists, the best option for every government is not to tax capitalists and to prevent intervening in the economy. Recently, this argument has been reinforced by the fact that under the current globalization process, international investors not willing to pay the taxes imposed by interventionist governments can now also decide to move their capital away to a country where 'cheaper' conditions for investment exist.

There are, as well, three reasons for rejecting the previous assertion that international investors are the policy-makers of today.

First, the welfare state consensus of the postwar years, which channelled the fight of the working class through capitalist democracy, in exchange for welfare systems and workers' participation on the distribution of the growing output generated by capitalist production (Przeworski, 1986), still holds today. Capitalists trying to break that consensus will again face fierce opposition by workers, mobilized at the domestic level by old trade unions, or at the international level by new anti-globalization movements.

Secondly, market integration and globalization increases the vulnerability of the population by increasing market dislocations and risk exposure, and thus increasing citizen's demands for political intervention in the economy to compensate wealth losses and provide new safety nets (Garrett, 1998).

And thirdly, it has been proved that those economies in which encompassing trade unions have made possible growth without inflation, are economies that provide better conditions for investment.[28] This is so because more equality in the distribution of income, in countries with comprehensive public health and education systems, generate economies with very productive workers and very stable societies, that grow more[29] and thus are very attractive to investors.

However, the assumption that ideology has a role to play in economic policy-making in general, and in fiscal policies and fiscal adjustment strategies in particular, is not only based on all those previous theoretical arguments. On the contrary, it is also based on the convincing empirical evidence found by prominent political economists which supported the thesis that politics and ideology matter for economic policy-making and economic policy outcomes.

The first literature on the subject provided empirical evidence that supported the thesis that left-wing governments fought unemployment while right-wing governments were especially worried about inflation (Hibbs, 1977, 1987).

This clearly meant that the former used Keynesian policies of demand management to achieve full employment, while the latter maintained small and balanced budgets to let the market achieve its full employment equilibrium, regardless of the consequences for equality. Nevertheless, many studies came immediately to demonstrate that after the oil shocks of the 1970s, governmental policies on the demand side only had temporary effects because of rational economic agents,[30] were inflationary except under certain underlying conditions of the labour market[31] and depended on the state[32] and on the evolution of the international economy.[33]

As a result, political parties were only left with the possibility of affecting economic policies on the supply side. Here again, partisan differences of economic policies were found. Boix (1996, 1997) demonstrated that left-wing governments are likely to implement interventionist supply-side policies, through the public provision of human and physical capital, to increase growth and the competitiveness of the economy, and to improve the position of the poorest in society. Capital will not fly out of the country to avoid higher taxation if public investment is expected to increase the overall level of productivity in the economy.

On the other hand, right-wing cabinets consider the public provision of capital to be inefficient and distortionary. They 'expect capital to invest in a way that will maximize its individual rate of return and, hence, in the absence of externalities, the social rate of return' (Boix, 1997: 818).

Updated empirical evidence for the 15 EU member states shown in Table 2.4 seems to offer further corroboration of these different approaches to public investment, even during the years of strongest fiscal consolidation in the EU previous to the 'Maastricht exam'. In countries with left-wing governments, the average share of public investment to GDP between 1993 and 1997 was almost half a point higher than the average public investment in countries with right-wing governments.

Table 2.4 Average public investment by cabinet's ideology in the EU, 1970–2000

Average public investment (per cent GDP) by government (EU-15)	*1970–89*	*1990–2000*	*1993–97 (Maastricht Adjustment)*
Right-wing governments	3.30 (n = 145)	2.68 (n = 59)	2.61 (n = 28)
Centre governments	3.75 (n = 60)	2.75 (n = 62)	2.73 (n = 31)
Left-wing governments	3.78 (n = 78)	2.88 (n = 43)	3.06 (n = 16)

Source: Own elaboration.

Therefore, after taking into account all of these previous considerations, the 'partisanship hypothesis' regarding the composition of the budget and the strategies of fiscal adjustment, has to be based on the two general assumptions under 'which scholars have modelled the impact of government partisanship on economic policies. In the first place, all political parties prefer policies that maximize growth ... [and] in the second place, parties adopt distinctive economic strategies depending on their redistributive consequences' (Boix, 1997: 816).

It is plausible to assume that social democratic parties have their principal electoral constituency among workers and the middle- and low-income part of the population (at least among those below the average income of the median voter). These sectors are the most vulnerable to cyclical downturns and suffer from different barriers to equal access to opportunities and services, as a consequence of their purchasing power and their education. Thus, social democratic parties, representing these sectors, while giving importance to economic growth, are also especially worried about how the benefits of economic growth are distributed and about equality in general.

Ideally, social democratic parties would use the public sector to smooth the impact that economic downturns have on the above-mentioned classes (through unemployment benefits and social transfers) and would try at the same time to redistribute income and promote equality.[34] Then, following the socialist preference for equality, redistribution, social benefits to the unemployed, and interventionist supply-side policies in the form of the public provision of human and physical capital, one should expect left-wing governments to be associated with higher levels of public expenditure on public consumption, social transfers, public investment and the government wage bill to pay for an extensive public administration.

To finance all these expenditures, left-wing governments would be expected to tax more and to tax more progressively. Higher public expenditures financed by higher public revenues do not mean that one should expect left-wing governments to run deficits more often than right-wing governments. A stronger state presence in the economy does not initially have to be associated with unbalanced budgets. Moreover, according to Keynesianism, demand management of the economy requires that surpluses are built during periods of economic growth, to be used for consumption-smoothing during periods of recession. Also, to intervene on the supply side of the economy through public investment socialist governments should prefer surplus or close to balanced budgets.

By contrast, right-wing parties obtain the majority of their votes from the economically accommodated part of the population (or at least from those with average income above the median voter's income). These people have more private resources to smooth their personal consumption in periods of economic downturn, are particularly concerned about inflation, and, as potential private investors, they suffer most from the crowding-out effect of public intervention in the economy.

Thus, right-wing governments would prefer to run balanced and small budgets, because this means a lower level of state intervention in the economy. As a result, right-wing governments would generally tax less and spend less than socialist governments. Lower levels of expenditures to GDP would require lower levels of public revenues, and ideally less distortionary taxes of market mechanisms and private incentives.[35]

In the framework of fiscal adjustments and as previously stated, one can initially hypothesize that both social democratic and conservative governments would be expected to start a fiscal consolidation with the same probability. Nevertheless, given their preferences, they would be expected to adopt opposite adjustment strategies, not in their timing and duration, but in terms of their composition. Left-wing governments should prefer revenue-based strategies, and if forced to freeze or reduce expenditures they should be expected to try and maintain the government wage bill, transfers payments and public investment, in order to maintain their capacity to intervene in the economy in future. By contrast, right-wing governments should prefer expenditure-based strategies, which subsequently allow them to reduce the most distortionary taxes and expenditures of the budget.

2.5 The five hypotheses of the book

The expected behaviour of governments willing to undertake a fiscal adjustment depends on the different interactions between the three sets of economic and the three sets of political factors detailed in the previous section. As illustrated above, alternative theories generate multiple expectations about the type of adjustment strategy that the government will implement, which may sometimes even seem contradictory. For example, some factors (such as a big coalition government) could induce a government to raise public revenues to consolidate the budget, while other factors (such as the proximity of elections) may discourage it. The relative explanatory power of these different factors is a matter of empirical testing.

It is therefore important to organize the different expectations raised in this chapter, and reformulate them in the form of different theoretical hypotheses within the framework of the book's questions. As summarized in Chapter 1, the book is motivated by five clear questions that deal with:

- the *timing* of fiscal adjustments: why and when are fiscal adjustments launched by governments in the first place?
- the *duration* of adjustment episodes: what makes fiscal consolidations last?
- the *composition* of fiscal adjustments: what factors explain why different countries implement different consolidation strategies in terms of budgetary composition, in a generalized process of deficit reduction?
- the *economic consequences* of fiscal adjustments: what is the macroeconomic impact of alternative consolidation strategies in terms of growth and equality?
- the *political consequences* of fiscal adjustments: what is the electoral impact of cutting the budget deficit?

The previous section of this chapter advances the likely impact of six sets of factors on fiscal adjustments (economic cycle and employment rate, prices and monetary conditions, debt accumulation, fragmentation of decision-making, proximity of elections, and government ideology). In order to answer the five questions above, the expected impact of these six sets of variables can be grouped around five different hypotheses.

The *fiscal stress hypothesis* Fiscal adjustments tend to start sooner when the structural budget deficit is high and when the relative cyclical position of the economy is positive. This means that the timing of fiscal adjustments is expected to depend heavily on initial fiscal and economic conditions, although elections may induce short-run deviations in the probability of starting fiscal adjustment, which in any case will be temporary. This hypothesis will be tested in Chapter 3 in order to answer the first question that motivates this book.

The *debt burden hypothesis* Fiscal adjustments tend to last longer when the debt burden is high, when there is a strong government in place, and when elections are not imminent. This means that the duration of fiscal adjustment is expected to depend heavily on initial fiscal conditions, although for stronger consolidations the probability of keeping the adjustment going will depend heavily on the relative cohesion of the cabinet and the proximity of elections. This hypothesis will be tested in Chapter 3 also, in order to answer the second question that motivates this book.

The *partisanship hypothesis* Fiscal adjustments tend to rely on revenue increases rather than on spending cuts when there is a social democratic majority in the government. The opposite applies for conservative governments. This means that despite the likely effect that other factors may have on the composition of fiscal adjustments (such as fragmented cabinets being associated with revenue-based consolidations), it is expected that the decision to raise revenues or cut expenditures depends very much on the ideological profile of the cabinet, motivated by the different preferences that right-wing and left-wing governments tend to have with respect to the relative role of the public sector in the economy. This hypothesis will be tested in Chapter 4 in order to answer the third question that motivates this book.

The *economic trade-off hypothesis* Expenditure-based fiscal adjustments can have, under certain accompanying conditions, a positive impact on economic growth but at the expense of growing income inequality. In this respect, the hypothesis is that if fiscal adjustments are based on spending cuts in the most rigid items of the budget, this can generate positive effects on growth *via* different supply-side and demand-side mechanisms. In contrast, the spending cuts on the rigid items (most likely wages and transfers) tend to reduce social redistributive policies and thus have a negative impact on inequality. This hypothesis will be tested in Chapter 6 in order to answer the fourth question that motivates this book.

The *fiscal voting hypothesis* Finally, fiscal adjustments are expected to diminish the probabilities of a prime minister's re-election. This is so because both tax increases and/or spending cuts associated with fiscal consolidations are usually disliked by voters. In fact, the negative effect that fiscal adjustments have on the probability of a prime minister's re-election can only be compensated for by good economic performance by the time the election takes place, or by a very credible commitment in this direction. This hypothesis will be tested in Chapter 7 in order to answer the fifth question that motivates this book.

As can be deduced from these different hypotheses, the whole underlying approach behind this book is that there exists a circular connection between causes and consequences of different fiscal adjustment strategies. This circular connection would go from economic and political factors affecting the three dimensions of fiscal adjustments (their timing, duration and composition) to the likely economic and political consequences associated with these strategies, which would in turn feed back to the initial stage of the whole decision-making process (see Figure 2.8)

The demonstration of this circular relationship and the empirical testing of the previous hypotheses is the subject of the rest of the book.

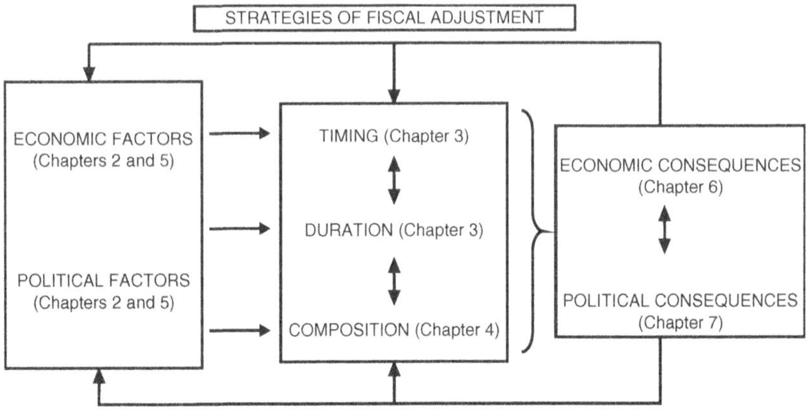

Figure 2.8 The circular structure of the causes and consequences of fiscal adjustment strategies

2.6 Conclusion

This chapter has developed the theoretical framework of the book. It has emphasized the direct role that fiscal policies play in the management of the aggregate demand, and their indirect impact on the aggregate supply of the economy. Today, this role is even more important because of the European context of the single currency and the condition of full capital mobility.

One could have expected that over the past three decades most European economies would show similar fiscal outcomes, given their strong interrelation. In general, there has been a common tendency in the past thirty years to spend more than what was collected, and thus to run deficits and accumulate debt. Nevertheless, despite this general picture, this chapter has presented abundant empirical evidence of wide variation in the level of public revenues, public expenditures, public deficits and public debt. Even more important is the evidence that shows that when EU member states decided to correct those imbalances, some have decided to undertake successive but short fiscal consolidations, while others pursued strong, one-off adjustments. Strategies of fiscal consolidation varied not only in timing, length and strength, but also in composition. Some countries decided to follow revenue-based fiscal adjustments, while others followed expenditure-based consolidations.

Economic theory is insufficient to explain this variation in fiscal policies and fiscal adjustment strategies, and this is why political explanations have been advanced. This chapter has formulated five hypotheses and has discussed in depth the theoretical reasons why the economic cycle and the unemployment rate, prices and monetary conditions, the accumulated level of debt, the degree of cabinet fragmentation, the proximity of elections, and the ideology of the party in government should be expected to affect the formulation of fiscal policies and the adoption of different strategies of fiscal adjustment. The following chapters will study their actual effects.

3
Timing and Duration of Fiscal Adjustments[1]

> 'Consolidation efforts that operate to a large extent on the spending side of the budget have a higher chance to survive than consolidations that relay mostly on increased revenues.'
>
> Von Hagen, Hallett and Strauch, 2001: 11

The first two questions that this book attempts to answer are why fiscal adjustments are undertaken in the first place, and what makes them last.

This chapter answers the first of these questions about the timing of fiscal consolidations, and half of the second question, in the part that refers to the duration dimension of fiscal adjustments. The chapter also constitutes the first step in the empirical effort of this book to validate or refute with actual evidence the theoretical hypotheses advanced in Chapter 2.

The first two sections of the Chapter outline what constitutes a fiscal adjustment, and discuss how many options governments face in the event of having to reduce their budget deficits. When confronted by the need to reduce the public deficit, governments have to design a strategy that determines the timing, the duration, and the composition of the fiscal consolidation episode. While section 3.3. of this chapter will deal with the timing decision, sections 3.4. and 3.5 will study the duration dimension of fiscal adjustments. The analysis of the composition dimension will then be the subject of Chapter 4.

The duration analysis will be divided into two parts:

The first presents the results of a non-parametric analysis of the duration of fiscal adjustments, which shows how the probability of ending a fiscal consolidation episode is dependent upon its accumulated duration.

Then, because time-dependency explains only part of the duration of fiscal adjustment episodes, the second part presents the results of a parametric analysis, in which different economic and political variables are included in order to fully understand what explains why some fiscal adjustments have lasted longer than others. The final section of this chapter will test whether or not the results presented in the previous sections are sensitive to changes in the definition of fiscal adjustments. It is very interesting to see how political factors gain importance in explaining the duration of fiscal consolidations, as the definition of what constitutes an adjustment is made more demanding. These results afford the conclusion that, for stronger fiscal efforts, economic determinants of duration lose explanatory power, while all of the political factors affecting the cabinet become crucial in sustaining the consolidation.

3.1 What is a fiscal adjustment?

The budgetary dimension of all economic activity developed by the public sector, already presented in Chapter 2, can be summarized as follows. The government buys goods and services and pays public employees (*G*). And it also makes transfers to households, in the form of unemployment benefits, pensions, or family allowances (*TR*). This constitutes the core of public expenditures that must be financed raising taxes from corporations and individuals (*TX*). A public deficit exists when total public revenues (*TX*) are insufficient to pay for total public expenditures ($G + TR$). This difference is covered annually by borrowing money, and this constitutes the public debt (*DB*), that every year renders some interest payments (rDB_{t-1}) that the government has to repay in the following year:

$$\text{Public Budget Balance} = \text{Public Revenues} - \text{Public Expenditures}$$
$$\text{Surplus or Deficit} = (TX_t) - [(G_t) + TR_t) + (rDB_{t-1})]$$

Therefore, each year public deficits can be either increased or reduced by the government. A fiscal adjustment takes place when in any given year the public deficit is reduced. Nevertheless, as explained in the previous chapter, there are two economic factors that every year can be influencing the budget balance and which are outside a government's immediate control. These are the economic cycle and the accumulated level of debt.

Because the intention is to focus on those fiscal adjustments that are politically driven, those in which the government takes a tight discretionary decision to reduce the budget deficit, a fiscal adjustment is defined as any improvement of the cyclically adjusted primary deficit from one year to the next. This means that after discounting the effect of the cycle on the budget,[2] and subtracting the amount paid as interest on debt (rDB_{t-1}), it is possible to look at the fiscal stance of a certain country in a certain year,[3] and determine if that year has been one of fiscal expansion or fiscal consolidation.

For example, if in a certain year the cyclically adjusted primary balance has increased by 1 per cent of GDP with respect to the previous year, then this year can be considered as a fiscal consolidation year, but if it has decreased by 1 per cent of GDP, then it has to be classified as a fiscal expansion year.

3.2 Strategies of fiscal adjustment: timing, duration and composition

In order to talk about fiscal adjustments, they have to occur first. As a response to the wave of fiscal expansions and the subsequent structural budget deficits accumulated during the 1960s and the 1970s in the European Union, fiscal adjustments have become more and more frequent over the past two decades (Table 3.1).

Once the government has decided about the timing of a fiscal adjustment, and it is totally committed to budget deficit reduction, it has to consider what is its preferred strategy to achieve the goal of re-equilibrating the budget.

In this respect, a strategy of fiscal adjustment can be defined as the group of measures needed to balance the cyclically adjusted primary budget balance, and approximate cyclically adjusted primary expenditures and cyclically adjusted revenues in a given year. The cabinet's decision over these measures is mainly a decision over two crucial dimensions of the fiscal adjustment strategy: (1) how long will it last (duration); and (2) what items of the budget will be affected by the consolidation effort (composition).

With respect to duration, fiscal adjustments can be either drastic or progressive. And with respect to composition, the public deficit can be reduced by increasing public revenues to pay for the same level of public expenditures (a revenue-based strategy), or by reducing public expenditures while public revenues are maintained or even reduced (an expenditure-based strategy). More concretely, the range of possible combinations that are available to any government willing to start a fiscal consolidation is:

—Type 1 Strategy (S1): To increase revenues more than it increases expenditures; $\Delta\Delta R$; ΔE
—Type 2 Strategy (S2): To increase revenues and freeze expenditures; ΔR; $= E$
—Type 3 Strategy (S3): To increase revenues and reduce expenditures; ΔR; ∇E
—Type 4 Strategy (S4): To freeze revenues and reduce expenditures; $= R$; ∇E
—Type 5 Strategy (S5): To reduce revenues less than it reduces expenditures. ∇R; $\nabla\nabla E$

Table 3.1 Number of years under a fiscal adjustment, by decade

1960–69	*1970–74*	*1975–79*	*1980–84*	*1985–89*	*1990–94*	*1995–2000*
1	6	20	29	28	24	53

Source: Own elaboration based on Table 2.2.

However, within these broad strategies more specificities arise. Apart from the speed with which they are implemented, the decision over the composition of the adjustment has to be even more specific. For example, the government has to decide if an increase in public revenues is going to be achieved through an increase in direct taxes, indirect taxes, or social contributions. Furthermore, direct taxes can be on labour or capital, and so on. The same happens with regard to public expenditures. Variation in expenditures can be achieved through different combinations of change in current or capital expenditures. In more detail these depend on the amount of subsidies, social transfers, public consumption, public wages (which is a function of the number of public employees), public investment, and so on.

For example, strategies of adjustment in the 1970s followed a general pattern of the expansion of the public sector. An increase in public expenditures was financed and surpassed by an even bigger increase in revenues. In the 1980s and the 1990s the strategies of adjustment became, however, increasingly divergent. During the 1980s, a majority of adjustments followed the previous pattern or the one characterized by increases in revenues and the freezing of expenditures. During the 1990s, finally, countries decided to reduce public expenditures, but the differences in the type of expenditures frozen or reduced increased.

In the process of deficit reduction to fulfil the Maastricht criteria, Austria, Denmark, Finland, Ireland, Spain and the United Kingdom decided to cut transfers, while the rest preferred to freeze them. Public consumption was reduced in France, Ireland, Spain and the United Kingdom, increased in the Netherlands and Belgium and maintained in the other countries. Public wages were reduced in Belgium, Finland, Sweden and the United Kingdom, while they were frozen in the rest of the EU, especially in Austria and Spain. In general, France and Greece reduced their public deficits during the 1990s by increasing their revenues and freezing their expenditures. Germany, Italy and Sweden and the United Kingdom increased public revenues and reduced public expenditures. And Belgium, Denmark and Spain followed the strategy of maintaining revenues and reducing expenditures, while Austria, Finland, Ireland and the Netherlands reduced both revenues and expenditures.[4]

3.3 The timing of fiscal adjustments: the 'fiscal stress hypothesis'

In order to test what are the economic and political conditions that have to be present before fiscal adjustment takes place, this section estimates a very simple probit model with a dependent variable that will take value 1 when a fiscal consolidation started, and value 0 otherwise. Note that I will consider that a fiscal adjustment has started when the change in the cyclically adjusted budget balance in one year exceeds 1 per cent of the cyclically adjusted GDP,[5] as reported by the AMECO database of the European Commission for the

15 member states. In the period 1960–2000, there were 115 such 'starts of fiscal consolidations'.

To discern the importance of initial and accompanying economic conditions to start a fiscal adjustment episode, the analysis includes as independent variables different measures of the three main economic factors influencing the budget: the economic cycle, monetary conditions, and debt accumulation. These three aspects will be captured using the following variables:[6]

1. Cyclical position of the domestic economy in the year before and during the start of the consolidation episode measured by the output gap. This is computed as the difference between the actual output and an estimated output trend, applying the Hodrick–Prescott (HP) filter, as explained at the end of the first section of this chapter. The hypothesis is that better economic conditions will lead to higher probabilities of starting a consolidation, since more revenues and less expenditures are naturally associated with periods of economic growth.
2. Cyclical position of the European economy. To describe this situation the analysis includes the EU-15 output gap and the EU-15 average structural budget balance.
3. Monetary policy stance. Following Von Hagen, Hallett and Strauch (2001: 11), I construct a *monetary conditions index* for each country. The index is the sum of the short-term real interest rate and the real exchange rate, each weighted by its sample standard deviation. An increase in the monetary conditions index thus indicates either an increase in the short-term real interest rate or a real appreciation of the currency. Both can be interpreted as a tightening of monetary policy. Because monetary policy and fiscal policy are usually inversely related, the hypothesis is that a tightening of monetary policy will reduce the probability of starting a fiscal adjustment.
4. Fiscal policy stance measured by the primary cyclically adjusted budget balance. An increase in this variable implies a worsening of the structural balance (typically meaning a higher deficit). Because unbalanced fiscal positions are unsustainable in the long run, the more negative the budget balance is, the higher the probability of starting a fiscal adjustment. Since this independent variable taken in first differences is the basis for the calculations of the dependent variable, the last two estimations in Table 3.2 are not calculated.
5. Debt accumulation. This can be easily captured by the debt-to-GDP ratio, and describes the fiscal position of any country before or during the consolidation episode. This is a continuous variable that measures the public debt with respect to Gross Domestic Product for each country. Given that the dependent variable has been built based on cyclically adjusted budget balances that include interest payments generated by the pending

debt, one would expect higher debt-to-GDP ratios will be associated with higher probabilities of starting fiscal consolidations.

In addition to these economic variables, political variables are also included in the analysis in order to capture the politico-institutional environment preceding or accompanying fiscal adjustments. These variables are the following:[7]

6. Coalition size: this variable measures the number of political parties in the government for each country and each year of the sample.[8]
7. Cabinet size: this variable measures the number of spending ministers in the cabinet[9] for each year and each country. The inclusion of both variables is related to the idea that fragmentation in decision-making is negative for expenditure control, that was fully presented in the previous chapter. Therefore, the larger the number of actors with a voice in the fiscal decision-making process, the stronger the pressure for more expenditures, and thus the larger the deviation from the optimal fiscal policy. This is why one would expect larger coalition governments and larger cabinets to be associated to lower probabilities of starting fiscal consolidations.
8. Election year: this variable takes value one when parliamentary and/or presidential elections that affect the designation of the prime minister and the cabinet take place. It takes value zero otherwise.[10] Because fiscal adjustments are unpopular, the hypothesis is that election years reduce the probability of starting fiscal consolidations.
9. Ideology of the party in government: this is captured by the degree of socialist control of the cabinet (government-left). This variable runs continuously from 0 to 100, according to the number of cabinet posts held by social democratic and other left parties, in percentage of total cabinet posts and weighted by days. As I discussed extensively in Chapter 2, one should not expect social democratic governments to run higher budget deficits than conservative governments, because long-lasting and effective intervention in the economy needs a policy of balanced budgets. On the contrary, the hypothesis is that both social democrats and conservatives will be driven more by economic and electoral considerations than by ideological ones, when deciding about the timing and duration of consolidation episodes.

Table 3.2 reports the results of a set of probit regressions of the dependent variable on the indicators of initial and accompanying politico-economic conditions defined above. The probit model estimates the likelihood of a fiscal consolidation to be started depending on the realizations of the explanatory variables in a given period. These results are very similar to those obtained by Von Hagen, Hallett and Strauch (2001: 12) using data for the OECD, although they did not include any political factors in their analysis.

The positive sign in the output gap shows that the probability of starting fiscal consolidations increases when the economy is growing. But, in contrast

Table 3.2 Probability of starting fiscal consolidations in the EU, 1960–2000

Probability of starting a fiscal adjustment	*Current level*		*Lagged level*		*First difference*	
	Univariate	*Multivariate*	*Univariate*	*Multivariate*	*Univariate*	*Multivariate*
Output gap	0.061	0.144***	−0.021	0.126**	0.151	0.078
	(1.26)	(2.95)	(1.06)	(2.70)	(1.67)	(0.99)
EU-15 output gap	−0.055	−0.301***	−0.190***	−0.221***	0.182***	−0.165
	(1.09)	(3.44)	(3.57)	(3.82)	(3.21)	(0.99)
EU-15 structural	0.023	0.169	−0.254***	−0.001	0.525***	0.614***
balance	(0.87)	(1.43)	(4.11)	(1.21)	(3.61)	(3.89)
Real monetary	0.097	−0.000	−0.048	−0.133**	0.127**	0.141**
condition	(0.85)	(0.04)	(0.56)	(1.99)	(2.23)	(2.17)
PCA Budg.balance	0.081***	0.450***	0.111***	0.499***	—	—
	(3.90)	(3.92)	(3.68)	(3.59)		
Debt–GDP ratio	0.010***	0.126***	0.009***	0.011	−0.001	0.029
	(3.67)	(3.86)	(4.01)	(1.05)	(0.65)	(1.22)
Government-left	−0.002	−0.012	0.067	0.007	−0.014	0.038
	(0.61)	(0.86)	(1.02)	(0.90)	(0.99)	(1.25)
Coalition size	−0.024*	−0.012*	−0.034	−0.042*	−0.002	−0.010*
	(1.85)	(1.88)	(1.17)	(1.78)	(0.88)	(1.86)
Cabinet size	−0.055*	−0.067**	−0.044*	−0.112**	−0.001	−0.009
	(1.89)	(2.12)	(1.74)	(2.19)	(0.78)	(0.87)
Election year	−0.009	−0.057**	0.003	0.056*	−0.010	−0.014
	(0.86)	(2.34)	(0.96)	(1.75)	(0.99)	(1.02)
Constant	−0.667*	−0.432*	−0.233	−0.788	−0.878*	−0.453**
	(1.84)	(1.81)	(1.02)	(1.22)	(1.89)	(1.99)
Observations	501	501	498	498	47	477
Log-likelihood	60.79	59.67	56.44	55.58	49.99	48.58
Pseudo R-squared	0.18	0.25	0.26	0.21	0.19	0.16
Prob > Chi2	0.000	0.000	0.000	0.000	0.000	0.000

Note: Absolute value of z-statistics in parentheses *significant at 10 per cent; **significant at 5per cent; ***significant at 1 per cent.

the EU-15 output gap enters with a negative sign in the current and the lagged levels. The combination of both signs can be interpreted as evidence showing that fiscal adjustments tend to be launched when the domestic economy is doing well relative to the EU-15 economy.

The stance of fiscal policy in the European countries decisively affects the probability of starting fiscal consolidations. This confirms the 'fiscal stress hypothesis' formulated in Chapter 2. While high European surpluses at the current level increase the probability of starting fiscal adjustments, the effect is the opposite when the lagged level is considered. Therefore, these two results point towards the existence of fiscal policy waves: a country is more likely to start a fiscal adjustment, if fiscal policy in other countries changes in that direction. The example of fiscal adjustments in Europe from the mid-1980s is very illustrative in this respect.

The effect of monetary policy on the probability of starting fiscal adjustments is only significant in the lagged levels and in first differences. In the first case the effect is negative, meaning that a tightening of monetary policy this year reduces the likelihood of starting a fiscal consolidation the following year (as predicted by some studies – for example, Mélitz, 1997). But this result is at odds with the negative effect of the same variable in first differences, which implies that a change of monetary policy this year in the direction of tightening reduces the probability of starting a fiscal adjustment during the same year.

Finally, the debt-to-GDP ratio has a very significant positive effect on the probability of starting a consolidation. The higher the current and the lagged level of public debt, the higher the probability of starting a consolidation the current year.

The effect of politico-institutional variables on the probability of starting fiscal consolidations is weaker than the effect of the economic cycle or the accumulated level of debt. For example, the ideology of the party in government does not affect the probability of starting fiscal consolidations. But the case of cabinet and coalition size, and election year, is different. Bigger coalitions and cabinets in the current and the lagged levels decrease the probability of starting fiscal consolidations, while current elections reduce the probability of launching an adjustment during the same year. Nevertheless, the result in the multivariate specification of the lagged level is relevant because it shows that the probability of starting a fiscal adjustment increases during the year after the election took place.

Both results confirm the hypothesized risk aversion that politicians have to arrive at the polls in the midst of a fiscal adjustment episode. They prefer to avoid fiscal adjustments during election years, and launch them immediately after elections have taken place and a new government arrives. One of the clearest examples of this behaviour occurred when Jacques Chirac called for early elections in 1997 in order to gain re-election before undertaking the necessary adjustment to fulfil the Maastricht criteria. This episode will be discussed in detail in Chapter 5.

3.4 The duration of fiscal adjustments: the 'debt burden hypothesis'

Given that fiscal adjustments can also vary in their duration and their composition, the chapter now focuses on the duration dimension. The duration concept is very simple to understand, because it is only related to the number of years for which the consolidation episode lasts. Nevertheless, the issue of duration is very important because it has both remarkable economic and political consequences. Very short and strong consolidation episodes can have very damaging deflationary consequences for domestic demand, because they give no time for the private sector to compensate the decreasing role of the state, and thus the country can enter a recession. But, on the other hand, if consolidations are managed more progressively and last for many years, they can be very difficult to handle politically, because the affected groups will fight harder against permanent reductions of the funding available for their programmes, than if these cuts were temporary.

Nevertheless, despite its relevance and despite the fact that in the literature on fiscal adjustments the success of fiscal consolidations has been defined in terms of duration,[11] direct and systematic studies that analyse the determinants of duration of fiscal consolidations are almost nonexistent. Only Alesina and Perotti (1995), Alesina and Ardagna (1998), Strauch (1999), and Von Hagen, Hallett and Strauch (2001) have studied the duration of consolidations, but all of them in an indirect way.

In the first two cases, the approach consisted in a two-step analysis: first, a pre-selection of consolidation episodes according to a predefined threshold; and second, a detailed account of the number of years contained in each period and a description of the main characteristics attributable to them. This approach allowed them to attribute certain characteristics as correlated with longer or shorter durations, and more or less successful experiences.

In the final two studies, Strauch (1999) and Von Hagen, Hallett and Strauch (2001) present a more detailed study of duration of fiscal consolidations in the EU, and they are the first, and indeed the only ones to date, to have used a duration model for this purpose. Nevertheless, their study only covers the period up to 1998, and probably because they focus on many more aspects of consolidations besides the determinants of duration of fiscal adjustments, the short section which they dedicate to this analysis lacks a serious discussion of the most adequate duration model for this type of analysis. But the most important gap in their study is that, although they find that some fiscal adjustments in countries like 'Belgium, Finland, France, Germany, Ireland, Portugal, Spain and the UK, occurred at times when the economic circumstances did not lead one to expect a consolidation to start' (p. 38), they did not look for any political factors that may have been influencing these economically unexpected behaviours, regarding the timing and the duration of fiscal consolidations in Europe.

Thus, it remains to be investigated why some consolidation experiences last longer than others. And it also has to be answered what are the main economic and political variables that affect the probability of ending a fiscal consolidation sooner or later. The resolution of these two questions is the core of this chapter and in order to do this a duration model will be applied. These models have been primarily used in labour economics[12] to study the duration of periods of employment and unemployment and the determinants of entry and exit rates, and they will be used here to study the duration of episodes of fiscal adjustment versus those of fiscal expansion. (See Kiefer (1988) for a literature review, and Appendix 2 for a technical description of these models.[13])

Table 3.3 Descriptive statistics: failure and duration

	Failure			*Duration*		
	All countries	*Unstable*	*Stable*	*All countries*	*Unstable*	*Stable*
Mean	0.479	0.493	0.458	2.055	1.959	2.194
Std. dev.	0.500	0.501	0.499	1.478	1.314	1.684
Variance	0.250	0.251	0.249	2.185	1.725	2.837
Skewness	0.085	0.027	0.170	1.844	1.533	1.921
Kurtosis	1.007	1.001	1.029	6.952	4.950	7.077
Obs.	237	45	92			

To apply duration analysis to fiscal consolidations implies analysing the time that passes between two consecutive years of fiscal expansion, or, in other words, the time spells between the beginning and the end of a fiscal consolidation. Using annual data on cyclically adjusted budget balances[14] between 1960 and 2000 for the 15 EU member states, I generate a dummy variable called '*Failure*', which takes value zero when the annual variation of the cyclically adjusted budget balance is bigger than zero[15] (years of fiscal consolidation), and changes to value one, when it is zero or lower than zero (years of fiscal expansion).

Using the dates in which a failure event occurs, I build a new variable called '*Duration*', which represents the time that passes between two consecutive failures – that is, the time that the fiscal consolidation lasts. In this sample, the minimum number of years that a consolidation lasts is one year, and the maximum is ten years. The sample covers five years, because there were very few observations (18) that lasted longer, but the sample still reflects 96.36 per cent of the observed data.

Table 3.3 presents the structure of the data on *Failure* and *Duration*. As can be seen, the total number of observations is 495. The average duration of fiscal consolidations is 2.06 years. The number of registered failures is 237, and the average probability of ending a fiscal consolidation is 48 per cent. The sample can be divided into two groups:

1. The group of *Highly-indebted* countries is integrated by those countries with an average Debt/GDP ratio above the EU-15 average ratio. These countries are: the United Kingdom, Greece, Netherlands, Ireland, Italy and Belgium. Their average duration is 2.19 years and the probability of ending the consolidation is 46 per cent.
2. The group of *Lowly-indebted* countries is made of those countries with an average Debt/GDP ratio below the EU-15 average ratio. These countries are: Luxembourg, Finland, France, Spain, Germany, Austria, Denmark, Portugal and Sweden. In this group the average duration of fiscal consolidations is 1.96 years, and its probability of failure is 49 per cent.

Table 3.4 Descriptive statistics: failure and duration by periods

	Failure		*Duration*		
Periods	*Mean*	*Std. dev.*	*Mean*	*Std. dev.*	*Freq.*
62/72	0.532	0.502	1.734	1.022	79
73/77	0.547	0.501	1.560	0.889	75
78/81	0.717	0.454	1.633	1.057	60
82/87	0.400	0.493	2.056	1.319	90
88/91	0.661	0.478	1.804	1.212	56
92/95	0.433	0.500	1.883	1.075	60
96/00	0.160	0.369	3.547	2.207	75
All	0.479	0.500	2.048	1.450	495

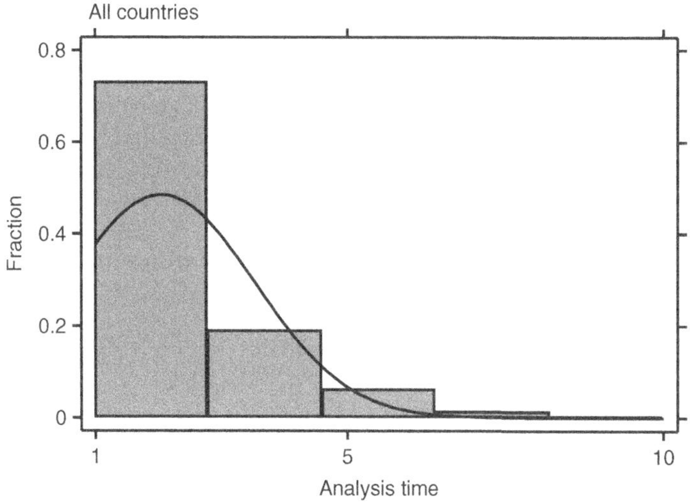

Figure 3.1 Duration of fiscal consolidations in the EU-15, 1960–2000

In addition, seven periods can be identified in the sample, all with different average durations and probabilities of failure (Table 3.4).

It is very interesting to observe that from 1962 to 1981, the average duration of fiscal consolidations was around 1.6 years, and the average probability of ending the consolidation was well above 50 per cent. Between 1982 and 1991, the average duration increased until it reached 1.9 years and the probability of failure decreased to remain in the 50 per cent range. Finally, during the 1990s, and especially from 1996 to 2000, the average duration of fiscal consolidations reached 2 years with a probability of ending the consolidation of only 16 per cent. This last result derives from the fact that at the end of 2000, which is the last year in the sample, 12 out of fifteen EU member states were still under ongoing consolidation episodes.[16] Most of those episodes were launched as a result of the Maastricht convergence criteria, and are currently reinforced by the Stability and Growth Pact. Because these consolidations were still ongoing in 2000, the probability of ending the consolidation during the period 1996–2000 is very low.

Figure 3.1 shows the duration of fiscal consolidations in the period 1960–2000. In that figure, it can be observed that 46 per cent of the fiscal consolidation episodes in the sample lasted one year, 21 per cent two years, 13 per cent three years, and 20 per cent lasted four or five years.

As could be expected, the group of *Highly-indebted* countries shows a flatter distribution than the *Lowly-indebted* ones (see Figure 3.2), because a smaller number of its fiscal consolidations finished in the first four years, and many more of them lasted five or six years.

Non-parametric estimation

Typically, duration analysis involves two steps, first a non-parametric analysis in which the dependence of duration of fiscal adjustments on time is analysed. And secondly, a parametric analysis in which other factors, apart from time dependency, are included as possible factors that can account for the observed variation in duration of adjustment episodes.

Starting with the non-parametric analysis, what this analysis tries to disentangle is the positive or negative dependence of fiscal consolidations on their accumulated duration. This is typically done by estimating the two following functions:

(a) The survivor function, which is defined as:

$$S(t) = \Pr(T \geq t) = 1 - F(t) \tag{3.1}$$

and gives the probability that the duration of the fiscal consolidation (T)[17] is greater than or equal to t.

(b) The hazard function, which is defined as:

$$h(t) = \Pr(T = t/T \geq \mathrm{t}) \tag{3.2}$$

and gives, for each duration, the probability of ending a consolidation episode, conditioned to the duration of the consolidation through that moment.

Figures 3.3 and 3.4 show the estimated survivor functions for the 15 EU member states, and by group of countries respectively.

The probabilities of continuing the fiscal consolidation after the first year and the second year drop dramatically in both groups of countries. As can be

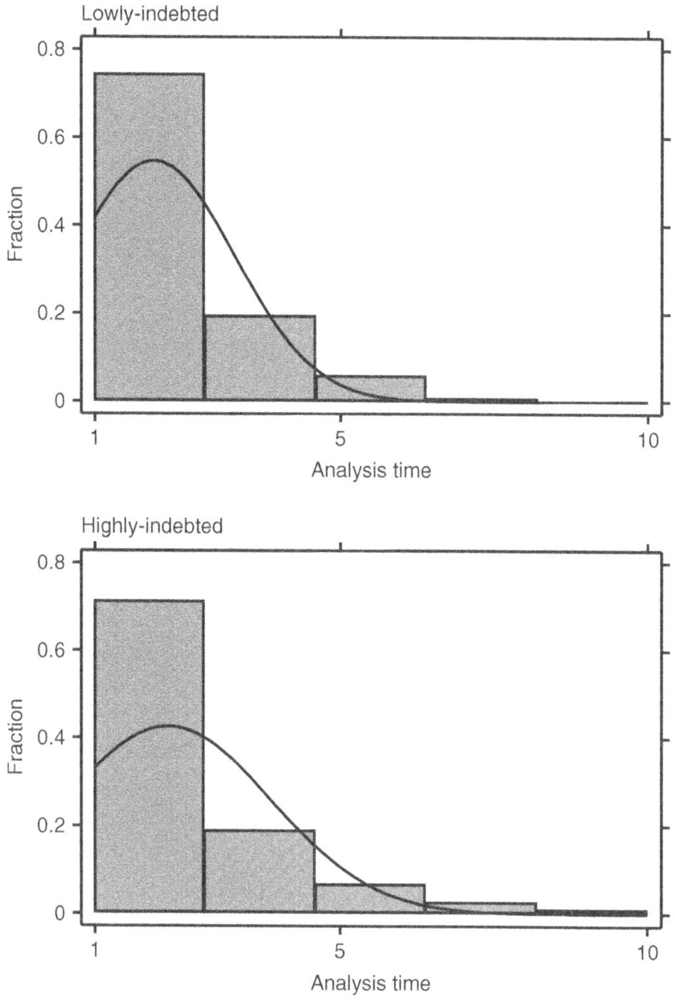

Figure 3.2 Duration of fiscal consolidations in the EU-15, 1960–2000. By group of countries

observed, the divergence between the groups increases after the second year. These results are influenced in the group of *Lowly-indebted* countries by such countries as Luxembourg and Finland, which combine very few periods of fiscal consolidation with very short durations when these few consolidations occur (average durations of 1.71 and 1.95 years, respectively). On the opposite side, in the group of *Highly-indebted* countries, Italy and Belgium combine a considerable amount of periods of fiscal consolidation with an average duration

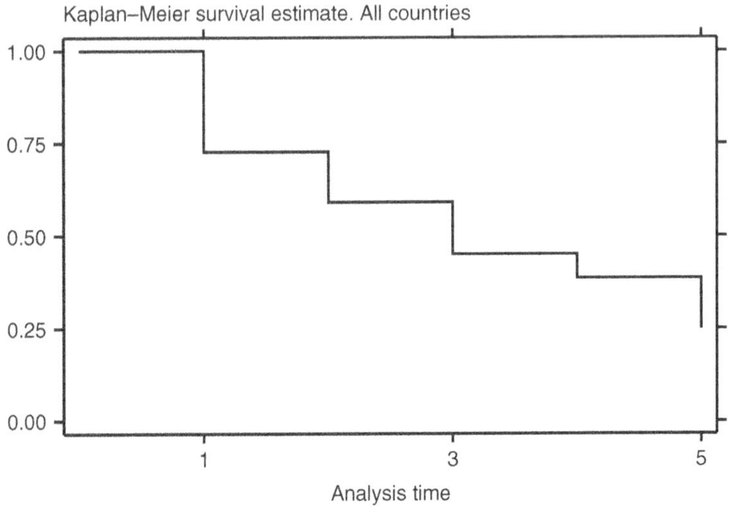

Figure 3.3 Kaplan–Meier survivor function. All countries

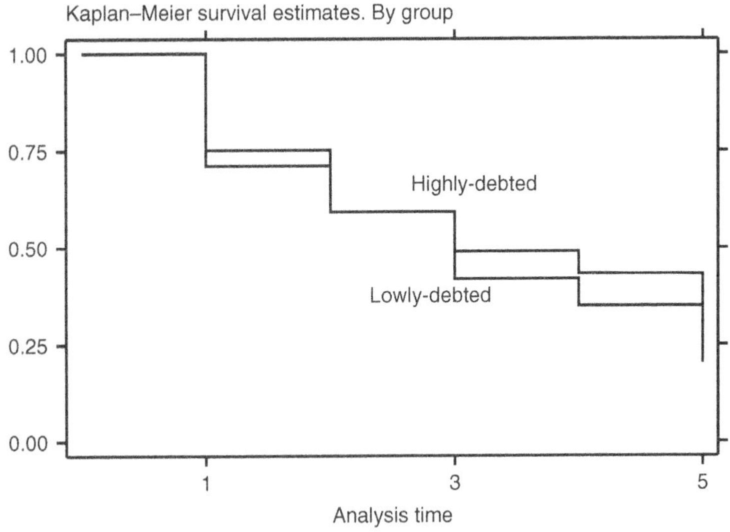

Figure 3.4 Kaplan–Meier survivor function by group

of 2.37 and 2.26 years, respectively. Italy shows the largest average duration of fiscal consolidations, but this result is a combination of a small number of consolidation episodes of medium length, and a single and very long consolidation effort of ten years in the 1990s.

It is very interesting to observe that in the strongest period of fiscal consolidation (1996–2000), when 11 countries entered the third stage of EMU, the probability of maintaining the consolidation remained close to 85 per cent almost independently of whether the consolidation had started one, two, three or four years before.

Figure 3.5 presents the estimated survivor function by periods.

The estimated hazard function, in Figure 3.6, gives further evidence of the positive dependence of fiscal consolidations on their accumulated duration. The convexity of that function implies that the probability of ending a fiscal consolidation is an increasing function in t, conditional on duration. This means that the longer the period of fiscal consolidation accumulated until t, the higher the probability that the consolidation will end in moment t. That hazard rate is higher after one year of consolidation, after three years of consolidation, and much higher after five years or more of uninterrupted consolidation.

Parametric estimation. The determinants of duration

The non-parametric analysis that was presented in the previous section is well suited to describing the actual duration of fiscal adjustment episodes and analysing the dependence of those consolidations on their accumulated duration. Nevertheless, it is very limited in analysing the other factors that explain the probability of ending fiscal consolidations. To address this issue, this section will perform a parametric analysis of duration. This will be done estimating a *Model of Proportional Hazard* (PH), which is the duration model that has usually been used to characterize the hazard function, and it assumes that the hazard function can be split as follows:

$$h(t,X) = h_0(t)^{*}g(X) \tag{3.3}$$

where $h_0(t)$ is the baseline hazard function that captures the dependency of data to duration, and $g(x)$ is a function of individual variables. This function of explanatory variables is a negative function usually defined as $g(x) = \exp(X'\beta)$. Note that in this proportional specification, regressors intervene re-escalating the conditional probability of abandoning the period of fiscal consolidation, not its own duration.

This model can be estimated firstly without imposing any specific functional form to the baseline hazard function, following the *Cox Model* (1972):[18]

$$h(t,X) = h_0(t)^{*}\exp(X'\beta) \tag{3.4}$$

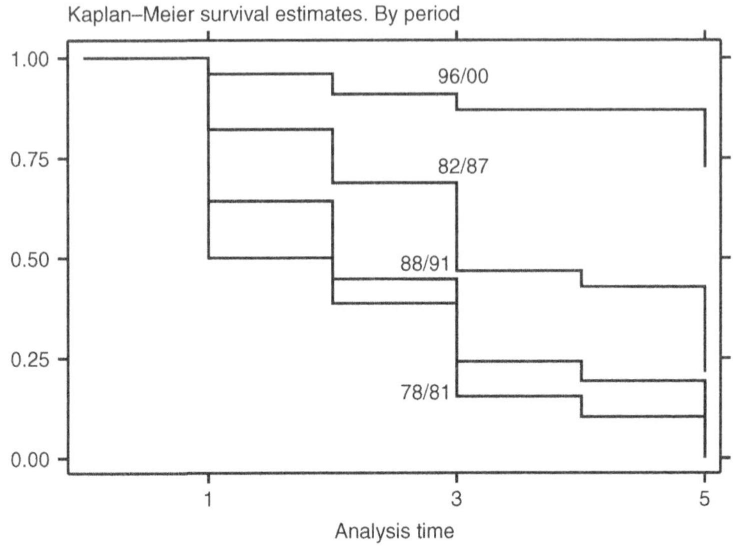

Figure 3.5 Kaplan–Meier survivor function by periods

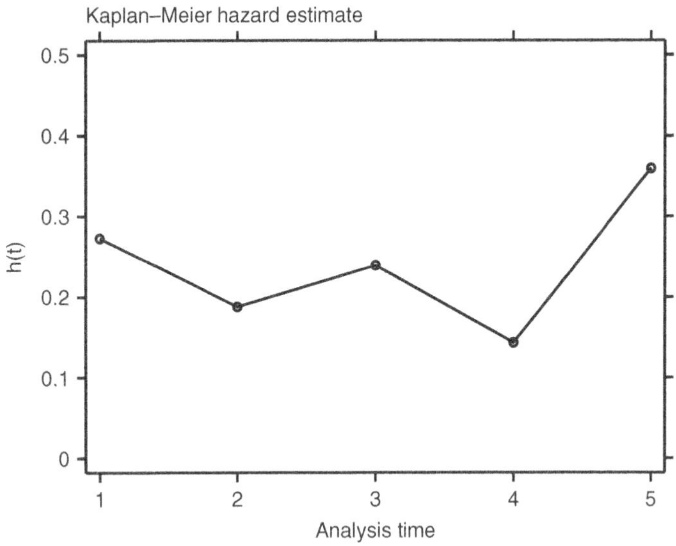

Figure 3.6 Kaplan–Meier hazard function. All countries

Or an alternative estimation can be undertaken by imposing one specific parametric form to the function $h_0(t)$. In this case, the models most commonly used are the *Weibull Model* and the *Exponential Model*. In the first one, $h_0(t) = pt^{p-1}$, where p is a parameter that has to be estimated. When $p = 1$, the *Weibull Model* is equal to the *Exponential Model*, where there exists no dependency on duration. On the other hand, when the parameter $p > 1$, there exists a positive dependency on duration, and a negative dependency when $p < 1$. Therefore, by estimating p, it is possible to test the hypothesis of duration dependency of fiscal consolidations.

As possible explanatory variables, the estimation includes all of those economic and political variables that can be directly related to the duration of fiscal adjustments, and whose theoretical justification was widely discussed in Chapter 2.

These variables are the following:[19]

1. Number of failures: this variable simply measures the accumulated number of failures (ends of fiscal consolidations) that have taken place in each country before the current consolidation. The hypothesis is that the higher the accumulated number of failures, the less stable is the country in maintaining a tight fiscal policy, and the more likely it is that the consolidation will end sooner than later.
2. Debt-to-GDP ratio: this variable is the same variable that was used in the timing analysis of section 3. The expectation is that higher debt-to-GDP ratios will be associated with longer periods of fiscal consolidation, and thus associated with lower probabilities of ending the consolidation.
3. Strength of consolidation: this continuous variable is the result in absolute terms of subtracting the annual variation of the cyclically adjusted budget balance to the chosen threshold that determines when a fiscal consolidation takes place. Remember that in this analysis the threshold is zero. This means that any given year is classified as a year of fiscal consolidation if the variation of the cyclically adjusted budget balance with respect to the previous year has been positive in any amount bigger than zero. Section 5 of this chapter will analyse the sensitivity of the results in section 4 to a change in the threshold from 0 per cent to 1 per cent.
4. Quality of the adjustment: this variable measures the contribution of primary expenditures (current public expenditures minus interest payments) to the total deficit reduction achieved in each consolidation year. Let the variable called *Contribution* $= (X_t - X_0)/(S_t - S_0)$ be the contribution of primary expenditures X to the adjustment in the surplus S, achieved between the first year of the consolidation episode *0*, and the year under consideration t.[20] Following all the literature on fiscal adjustments mentioned in chapter 2 and at the beginning of this chapter, the hypothesis is that the higher the contribution of primary expenditures to the overall amelioration of the budget, the lower the probability that the consolidation will

end, because expenditure-based consolidations are expected to last longer than revenue-based adjustments.

5. Coalition size: this variable is the same that was used in section 3 of this chapter, and measures the number of political parties in government for each country and each year of the sample.

6. Cabinet size: again this variable measures the number of spending ministers in the cabinet for each year and each country. More parties and more ministers in the government are expected to increase the probability of ending the consolidation, therefore reducing its duration.

If fragmentation of decision-making has a role to play in fiscal policy decisions, both cabinet and coalition size must have an important impact on the duration of fiscal adjustments in Europe, because most EU countries use varying systems of proportional representation that usually generate many coalition governments as a result of very heterogeneous parliaments. For example, in 1992, when the Maastricht Treaty was signed, 'there were eight parties represented in the Danish Folketing, nine parties in the Dutch Second Chamber, thirteen in the Spanish Congress of Deputies, and thirteen in the Belgian Parliament (although that also reflects the division of the main parties into separate French-speaking and Dutch-speaking wings)' (Dale, 1993: 2).[21]

7. Months to next election: This variable is slightly different from the one used in the analysis of the probability of starting fiscal consolidations in section 3. There I used a dummy variable with value 1 for election years and 0 otherwise. Since now the purpose is to capture the dynamic influence that coming elections have on the probability of ending a consolidation that is already taking place, I use a new variable that takes values 0, 12, 24, 36 and 48 to measure the distance in months between each year under consideration and the year in which the next general election will be celebrated. When governments design their strategies of fiscal adjustment, they usually implement every unpopular measure at the beginning of their mandate, and they normally try to have all the process ended by the time the next election arrives. Together with the possibility of ending the consolidation just before the election, European prime ministers willing to undertake a consolidation without the pressures of the electorate, face also the alternative of calling an early election when they judge it most politically advantageous. As has been already mentioned, the most illustrative example again is that of Jaques Chirac who called an early election in 1997, expecting that a renewed right-wing majority would give Alain Juppé's cabinet enough strength 'to push through further painful spending cuts or tax increases'[22] during the last year before the 'Maastricht exam'. His miscalculation gave the government to the left, and to Lionel Jospin the leadership of the French executive.

But because this type of electoral calendar management usually undermines democratic stability, early calls normally take place in the last year of the mandate, and thus on many occasions consolidation efforts and elections have coincided (especially during the run-up to EMU). Very illustrative of this point is an article that appeared in *The New York Times* in March 1997, that affirmed: 'Europe is really very unlucky. There is a collision of calendars, including the French and German election calendars and the Maastricht single-currency decision calendar in 1998'.[23]

Therefore, assuming that fiscal adjustments are unpopular, and politicians tend to spend more just before the election discounting fiscal illusion and misinformed voters,[24] one should expect election years to increase the probability of ending the consolidation.

8. Socialist control of the cabinet (Government-left). This is the same variable that was used in section 3 for the timing analysis. As was the case then, the ideology of the cabinet is not expected to play any significant role in the duration of fiscal adjustments, except for the fact that stronger and more cohesive governments (those in which a higher percentage of cabinet posts are held by members of the same party – either left or right), may be associated with longer duration, because their cohesion can make it easier for them to stick to the decided path, in front of lobbyists' pressures and the electorate's discontent.

In order to decide if country or time dummies should be included in the specification, I perform the usual Cox-regression-based test for equality of survival curves.

Results from Table 3.5 show that the null hypothesis that equality of countries exist cannot be rejected, and therefore the sample can be considered as an homogeneous sample, for which no country dummies are needed. Nevertheless, when I undertake the same test differentiating the sample by periods and groups of countries, I obtain somewhat different results. Tables 3.6 and 3.7 contain the results of the Cox regression-based test for equality of survival curves by group and by period, respectively.

As the *p-values* show, the null hypothesis of equality of groups cannot be rejected. Instead, it is possible to reject the hypothesis that equality of periods exists. Thus, the sample of study shows temporal heterogeneity, but no spatial heterogeneity. Therefore, time dummies must be included in the parametric analysis, in order to control for time heterogeneity, such as the one caused by periods with important accumulation of consolidation episodes.

After taking into account all these factors, the three functional forms presented at the beginning of this section are estimated by maximum likelihood, using 412 observations and 195 failures.

Table 3.8 presents the parameter estimates for these alternative hazard function models. Recall that a positive parameter indicates an increase in the hazard rate, that is, an increase in the probability that the consolidation will end in period $t + 1$, given that it lasted through period t. As can be observed, the three alternative specifications give almost identical results. All explanatory variables show the expected signs, but the only explanatory variables that

Table 3.5 Cox regression-based test

All countries	*Events observed*	*Expected*	*Relative hazard*
Austria	19	16.68	1.171
Belgium	17	20.66	0.834
Denmark	13	14.63	0.905
Finland	20	15.97	1.293
France	16	13.86	1.177
Germany	18	19.88	0.923
Greece	21	15.91	1.361
Ireland	14	13.04	1.098
Italy	12	16.69	0.727
Luxembourg	11	12.03	0.934
The Netherlands	15	13.6	1.132
Portugal	18	18.81	0.978
Spain	15	12.19	1.267
Sweden	15	12.71	1.208
UK	13	20.33	0.651
Total	237	237	1
LR Chi2(14)		10.18	
Pr > Chi2		0.75	

Table 3.6 Cox regression-based test for equality of survival curves, by country-group

Group	*Events observed*	*Expected*	*Relative hazard*
Lowly-indebted	145	136.77	1.063
Highly-indebted	92	100.23	0.929
All	237	237	1
LR Chi 2(1)		1.19	
PR > Chi 2		0.27	

Table 3.7 Cox regression-based test for equality of survival curves, by period

Periods	*Events observed*	*Expected*	*Relative hazard*
62/72	42	33.11	1.67
73/77	41	28.94	1.90
78/81	43	24.03	2.35
82/87	36	43.58	1.04
88/91	37	24.49	1.93
92/95	26	27.05	1.24
96/00	12	55.8	0.24
All	237	237	1
LR Chi2(6)		83.3	
Pr > Chi2		0.00	

Table 3.8 Parametric estimation of proportional hazard model

Probability of ending the fiscal adjustment if it lasted until t	*Cox*	*Exponential*	*Weibull*
N. Failures	0.015***	0.012***	0.031***
	(8.67)	(9.53)	(13.25)
Debt-to-GDP	−0.011***	−0.010***	−0.014***
	(−5.29)	(−5.04)	(−5.70)
Strength of adjustment	0.081	0.069	0.108*
	(1.62)	(1.45)	(1.81)
Quality of adjustment	−0.043***	−0.042***	−0.048***
	(−4.63)	(−4.94)	(−4.17)
Coalition size	0.016	0.009	0.036
	(0.38)	(0.22)	(0.71)
Cabinet size	0.110***	0.101***	0.145***
	(3.91)	(3.83)	(3.90)
Months to election	−0.005	−0.005	−0.007
	(1.15)	(1.17)	(1.40)
Government-left	−0.003	−0.002	−0.003
	(1.61)	(1.41)	(1.41)
1962–72	1.927***	2.122***	2.253***
	(5.01)	(5.15)	(5.22)
1973–77	1.579***	1.878***	1.977***
	(4.25)	(4.02)	(4.7)
1978–81	1.893***	1.987***	2.247***
	(5.27)	(5.32)	(5.61)
1982–87	1.267***	1.323***	1.474***
	(3.75)	(3.87)	(4.07)
1988–91	1.745***	1.845***	1.947***
	(5.21)	(5.12)	(5.18)
1992–95	1.424***	1.555***	1.697***
	(4.19)	(4.98)	(5.03)
Constant			−6.292***
			(−11.32)
P			2.844***
			(20.46)
Observations	412	412	412
No. of failures	195	195	195
Wald Chi2(8)	154.43	174.67	257.41
Prob > Chi	0.0000	0.0000	0.0000
Log-likelihood	−1027.06	−351.41	−251.56
AIC	2072.12	722.82	525.12

Note: Robust z-statistics in parentheses. *significant at 10 per cent, **significant at 5 per cent; ***significant at 1 per cent.

are statistically significant are the number of failures, the debt-to-GDP ratio, the strength of the adjustment (only in the Weibull estimation), the quality of the adjustment, and the size of the cabinet.

The higher the debt-to-GDP ratio and the higher the contribution of primary expenditures to deficit reduction, the less probable it is that the consolidation ends. This clearly confirms the 'debt burden hypothesis' formulated in Chapter 2. In addition, the higher the number of accumulated failures, the stronger the adjustment, and the larger the number of spending ministers in the cabinet, the higher the probability that the fiscal consolidation ends, and a fiscal expansion starts. The p parameter in the Weibull estimation is statistically significant, positive and bigger than one, which means that the hazard function grows with time, and this is consistent with the empirical hazard function previously commented upon in the non-parametric analysis (see Figure 3.6), that predicted positive duration dependence of consolidation episodes.

These results confirm that all economic variables pointed out by other authors are significant explanatory factors to account for different durations of fiscal consolidations in Europe. Of the four political variables, only cabinet size (the number of spending ministers) is statistically significant and shows that more fragmented cabinets find it problematic to maintain long consolidation efforts. The role of elections, although not significant, behaves as expected, because its negative sign indicates an association between lower number of months to next election, and a higher probability of ending the consolidation effort.

Finally, given the fact that the application of duration models to the study of fiscal consolidations is almost nonexistent, and because none of these attempts has offered a discussion of what would be the most appropriate functional form to be used in these cases, it is useful to compare very briefly the three models estimated. Out of the three functional forms included in Table 3.8, the one that best fits the data according to all the possible tests,[25] is the Weibull specification. The superiority of this model becomes even clearer by looking at the Cox–Snell residuals plots, in Figure 3.7.

If the model fits the data, then the plot of the cumulative hazard function versus the Cox–Snell residuals should be a straight line with slope equal to unity and beginning at the origin. Comparing the plots below, it becomes clear that the *Weibull plot* satisfies the exponential requirement for most of the time, except in the part of larger residuals where the slope appears to exceed the unity. This confirms that the Weibull model should be the preferred model for the parametric analysis of duration of fiscal adjustment episodes.

3.5 Economic and political factors during stronger consolidations

Any study of fiscal adjustments is incomplete if it does not deal with the problem of arbitrariness of different definitions of fiscal consolidations. Until now I have been working with the loosest possible definition. Nevertheless, under this arbitrariness problem no results from the duration analysis can be taken as definitive until they are tested for a different definition of fiscal adjustment.

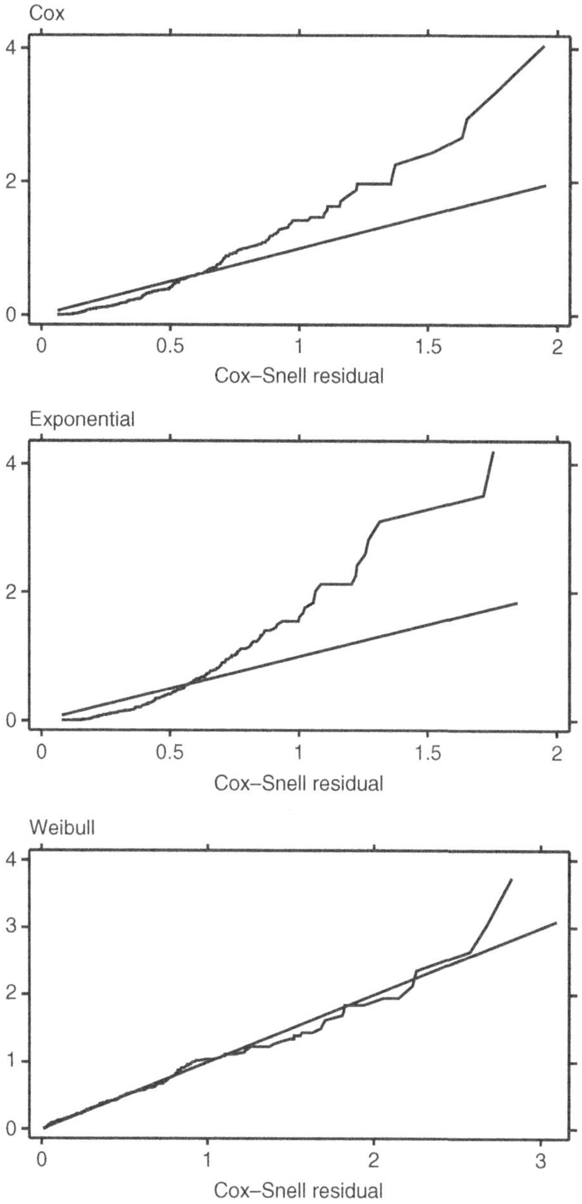

Figure 3.7 Cox–Snell residuals to evaluate fit of 3 regression models

Thus, in this final section I will replicate the parametric analysis of section 3.4 of this chapter, but changing the definition of fiscal consolidation.

Now I will consider that a fiscal consolidation takes place in a given year if the cyclically adjusted budget balance with respect to GDP in that year increased by 1 per cent or more from the previous year. By changing the threshold from 0 per cent to 1 per cent, it will be possible to test the sensitivity of the previous results to different definitions of fiscal adjustment. It can be considered that the 0 per cent threshold is the minimum threshold that one can impose to differentiate fiscal consolidation years from fiscal expansion ones. On the other hand, the 1 per cent threshold is the most common in the literature on fiscal adjustments, since it discriminates in favour of stronger consolidation experiences, where the political commitment to reduce the public deficit needs to be firm and the adjustment is typically the result of intended policies specially designed for that purpose.

That literature follows in general the trend started by Alesina and Perotti (1995, 1996a, 1996b), and defines episodes of fiscal consolidations as those in which the cyclically adjusted primary budget balance increased by at least 1.25 per cent of GDP in two consecutive years, or if the change in the cyclically adjusted primary balance (excluding interest payments) exceeded 1.5 per cent of GDP in one year and was less than 1.25 per cent of GDP in the following or the precedent year. Note that because this chapter has, upto this point, used cyclically adjusted budget balances (including interest payments) in order to assess the dynamic impact of debt accumulation on duration of adjustment episodes, the new threshold that will be used for the sensitivity test can be considered as 'identical' to the one used in the literature.

Under the new definition, all the duration analysis changes. As can be seen in Table 3.9, the number of failures under the *Stronger* definition (the 1 per cent threshold) is bigger than under the *Weaker* definition (390 versus 237).

Furthermore, under the *Stronger* definition, the average probability of ending the fiscal consolidation is much higher than under the previous definition (77.8 per cent versus 47.6 per cent), and the average duration is much lower

Table 3.9 Descriptive statistics: failure and duration by threshold

	Failure		*Duration*	
	Weaker	*Stronger*	*Weaker*	*Stronger*
Mean	0.476	0.778	2.048	1.295
Std. dev.	0.500	0.416	1.450	0.623
Variance	0.250	0.173	2.103	0.389
Skewness	0.095	−1.341	1.690	2.322
Kurtosis	1.009	2.798	5.787	8.343
No of failures	237	390	237	390
Observations	495	501	495	501

(1.29 years versus 2.05). The maximum duration under this new threshold is four years.

Figure 3.8 presents the Kaplan–Meier survivor and hazard estimates for both definitions of fiscal adjustments.

As can be observed, the probability of maintaining the consolidation after the first year decreases even more under the new definition (0.6 versus 0.4) than it did under the initial definition. These differences are maintained for longer durations, because the probability of maintaining the consolidation after the second year decreases 0.2 under the new definition, when it only

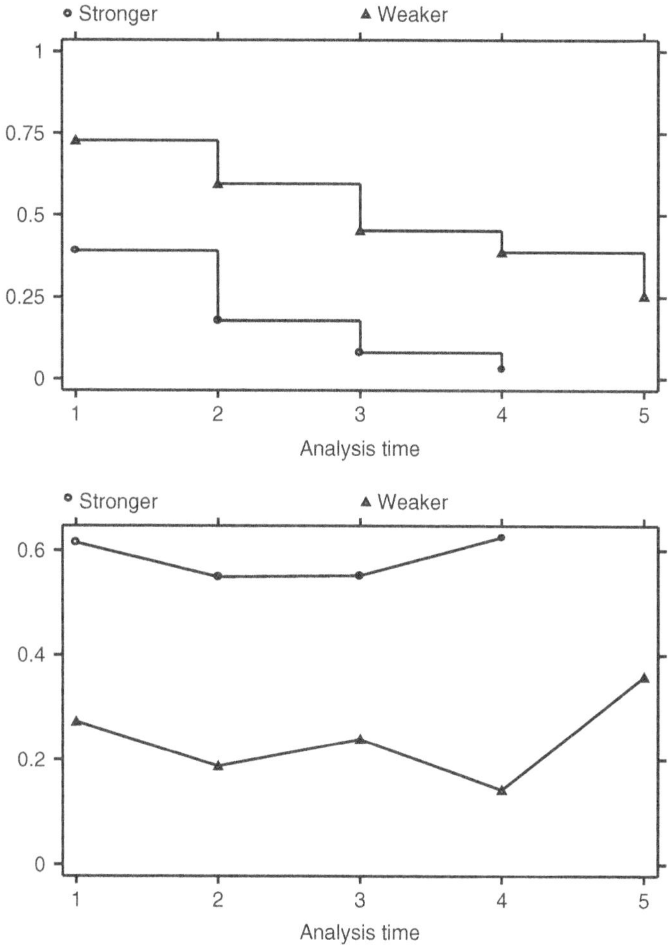

Figure 3.8 Kaplan–Meier survivor and hazard functions by threshold

decreased by about 0.1 under the initial definition. This behaviour is translated into a smoother estimated hazard function, which clearly shows higher positive dependency on accumulated duration under the *Stronger* definition than under the *Weaker* one.

But the most important results arise when the same parametric model is estimated using the new definition of fiscal consolidation.

As can be observed by looking at the results reported in Table 3.10, the most important difference between the results under the two thresholds is that political factors become much more important in explaining the duration of fiscal adjustments, when the definition of consolidation is made stricter. In fact, all political factors gain statistical significance, while some important economic variables lose explanatory power.

Again, the larger the level of debt, the less likely it is that the consolidation ends; and the larger the cabinet and the number of accumulated failures, the more probable is that the consolidation finishes.

Nevertheless, under the stronger definition, the two remaining economic variables, such as the strength of the adjustment and its quality, stop being statistically significant. Together with this loss of predictive power among economic variables, the other three political variables, such as coalition size, months to next election, and Socialist control of the cabinet, suddenly gain statistical significance.

Therefore, under the stricter new definition, larger coalitions, larger cabinets, and closer elections increase the probability of ending a fiscal consolidation.[26] In addition, the negative and significant coefficient of leftist cabinets should both be interpreted as the proof that social democrats are not necessarily more reluctant to balance the budget, and most importantly, as the confirmation that ideological homogeneity in the cabinet allows governments to stick to longer adjustment efforts.

These results indicate that stronger fiscal adjustments are the result of strong and very committed governments, not threatened by the fear of unpopularity or adverse election results, willing to pursue the necessary policies to balance the budget. If these conditions of cabinet cohesion and medium-run electoral stability are not met, governments find it very difficult to maintain fiscal consolidations for a long time (Hannon, 2001).[27]

3.6 Conclusion

Let me summarize the main findings of this chapter so far. After presenting the definition of fiscal adjustment on which this book is based, this chapter has examined the economic and political determinants of timing and duration of fiscal consolidations in the European Union.

To analyse the initial conditions that influence the probability of starting fiscal consolidations, the analysis has been based on a series of probit estimations. Results from this section have shown that the domestic economic cycle,

Table 3.10 Parametric Weibull estimation by threshold

Duration	*Weaker definition*	*Stronger definition*
Number of failures	0.031***	0.010***
	(13.25)	(15.49)
Debt-to-GDP	−0.014***	−0.013***
	(−5.70)	(5.31)
Strength of adjustment	0.108*	−0.024
	(1.81)	(0.47)
Quality of adjustment	−0.048***	−0.026
	(−4.17)	(1.64)
Coalition size	0.036	0.093*
	(0.71)	(1.91)
Cabinet size	0.145***	0.073***
	(3.90)	(2.96)
Months to election	−0.007	−0.006**
	(1.40)	(2.08)
Government-left	−0.003	−0.004**
	(1.41)	(2.18)
1962–72	2.253***	2.853***
	(5.22)	(5.52)
1973–77	1.977***	1.897***
	(4.7)	(4.74)
1978–81	2.247***	2.457***
	(5.61)	(5.41)
1982–87	1.474***	1.436***
	(4.07)	(4.11)
1988–91	1.947***	1.958***
	(5.18)	(5.23)
1992–95	1.697***	1.598***
	(5.03)	(4.78)
Constant	−6.292***	−2.865***
	(−11.32)	(7.00)
P	2.844***	−3.543***
	(20.46)	(30.55)
Observations	412	404
No. of failures	195	307
Wald Chi2(8)	257.41	337.96
Prob > Chi	0.0000	0.0000
Log-likelihood	−251.56	−159.70
AIC	525.12	341.48

Note: Robust z-statistics in parentheses: *significant at 10 per cent **significant at 5 per cent ***significant at 1 per cent.

the relative growth rate, and the accumulated level of debt are very important factors influencing the probability of starting fiscal consolidations. The effect of politico-institutional variables in this context is weak, except for the proximity of elections.

Once the analysis on timing was completed, the chapter has turned to apply the methodology of duration models to annual data on cyclically adjusted budget balances for the 15 EU member states between 1960 and 2000.

First, I have carried out a non-parametric analysis that has only taken into account time, in order to assess the impact of accumulated duration on the probability of ending a fiscal consolidation. Results have shown that the probability of ending a fiscal adjustment episode increases with the accumulated number of years of the tightening effort.

Secondly, I have performed a parametric analysis, in order to include more variables that could influence the probability of ending the fiscal consolidations. This analysis has shown that the accumulated level of debt and the fragmentation of the cabinet are the most important determinants of the duration of fiscal efforts. In fact, under a stronger definition of fiscal consolidation, political variables such as the number of parties in the coalition, and the proximity of elections, gain importance as predictors of duration of fiscal consolidations, while those economic variables such as quality of the adjustment, that have been traditionally pointed by the literature as the key variable for the success of fiscal adjustments, lose their predictive power.

This chapter has demonstrated that the statement:

> Consolidation efforts that operate to a large extent on the spending side of the budget have a higher chance to survive than consolidations that rely mostly on increased revenues. (Von Hagen, Hallett and Strauch, 2001: 11)

is no longer sufficient to characterize the determinants of duration of fiscal adjustments, if a group of alternative economic and political factors is not taken into account as well. But what this chapter has not answered yet is why during long and short episodes of fiscal adjustment, some countries decide to operate on the spending side, while others relay mostly on increased revenues.

The composition dimension of fiscal consolidations is the subject of the next chapter.

4
The Composition of Fiscal Adjustments*

> 'In a capitalist democracy, politics is nothing but the matter of who gets what, when, and how.'
>
> Laswell, 1936: 19

The choice of which budget components will be increased or decreased during a fiscal adjustment episode in order to achieve a balanced budget is the crucial dimension of any strategy of fiscal consolidation.

Following the exploration in the previous chapter of the importance that different economic and political factors have in determining the timing and duration of fiscal adjustment experiences, this chapter will present a detailed account of how those factors affect any government confronted with the decision of choosing among different budgetary compositions for their fiscal adjustment strategy.

In order to do this, the chapter will be divided into three main blocks: The first section will focus entirely on explaining why the composition of the budget is important for the level of growth and equality of any economy: Then, the second section will be devoted to explore empirically what are the economic and political factors that determine the general composition of the budget. And, finally, the third section will focus on the effect that these same factors have on the composition of fiscal policies, but only during episodes of fiscal adjustment

Because the second section will present strong empirical evidence confirming that the ideology of the party in government is a crucial factor in explaining the composition of the budget, during both years of fiscal expansion and years of fiscal adjustment, the third section of this chapter will test if this role of ideology is maintained when the focus of the study is narrowed and only considers longer episodes of fiscal consolidation.

While in the previous chapter economic variables, such as the economic cycle and the level of debt, were shown to be very powerful predictors of the timing and the duration of fiscal adjustment episodes, this chapter will conclude that political factors are more important in understanding their composition.

4.1 Why is composition of the budget important?

The composition of the budget is important for two reasons: (1) according to most economists, the composition of the budget has macroeconomic effects; and (2) it implies a political decision over who pays and who receives what in a country.

With respect to the economic consequences of fiscal adjustments, Chapter 6 of this book offers a detailed analysis. However, it is very useful to borrow the basic theoretical concepts from its first section and bring them here to put the analysis of budget composition in context.

Most recent work has focused on the theoretical and empirical discussion surrounding the idea that different composition of fiscal adjustments can have very different effects on economic growth. As was explained in Chapter 2, conventional macroeconomics holds that fiscal retrenchment can only be achieved at the cost of reduced output and employment, because tight fiscal policy reduces aggregate demand for goods and services, and with rigid prices, this decline in nominal demand results in a fall in real output.

This 'Keynesian-conventional' view was first challenged in the 1980s by Hellwig and Newmann (1987). The idea was that when the private sector realizes that a fiscal consolidation will imply a lower tax burden in the future, and, assuming that consumption depends on permanent income and investors are forward-looking, both consumption and investment will rise even above the levels previous to the fiscal consolidation. This 'rational expectations' interpretation gained popularity after the work of Giavazzi and Pagano (1990), who demonstrated that fiscal adjustments in Ireland and Denmark had caused an increase in the private sector's demand.

More recently, this so-called non-Keynesian effect of fiscal adjustments has been refined,[1] and has been directly associated with the type of adjustment in terms of composition. According to McDermott and Wescott (1996), Alesina and Perotti (1995, 1996a, 1996b, 1998), Buti and Sapir (1998) and Von Hagen, Hallett and Strauch (2001), fiscal adjustments that rely primarily on spending cuts in transfers and the government wage bill can be expansionary and have a better chance of success than do fiscal adjustments that rely primarily on tax increases and cuts in public investment (which tend to be short-lived and are contractionary).

One explanation for this evidence is the mentioned demand effect of serious fiscal tightening, according to which wealth rises when the future tax burden declines, and when interest rates decline credibility is restored and inflation and default risks abate. Both consumption and investment rise.

However, a newer alternative supply-side explanation affirms that cuts in wage government consumption and in transfers can start a virtuous cycle that makes the economy more competitive. Particularly in highly unionized and very open countries (most European countries), a cut in wage government consumption causes a fall in the demand for labour, while a cut in transfers reduces the alternative income available to union members, respectively; both effects reduce the bargaining power of unions, thus increasing the competitiveness of the tradable sector and increasing exports.

But the composition of the budget is not only important for raising the level of income in the economy, it also has very important implications for the distribution of this income among citizens.[2] A superficial approach to public spending would erroneously lead to the conclusion that higher levels of public expenditure are always enough to reduce inequalities. But nothing is more mistaken. Some public expenditures are productive, some unproductive, some redistribute income, and some others just subsidize big but not always efficient bureaucracies.[3]

The decision over who gets what in a country and who pays to finance the public sector's activity, immediately implies a reallocation of resources. This reallocation effect can be the unintended outcome of public policies not directly conceived to affect the distribution of income, or in many occasions it can be the direct result of a carefully designed policy aimed at increasing the degree of equality in the economy.[4]

There are numerous ways in which equality can be promoted through fiscal policy. Some countries have, for example, promoted very actively direct transfers of income from public resources to improve the situation of the bottom tier of income distribution, while others have focused on the top percentiles by introducing highly progressive taxes.

These measures can be complementary to each other, and labour market policies have also been considered complementary to fiscal policies to reduce inequality in European countries (the rationale being that relative wages exert a strong influence on income inequality).

Among these labour market measures, the most common have been the introduction of minimum wages, generous unemployment benefits, and a wide range of job-creating measures such as low payroll and income taxes for low-waged workers, or measures to reduce labour market rigidities. In addition, improved access to education and health, as long as new investments in formation of the low-skilled, investments in human capital and new technologies, are commonly accepted measures which lead to an increase in equality.

But normally, when fiscal adjustments are to be implemented, many of those policies of income redistribution and the most extensive benefits schemes will need to be reduced, or if maintained, it will be at the cost of a higher tax burden. The effect of fiscal adjustments on public initiatives to diminish income inequalities has generally 'meant doing more with less'.[5]

Although there is a lack of empirical studies that address the impact of fiscal adjustments on income redistribution,[6] the intuitive idea could be set out as follows: when a fiscal consolidation is going to take place, and the impact on redistribution policies is to be minimized, governments should focus on reducing unproductive expenditures (such as military expenditures, bureaucratic wasted resources, etc.), and should at least maintain public consumption and public investment on education, health and infrastructures, for long-run equality purposes.

Finally, the composition of the budget is not only important because of its economic effects on the generation and the distribution of income: it is also important because of the political use that policy-makers can make of their budgetary decisions. When a government decides 'who gets, what, when, and how' (Laswell, 1936: 19), it is not only reallocating resources in order to improve the growth rate or the degree of equality in a certain country, but it is also benefiting some social groups (most likely its electoral constituency) at the expense of others.

How the composition of the budget can be used by policy-makers to profit electorally from it, has been already discussed in depth in the previous chapters. Higher public consumption before the election will increase momentarily economic growth and the employment level, and this will normally be rewarded by the electorate.[7] Direct targeted transfers and lower taxes will collect a higher percentage of votes among the benefited groups. Sometimes, even a credible promise of future tax decreases will be welcomed by the electorate.[8] And, finally, an increase in public wages can also gain a good portion of the electorate in countries with extensive public employment, such as Sweden, where around 60 per cent of women work in the public sector.

4.2 Economics, politics and composition of the budget

Given such remarkable economic and political consequences, decisions about the budget's composition are probably the most important annual decision that any government takes. Thus, it is the purpose of this section to investigate what are the causes of that decision, or, in other words, what are the economic and political factors that influence that transcendent choice.

The possible explanatory factors that will be tested to answerr this question are those that have been discussed and tested in the two previous chapters.

Within this conext and on the economic side, the composition of the budget might be influenced by the economic cycle (in terms of growth, unemployment rate and inflation), the accumulated level of debt (basically through its effect on interest payments) and the fiscal record of previous years (most importantly, the public deficit of the previous year).

On the political side, the degree of fragmentation of the cabinet is expected to increase the total level of public expenditures, mainly via public transfers. The electoral calendar is supposed to have an impact both on increased public consumption (to increase aggregate demand) and on a decrease in taxes. And, finally, the effect of cabinet ideology is expected to influence both revenues and expenditures. Normally, it would be reasonable to expect higher expenditures and revenues (although not necessarily deficits) to be associated with social democratic governments. Also, these higher expenditures are likely to be concentrated on public consumption, public wages, public transfers and public investment, typically financed with the corresponding increase in direct taxation under progressive tax systems.

To test all of these hypotheses, I run the following regression of time-series cross-national data for the period from 1970 to 2000 in the 15 European Union member states:[9]

$$\Delta Y_{i,t} = \alpha_0 + \alpha_1 PCABB_{i,t-1} + \delta_1 \Delta U_{i,t} + \delta_2 \Delta P_{i,t} + \beta_K X_{i,t} + T_t + C_i + \varepsilon_{i,t} \quad (4.1)$$

Where $Y_{i,t}$ is any item of the budget cyclically adjusted (to partial out the evolution of the cycle and the interest payments which are out of the control of politicians) in country *i* during year *t*;

1. *PCABB* is the cyclically adjusted budget balance minus interest payments (a positive balance is a primary surplus and a negative balance is a primary deficit);
2. ΔU is the change in the unemployment rate;
3. ΔP is the rate of inflation of the consumer price index;
4. *X* is a vector of four political independent variables (percentage of total cabinet posts held by social democratic and other left parties; number of parties in government; number of spending ministers in the cabinet; and number of months before next election);[10]
5. *T* is a vector of time effects;
6. *C* is a vector of country dummy variables or fixed effects.

The use of fixed effects is particularly important in this model since most variables vary more across units than over time.[11]

The specification is identical to that used by Perotti and Kontopoulos (2002) to explore the same question, though with a different sample. As they explain: 'the use of variables representing the economic environment – ΔU and ΔP – has two basic justifications: first, to capture the effects of, say, unemployment on expenditure via unemployment-related subsidies and similar types of expenditures;[12] secondly, to capture the reaction function of policymakers implementing countercyclical policies' (p. 15).

By introducing the independent variables of coalition size and cabinet size, as in the chapter on timing and duration, I also follow Perotti and Kontopoulos (2002) in abandoning the classical 'Type of Government' variable.[13] In contrast to other studies, the electoral system is not included among the independent variables because this is a variable that correlates strongly with coalition size, since more proportional systems tend to produce larger coalition governments.[14] For similar reasons, the number of parliamentary seats held by the party in government is excluded from these regressions.[15]

In addition, as in the duration analysis, the composition analysis excludes any variable that accounts for procedural fragmentation (such as the existence of spending limits, the nature of the budget negotiations or the existence of strong finance ministers), because they are time-invariant and cannot be distinguished from country dummies, and because Perotti and Kontopoulos (2002) already demonstrated that, contrary to previous findings, the impact of those variables on fiscal outcomes is rather insignificant.[16]

To study the effect of the same independent variables in the composition of the budget, the same regression has been run several times with the following dependent variables:

1. The government's primary cyclically adjusted budget balance;
2. Total revenues of general government cyclically adjusted, and: Taxes on income and wealth (direct taxes); Taxes on production and imports (indirect taxes); Social contributions;
3. Total primary expenditures of general government cyclically adjusted, and: Subsidies; Final government consumption (public consumption); Collective consumption; Social benefits in kind; Social transfers other than in kind (social transfers); Compensation of employees (public wages); and Gross fixed capital formation (public investment).

These estimations have been carried out for the whole 1970–2000 period, and two sub-periods, 1970–94 and 1995–2000, in order to avoid the inconsistencies that the change from ESA-79 to ESA-95 generate in the AMECO Database of the European Commission.[17]

All these regressions follow the methodology suggested by Beck and Katz (1995, 1996) using Ordinary Least Squares with panel-corrected standard errors to deal with panel heteroscedasticity, spatial correlation and serial correlation.[18]

Table 4.1 presents the estimated coefficients for all regressions on main aggregates (revenues, expenditures and budget balance). These results show that the better the budget balance in year $t - 1$, the stronger the deterioration in the budget balance in year t, meaning that governments tend to run deficits more often when their budgetary position in previous years was not under pressure.

The effect of unemployment on public revenues and public expenditures is very cyclical. A worsening of the unemployment rate reduces public revenues and increases public expenditures. Similarly, an increase in the level of prices increases both public revenues and expenditures. The positive effect that prices have on the change in the budget balance confirms the hypothesized impact formulated in Chapter 2 that monetary easing (normally conducive to price increases) drives the budget balance in the direction of tightening.

As can also be observed in Table 4.1 between 1970 and 2000 left-wing governments were not associated with budget deficits, although they tended to be positively associated with higher revenues and expenditures.

Table 4.1 Composition of the budget: main aggregates, 1970–2000

First differences (Δ)	*1970–2000* Δ*Bbal*	*1970–2000* Δ*Rev*	*1970–2000* Δ*Exp*	*1970–1994* Δ*Bbal*	*1970–1994* Δ*Rev*	*1970–1994* Δ*Exp*	*1995–2000* Δ*Bbal*	*1995–2000* Δ*Rev*	*1995–2000* Δ*Exp*
PCA Budg. balance$_{t-1}$	−0.182***	−2.805	1.907	−0.177***	−3.917*	1.125	−0.725***	−4.723**	−1.798
	(4.18)	(1.52)	(0.96)	(3.21)	(1.81)	(0.46)	(10.47)	(2.60)	(0.32)
Δ Unemployment	−0.003	−4.114***	3.751**	−0.024	−3.672*	2.086	0.019	−2.381	3.011
	(0.03)	(2.91)	(2.27)	(0.23)	(1.87)	(1.64)	(0.11)	(0.14)	(0.27)
Δ Prices	0.080***	2.963***	0.207	0.083***	3.217***	0.240	0.058*	3.913**	−0.316
	(3.02)	(3.11)	(0.17)	(2.61)	(3.21)	(0.18)	(1.80)	(2.07)	(0.13)
Government-left	−0.002	0.197*	0.114*	−0.003	0.070	0.134*	0.017***	1.305***	−0.460
	(0.79)	(1.80)	(1.90)	(1.06)	(0.57)	(1.86)	(3.63)	(2.97)	(1.47)
Coalition size	−0.107	1.515	2.166	−0.110	3.143	2.588*	−0.354***	2.364**	−1.147
	(1.19)	(0.30)	(0.42)	(1.01)	(0.53)	(1.75)	(2.83)	(2.22)	(0.76)
Cabinet size	−0.168**	1.568**	2.712*	−0.159*	2.705	3.433***	0.214	2.021	−2.626
	(2.41)	(2.03)	(1.88)	(1.79)	(1.17)	(2.80)	(1.32)	(0.38)	(1.60)
Months – election	0.014***	0.384	−0.433*	0.017***	0.201	−0.700**	0.008	0.947	0.228
	(2.91)	(1.37)	(1.73)	(2.93)	(0.60)	(2.36)	(1.36)	(1.60)	(0.45)
Constant	1.773**	84.758**	12.491	1.387	92.954**	−35.223	−0.216	13.766	37.593**
	(2.30)	(2.10)	(0.29)	(1.48)	(2.03)	(0.78)	(0.12)	(0.07)	(2.13)
Observations	412	413	413	339	340	340	88	88	88
Number of groups	15	15	15	15	15	15			
R-squared	0.30	0.36	0.37	0.29	0.33	0.36	0.75	0.63	0.55
Wald-Chi2	2002.77	1892.16	4628.05	5952.09	5952.97	20423.28	11.16	7.40	7.76
Prob > Chi2	0.0000	0.0000	0.0000	0.0000	0.0000	0.0000	0.0000	0.0000	0.0000

Notes:

1. Panel-corrected z-statistics in parentheses; *significant at 10 per cent; **significant at 5 per cent; ***significant at 1 per cent.
2. Regressions for 1996–2000 were OLS with robust standard errors, because panel-corrected standard errors cannot be used when number of years is smaller than the number of countries in the panel.
3. For presentation purposes, the 14 country and 30 time dummy variables are not included in this table.

The positive impact in revenues was stronger in the 1990s, while during that period the positive impact in expenditures became negative, associated with the process of fiscal adjustment in the run-up to EMU. Also, as expected, a growing number of parties in the coalition and a growing number of ministers in the cabinet were positively associated with higher expenditures, though these positive correlations were only statistically significant in the period 1970–1994. In the second half of the 1990s, as happened with ideology, more fragmented governments became associated with revenue-based strategies of fiscal adjustment, translated into a significant positive impact of these variables on revenues, and a non-significant negative impact on expenditures.

Finally, the effect of the number of months before the next election also confirms the initial electoral cycle hypothesis: the longer the time before the next election, the higher the cyclically adjusted primary deficits; and in the period 1970–1994, the closer the election, the higher the adjusted expenditures. Again, during the second half of the 1990s, the effect of elections on the budget becomes insignificant.

Looking in more depth at the different components of public revenues and public expenditures between 1970 and 1994, just before the stronger fiscal efforts to qualify for EMU took place, gives a better perspective on the influence that each economic and political factor had on the budget's composition.

Results in Table 4.2 show that between 1970 and 1994, the budget balance in $t - 1$ had a negative effect on public revenues coming from direct and indirect taxes, showing that governments tended to lower taxes when the budget balance had improved in the previous year. In addition, a positive change in the unemployment rate lowered the revenues coming from direct taxation and increased collective consumption, social benefits, and social transfers, while a positive change in the level of prices increased revenues coming from both direct and indirect taxes.

Both of the results above confirm the cyclical effect that unemployment and prices have on the different components of the budget. In addition, these results also show that during that period leftist governments, coalition size and number of spending ministers were positively and very significantly correlated with higher social transfers.[19] In addition, leftist governments and big cabinets were associated with higher collective consumption, higher social benefits, and higher public investment. Finally, by looking at the effect of independent variables on the individual items of public revenues, the effect that closeness to elections had on certain aspects of the budget is very illustrative. The longer the period before elections, the higher the revenues from direct and indirect taxes, or, in other words, the closer the elections, the lower the revenues from taxes. Also, although not both are statistically significant, the negative coefficient of Months to Next Election in the social transfers regression, and the positive coefficient in the public

Table 4.2 Composition of the budget: individual items, 1970–94

First differences (Δ)	*Δ Indtax*	*Δ Dirtax*	*Δ Pwages*	*Δ Fconsu*	*Δ Colcons*	*Δ Sbenef*	*Δ Stransfer*	*Δ Pinvest*
PCA budg. balance$_{t-1}$	−3.115***	−2.835**	0.807	1.061	0.531	0.543	0.541	0.267
	(2.70)	(1.96)	(0.66)	(0.78)	(1.02)	(0.72)	(0.40)	(0.26)
Δ Unemployment	1.287	−4.647*	3.292*	2.400	2.510**	2.975*	1.379***	−1.524
	(0.30)	(1.72)	(1.86)	(1.16)	(2.39)	(1.68)	(3.28)	(0.57)
Δ Prices	1.755**	1.014*	0.080	0.529	0.004	−0.168	−1.052	−0.456
	(2.223)	(1.81)	(0.15)	(0.77)	(0.02)	(0.70)	(1.33)	(0.83)
Government-left	−0.003	−0.059	0.123*	0.026	0.126***	0.161***	0.231**	0.042*
	(0.03)	(0.61)	(1.71)	(0.30)	(3.58)	(3.32)	(2.11)	(1.92)
Coalition size	2.812	−2.278	−1.940	0.880	2.748*	2.394	2.041*	0.012
	(1.63)	(0.52)	(1.65)	(0.28)	(1.96)	(1.34)	(1.81)	(0.00)
Cabinet size	−2.882*	2.823*	3.000	1.225	2.644**	2.787***	3.365***	0.540*
	(1.65)	(1.68)	(1.38)	(0.48)	(2.28)	(3.09)	(2.62)	(1.71)
Months – election	0.473**	0.577**	0.198	−0.115	−0.089	−0.076*	−0.207*	0.153
	(2.27)	(2.23)	(1.15)	(0.54)	(1.16)	(1.76)	(1.93)	(1.05)
Constant	10.547***	42.941	8.182	18.043	18.271	8.387	−43.905	24.392
	(3.10)	(1.33)	(0.34)	(0.63)	(1.34)	(0.43)	(1.22)	(1.00)
Observations	340	340	340	340	322	322	340	340
Number of groups	15	15	15	15			15	15
R-squared	0.28	0.15	0.34	0.38	0.62	0.57	0.39	0.20
Wald-Chi2	4723.64	4673.66	24960.10	20038.3	11.17	9.00	52733.74	814.73
Prob > Chi2	0.0000	0.0000	0.0000	0.0000	0.0000	0.0000	0.0000	0.0000

Notes: Panel-corrected z-statistics in parentheses. *significant at 10 per cent; **significant at 5 per cent; ***significant at 1 per cent. Regressions for variation of collective consumption and variation of social benefits were OLS with robust standard errors, not panel-corrected standard errors. Regressions for Collective Consumption and Social Benefits in Kind are OLS-robust, since due to the important number of missing cases, the number of observations per panel used to compute the disturbance covariance matrix in the panel corrected standard errors technique is less than half the average number of observations.

investment one, are consistent with Rogoff's model predictions (Rogoff, 1990), where opportunistic policy-makers cut public investment before elections because they are less visible to voters than transfers.

Nevertheless, evidence from the second half of the 1990s shows that the process of fiscal consolidation required to qualify for the third stage of EMU did not significantly affected the way in which economic variables influenced fiscal outcomes, but it reversed the effects that political variables had on the budget composition in the previous period.

As can be observed in Table 4.3, the main finding for the second half of the 1990s is that leftist governments, larger coalitions, larger cabinets and proximity to elections are no longer associated with higher expenditures and higher transfers. The most important result, however, is the one related to ideology of the cabinet in the fourth line of Table 4.3.

As can be seen from Table 4.3, during the second half of the 1990s leftist governments increased their revenues (mainly from direct taxes) to finance increases in the government wage bill[20] and in public investment. These two items on the expenditure side of the budget were already positively associated with left-wing governments before 1995, but they were both less statistically significant and less important than social transfers. It appears that, in the run-up to EMU, left-wing governments readapted their preferences, and when forced to cut expenditures they preferred to maintain public wages and public investment, even at the expense of social transfers.

These results are very important because they support the argument that when demand policies have proved to have only temporary effects in the long run and its short-term success depends on certain conditions of the labour market, the state and the international economy, leftist governments have been only left with the possibility to affect economic policies on the supply side. Boix (1996, 1997) demonstrated that left-wing governments are likely to implement interventionist supply-side policies, through the public provision of human and physical capital, to increase growth and the competitiveness of the economy, and improve the situation of the poorest members of society. According to this new approach to economic policy management, capital will not fly out of the country to avoid higher taxation if public investment is expected to increase overall productivity in the economy (Boix, 1997: 818; Garrett, 1998). Results from Table 4.3 confirm these findings as well, but in the field of fiscal policy show that the social democratic preference for public investment crucially affect the budget composition.

4.3 Composition of the budget during fiscal adjustments: the 'partisanship hypothesis'

Once the economic and political determinants that affect the composition of the budget have been investigated in the previous section, this section replicates the analysis, but only for the sub-sample of fiscal adjustment

Table 4.3 Composition of the budget: individual items, 1996–2000

First differences (Δ)	*ΔIndtax*	*ΔDirtax*	*ΔPwages*	*ΔFconsu*	*ΔColcon*	*ΔSbenef*	*ΔStransfer*	*ΔPinvest*
PCA budg. balance$_{t-1}$	3.165	−4.443*	−2.208	1.765	3.112	2.538***	−0.082	2.981**
	(0.56)	(1.82)	(1.15)	(0.26)	(1.38)	(4.58)	(0.02)	(2.34)
Δ Unemployment	0.465	−1.412	2.483	1.587*	1.767	3.057	1.970*	−1.869
	(0.04)	(1.33)	(0.95)	(1.88)	(0.56)	(1.19)	(1.82)	(0.28)
Δ Prices	1.520	1.068**	0.383	2.316	1.070	−1.656	−1.300	−0.77*
	(0.93)	(2.43)	(0.12)	(0.68)	(0.72)	(0.59)	(0.85)	(1.94)
Government-left	0.202	1.045**	0.143	−0.213	−0.037	−0.307	−0.547*	0.523**
	(0.62)	(2.60)	(1.69)	(0.56)	(0.29)	(1.54)	(1.80)	(2.44)
Coalition size	−1.761	2.490*	−1.935*	−1.933	−2.102	−3.531	−3.179	−3.732
	(0.98)	(1.89)	(1.73)	(1.30)	(0.70)	(0.74)	(0.80)	(0.51)
Cabinet size	4.054	1.751*	−1.586	−2.023**	−4.281	−1.809**	−2.033	−1.653
	(0.23)	(1.76)	(1.64)	(2.13)	(1.10)	(2.66)	(0.56)	(1.24)
Months – election	−0.104	0.756	−0.166	0.005	−0.050	−0.027	0.137	−0.449
	(0.20)	(1.54)	(0.55)	(0.01)	(0.28)	(0.14)	(0.52)	(1.40)
Constant	135.353	184.155	226.85**	285.80**	66.542	168.610**	125.552	136.928
	(0.74)	(1.01)	(2.40)	(2.35)	(1.23)	(2.45)	(1.24)	(1.46)
Observations	88	88	88	88	88	88	88	88
R-squared	0.38	0.49	0.41	0.48	0.48	0.58	0.50	0.46
F(25,47)	4.576	5.9	3.57	3.81	3.89	5.29	9.43	7.23
Prob > F	0.000	0.0000	0.0001	0.0000	0.0000	0.0000	0.0000	0.0000

Notes: Panel-corrected z-statistics in parentheses. *significant at 10 per cent; **significant at 5 per cent; ***significant at 1 per cent. All these regressions are OLS with robust std errors, because panel-corrected std errors cannot be used when T > N.

episodes. By concentrating only on those years when a consolidation is taking place, one can explore whether the factors that influence the composition of the budget in general are also relevant for explaining the composition of the budget, during fiscal adjustments in particular.

In principle, it can be assumed that the same economic and political factors that affect the budget composition in general, are those that affect the budget composition during periods of fiscal consolidation. Therefore, all these factors will be included in the analysis, but special attention will be paid to the role of ideology of the party in government.

As the previous section has shown, during the second half of the 1990s, when the strongest fiscal adjustments were taking place in Europe, economic predictors behave similarly to the pre-1995 period, fragmentation and electoral variables lost statistical significance, and the only factor that reaffirmed its salience as an important variable to understand the composition of the budget was the ideology of the cabinet. Therefore, it is reasonable to assume that this factor will become increasingly important in explaining the composition of the budget during fiscal adjustment episodes.

Before proceeding to the statistical analysis, let me give a fuller consideration of what a 'partisan strategy of fiscal adjustment' might mean in terms of composition. If one recalls from Chapter 3 that any government willing to reduce the public deficit has five possibilities: (S1) to increase revenues more than it increases expenditures; (S2) to increase revenues and freeze expenditures; (S3) to increase revenues and reduce expenditures; (S4) to freeze revenues and reduce expenditures; or (S5) to reduce revenues less than what it reduces expenditures, then the 'partisan strategy of fiscal adjustment' can be characterized in terms of these choices as follows:

A purely revenue-based strategy of adjustment would be any strategy like S1 or S2. A purely expenditure-based strategy of fiscal adjustment would be any strategy like S4 or S5. And, finally, S3 could be defined as a 'mixed-strategy'.

Because S1 and S2 are strategies that despite the consolidation effort still increase the role of the public sector in the economy, one can expect left-wing governments to be associated with those strategies. Left-wing governments should prefer revenue-based strategies because their preference for equality and for a bigger presence of the state in the economy increases public expenditures, that call for higher revenues in order to consolidate the budget. By contrast, because S4 and S5 imply a decrease in the size of the public sector and its coverage, one expects that these strategies should be preferred by right-wing governments. S3 is a middle strategy that could be chosen by either social democratic or conservative governments, and, most likely, by coalition governments with 'mixed' ideologies.

If the previous set of expectations are represented more formally in a graph like the one in Figure 4.1, one would expect all governments undertaking a

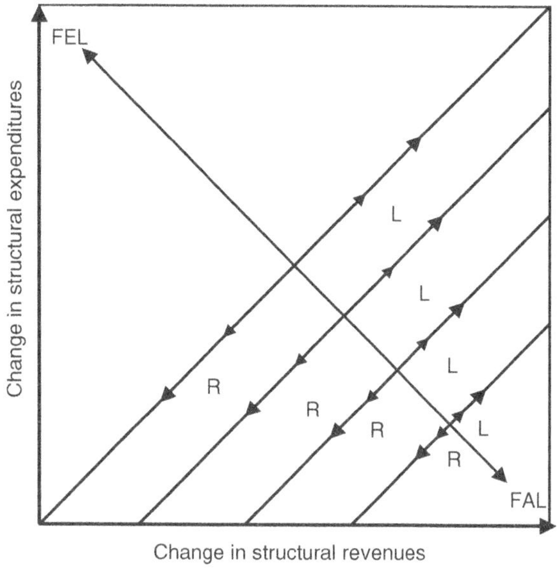

Figure 4.1 Strategies of fiscal adjustment: ideal types

fiscal adjustment to place themselves to the right of the 45° line, when the FEL (Fiscal Expansion Line) becomes the FAL (Fiscal Adjustment Line). And at each level (levels defined by the degree of the adjustment), one would expect leftist governments to choose those strategies that imply both higher levels of public revenues and public expenditures (to the right of FAL). Similarly, preference for a weaker public sector should place right-wing governments making a fiscal adjustment below the Fiscal Adjustment Line (FAL).

Whether the previously described partisan strategies of fiscal adjustment, in which leftist governments would prefer revenue-based strategies and rightist governments would prefer expenditure-based ones, has any predictive power is still a matter for empirical testing.

Simple plotting of the 53 adjustment episodes that occurred between 1960 and 2000,[21] labelled by the ideology of the party in government that undertook the adjustment, gives an idea of how well the data fit the partisanship hypothesis formulated in Chapter 2, for the years preceding the signing of the Maastricht Treaty.

As can be observed in Figures 4.2 and 4.3, both left-wing and right-wing governments followed their expected behaviour when they chose the composition of their fiscal consolidation strategy.

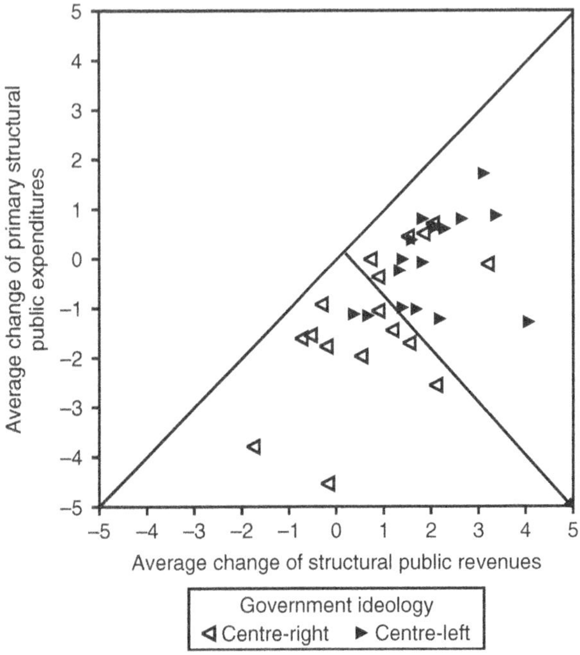

Figure 4.2 Strategies of fiscal adjustment, 1960–91[22]

Nevertheless, it appears that between 1960 and 1991 some rightist governments followed leftist strategies of fiscal adjustment, increasing revenues substantially to finance increases in expenditures. This probably reflects the welfare state consensus of the 1960s and 1970s in Europe, a period during which the welfare state developed in all European countries independently of the party in government.

The picture is less clear during the fiscal adjustment episodes in the post-Maastricht period, even though the ideological hypotheses still fits very well. As can be seen in Figure 4.3, during the 1990s the strongest fiscal adjustments were taken by leftist governments. This makes the comparison more difficult, since the number of adjustments held by leftist governments doubles the number of adjustments held by rightist ones.[23]

Moreover, the fact that some rightist governments followed revenue-based strategies of adjustment (France 1995–96 or Portugal 1992–93), and some leftist governments followed expenditure-based ones (Denmark 1996–99 and Sweden 1995–98), confuses the picture to some extent.

These illustrative results stress the importance of looking at the detailed composition of each adjustment strategy. That is, when the effect of variables lose presence in aggregated magnitudes, it is necessary to consider minor components before arriving at definitive conclusions.

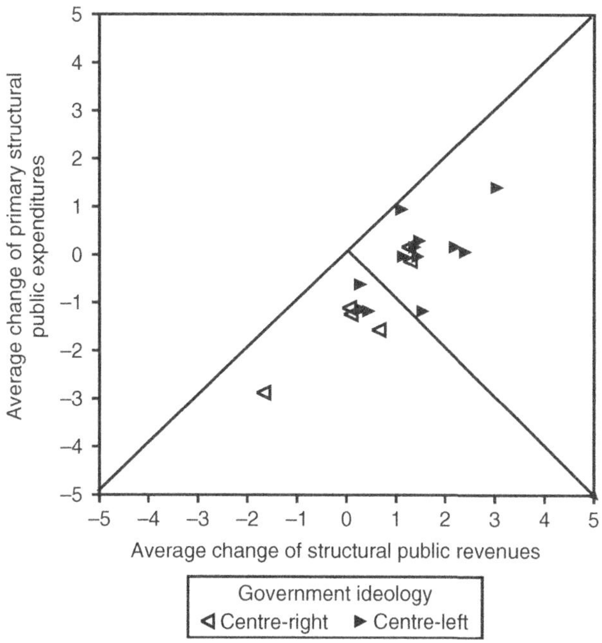

Figure 4.3 Strategies of fiscal adjustment, 1992–2000

For that purpose, this section will again use regression analysis to see if the same economic and political factors that showed a remarkable importance in explaining the timing and duration of consolidations (in Chapter 3), and composition of the budget during both years of adjustment and expansion (section 4.2), are still relevant to explain the composition of the budget, only during episodes of fiscal consolidation.

Hypotheses of the effects that political variables may have on fiscal adjustment strategies must be logically based on the effects that have already been observed during the composition analysis in both adjustment and non-adjustment years. Because more fragmented governments, more leftist governments and the proximity to elections tended to be associated with higher expenditures, one can expect these variables to be associated now with revenue-based strategies of fiscal adjustment, because the only way to reduce the deficit while expenditures are maintained or even increased, is to increase revenues by a greater amount.

Bigger coalitions and bigger cabinets are expected to maintain their preference for social transfers and expenditures, and in principle one should not expect them to cut these expenditures even during periods of fiscal adjustment.

On the contrary, the effect of elections on the strategies of fiscal adjustment cannot be expected to be the same as in the case of non-adjustment periods. Politicians may still want to manage the cycle electorally. The closer the elections, the lower the taxes (and thus the revenues) and the higher the expenditures. Nevertheless, this is a combination of policies that can easily lead to budget deficits. Thus, if the election is close, it is unlikely that the government will start a fiscal adjustment, and most likely that it will end the consolidation (as was highlighted in Chapter 3). Consolidations will only take place during elections in cases where the fiscal adjustment is 'unavoidable', and has to comply with an unalterable calendar.[24] This was the case in the run-up to EMU in the 1990s, and the strong influence of this event in the whole sample of fiscal adjustments in Europe, makes one expect a different effect of elections on fiscal policies than was seen in the previous section.

Finally, taking into consideration the effect that the ideology of the government demonstrated as a strong predictor of the composition of fiscal policy, and looking at the plots in Figures 4.2 and 4.3, it is very clear that socialist control of the cabinet should be expected to play a significant role in explaining why some countries chose revenue-based strategies, while other preferred to follow expenditure-based adjustments. In principle, one should expect left-wing governments to increase revenues in order to maintain the level of expenditures. But if forced to freeze or reduce expenditures as could have been the case during the Maastricht period or under the pressure of the Stability and Growth Pact, one should still expect leftist governments to maintain the government wage bill, transfer payments and public investment, due to their redistributive and supply-side implications.

To study the effect that all economic variables, plus the fragmentation of decision-making, the ideology of the party in government and the proximity to elections have had on strategies of fiscal adjustment and the composition of the budget only during episodes of fiscal consolidation, this section runs the same regressions as in section 2 of this chapter, but now only for the 53 episodes of consolidation.

$$\Delta Y_{i,t} = \alpha_0 + \alpha_1 PCABB_{i,t-1} + \delta_1 \Delta U_{i,t} + \delta_2 \Delta P_{i,t} + \beta_K X_{i,t} + C_i + \varepsilon_{i,t} \qquad (4.2)$$

The technique now is OLS with robust standard errors, with country dummies and no year dummies, because the panel is markedly unbalanced, and the environment is assumed to be common for every EU country in the 1990s.[25]

Given the fact that now observations are episodes of fiscal adjustment that normally last for more than one year, the values in levels and first differences of the different dependent and independent variables are averages of the levels and first differences of the whole episode of adjustment.

A new dependent variable was created, 'Strategy Type', which is the sum of the average variation of cyclically adjusted revenues and cyclically adjusted primary expenditures. The higher the value of 'Strategy Type' in a fiscal adjustment episode, the more expansionary of the public sector was the strategy followed by the corresponding government.

Results for aggregate measures of the adjustment composition are presented in Table 4.4. As can be seen, results confirm the initial hypotheses. The effect of economic variables is not very important, except for the rate of unemployment that has a very positive effect on public expenditures, and thus require higher revenues in order to maintain the fiscal adjustment.

During episodes of fiscal adjustment between 1960 and 2000, bigger coalitions, bigger cabinets, and more leftist governments were associated with growing revenues and expenditures, and thus followed revenue-based strategies of adjustment.[26] The effect of ideology was the only statistically significant variable. Though not statistically significant, the effect of closeness to elections was contrary to what might be expected (revenues increased and expenditures decreased as the election was closer). This is probably the result, as was previously hypothesized, of the overlapping of

Table 4.4 Strategies of fiscal adjustment: main aggregates, 1960–2000

Av. first differences	*Δ Reven*	*Δ Expend*	*Strategy type*
PCA budg. balance$_{t-1}$	−0.092**	0.023	−0.068
	(2.32)	(0.67)	(1.13)
Δ Unemployment	−0.349**	0.442***	0.791***
	(2.42)	(2.89)	(2.89)
Δ Prices	−0.008	−0.016	−0.024
	(0.61)	(0.95)	(0.91)
Government-left	0.015***	0.012***	0.028***
	(3.26)	(3.05)	(3.37)
Coalition size	0.241**	0.193*	0.434**
	(2.46)	(1.69)	(2.13)
Cabinet size	0.023	0.062	0.085
	(0.40)	(1.06)	(0.84)
Months – election	−0.441	0.215	−0.227
	(1.65)	(0.70)	(0.45)
Constant	0.150	−2.363***	−2.217**
	(0.26)	(3.36)	(2.05)
Observations	53	53	53
R-squared	0.40	0.40	0.43
F(7,45)	4.09	3.56	4.14
Prob > F	0.0015	0.0040	0.0014

Notes: Robust *t*-statistics in parentheses. *significant at 10 per cent; **significant at 5 per cent; ***significant at 1 per cent.

Table 4.5 Strategies of fiscal adjustment: individual items, 1960–2000

Av. first differences	*Δ Indtax*	*Δ Dirtax*	*Δ Fincon*	*Δ Pwages*	*Δ Stransf*	*Δ Pinvest*
PCA budg. balance$_{t-1}$	−0.032	−0.023	0.024	0.018	−0.010	0.025**
	(1.47)	(1.20)	(1.22)	(1.43)	(0.44)	(2.24)
Δ Unemployment	0.045**	−0.031*	0.064	0.083	0.372***	0.007
	(2.06)	(1.72)	(0.60)	(1.43)	(3.12)	(0.22)
Δ Prices	0.011	0.007	−0.001	−0.003	−0.004	0.010
	(1.40)	(0.67)	(0.20)	(0.44)	(0.33)	(1.41)
Government-left	0.003	0.006**	0.007***	0.005***	0.001	0.012**
	(1.42)	(2.39)	(2.99)	(3.18)	(0.30)	(2.06)
Coalition size	0.025	0.109	0.079	0.030	0.001	0.020
	(0.49)	(1.48)	(0.86)	(0.66)	(0.30)	(0.86)
Cabinet size	0.016	−0.010	−0.004	−0.010	0.035	0.027*
	(0.60)	(0.21)	(0.10)	(0.43)	(0.75)	(1.85)
Months – election	−0.214	0.040	−0.082	0.011	−0.056	−0.023
	(1.61)	(0.22)	(0.40)	(0.11)	(0.23)	(0.32)
Constant	0.050	0.024	−0.383	−0.237	−0.468	−0.659*
	(0.18)	(0.05)	(1.09)	(1.41)	(0.98)	(2.01)
Observations	53	53	51	53	53	53
R-squared	0.18	0.12	0.12	0.32	0.19	0.28
F(7,45)	3.83	1.28	2.89	3.84	2.92	2.81
Prob > F	0.0024	0.2799	0.0145	0.0024	0.0132	0.0163

Notes: Robust *t*-statistics in parentheses. *significant at 10 per cent; **significant at 5 per cent; ***significant at 1 per cent.

the 'electoral calendar' and the 'Maastricht calendar'[27] which took place in some European countries between 1995 and 1998.

The analysis of the effect that economic and political variables have on the individual components of the budget during episodes of fiscal adjustment (see Table 4.5), confirm again the main hypotheses that had been previously formulated in this respect.

As in previous regressions, the unemployment rate was the only statistically significant economic variable. In order to consolidate the budget in countries where the unemployment rate is growing, the only possible strategy available to government was to increase those public revenues coming from indirect taxes (since those from direct taxes tend to fall), in order to pay for a growing level of expenditures on unemployment subsidies.

Coalition size and cabinet show the expected signs in all specifications and were positively associated with increases in transfers during fiscal adjustment episodes, though these effects were not statistically significant.

Most importantly, results show that the ideology of the party in government was the most important political variable affecting the evolution of different items of the budget during episodes of fiscal consolidation. Leftist governments followed strategies of adjustment that increased revenues (mostly from direct taxes) to finance the maintenance or even an increase of public expenditures – in particular, public consumption, the government wage bill and public investments. Other public expenditures were also positively affected by leftist governments, though these effects were not statistically significant.

These results are very important because they present very clear evidence that, even under the strongest pressures for further convergence of fiscal policies, there is still room to formulate different approaches to fiscal policy at sub-aggregate levels of the budget's composition.

Particularly important in this respect is the evidence that leftist governments still tried to affect the supply side of the economy by investing relatively more than rightist governments. This preference was so strong that it was maintained even during periods of fiscal adjustment, when public investment is typically either frozen or reduced. The fact is that under a general trend of decreasing public provision of physical capital since the 1970s, during the 1990s socialist governments seemed to be successful in maintaining or even increasing the share of GDP dedicated to public investment (see Table 2.4).

4.4 Conclusion

This chapter has answered the following two questions: what determines the composition of the budget in general?, and what explains that different countries follow different strategies of adjustment in periods of fiscal consolidation?

Results have confirmed that economic variables that were very strong predictors of the timing and duration of fiscal consolidation analysed in chapter 3, lose predictive power in favour of political variables as predictors of the budget's composition during fiscal adjustment episodes.

In this respect, bigger coalitions, bigger cabinets, more leftist governments and proximity of elections had a positive effect on the increase in public expenditures, especially social transfers, between 1970 and 1994. Nevertheless, this influence was reversed during the second half of the 1990s. Interestingly, evidence shows that ideology was the strongest determinant of the budget's composition during this period, when leftist governments reoriented their policies and used increasing revenues from direct taxes to balance the budget and maintain or increase the government wage bill (public employment and wages) and public investment (to affect the economy in the supply side), even at the expense of cuts in subsidies, consumption and social transfers. The importance of political variables was confirmed in the section dedicated to the study of the budget's composition during episodes of fiscal adjustment.

Because the composition of the adjustment is related to its likelihood of success,[28] apparently decisions such as those taken by some European countries in the 1990s that followed a revenue-based adjustment to qualify quickly for EMU, should have never been adopted because they were not optimal in the medium run. In fact, some of these countries had already experienced difficulties in order to keep their budgets balanced at the beginning of the next decade during the first economic slowdown of the euro era, and were warned by the European Commission for breaching the limits of the Stability Pact.

By pointing out the influence that political factors have on fiscal policy, and the special relevance that partisan strategies of adjustment played in the process towards EMU, this chapter is crucial in understanding why those decisions were made and those strategies were chosen.

5
Fiscal Adjustments in the 1990s: Case Studies

'If quantification produces precision, it does not necessarily encourage accuracy ... Case studies are essential for description and accuracy, and are, therefore, fundamental to social science.'

King, Keohane and Verba, 1994: 44

In the context of the clear limits established by the Maastricht Treaty and the Stability and Growth Pact, to affirm that fiscal policy is not as homogeneous across Europe as could be expected in a monetary union because domestic economic and political factors still have a strong influence, may appear unconvincing in spite of the statistical evidence presented until now.

In this respect, the first questions that arise in view of the empirical results presented in Chapters 3 and 4 regarding the influence of domestic economic and political factors on the timing, the duration and the composition of different fiscal adjustment strategies, are the following: if governments at the national level have traditionally sought to formulate differentiated fiscal policies, why did they tie their hands in the first place by setting the Maastricht convergence criteria? Why was monetary union a project that attracted all European national governments to such an extent that they gave up their sovereignty in monetary policy and constrained their ability to manage fiscal policy in the future? Also, if social democratic parties have usually formulated their economic policies within the limits of the nation-state, why did they sign and promote the project of monetary union?

The first part of this chapter will consider the answer to these questions. The project of monetary union arrived in Europe at a time when the internationalization of capital had created the conditions for cooperative solutions to the problems of slow growth and inflation that Europe had experienced since the 1970s. Aiming to isolate European countries from the exchange-rate volatility of the 1970s, they agreed on a common exchange rate mechanism (the EMS). By the end of the 1990s, the asymmetries in the EMS created a need to counterbalance German monetary power in Europe. EMU was conceived as a mechanism to redistribute the costs derived from a unique monetary policy managed by the Bundesbank, as well as a mechanism to consolidate the postwar project of European peace and stability in the midst of the uncertainty created by German reunification.

The second part of this chapter considers the second set of possible objections that the results presented in the first part of the book could generate. These objections would generally take the form of concrete case studies where the main predictions made by the model do not appear to fit. Typically, when we find a country where one political variable works in the opposite direction to the one predicted by the model, it usually occurs because there has been a very strong influence exerted by the other variables. For example, when we find a social-democratic cabinet that has implemented an expenditure-based adjustment, it is typically the case that economic conditions, political fragmentation or electoral pressures have displaced the influence of ideology on certain fiscal policy decisions.

Therefore, the second part of this chapter presents country studies that offer pure paradigmatic examples of the different interactions that have taken place between economic and political variables in real adjustment episodes occurred during the 1990s. It starts by comparing two paradigmatic cases in which the ideology of the party in government played a crucial role as the main determinant of the fiscal adjustment strategy. Spain, between 1996 and 2000, epitomizes the typical conservative expenditure-based adjustment, while Portugal between 1995 and 1999 was paradigmatic of the opposite revenue-based social democratic approach. In a similar way, the UK and Italy are compared with each other to exemplify the influence of the fragmentation of decision-making. Italy, the European country with one of the most fragmented political systems and a very weak budgetary process, was also the one where the effect of partisanship had been more blurred during the 1990s, while the UK, with the least fragmented system, has historically tended to witness the clearest patterns of partisan management of fiscal policy until the 1990s. Finally, during the 1990s France and Germany became clear examples of the strong influence that electoral considerations have on the formulation of fiscal policy. Elections can affect the strategic timing of consolidations (the French case in 1995–97), or can motivate the weakening of domestic fiscal institutions with electoral purposes (the German case).

Therefore, the aim of this chapter is to go beyond the results of the quantitative analysis of previous chapters, and to shed light around the same issues through concrete and real examples. At last, 'in comparative analysis we work with concepts ... [but] when we confront them with political and social realities we sometimes realize that they do not fit; or indeed that the concepts obscure or confuse. Then our task is to reformulate them, highlight different dimensions, and sometimes to introduce new conceptualizations' (Stepan, 2001: 4).

5.1 The Maastricht Treaty and the decision of monetary union

The Maastricht Treaty

In February 1992, the final version of the Treaty on the European Union was signed by the Heads of State Government of the 12 members of the former European Community. They did so following two months of 'polishing-up' of the text that was agreed in the European Council meeting of 9–10 December 1991 in the Dutch city of Maastricht. Finally, following delays in the ratification process at the national level (especially its rejection in the Danish referendum), the Treaty on European Union came into effect on 1 November 1993.

The Treaty had three pillars, the most important of which was monetary union. That section of the Treaty stated that EMU would be fully in place by 1999 at the latest, and possibly as early as 1997. Monetary union would be managed by an European Central Bank (ECB), independent of national or supranational governments whose primary objective would be price stability. During the transition period full capital mobility should be ensured in all member states, and full independence of national central banks should also be granted. The European Monetary Institute would be the seed of the future ECB, but adoption of the single currency would only happen after nominal convergence among European economies. The famous Maastricht convergence criteria laid out in the Treaty established that every country moving to stage 3 would display: (1) a rate of inflation in the consumer price index no higher than 1.5 per cent higher that the average of the three states with the lowest inflation; (2) interest rates on long-term government bonds no higher than 2 per cent above the average of the three countries with the lowest rates; (3) a central government budget deficit no greater than 3 per cent of GDP; (4) a public debt-to-GDP ratio below 60 per cent of GDP; and (4) a national currency that had remained within the narrow (2.25 per cent) fluctuation margins of the exchange rate mechanism of the EMS for the previous two years and had not been devalued against other member state currency over the same period.

In general terms, the agreement on monetary union followed very closely the recommendations of the previous 'Report on Economic and Monetary Union in the European Community', also known as the *Delors Report*. This report was prepared by the European Commission and endorsed by the European Council held in Madrid in June 1989 (see Table 5.1). Some changes were, however, included in this proposal during the intergovernmental conference (IGC) to study monetary union[1] that started in December 1990 in Rome and finished in Maastricht in 1991.

However, the agreement on monetary union was a long process.[2] As early as the 1960s, the Werner Report presented at the Hague EC summit in

Table 5.1 Key recommendations of the 'Delors Report'

Stage	*Objectives*
Stage 1 (1992)	Complete the internal market (the 1992 programme) Coordinate the economic policies of the member states Remove all exchange and capital controls Bring all European Community (EC) currencies into the exchange rate mechanism Eliminate obstacles to the private use of the European Currency Unit (ECU) Give the committee of central bank governors a role in assessing monetary policies and advising national governments and the Council of Ministers Prepare a treaty on monetary union
Stage 2 (1994)	Establish a European System of Central Banks (ESCB) with a federal structure Transfer the functions of existing EC monetary institutions to the ESCB Leave monetary policy decisions in the hands of national authorities Narrow the fluctuation margins in the exchange-rate mechanism
Stage 3 (1997 or 1999)	Move to irrevocably fixed exchange rates, with eventual replacement of national currencies by a single EC currency Transfer full monetary policy authority to the ESCB Create binding rules to constrain national budget deficits
2002	Circulation of the euro

Source: Committee for the Study of Economic and Monetary Union (EC, 1989: 27–38). In Sandholtz (1993: 15).

December 1969 mentioned for the first time the project of a future monetary union. These first thoughts were motivated by the mounting tensions in the Bretton Woods system of fixed exchange rates, and by growing French dissatisfaction both with US leadership in European affairs, and growing German leadership on monetary policy in the continent.

Later, after the first oil shock, and the demise of the Bretton Woods system, German Chancellor Helmut Schmidt proposed the European Monetary System (EMS) at the April 1978 European Council in Copenhagen. Between April and December, EC policy-makers bargained over the proposed system's institutional framework, creating an exchange rate system based on a bilateral parity grid, centred around the Bundesbank and supported by restrictive financial mechanisms 'that asymmetrically placed the costs of exchange rate stability upon weak-currency policymakers' (Oatley, 1997: 47). The system, a 'snake' that established the upper and lower limits for currency fluctuations, began operating in March 1979, but at first it consisted of only France and Germany, together with the rest of the smaller member states. Italy joined but subject to partial membership, while Britain refused altogether to enter the exchange rate mechanism.[3] Then, between 1987 and 1991, EMS institutions evolved towards greater exchange rate stability. The achievement of a high degree of nominal convergence, the integration of financial markets in conjunction with the Single European Act (1986), and reforms that placed less emphasis on exchange rate realignments and more emphasis on interest rate coordination to manage the system (the Basel–Nyborg reforms) combined to push the EMS first towards a more rigid exchange rate system and then towards monetary union (Oatley, 1997: 143).

Finally, in June 1988 at the Hanover summit, EU Heads of State Government called, in the face of British objections, for a committee of experts to draw up a plan for monetary union. The committee, composed by central bank governors and chaired by the European Commission's President, Jaques Delors, produced the above-mentioned 'Report on Economic and Monetary Union in the European Community' in April 1989. Discussions following this were hard, mostly regarding the issue of whether entering stage 1 already implied acceptance of stages 2 and 3. The dates when each stage should start, the conditions of entry,[4] and the powers of the future European Monetary Institute (later the ECB), also caused some conflict. However, the decision to proceed was firm and became clearer as German reunification appeared increasingly inevitable. Despite Margaret Thatcher's continued efforts to delay the process, the steps towards monetary union accelerated through the Spanish, the French, the Italian and the Dutch consecutive presidencies, and ended with the signing of the Maastricht Treaty in December 1991.[5]

Why monetary union? Why was it embraced by most governments?

This question has no single straightforward answer, but can be solved through a combination of various perspectives.

Certainly, the movement towards monetary union would have not taken place without the previous shift in European domestic political economies towards macroeconomic discipline during the 1980s (Sandholtz, 1993). Germany, being the largest economy in Europe and the most vigilant of monetary stability, would have never agreed to monetary integration with countries that had long pursued economic strategies based on cycles of inflation and devaluation. Technological changes that speeded the mobility of capital, together with the failure of the Keynesian approach to macroeconomic policy management during the 1970s, created the momentum for a radical change in the economic policy ideas of the governing elites across Europe. In France, this shift towards restrictive economic policies began in 1976 when the Barre government was installed with the explicit mandate to adopt a policy of economic austerity. After the failed Keynesian expansion of the first Mitterrand government in 1981, French political elites adhered to the *franc fort* policy based on macroeconomic stability, a commitment which still holds today. Italy followed France in the 1980s, under the leadership of a small elite from the Bank of Italy, and other countries such as Belgium, Luxembourg, Denmark, Ireland and the Netherlands had all made their transitions to macroeconomic discipline by the mid-1980s.

Nevertheless, although this generalized conversion to the new disinflationary zeal was a necessary precondition for talks on monetary union to start, it is not sufficient to explain the choice that EU countries finally made. In principle, in order to sustain low inflation across the continent, monetary union is not necessary. EU countries could have maintained low inflation without surrendering their sovereignty on monetary policy. It is not even clear among economists that the EU met the minimum standards of an optimal currency area, or that monetary union was a real economic necessity to complete the Single Market.[6]

European countries could have tried to maintain their commitment to low inflation under a floating exchange regime, by taking credible steps in this direction (primarily the establishment of truly independent central banks, obligated by law to pursue low inflation). In addition, they could have tried to strengthen the EMS, which in fact could have been seen as superior to monetary union because it would have given the chance to low growth/low productivity countries to adjust to asymmetric shocks via minor realignments, instead of via factor mobility across countries. However, they finally decided to push for monetary union. Why did they take this course of action?

The advantages that the European Commission and other European policy-makers put forward throughout the process were certainly important aspects that contributed to the final decision. Some of the crucial arguments that were raised in this respect were: (1) for each member government, a single currency would constitute the most credible possible commitment to low inflation, since they could no longer resort to devaluation to compensate for high inflation or low productivity; (2) low inflation would provide the basis for increased investment, and therefore higher growth and employment; (3) a single currency would eliminate exchange-rate risk and the transaction costs of exchange currencies within the European market. These costs were considerable, as intra-communitarian trade kept growing. By the end of 1991, the European Commission estimated these savings to range between 13 and 19 billion ECU, or 0.5 per cent of GDP per year for the larger countries, and 1 per cent for the smaller ones; (4) the ECU (euro) would become a major international currency for trade, international bond issues, and reserves (the savings in exchange reserves for the EU were estimated to be around ECU 230 billion) (5) the monetary union could handle asymmetric shocks in a variety of ways, including wage and price flexibility, increased factor mobility, and investment (public and private); (6) and, finally, a single currency would boost the European identity, and would thus become a further step towards permanent peace and future political integration in Europe (EC, 1990).

However, in addition to all these advantages, the decisive reasons for the final choice in favour of monetary union had to do with the coincidence of a variety of factors among which foreign policy motivations in France and Germany played a crucial role.

Among these various factors that coincided as driving forces of European monetary union, five can be mentioned as the most important:[7]

1. *Spillovers from the 1986 and 1992 processes*: according to this proposition, the completion of the single market in 1992, as projected in the Single European Act of 1986 would have created internal dynamics by which only through monetary union all the parts could obtain the full benefits of integration in the economic area. The theoretical case for spillovers was initially developed in neofunctionalist theories of integration in the 1960s (Haas, 1958).[8] Even in its revised formulation (Schmitter, 1970) the spillover argument sustains that integration in one issue-area (trade integration) would reveal functional linkages to other issue areas (monetary union), and then to other issue areas (single economic government or political union).

This argument was very much used by the European Commission in their first arguments in favour of monetary union. In several documents the Commission repeated that the single market project would never be fully completed without monetary union. In their own words: 'A single currency is the natural complement of a single market. The full potential of the latter will not be achieved without the former' (EC, 1989: 11). Therefore, 'the economic advantages of 1992 are certainly not fully achievable without a single currency' (EC, 1990: 17), because with complete capital mobility, capital would flow from European countries with high inflation to those with lower inflation, creating massive fluctuations in the exchange rates. In that situation, either the EMS would become a much more unstable mechanism in the future, or full capital mobility could not be completed by 1992 as initially scheduled (Padoa-Schioppa, 1998).

The most important drawback of this argument is that, as with any functional logic, it explains the intermediate steps but not the initial decision. Also, it inherently implies a learning process by which actors realize that they are not obtaining all the benefits from the previous step, before deciding to move to the next one. This learning process did not happen in Europe, because discussions on monetary union started long before the official proposal of 1989, but in any case at least three years before the expected completion of the single market in 1992.

2. *Domestic business actors*: According to this proposition, the motivation of business groups and European multinationals, supported by the European

enthusiasm of the general public, motivated national politicians to engage into negotiations for further European integration. In this respect, the creation of the two business lobbying groups in favour of monetary union (the Committee for the Monetary Union of Europe and the Association for Monetary Union in Europe) before the formal discussion of EMU started by European governments is generally interpreted as evidence in favour of this argument (Frieden, 1991).[9] However, the idea was circulating in European circles for quite a long time, and it looks like the support of this group once formal discussions started played a more important role than before this happened.[10]

With respect to a second argument in a similar direction, according to which the coincidence of peaks in the public opinion's support for further integration in the late 1980s would have moved national politicians in the direction of monetary union, the evidence is much weaker or points in precisely the opposite direction. It is true that public support for European integration had risen by the late 1980s and the beginning of the 1990s. However, there is also evidence that national politicians and European proposals ignited this public enthusiasm, instead of the other way around. Moreover, some of these countries that took the lead in the drive towards monetary union were among those with the lowest rates of public support for the single currency (in Germany the level of public support was slightly under 50 per cent in 1990).

3. *Concerns about credible binding commitments*: A third factor traditionally seen as an important motive driving towards monetary union has been the existing concerns at the time in various member states about the impossibility of convincing the markets of their serious commitment towards achieving price stability. For some of those countries with a bad inflation history and frequent use of competitive devaluations, to bind their hands in a monetary union was the best way to gain this definitive credibility. This was evidently the case because accepting monetary union was the strongest binding commitment in which these countries could engage.

The evidence favouring the 'tying hands' hypothesis is the broad consensus on the nature of monetary union. All European governments concurred that the future ECB would be granted complete independence from political authorities, and that its first mission would be to control inflation. They also agreed immediately that for this commitment to be regarded as decisive from the outset, national central banks should be granted full independence before any further decision towards monetary union was taken.

4. *Politics of the European monetary system*: This proposition affirms that some countries, such as France and Italy, would have pushed for monetary union in an attempt to gain greater voice in European monetary policy-making against German dominance of the EMS. This argument reinforces the 'neorealist' view according to which countries cooperate with each other only in order to balance the power of a hegemonic state.

The idea is that in 1983 France found it more costly to exit the EMS than to gain greater voice in the system by setting the conditions of monetary policy in Europe. The French were disappointed with what they perceived to be a fundamental asymmetry of the system, namely that the burden of the adjustment so as to maintain parities relied predominantly on the weak currency country. In the meantime, the Germans only needed to consider domestic objectives and consequences.

What in its origins was conceived as a mechanism to force from abroad internal consensus around price stability was now seen as the source of important asymmetries. When Chancellor Schmidt proposed the EMS in 1978, he was facing pressure to increase employment from those traditional labour unions close to the SPD. At the same time he was constrained by a coalition government and by the independent Bundesbank committed to price stability that was increasing interest rates, appreciating the currency and damaging the trade balance. For the Schmidt government, 'a community exchange rate system, by stabilizing the mark, and perhaps also forcing the Bundesbank to adopt a less restrictive monetary policy, could help them to achieve labour's demands. Thus Schmidt proposed the EMS to try to achieve domestic objectives he could not achieve otherwise' (Oatley, 1998: 48). Similarly, France accepted the proposal because monetary restriction was fully consistent with President Giscard d'Estaing's domestic monetary policy objectives centred on disinflation, and helped to curb domestic opposition, and the domestic tendency to wage–price spirals exhibited in the late 1960s and the 1970s.

By the beginning of the 1980s, the EMS had fulfilled all its objectives by achieving a high degree of exchange rate stability and disinflation. However, French perceptions of unfair asymmetries forced the EMS revisions of 1987, leading to the Basle–Nyborg reforms and the December 1987 realignment.[11] However, even this was not enough. In January 1988, the French Finance Minister, Édouard Balladur, circulated a letter to his counterparts calling for an open discussion on the topic of a European Central Bank that would manage a single currency, and would therefore avoid the current situation where one country dictated the monetary policy of all the others. Giuliano Amato immediately expressed Italian support for this initiative. Other countries also supported the proposal, including Belgium and even the Netherlands, who finally hosted the signing of the Maastricht Treaty.[12]

5. *Foreign policy interests*: The previous argument, however, gives no explanation of German acceptance of the French proposal to counterbalance its power. One interpretation for this acceptance by Kohl's government is that the German executive saw in EMU an instrument to circumvent the strong power of the Bundesbank which was raising interest rates in view of the fiscal expansion that was taking place to finance German reunification. This restrictive monetary policy was damaging other European economies and also the investment prospects in Germany. In this sense, Kohl would

have accepted EMU for the same reasons that Schmidt had proposed the EMS ten years before: to place external pressure on the Bundesbank to soften monetary policy. However, this interpretation lacks strength, since Kohl was not subject to the strong domestic pressures from trade unions from which Schmidt had suffered. Also, at the time Germany needed tight monetary policy, in order to prevent inflation from spiralling in the context of the strong fiscal expansion that massive transfers to the East motivated. Therefore, the question remains, why did Germany move to the front wagon and lead monetary union?

The main reason, it is argued by defendants of this proposition, has to do with Germany's desire to prove to its European counterparts that despite German reunification after the fall of the Berlin Wall, German would remain loyal to the Western European postwar principles. According to this proposition, France, the Netherlands, Belgium, and other European states suggested the acceleration of the plans on monetary union, as a response to the rapid strengthening of Germany in European geopolitics by means of its reunification with the former Democratic Republic. At the same time, German foreign policy officials considered than in order to gain the support of their European counterparts for German reunification, they had to reaffirm their commitment towards European integration. 'According to some reports, German support for monetary (and political) union was a bargain, the other one half of which was French assent to rapid German unification' (Sandholtz, 1993: 33).

The fact that Hans-Dietrich Genscher, the then German Foreign Minister, took the lead in sending the message to all European governments that Germany would push for monetary union, in spite of the reticence expressed by the Finance Minister, Gerhard Stoltenberg, and the President of the Bundesbank, Helmut Schlesinger, offers strong support for the idea that Kohl's definitive support of monetary union was a political decision largely based on foreign policy considerations.[13]

None of the five factors listed above can explain the whole story about the motivations that drove the move towards EMU, but together they provide the basis for a very comprehensive explanation. The first three factors – the 'spillovers' argument, the 'business interests' argument, and the 'credible commitment' argument – exemplify the influence that supranational institutions, actors and ideas played in generating the appropriate background for monetary union. The last two arguments – that on 'the politics of the EMS', and that on 'foreign policy motivations' – help, however, to explain the concrete motivations that made each country take the final decision of signing the treaty.

These last two arguments are also very useful in answering the question of why social democratic governments supported EMU, even though monetary union considerably constrained their traditional preference for active fiscal policies and national economic management.

There are different ways to answer this question. First, it could be argued that of the 12 Heads of State Government that met in Maastricht in December 1991, only three were social democrats. This would be why, although the socialist French president, François Mitterrand, played an important role in Maastricht, the institutional set-up for monetary union that was agreed there was much closer to German than to French preferences, and resulted therefore in institutions that guaranteed restrictive policies in the future. It could be also argued, in this respect, that the three Scandinavian countries, traditionally considered among the paradigmatic examples of social democratic welfare states, joined the EU later in 1995, and had to take Maastricht as given. Nevertheless, although true, this argument would not be able to explain why social democratic parties in opposition backed their respective national governments in their decision of signing EMU, and never attempted later to reverse or modify the process once they reached power in the second half of the nineties.

A second alternative way to answer to these objections consists of reinterpreting EMU as a device that was in fact favourable to the social democratic goals of macroeconomic policy management. This reinterpretation would argue that EMU offers a framework for the cooperation of social democratic governments at the European level (Ladrech, 2000), where they can finally pursue coordinated demand stimulation at the European level, and can agree on welfare state harmonization to prevent a 'race-to-the bottom' of the European welfare model. Finally, EMU can be interpreted as providing the new institutional set-up that can serve as the anchor that assures the wage restraint that was lost in the 1970s when the corporatist centralized wage bargaining model disappeared and opened the door for the end of Keynesian approaches to demand management (Notermans, 2001a). Again, although theoretically plausible, this argument is not supported by strong empirical evidence. During the late 1990s, when 12 out of 15 governments in the EU were social democratic, no step forward was taken in the direction of welfare state harmonization or common economic stimulation.

This is why, in my opinion, the social democratic consensus around EMU has to be interpreted as the result of two different factors: (1) the genuine conviction among social democrats that monetary union and fiscal restraint was the basis for sustainable growth, because fiscal balance was a precondition for the viability of supply-side policies and sustainable welfare systems; and (2) the logical support that opposition parties traditionally grant to their governments in issues that affect the national interest.

In this respect, EMU was interpreted as a foreign policy issue that was in the national interest of Germany, France, Italy and other European countries. In these circumstances, none of the social democratic parties in opposition in these big states hesitated in giving their support to the project (Ross, 2001; Notermans, 2001b). Once the decision was taken, small countries such as the Netherlands, Austria, and Belgium, which were traditionally pegged to

Germany's monetary policies, followed without delay.[14] The argument of national interest was always present among domestic political elites and all social democratic parties pledged to it. For example, the PvDA leadership in the Netherlands kept insisting throughout the whole process that monetary union meant more integration, and that this, by bringing more trade gains to the country, could be very beneficial for the middle classes and the poor, as long as these gains were channelled properly through the correct institutions (de Beus, 2001). In the European periphery, countries such as Ireland, Spain, Portugal, and Greece, not only exchanged their support to EMU for cohesion funds,[15] but interpreted monetary union as something beyond an economic project. These countries saw in EMU a unique opportunity to achieve modernization, democratic consolidation, and future social prosperity. The objective of 'not missing the train this time' became a national objective in these countries that the electorate supported and that no party disputed.

Finally, the case of Scandinavian countries presents a heterogeneous picture. Meanwhile Finland supported full EMU membership with the social democratic party taking the lead in this decision, the Swedish socialist party (SAP) opposed it frontally, and the Danish supported it but with conditions.

The Finnish support was a foreign policy decision that aimed to strengthen the European ties after the collapse of the Soviet Union (Pekkarinen, 2001). This foreign policy objective coincided with the social democratic party revision of its economic strategy after the unprecedented economic crisis of 1990. Economic austerity and a firm commitment to exchange rate stability in a very open economy became central objectives of this new approach, what facilitated considerably the full embracement of EMU by Finnish social democrats.[16]

In the Swedish and the Danish cases the story was somewhat different. The neutrality identity of their citizens and political elites seems to have played an important role in shaping their common reticence towards EMU (Aylott, 2001; Haar, 2001). However, differences can be found in their respective attitudes. While the social democratic party in Denmark defended the country's participation in EMU as the only way to have a voice at the European level in a policy area that might endanger their social model, the Swedish social democrats openly opposed it. With an argument similar to that adopted by the British,[17] Sweden opted out of joining EMU in the first wave. Social democrats embraced fully what was a foreign policy decision, based on the argument provided by the Calmfors Report (1999), according to which they should not support monetary union because the Swedish economy was not in the same economic cycle as the rest of Europe. This could result in unfavourable asymmetric shocks to its economy, which could not be counterbalanced through devaluation because of the constraints of a monetary union.

5.2 Case studies: complying with the Maastricht criteria and the influence of political variables

The fact that national interests and foreign policy considerations were the driving forces that motivated member states to agree on monetary union and sign the Maastricht Treaty does not contradict the fact that during the post-Maastricht period, in the process of meeting the Maastricht criteria, domestic factors have had a decisive influence on the strategy of adjustment that was finally adopted by each country.

As Chapters 3 and 4 have demonstrated, country differences in the timing, the duration, and the composition of fiscal adjustment strategies across Europe were still heavily influenced during the 1990s by factors such as the economic cycle, the accumulated level of debt, the proximity of elections, the fragmentation of decision-making, and the ideology of the party in government. Therefore, once countries decided to sign the Maastricht Treaty based on foreign policy considerations, and committed themselves to fiscal deficit reduction, these domestic economic and political constraints started to play their role in affecting the decision over the adjustment strategy that each government chose to follow. Regarding partisan politics, this means that the fact that social democratic parties supported monetary union for foreign policy reasons and/or for their true belief in economic stability, does not contradict the fact that they decided to implement adjustment strategies that were different from those chosen by conservative governments. To sign up for EMU and still try to preserve the role of the state in the economy, and its capacity to launch supply-side policies and affect income distribution, does not imply any contradiction.

Of course, during the process of convergence, between 1992 and 1997, state-level 'realpolitik' in the European arena still played a role. This was especially the case around the decisions over how many countries would join the third stage of EMU in the first phase, and how strictly the convergence criteria would be interpreted. Both decisions were, of course, interrelated. After the exchange rate crisis in the EMS of 1992 and 1993, when the pound and the lira were expelled from the system, several currencies depreciated and fluctuation boundaries had to be widened to +/−15 per cent, the criteria on exchange rate stability was completely relaxed. The issue then became how to fulfil the deficit and debt criteria in the midst of a strong economic recession. When the effects of the recession were not still very acute in Germany, this country insisted on the strict application of the criteria, and therefore on a small first group of core countries joining stage 3 of EMU. The problem was that Belgium and Italy, two of the founding members of the European Community back in 1957, had accumulated debt figures that doubled the limits established in the Maastricht criteria. The group of Germany, the Netherlands, Austria and Luxembourg was more reluctant to exclude Belgium (for obvious economic ties), than Italy. However, if criteria were strictly applied to one, no exception could be made with the other.

Things remained like that until 1997, when a final decision had to be made on the final membership of the euro, meanwhile all countries struggled to meet the 3 per cent limit. Only Germany took one step further its obsession to secure the German public that the euro would be as stable and strong as the Deutsche Mark, and in 1995 forced the negotiations over the Stability and Growth Pact, that was finally signed at the Amsterdam summit in June 1997. This pact established that budget deficits would remain below 3 per cent after stage 3 of EMU, and that they would aim at balance or surplus, to be able to accommodate economic downturns without exceeding the limit. Fines of up to 0.5 per cent of GDP would be imposed on those countries violating the Treaty provisions, except if they were hit by a permanent recession.

Ironically, at the beginning of 1997 it became clear that countries such as France and Germany were struggling to meet the '3.0 per cent limit' (as the German Finance Minister Theo Waigel had insisted in calling it). As France and Germany introduced a series of last-minute one-off measures, the rest followed the example.[18] France obtained the equivalent of 0.5 per cent GDP from France Télécom in exchange for assuming the pensions of its employees in a future privatization, while Portugal did the same with Banco Nacional Ultramarino and received a payment equal to 0.3 per cent of GDP. Germany sold some gold reserves and tried to revalue the rest, and cash-in the surpluses; Belgium followed the same example and sold part of the Central Bank's gold reserves; Austria sold a third-generation mobile phone licence, received a payment from the Sparkasse (both amounting to 0.25 per cent of GDP), and reclassified municipal agencies and road-financing agencies out of the government structure. Finally, Italy levied an special euro-tax on all incomes, and the UK levied a 'windfall tax' on the profits of recently privatized public enterprises.

Despite all these one-off measures, acknowledged and 'permitted' by the European Commission (EC, 1998a), there was tension until the last moment surrounding the question of Italy. Germany did not want Italy in the first group, but Jospin, in one of his first foreign policy statements as prime minister, said that France would not join without Italy. Finally, there was a flexible interpretation of the criteria (mainly the debt criteria), and in an extraordinary European Council held in Brussels on 2 May 1998 it was agreed that 11 states would join stage 3 (all member states except the three opt-outs and Greece). The ECB board was also appointed and the dates of 1999 for blocking exchange rates, and of 2002 for the circulation of euro coins and notes, were confirmed.

It must be also noticed, however, that, despite the above accounting tricks, and the inter-states fights over the 'ins' and 'outs', it is undisputable that the 1990s witnessed some of the strongest episodes of fiscal adjustments in the last three decades of European economic history. It is also undisputable that different countries followed different strategies of adjustment, and that in these choices, domestic economic, institutional and political factors played a crucial role.

In what follows, the rest of the chapter will deepen into the details of some paradigmatic case studies, with the purpose of illustrating with concrete empirical evidence some of the most important conclusions reached in the previous statistical chapters. The cases of Portugal, Spain, the UK, Italy, France, and Germany, illustrate, each in its own way, how domestic political factors such as the ideology of the party in government, the fragmentation of the cabinet, and the proximity of elections, affected fiscal adjustment strategies in these countries during the nineties.

The ideology of the party in government: Portugal vs Spain

During the 1990s, several examples of 'partisan strategies' of fiscal adjustment can be observed. In France, for example, the Socialist government of Jospin followed a fiscal adjustment strategy that combined relative increases in revenues from direct taxation, the freezing of unproductive expenditures, and expansion of public investment, following the archetypical supply-side economic strategy of social democratic parties after the fall of Keynesianism. The same strategy was followed by the Finnish government from 1999 on, under a centre-left coalition, as well as in the Netherlands (1990–94) or Greece (1994–99). There are other examples as well of centrist coalitions and conservative governments undertaking expenditure-based fiscal adjustments. These were the cases of Austria (1995–97), Ireland (1990–93, and again 1998–2000), Finland (1993–95), Denmark (1990–93), Germany (1995–97), Italy (1990–93), or the United Kingdom under John Major (1993–96).

However, probably the two most salient cases of opposite partisan influence on fiscal policy were those of Portugal and Spain in the second half of the 1990s. Both countries achieved remarkable reductions of the public deficit and the stock of debt after 1995, starting at levels around 6 per cent deficit and 65 per cent debt in 1995 and qualifying for EMU in 1997 below the 3 per cent deficit limit and close to the 60 per cent debt limit (see Table 5.2).

During the second half of the 1990s both countries grew at above the EU average recording sustained rates of real GDP growth – around 3 per cent per year. And, if any, only small differences can be seen in the sources of aggregate demand expansion. Portugal's growth was more export-driven, and Spain's expansion contained a stronger component of domestic consumption and investment. In both cases, interest rates and inflation rates converged rapidly towards the EU average from 1995, and in both cases too, a currency devaluation preceded the fiscal adjustment.

Probably the strongest differences between both countries can be found in the level of structural and cohesion funds that each country received during

Table 5.2 Macroeconomic situation in Portugal and Spain, 1990–2000

	Portugal						*Spain*					
	1990–95	*1996*	*1997*	*1998*	*1999*	*2000*	*1990–95*	*1996*	*1997*	*1998*	*1999*	*2000*
GDP per capita (PPS, EU-15 = 100)[a]	66	71	74	76	78	80	80	81	82	84	86	87
GDP growth rate	2.2	3.2	3.7	4.2	3.4	3.6	1.7	2.4	3.5	3.8	3.6	3.5
Private consumption	3.2	2.5	2.9	3.6	3.4	3.4	1.5	2.0	3.1	3.4	3.7	3.5
Gross fixed investment	2.9	5.7	11.3	8.4	10.3	7.2	0.4	1.3	5.1	8.8	8.0	8.5
Domestic demand	3.3	2.8	4.7	4.7	4.0	3.9	1.4	1.6	2.9	4.6	4.5	4.6
Exports	5.2	10.2	8.4	10.3	6.1	7.9	8.9	10.6	14.8	9.8	7.0	8.3
Imports	7.4	7.5	10.4	10.4	7.1	7.7	6.7	7.4	12.2	11.6	9.3	10.5
Unemployment (per cent Civil LabForce)	5.5	7.3	6.8	5.7	5.1	4.7	20.2	22.2	20.8	18.9	17.2	15.7
Inflation	8.4	3.6	2.5	2.6	2.4	2.1	5.7	3.4	2.5	2.3	2.1	2.1
Current account balance	−3.1	−5.1	−2.0	−2.1	−1.8	−2.0	−2.2	0.2	0.4	0.1	−0.4	−0.8
Nominal short-term interest rate	14.2	7.4	5.7	4.5	—	—	11.8	7.5	5.4	4.3	—	—
Real effective exchange rate	4.8	2.0	0.4	0.8	2.2	—	−0.9	2.2	−4.5	0.3	1.1	—
Government budget balance (per cent GDP)	−5.3	−3.3	−2.5	−2.3	−2.0	−1.8	−5.6	−4.7	−2.6	−2.1	−1.6	−1.3
Primary bud. bal. (per cent GDP)	1.7	1.5	1.8	1.2	1.1	1.1	−0.9	0.4	1.8	2.1	2.3	2.5
Structural and cohesion funds*	2.7	2.7	3.7	3.1	3.2	3.0	0.7	1.4	1.3	1.3	1.2	1.2

Source: *Annual Economic Report*. Part 2. Country Section (EC, 1999). [a] *European Economy*, 2000. No. 1, p. 195. * *European Economy*, 2000. No. 71, p. 213. (EC, 2000c).

the period (with Portugal doubling Spanish figures, in response to their differences in economic development), and their unemployment rates (much lower in Portugal than in Spain). However, both countries showed too a very similar rhythm of employment creation in both countries during the period of study.

All these commonalities in the economic sphere would have pointed towards a common strategy of fiscal adjustment in both cases (Von Hagen, Hallett and Strauch, 2001). However, this was not at all the case.

Portugal dramatically reduced its budget deficit between 1995 and 1999 (around 3.6 percentage points), and in fact qualified in a better position than Spain for the third stage of EMU, following a revenue-based strategy of adjustment. This strategy consisted of collecting more revenues from direct taxation and reducing interest payments, in order to enable the government both to consolidate the budget and increase social spending, public wages, and, most importantly, public investment in education and infrastructures.

In contrast, Spain consolidated its budget during the second half of the 1990s (around 4 percentage points) following an expenditure-based strategy consisting in cutting primary spending, mainly interest payments, social transfers, public wages, public consumption and public investment, and then using the surplus to reduce general direct taxation for businesses and individuals.

This section argues that the main difference driving the different strategies of adjustment chosen by each country, given their initial economic similarities, was the ideology of the party in government during each consolidation episode. While the socialist government of Antonio Guterres launched a revenue-based adjustment in Portugal aiming at preserving and increasing the role of the state in the economy, the strategy followed by the conservative government of José María Aznar was exactly the opposite.

Portugal: left-wing government and revenue-based fiscal adjustment, 1995–1999

During the 1990s, Portugal experienced two fiscal adjustments in 1991–92 and in 1995–98. The first fiscal adjustment was launched by the right-wing PSD government of Prime Minister Cavaco Silva, who led the country between 1985 and 1995 in cohabitation with the socialist president, Mario Soares. This adjustment episode was short and sharp, achieving a reduction of 3 percentage points in the deficit, from (−5.9 per cent of GDP to −2.9 per cent) in only one year.[19] Some view it as unintentional, meaning that the fiscal adjustment was more the result of a broader economic policy attempting to stabilize the economy, reducing inflation and controlling the exchange rate (Torres, 1998), than an objective in its own right, since the fiscal policy was at the time accommodating to the inflation target established every year.

After the IMF adjustment programmes of the 1980s, the accession to the EC, and the elections of 1985, Cavaco Silva pursued a strategy of gradual convergence towards European standards that comprised a sequence of economic adjustment programmes. The first adjustment programme, the PCEDED, was launched after the PSD won a parliamentary majority in 1987. Its successor, P2, featured initial fiscal adjustment measures based on the privatization of state-owned enterprises and increases in indirect taxation that ran parallel to the introduction of VAT. Forty per cent of the revenues from privatizations were used to bring the accumulated debt down to 63.3 per cent from a previous level of 72 per cent, what helped to reduce interest payments by 1.7 per cent of GDP between 1991 and 1993. Freezing of public consumption and public investment, together with the revenues coming from the new indirect taxation (that increased 2 per cent of GDP in only one year), were responsible for the additional fiscal consolidation. This episode was however very short, since the economic recession of 1992–93 and a sweeping increase of the public sector wage scale, raised substantially the spending in social transfers and the government's wage bill by the end of 1992.

By contrast, in the mid-1990s the government of Antonio Guterres pursued a completely different strategy that epitomizes the type of revenue-based adjustment that the model presented in Chapter 4 predicted for left-wing cabinets undertaking a fiscal consolidation. As shown in Table 5.3, Portugal's fiscal adjustment relied on increasing revenues, mainly from direct taxation, and the redistribution of expenditures through the reduction of interest payments, and the increase of social transfers, and public investment in human and physical capital.

The process of adjustment was smooth and constant, and started with a 'rigorous but socially conscious budget, in an attempt to stimulate the economy, while promoting investment, disinflation and fiscal consolidation'.[20]

The government passed[21] its first budget in 1996 planning to increase nominal current spending by 7.6 per cent, and capital spending by 11.6 per cent. Among current spending, social spending was to increase by 10.4 per cent, underlining the greater emphasis on social programmes.

To fulfil its goal of investing more in education as a means to increase the competitiveness of the workforce, the government increased education outlays by 12 per cent, while health-related categories rose by 7.7 per cent.

These increases were partially made possible by cuts in defence, agriculture and administrative expenditures. Most importantly, within capital expenditure, public investment was projected to rise 17.3 per cent (half of this to be financed by EU Structural and Cohesion funds), while the increase in infrastructure and transport spending rose by 35 per cent. These measures ran against the predictions of 'many observers who speculated that the government would take the easy choice of slashing infrastructure spending in order to meet its 1996 deficit target'. In contrast, 'Antonio Guterres reaffirmed the importance of the ambitious investment programme, not only to upgrade deficient networks but also to counteract slower growth in Europe' (EIU-Portugal Country Report, 1996: 12). This overall picture was maintained throughout the adjustment episode: social spending was budgeted to increase by 8.4 per cent in 1997, and by 6.2 per cent in 1998. The effort in education spending and public investment was also sustained at similar levels of annual increases of 10 per cent during the following years.

On the revenue side, with current revenue projected to rise by 9.7 per cent in 1996, the government aimed at keeping its promise not to increase major tax rates. In order to do this, it raised excise taxes on petrol and alcohol, used most of the Esc380bn from privatizations to write off the public debt[22] and reduce interest payments, and emphasized the intention of the government to increase revenues from direct taxation, not through higher tax rates, but through greater efficiency in tax collection and a crackdown on tax evasion. In this respect, some important measures were implemented: tax brackets and allowances were adjusted at the inflation rate, the tax base was broadened by a reduction of exemptions, and deductible accumulated losses were diminished (Banco de Portugal Annual Report, 1996: 109; 1997: 109–10). Moreover, direct corporate and income taxes rose due to the greater effectiveness of the tax collection (Banco de Portugal Annual Report, 1997: 109–10; 1998: 119). Here, the government benefited from the effectiveness of the 'Mateus Plan' which provided incentives for taxpayers to formalize their tax situation and pay arrears to the tax and social security system, before 31 December 1997. Also, the VAT system was revised on various occasions during the consolidation episode, and a small tax was imposed on self-employed workers. The car tax was strongly raised due to a broadening of the tax base and the introduction of a new tax scale in 1995 and 1996 (EC, 1996; Banco de Portugal Annual Report, 1997: 111; 1998: 120). In order to tackle firms' tax evasion, in 1998 the government introduced a corporate minimum tax payment, independent of profit or losses. And again in 2001 the government introduced further measures against fraud, such as requiring taxpayers to prove the veracity of their declaration, the total abolition of bank secrecy, and the use of external signs of wealth as indicators of income (EIU-Portugal Country Report, 2001: 18).

But, most importantly, during the adjustment episode the government also introduced some minor income tax reforms aimed at increasing the progressiveness of the system. Between 1998 and 1999, a lower income tax was introduced for the low paid, diminishing it from 15 per cent to 13 per cent. Also, the upper income limit for the 25 per cent band was increased, while the upper brackets of 35 per cent and 40 per cent did not benefit from any measure. The tax rates for small companies were cut from 34 per cent to 20 per cent in 1999, and again in 2000. Furthermore, the 2001 budget projected cuts in income tax for salaried employees, reducing revenues by an estimated Esc100bn a year, or 0.5 per cent of GDP, that were to be offset by equally growing revenues from taxes on capital gains, 'following changes in the way CGT was assessed, and a series of measures to tackle endemic rates of capital tax evasion and fraud' (EIU-Portugal Country Report, 2001: 18).

Therefore, the mentioned increase in revenues was the result both of the growing economic cycle, and of a bunch of very concrete measures to improve tax collection and make it more progressive. As a result, public revenues that represented 38.3 per cent of GDP in 1994, rose to 41.6 per cent in the first year of the socialist-led fiscal consolidation, and ended the episode in 1998 at a level of 41.8 per cent (see Table 5.3). The government then, still maintained its strategy of increasing the presence of the public sector in the economy and raising public revenues until they reached the 43.8 per cent of GDP at the end of 2001. With more revenues flowing into the public budget, a typical leftist strategy of welfare state expansion and supply-side policy was made compatible with the Maastricht criteria. In order to make it possible, the composition of public expenditures was also modified. While public consumption, public wages and public transfers remained frozen at the levels of 19 per cent, 14 per cent and 11.8 per cent of GDP respectively during the strongest part of the adjustment period (1995–98), they grew in the aftermath and reached levels of 20.6 per cent, 14.9 per cent and 12.4 per cent of GDP in 2001. Other expenditures increased in spite of the consolidation effort. This was especially the case with education spending and public investment, which rose to 4.5 per cent of GDP in 1998 from a previous level of 3.5 per cent in 1994. Besides the increase in revenues, this redistribution of expenditure was possible mainly because the public debt was reduced from 64.7 per cent of GDP in 1995 to 56.5 per cent in 1998, and then again to 55.1 per cent in 2001, driving down interest payments from 6.2 per cent of GDP in 1995, to 3.5 per cent in 1998, and then 3.1 per cent of GDP in 2001.

Such a revenue-based strategy allowed the Portuguese socialist government successfully to reduce the budget deficit and to qualify for the single currency in 1999, without renouncing to develop its programme of expanding welfare programmes to alleviate the situation of the poorest strata of the population, and investing strongly in education and infrastructures to increase the competitiveness of the economy in the long run. This was in fact a sustained commitment of the government. Even 'when the European Commission and the OECD criticized the government for timidity in tackling public finances, the government insisted that budgetary policy must strike the right balance between fiscal rigour and its social objectives, with spending on health, education and infrastructures projected to rise until 2002' (EIU-Portugal Country Report, 1999: 14).

Together with the outstanding effort to increase public investment in education and infrastructure, there were two typically leftist expenditure initiatives taken while the fiscal consolidation was still ongoing in 1995–98. These were the extension of the coverage of the income maintenance programme in line with the social objectives set by the socialist cabinet (Von Hagen, Hallett, and Strauch, 2001: 109), and the rise of public wages. Expenditures related to the means-tested minimum programme were actually multiplied by five, reaching Esc33.8bn in 1998 (Banco de Portugal Annual Report, 1999: 137).

Table 5.3 Fiscal policy in Portugal, 1993–2001

			Fiscal adjustment episode						
	1993	*1994*	*1995*	*1996*	*1997*	*1998*	*1999*	*2000*	*2001*
Total current resources	36.9	36.6	38.4	38.1	39.1	39.6	40.3	41.8	42.7
Taxes on production and imports	13.0	13.4	14.3	14.4	14.2	14.2	14.6	14.8	14.7
Current taxes on income and wealth	9.0	8.8	9.3	9.5	10.1	10.6	10.7	10.8	11.9
Social contributions	11.8	11.5	11.0	11.0	11.1	11.4	11.5	11.9	12.0
Other current resourses	3.1	2.6	3.9	4.1	3.8	3.5	3.5	4.3	4.2
Capital transfers received	:	:	1.9	2.1	2.3	1.6	2.2	1.6	1.6
Total public revenues	**36.9**	**36.3**	**40.4**	**41.6**	**41.7**	**41.8**	**42.7**	**43.4**	**44.7**
Total current expenditures	39.0	39.1	39.7	39.6	38.2	37.8	38.1	39.5	39.4
Government consumption expenditure	17.5	17.2	18.7	19.0	19.1	19.1	19.7	20.6	20.6
Of which compensation of employees	14.2	13.7	13.7	13.7	13.8	14.0	14.4	14.9	14.9
Social transfers other than in kind	12.9	12.8	11.8	11.8	11.7	11.7	11.8	12.4	12.4
Interest payments	6.1	6.1	6.2	5.4	4.2	3.5	3.2	3.2	3.1
Subsidies	1.3	1.2	1.4	1.5	1.2	1.5	1.0	0.9	0.9
Other current expenditure	:	:	1.6	1.9	1.0	2.1	2.3	2.5	2.5
Gross fixed capital formation	3.9	3.5	3.7	4.2	4.4	4.5	4.3	4.3	4.3
Other capital expenditure	:	:	1.4	1.7	1.6	1.7	2.2	1.4	2.2
Total public expenditures	**42.9**	**42.2**	**44.9**	**45.6**	**44.2**	**44.1**	**44.8**	**45.1**	**46.2**
Tax burden	34.5	34.7	34.5	35.3	35.4	35.8	36.8	37.5	38.5
Budget balance	**−6.0**	**−5.9**	**−4.6**	**−4.0**	**−2.7**	**−2.3**	**−2.1**	**−1.4**	**−1.5**
Cyclically adjusted budget balance	5.5	−5.0	−3.9	−3.6	−2.5	−2.4	−2.2	−2.0	−1.7
Consolidated gross public debt	62.1	63.7	64.7	63.6	60.3	56.4	56.7	57.2	55.1

Source: (EC, 2002).

The final agreement with the unions to concede a wage rise of 3 per cent to 500,000 public workers increased the government's wage bill, and showed a firm commitment towards public employment, which contrasts with exactly opposite measures in other converging countries such as Spain.[23] Because in Portugal public wages serve as a bottom reference to wage-bargaining in the private sector, the socialist cabinet immediately achieved a private sector wage deal too, based on an annual wage rise of 3.5 per cent over the period 1997–2000, in exchange for an additional investment of Esc140bn in job creation, with the purpose of controlling inflation in the run-up to EMU. This corporatist-style income policy initiative proved successful in keeping inflation inside the limits set by the Maastricht criteria.

At the time of writing, many analysts say that this overall strategy of revenue-based fiscal adjustment designed and implemented by the socialist cabinet of Antonio Guterres was responsible for the economic and fiscal problems faced by Portugal after 2002. In any case, the immediate consequences of such strategy were clearly beneficial. Portugal gained the confidence of the markets, and easily fulfilled the Maastricht criteria with even better numbers than core countries such as the Netherlands, France, Italy, and also Spain. It also granted the cabinet strong domestic and external political support, translated into notable achievements during the first semester of European presidency in 2000, and contributed to the re-election just one seat short of the absolute majority (215 of 230 seats) the same year. This growing popular support became evident in the strong victory and re-election of Jorge Sampaio as president, beating the right-wing AD electoral alliance between the PSD and the PP, and sending both parties into internal battles and mutual doubts about the continuation of the coalition. In addition, the government also achieved remarkable economic outcomes until 2001, in a framework of generalized economic growth in Europe.

Spain: right-wing government and expenditure-based fiscal adjustment, 1996–2000

Similarly to Portugal, Spain experienced two fiscal adjustments during the 1990s, in the same years but under cabinets of different political 'colours'. The first episode of adjustment, between 1992 and 1993, was also short, but weak and revenue-based. The second one, between 1995 and 1999, was longer, stronger and expenditure (mixed)-based. While between 1992 and 1993 the conservative cabinet of Cavaco Silva attempted an expenditure-based fiscal adjustment in Portugal, the socialist government of Felipe González launched a revenue-based one in Spain. Later, when a second and stronger adjustment was required in both countries in order to qualify for EMU, Guterres pursued a revenue-based fiscal adjustment between 1995 and 1999 in Portugal, at the same time that the conservative government of José María Aznar chose to pursue an expenditure-based consolidation strategy. In Spring 1998 both countries were admitted to the third stage of EMU along with nine additional member states.

In April 1992, the government of Felipe González, under the auspices of his minister of finance, Carlos Solchaga, launched its first Convergence

Programme that included fiscal policy

> in a broader two-pronged strategy: a radical change towards a balanced macroeconomic policy-mix and structural reforms particularly in the labour market and service sector. Within that framework, the government proposed a continuous reduction of the deficit from 4 per cent in 1992 to 1 per cent in 1996. The course of this adjustment, however, was based on excessively optimist growth assumptions of more than 3 per cent of GDP per year. (Von Hagen, Hallett and Straucht, 2001: 110)

In spite of some attempts to tighten some unemployment benefits, and the transference of some disability benefits to private companies, the adjustment maintained the level of expenditures untouched, and relied greatly on higher revenues. On the revenue side of the budget, the personal income tax schedule was revised upwards and the related withholding rates adjusted; the VAT rate was raised from 13 per cent to 15 per cent, excise tax rates also increased, and the employers' social security contributions for unemployment were raised by 1 per cent in 1992 (Banco de España Annual Report, 1992; OECD Economic Survey, 1993: 37). The consolidation of 1992 that relied on the freezing of expenditures and increases in revenues ended in 1993, a crucial calendar year for the government after 14 years in power, when the government changed its policy stance to give more importance to measures offsetting the effects of the economic crisis. 'Primarily transfer payments to social security funds, such as the labour office INEM, and other public companies and entities were responsible for the deterioration of the deficit in 1993. In addition, growing interest payments and government purchases contributed to the strong expansionary trend' (Von Hagen, Hallett and Strauch, 2001: 111). Particularly, however, expenditure policies among the Autonomous Communities did not pledge to the fiscal austerity that they had promised in 1992. 'At least, transfers from the central government to the regions remained a source of fiscal overrun until 1995' (OECD Economic Survey, 1995: 28). This fiscal expansion at the end of 1993 has been interpreted by some analysts as a clear example of the political fiscal cycle, motivated by the imminent general elections of 1993 (Von Hagen, Hallett and Strauch, 2001).

Soon after his election on 3 March 1996, the minority government (156 seats of 350)[24] led by the new President José María Aznar and his minister of finance, Rodrigo Rato, showed a convincing commitment to place Spain in the first group of qualifying countries in 1999. They were explicit at the expenditure-based strategy of adjustment,[25] since in their campaign they promised a general reduction of taxes that had to be coupled with cuts in inefficient public spending, and amelioration of the whole system of public administration. After the presentation of the 1997 budget, in September 1996, the government started to implement its plan very rapidly, since it had

Table 5.4 Fiscal policy in Spain, 1993–2001

				Fiscal adjustment episode					
	1993	*1994*	*1995*	*1996*	*1997*	*1998*	*1999*	*2000*	*2001*
Total current resources	40.9	39.8	38.0	37.8	38.1	38.2	38.6	38.6	38.8
Taxes on production and imports	10.1	10.6	10.2	10.2	10.4	11.1	11.7	11.6	11.8
Current taxes on income and wealth	11.5	11.0	10.7	10.5	10.4	10.2	10.3	10.5	10.3
Social contributions	14.3	14.0	13.0	13.1	13.1	13.1	13.	13.4	13.4
Other current resources	5.0	4.2	4.1	4.1	4.0	3.7	2.6	3.1	3.2
Capital transfers received	:	:	1.4	1.4	1.3	1.3	1.4	1.2	1.3
Total public revenues	**40.9**	**39.8**	38.4	**38.8**	**39.1**	39.1	**39.6**	**39.5**	**39.8**
Total current expenditures	42.6	41.3	39.2	39.0	37.6	37.0	35.9	35.2	34.8
Government consumption expenditure	16.8	16.2	18.1	17.9	17.6	17.5	17.3	17.1	16.9
Of which compensation of employees	11.8	11.3	11.3	11.3	10.9	10.7	10.5	10.4	10.2
Social transfers other than in kind	16.2	15.8	13.9	13.8	13.3	12.8	12.4	12.4	12.3
Interest payments	5.0	4.7	5.2	5.3	4.8	4.3	3.6	3.3	3.2
Subsidies	3.1	2.9	1.1	1.0	0.9	1.1	1.2	1.1	1.1
Other current expenditure	:	:	0.9	1.0	1.1	1.2	1.3	1.3	1.3
Gross fixed capital formation	4.1	4.0	4.0	3.2	3.1	3.1	3.2	3.3	3.3
Other capital expenditure	:	:	2.3	2.0	1.9	1.9	2.0	1.7	1.8
Total public expenditures	**47.6**	**45.9**	**45.0**	**43.7**	**42.2**	**41.7**	**40.8**	**39.9**	**39.7**
Tax burden	36.5	36.1	35.0	34.4	34.8	35.1	35.7	36.2	36.2
Budget balance	**−6.7**	**−6.1**	**−6.6**	**−4.9**	**−3.0**	**−2.6**	**−1.2**	**−0.3**	**0.1**
Cyclically adjusted budget balance	−6.1	−5.4	−5.9	−4.0	−2.6	−2.4	−1.2	−0.8	−0.2
Consolidated gross public debt	57.9	60.4	63.2	68.1	66.7	64.9	63.5	62.3	59.9

Source: EC (2002).

only one and a half years to reduce the budget deficit by two percentage points.

Measures on both the revenue and the expenditure side of the budget were simultaneous, and aimed at both reducing the deficit, and reducing the presence of the public sector in the economy (see Table 5.4). These combined measures aimed also at providing new incentives to the private sector, that should 'crowd-in' and push the economy decisively towards an economic expansion.

On the revenue side, the government pursued exactly the opposite policy to that outlined in the Portuguese case. At the end of 1996 it started cutting the corporate tax rates for small companies (defined as those with a turnover of less than Pta250bn) from 35 per cent to 30 per cent, and prepared measures to make private pension funds more attractive, increasing from 15 per cent to 20 per cent the proportion of contributions that were tax-deductible. In addition, the withholding rate of the income tax was reduced by 2.7 per cent to increase disposable income in the hands of consumers (EIU-Spain Country Report, 1997: 15).

In addition to these small cuts on some secondary sources of revenue, the government announced that it would commit to its electoral promise of cutting personal income taxes, reducing the top rate of tax from 56 per cent to as low as 40 per cent, and reducing the number of tax bands from eight to three. These tax cuts were approved in 1998 and finally became effective in January 1999.

The government took these measures under the assumption that the income tax bill would fall by around 11 per cent during that year, and hoping that the subsequent injection of an additional Pta776bn into the economy (0.9 per cent of GDP) coming from the economic expansion would mitigate the decline in revenue. Finally, the government also decided to cut taxes on capital gains – these were reduced from 20 per cent to 18 per cent in 2000.

If these reductions in public revenues were to be compatible with the fulfilment of the 3 per cent deficit limit set in Maastricht and the Stability Pact, either additional revenues had to be levied from alternative sources, or public expenditures had to be cut significantly. There was a little of the former and much more of the latter. The only revenues that were discretionarily raised were those coming from excise duties on alcohol, tobacco and beverages (Banco de España Annual Reports, 1996 and 1997), while the bulk of the adjustment took place on the expenditure side. During the first two years of the PP-government, one of the main sources of cuts in public expenditure was the reduction of interest payments as a consequence of debt repayment after massive privatization of public enterprises. Only in 1997, the government raised Pta1.7trn in privatization receipts, which amounted for more than the total receipts for the preceding ten years put together. 'The main operations were the flotation of the state's remaining shares in the telecommunications group, Telefónica, and the energy group, Repsol, as well as a 25 per cent stake in the electricity utility, Endesa, and a 53 per cent stake in the new steel company, Aceralia' (EIU-Spain Country Report, 1998: 18).

In addition to these, some very important policy measures helped to reduce other important items in the budget. 'Regarding public consumption, an agreement was reached with the unions that public wages and pensions were to be raised in line with the official inflation target and not actual inflation during 1996 and 1997' (Von Hagen, Hallett and Strauch, 2001: 112). This was complemented by several directives to freeze the public sector's employment and payments (Banco de España Annual Report, 1997). In 1998, the central government and the unions reached another agreement on a new Civil Servant's Charter, also agreed with the territorial governments, under which wages were to be set centrally (EC, 1998b). This strengthening of the central government's position vis-á-vis subnational governments, which had traditionally tended to pay less attention to fiscal austerity, was reinforced by the end of 2000, when the government passed a draft bill 'obliging all levels of government (central, local and regional) to balance their budgets. Under this legislation, deficits would only be permitted in times of recession or natural catastrophe' (EIU-Spain Country Report, 2001: 18). This overall strategy of curtailing the most rigid items of the budget, achieved a general reduction in public consumption – from 18.1 per cent of GDP in 1995 to 17.3 per cent of GDP in 1999, and 16.9 per cent of GDP in 2001. Similarly, public wages were reduced from 11.3 per cent of GDP in 1995 to 10.5 per cent of GDP in 1999, and finally, to 10.2 per cent of GDP in 2001 (see Table 5.4 above).

During the run-up to EMU social transfers were curtailed even more sharply than public wages or government consumption (from a level of 13.9 per cent of GDP in 1995 to 12.4 per cent of GDP in 1999). This was the combined result of two factors: the upturn in the economy which alleviated the pressure coming from unemployment benefits, and some other specific policy measures aimed at reducing other sources of social spending. For example, in 1997, the *Social Security Consolidation and Rationalization Act*, signed in October 1996, came into force. This Act guaranteed the purchasing power of pensions in terms of the CPI. It also raised from 8 to 15 the number of years needed to determine the regulatory base, and widened the pension base, reducing the percentage applied to that base. According to the OECD, 'these measures achieved an approximate reduction of the average pension of 5 per cent' (OECD Economic Survey, 1998: 71).

Finally, and in contrast to what occurred in other 'Cohesion countries' such as Greece, Ireland, and especially Portugal, public investment was severely curtailed in Spain (Banco de España Annual Report, 1998: 62–3). In only one year, gross fixed capital formation by the public sector was reduced from 4.0 per cent of GDP in 1995 to 3.2 per cent of GDP in 1996 and it remained at that level until Spain joined the EMU (see Table 5.4 above).

Public works were postponed or cancelled, and in some cases were transferred to private companies in packages that delayed payments in the future (Mauro and Spilimbergo, 2001).

Finally, public spending on health and education, the other two components of a classic social democratic strategy, were also either frozen or reduced (see Table 5.5).

As a result, the total share of social spending with respect to GDP in Spain fell from 22.5 per cent in 1996 to 20 per cent in 1999, compared to a 0.9 per cent decrease in the EU-15 average during the same period (OECD, Economic Survey, 1999: 85).

In summary, the expenditure-based strategy of fiscal consolidation implemented by the cabinet of José María Aznar between 1996 and 2000 resulted in a reduction of the weight of public expenditures in the economy, from 45 per cent of GDP in 1995 to 40.8 per cent in 1999 (and 39.7 in 2001), while public revenues remained at a constant level of 39.2 per cent of GDP throughout the whole period. Because the fiscal consolidation took place during a period of very strong economic growth, the additional incoming revenues coming from increasing social security contributions and taxes on general

Table 5.5 Total expenditure on health, education and public investment, 1990 and 1998 (per cent GDP)

	Health		*Education*		*Public investment*	
	1990	*1998*	*1990*	*1998*	*1990*	*1998*
Austria	5.3	6.0	0.3	0.4	3.2	1.9
Belgium*	6.6	7.9	1.2	1.3	1.3	1.5
Denmark	7.0	6.8	1.1	1.9	1.6	1.7
Finland	6.4	5.3	1.0	1.2	3.7	2.9
France*	6.7	7.3	0.8	1.4	3.5	2.9
Germany	6.7	7.9	1.0	1.3	2.3	1.8
Greece*	4.8	4.7	0.4	0.3	2.8	3.6
Ireland*	5.0	4.8	1.4	1.7	2.0	2.7
Italy*	6.3	5.7	1.4	1.1	3.3	2.4
Luxembourg*	6.1	5.4	0.3	0.3	4.5	4.6
The Netherlands	6.1	6.0	1.3	1.7	1.9	3.0
Portugal*	**4.2**	**5.8**	**0.6**	**0.9**	**3.2**	**4.0**
Spain	**5.4**	**5.4**	**0.9**	**0.7**	**4.9**	**3.2**
Sweden[a]	7.9	7.4	1.7	2.0	2.3	2.7
United Kingdom*	5.1	5.9	0.6	0.4	2.3	1.2

Notes:

1. [a]For Sweden year 1990 refers to 1990–91.
2. *For Belgium, France, Luxembourg, and Portugal year 1998 refers to 1997, for Italy and Ireland to 1996, and for Greece to 1994. Finally, for UK year 1990 refers to 1990–91, year 1998 to 1997–98. These exceptions only apply to data on education spending.

Sources: OECD, Labour Market Expenditures,1999; OECD Health Data.

consumption, allowed the government to reduce direct taxation, through a general reform of the IRPF (personal income tax) in 1998 and 2002.

Summing up, evidence shown in previous paragraphs confirms that Portugal and Spain implemented opposite strategies of fiscal adjustment during the second half of the 1990s. These differences were the result of opposite ideologies regarding the role of the state in the economy, rather than the result of different initial economic conditions. While, the centre-left socialist cabinet of Antonio Guterres was convinced of the role to be played by the state in reducing income inequalities and leading public investment in infrastructures and education, the centre-right popular cabinet of José María Aznar cared less about income redistribution, and believed in the non-Keynesian positive effects on growth that spending cuts could bring about. These two different approaches to economic policy led them to adopt opposite strategies of fiscal adjustment.

On the one hand, the socialist cabinet in Portugal maintained labour tax rates, increased corporate taxes for big enterprises, extended the tax base and attacked tax evasion. With the growing public revenues generated by these initiatives and by economic growth, the Portuguese socialist government not only consolidated the budget, but it recorded increases in public wages and maintained general public transfers (increasing them to the poorest) and boosted public investment in education and infrastructure. This strategy placed Portugal in 1999 among the group of countries where the public sector represented the highest shares of GDP, close to Germany, the Netherlands and Italy, and only below the Scandinavian countries and Austria, when only in 1994 it was in the lowest position with Greece (see Figure 5.1).

By contrast, the conservative government of José María Aznar reduced public spending and maintained public revenues.[26] Overall, personal income taxes and corporate taxes were cut, and nominal public revenues remained constant only thanks to the strong economic performance that coincided with the consolidation episode. Nevertheless, these initiatives on the revenue side left the burden of the adjustment to public expenditures. Public consumption was significantly curtailed, public wages were frozen first, and then reduced, and social benefits schemes were tightened. Finally, education spending and public investment on infrastructures were cut first, and then maintained at constant levels. This strategy placed Spain, in only four years, among the group of countries where the public sector represented the lowest shares of GDP in Europe, close to United Kingdom and Ireland.

Nonetheless, the crowding-in of the private sector in the Spanish economy motivated by this expenditure-based strategy of adjustment boosted private investment, employment creation and economic growth during the following years. It also gave José María Aznar re-election with a comfortable absolute majority in March 2000 that sent the Socialist Party into a profound period of renewal and weak opposition.[27]

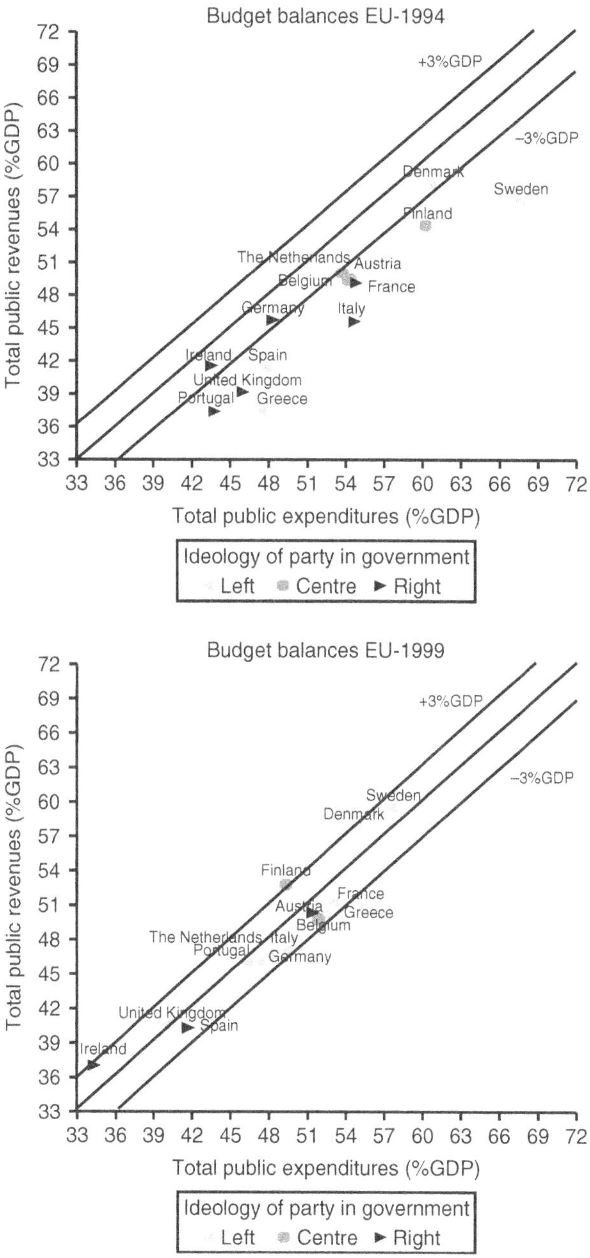

Figure 5.1 Relative size of public sector in EU member states, 1994 and 1999

At the same time, however, these achievements ran parallel to growing income inequalities in Spain, recording increases in the inequality index of 6 per cent in four years, significantly above most countries in the EU and only below Italy, Finland, Austria and the UK (see Chapter 6, Table 6.5).

Fragmentation of decision-making: UK vs Italy

The degree of fragmentation in decision-making over the public budget is the variable that usually explains why in some countries partisan patterns of fiscal adjustment cannot be identified. Coalition governments, fragmentation of decision-making, and the weak influence of the parties' ideologies in cabinet decisions, are mutually associated. The explanation runs as follows: because the degree of fragmentation is highly correlated to the electoral system, in countries where proportional systems tend to create the conditions for coalition formation in the cabinet, the partisan pattern of fiscal policy appears diluted. This is the case in countries such as Belgium, the Netherlands, Finland or Italy. In these countries, also as a consequence of their institutional structure, deficits are more difficult to control, and public debt tends to accumulate, generating a vicious cycle of 'more debt–more interests–more debt', known as the 'snow-ball effect'.

As previous chapters have shown, it is easier to implement expenditure-based adjustments in countries with low degrees of fragmentation, while revenue-based adjustments are normally associated with higher degrees of fragmentation. This is usually the case because the larger the number of actors who have a say in the spending decision, the more difficult it is to cut expenditures. Each member in the coalition claims a part for its constituency, and threatens to abandon the cabinet and bring down the government if its demands are not satisfied. Every member in the coalition has an incentive to spend because the benefits will be enjoyed by its constituency, while the total cost of an additional unit of spending will be paid by all the population. 'Italy's experience with growing welfare payments is a prime example for this mechanism. In the past 30 years, Italian politicians used the disability pension system quite openly to buy voter support' (Von Hagen, Hallett and Strauch, 2001: 41). Consequently, a low centralization index[28] has placed Italy among the worst fiscal performers in Europe, recording the second highest average deficit, and the third highest debt-to-GDP ratio among member states.

On the other hand, the UK represents the country with the most centralized process of budget negotiation (Figure 5.2), which contributed to placing the UK as the country with the second lowest average deficit and the third lowest debt-to-GDP ratio in the 15 years previous to 1996, before most of the strongest fiscal consolidations to qualify for EMU took place across Europe.

The coordination problem produced by the fragmentation of decision-making cannot be overcome unless the rules that regulate the process of budgetary decision-making change the internal mechanism itself, and create

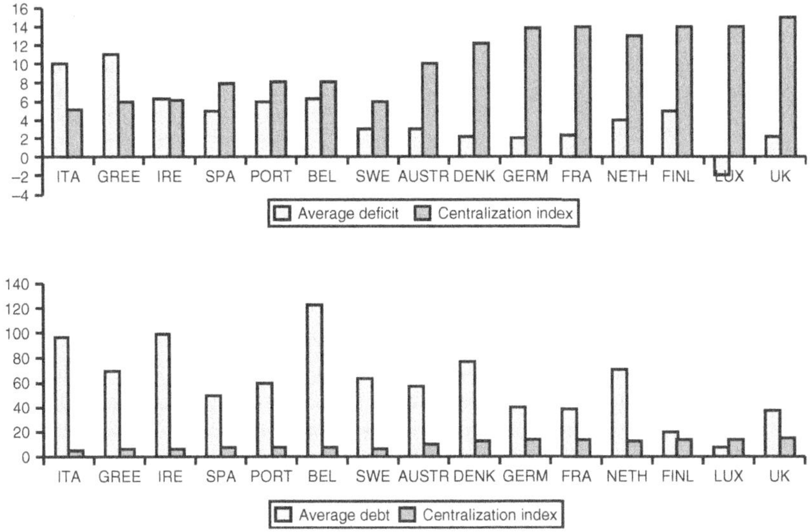

Figure 5.2 Budget processes, deficits and debt, 1981–95
Source: Von Hagen, Hallett and Strauch (2001: 44).

a different structure of incentives that allow coalition members to control the level of spending.

Therefore, the solution to fragmentation is centralization. There are two basic institutional approaches to achieve more centralization: the 'delegation approach' and the 'contracts approach' (Von Hagen, 1992). The 'delegation approach' emphasizes hierarchical relationships, and usually consists in vesting the finance ministers with more power over the rest of spending ministers. This approach normally takes the form of a finance minister being vested with strong agenda-setting power relative to the rest of members of the executive; a finance minister with strong monitoring capacity in the implementation of the budget; and/or a strong position of the executive relative to the legislature in the parliamentary phase of the budget process.

On the contrary, the 'contract approach' emphasizes 'horizontal relationships among the relevant policy makers ... being the process of negotiation what makes the participants realize the externalities created by the general tax fund' (Von Hagen, Hallett and Strauch, 2001: 42). This approach normally takes three forms:

> A strong emphasis on budgetary targets negotiated among all members of the executive at the beginning of the annual budget cycle ... a finance minister vested with strong monitoring capacities in the implementation of the budget, yet little agenda setting powers; and/or a weak position of

> the executive relative to the parliament exemplified by weak or no limits on parliamentary amendments to the budget proposal, and strong monitoring capacities of parliamentary committees overseeing the activities of individual departments of the executive. (Von Hagen, Hallett and Strauch, 2001: 43)

The type of approach that best suits each country depends heavily on the electoral system. The 'delegation approach' is better suited to plurality systems that produce single-party governments, while the 'contract approach' is better suited to proportional systems that produce coalition governments (Hallerberg and Von Hagen, 1999). As Table 5.6 shows, there is a significant relation between the electoral system and the institutional choice of the budget process. Historically, countries with proportional systems chose a 'contract approach' to the budget process to achieve a higher degree of centralization, while countries with plurality systems chose a 'delegation approach' to achieve the same solution.

The exceptional case in Table 5.6 is Germany. Although Germany has a proportional system, it is augmented by a minimum vote requirement. According to this requirement, parties winning less than 5 per cent of the vote secure no seats in parliament. As a consequence, this has traditionally produced two-party governments consisting of one big party and one small party (the liberal democrats). 'In this situation, neither coalition partner could threaten effectively to break up the coalition, since neither one would easily find an alternative partner for a new coalition. The ineffectiveness of the threat

Table 5.6 Electoral systems and electoral choice

	Institutional choice		
Electoral system	*Contract*	*Delegation*	*Fragmentation*
Proportional representation			
AUS, BEL, DENK, FIN, IRL, ITA, LUX, NETH, POR, SPA, SWE	AUS, BEL, DENK, FIN, IRL, LUX, NETH, POR, ITA*, SPA*, SWE*		ITA*, SPA*, SWE*
Plurality system or PR with restrictive minimum vote requirements			
GERM, FRA, GREE, UK		GERM, FRA, UK	GREECE

Note: *Italy, Sweden and Spain introduced measures moving towards a contract model in the 1990s.

Source: Von Hagen, Hallett and Strauch (2001: 45).

implies that the contracting approach does not work, making Germany a delegation country instead' (Von Hagen, Hallett and Strauch, 2001: 45).

Another interesting feature partially outlined by Table 5.6. is the institutional changes that occurred in Sweden, Italy, Spain, Belgium, and Austria during the 1990s. The Swedish case is somewhat different to the other four. In that country the reform of the budgetary process in the 1990s was designed to give more visibility to the budgetary process, and to constraint the different parties in parliament by forcing them into a system of expenditure ceilings, negotiated and established in advance on the basis of economic forecasts, that cannot be modified except if more spending in one item is offset by less spending in another (Molander, 2001).

In contrast, Italy and Spain during the 1990s moved towards 'contract approaches' that were more oriented towards controlling the level of deficit and debt in local and regional units of government. This strategy was also followed by Belgium and Austria: although they did not make any formal change to their previous models, they substantially reinforced some of their existing institutions. In all four of these cases the progressive process of expenditure decentralization to subnational levels of government was compensated by 'contractual approaches' aimed at negotiating indebtness ceilings for the lower levels of government. In Belgium, this was undertaken by strengthening the High Council of Finances (HCF), which monitors the compliance of all parts of government with Belgium's Convergence Programme, and decides how much each level of government has to contribute to the desired reduction in the debt-to-GDP ratio and the deficit (Stienlet, 2000; Hallerberg, 2000a, 2000b). In Austria, the mechanism that was put in place was a series of coordination committees in charge of monitoring public finances at each level of government, and making further transfers of competencies subject to good fiscal performance (Huttner, 1999). And in Spain, an Internal Stability Pact between the central government and the regions gave the central government the veto-power to deny or accept the debt and deficit proposals sent by lower levels of government. This process was coordinated by the Fiscal and Financial Policy Council (Gordo and Hernández de Cos, 2000; González-Páramo, 2001).

But it was in Italy that initiatives were more numerous, and in fact where changes were more effective in contributing to the final qualification of Italy among the group of countries joining EMU in 1999. As was shown in Figure 5.2, Italy was the country with the lowest score in the fragmentation index developed by Von Hagen (1992). For three decades, this had gone hand in hand with the second highest average deficit and debt-to-GDP ratios in Europe, and placed Italy at the beginning of the 1990s 'surely off the list, for immediate consideration' to enter stage 3 of EMU (Dornbusch, 1996: 11). The fact that Italy finally qualified in the first wave of countries joining the euro is related to many factors, among the most important of which was the institutional change directed towards centralizing decision-making.

The fact that over many years, fiscal policy in Italy had almost always relied on uncontrolled spending whichever party was in government was the result of the political fragmentation generated by its electoral system. As such, Italy is a paradigmatic example of how, in very fragmented systems, the ideology of the party in government does not predict the possible strategy of adjustment, because either the adjustment never takes place, or if it does, it is almost always revenue-based in response to the high degree of fragmentation. The opposite case, the UK, would constitute a clear example of how the party in government, always alone in the cabinet, can implement any initiative to increase or decrease the role of the public sector in the economy, but always keeping the budget as close to equilibrium as desired.

Because these two cases represent the two opposite extremes in terms of fragmentation of decision-making, the next two sections will describe the strong fiscal adjustment episodes that they experienced during the 1990s. Under the government of John Major, the UK pursued a strong expenditure-based fiscal adjustment, without encountering major political difficulties, in terms of parliamentary opposition. Italy, however, pursued a general strategy based on raising revenues, independent of the 'colour' of the cabinet, because of the strong coalitional component and the instability of these governments. Nonetheless, the fact that Italy pursued an overall revenue-based strategy of fiscal adjustment cannot hide the important fact that many measures were taken on the spending side, so as to almost make it a mixed strategy of adjustment during the second half of the 1990s.

When and how this was done had a lot to do with the institutional changes undertaken by the Italian legislature in order to make it a less fragmented system, although the 'contract approach' chosen then to centralize the process was still very distant to the more hierarchical delegation system present in the UK. In addition, in Italy the external component of the Maastricht Treaty and the 'national pride factor' played a major role in forcing all the changes through which Italy went between 1996 and 1999. For this reason, Italy is also the best example to illustrate an additional 'external contract' between supranational bodies and the nation-states that took place in many countries in the run-up to EMU, and that clearly acted as a complementary mechanism that reduced the effect of fragmentation in those political systems.

The United Kingdom: low fragmentation of decision-making and expenditure-based adjustment, 1993–97

The budget process in the United Kingdom is highly centralized, as is appropriate for the only country in the European Union that uses a pure plurality electoral system. Indeed, the structure of its budget process epitomizes the 'delegation approach'. The prime minister is exceptionally strong, and the Chancellor of the Exchequer (the finance minister), considered the second in the cabinet, has the power to negotiate one-on-one with spending ministers about their budget allocations. If there is a dispute between the finance minister and other spending ministers, it goes to a committee of non-portfolio ministers (not the whole cabinet) who usually resolve in favour on the minister of finance. Together with this low fragmentation inside the cabinet, the budgetary process in the UK is also safe from any additional fragmentation coming from the legislature. The possibility of the Parliament to include amendments in the budget is very limited. With such a system, changes in taxation rates against the desire of the government have been very rare in the House of Commons, while changes in expenditures have never been included in opposition to government's plans, except if they were to reduce the level of budgeted expenditures.[29]

As a direct consequence of this institutional structure, parties have always found it easy to implement their preferred policies once in government. The only limit to the government's formulation of fiscal policy came from the electorate's preferences.

Over the years, ideological differences between Conservative and Labour attitudes to fiscal policy were at the top of the political agenda. Only after the end of the Labour government of James Callaghan in the 1970s, did the consensus around fiscal conservatism seemed to reach both parties. Moreover, Thatcherism and its open neoliberalism were inherited by the two Major governments, and in fact the Labour Party had to go through the 1987 and 1997 Policy Reviews in order to win the election defending a fiscal approach that was almost identical to that of the Conservatives (Gamble and Kelly, 2001). This is important, because the well-known shift in the traditional Labour policies under Tony Blair is the result of a strategic redefinition of the Labour party postulates in search of the median voter that returned them to power after 18 years, and not the result of any variation in the institutional setting of the budget process that may have disrupted the traditionally strong influence of party ideologies in the formulation of fiscal policy in Britain. If any, the reorientation of the British left towards more conservative positions had to do with the fiscal conservatism towards which the British electorate shifted during the 1980s and 1990s. Nevertheless, when the composition of the fiscal adjustments under Major and Blair are analysed together, still some differences can be found, although both are embedded in a general trend of lowering the role of the public sector in the economy.

The United Kingdom started the decade of the 1990s entering a strong recession that caused a strong deterioration of the budget balance. The budget deteriorated from −0.9 per cent of GDP in 1990 to −7.8 per cent of GDP in 1993. This deterioration can be substantially attributed to the cyclical effect of decreasing revenues from direct taxation and growing transfer payments, which rose by 3.5 per cent of GDP.

The fiscal consolidation started by the second cabinet of John Major in 1994 reversed the previous unsustainable path of public spending. During the first year of the adjustment episode most of the amelioration of the budget came from increased revenues from direct taxation and social contributions, reflecting the new expansion of the economic cycle. In addition, some tax measures in 1993 and 1994 raised revenues from mineral oil and tobacco products, while tax breaks ended (EC, 1998a: 187). However, after 1995, revenues remained constant around 40 per cent of GDP, and most of the adjustment came from spending cuts.

The reduction was especially important in the government's wage bill and in public investment. Wage payments fell from 10.7 per cent of GDP in 1993 to 7.4 per cent of GDP in 1998. 'The fall of wages was produced by an impressive amount of employment reduction between 1993 and 1995. During these years, several public firms were privatized, most importantly British Rail and British Coal in 1994 and 1995' (Von Hagen, Hallett and Strauch, 2001: 116).[30] Similarly, gross fixed capital formation by the public sector fell from 2 per cent of GDP in 1994 to 1.2 per cent of GDP in 1997 and 1998, contributing to the general decrease of public expenditures as a percentage of GDP from 45.8 per cent in 1994 to 40.7 per cent in 1998 (see Table 5.7).

While the expenditure-based adjustment of the Major government in the UK exemplifies how partisan strategies of fiscal adjustment can be more easily pursued in countries where the institutional set-up prevents the cabinet from dealing with additional coalition partners either in government or in parliament, a word should be also said about the fiscal conservatism during the Blair administration.

Despite all that has been said since 1997 about the Labour government's strategy of not raising taxes (Labour lost the 1992 election after advocating new taxes), not re-nationalizing former public enterprises, and its solid commitment to a balanced budget at the expense of reducing the role of the state in the economy (Rasmussen, 1997), some differences can still be identified when the composition of fiscal policy during its mandate is compared to that of the previous Conservative government.

As Table 5.7 shows, between 1997 and 1998, total public revenues rose by 1 per cent of GDP. This was the result of a windfall tax on the gains of privatized public utilities in 1997 and 1998, but this level of revenues was maintained throughout the following years. In addition, at the beginning of 2002 Tony Blair decided to break his electoral promise of not raising taxes and ordered an increase in the Social Security tax rates in order to collect additional 65 billion euros to renovate the National Health System (*El País*, 18 April 2002).

Most importantly, payments of public wages rose by 0.8 per cent between 1998 and 2001, and similarly public investment started to grow again after 1997, showing an increase of 0.5 per cent of GDP during the same period. Although the purpose of this section is not to repeat previous conclusions with new examples, these timid developments seem to be particularly consistent with the postulated supply-side social democratic policies and the new approach of the New Labourism to social justice. According to these new ideas, equality should no longer be conceived as a question related to

Table 5.7 Fiscal policy in the United Kingdom, 1993–2001

			Fiscal adjustment episode						
	1993	*1994*	*1995*	*1996*	*1997*	*1998*	*1999*	*2000*	*2001*
Total current resources	35.2	35.8	38.6	38.6	38.9	40.2	40.5	41.1	40.6
Taxes on production and imports	15.4	15.5	13.2	13.3	13.6	13.5	14.0	14.1	13.9
Current taxes on income and wealth	11.5	11.9	15.0	14.8	15.0	16.5	16.3	16.9	16.7
Social contributions	6.1	6.2	7.6	7.5	7.5	7.6	7.5	7.6	7.5
Other current resources	2.2	2.2	2.9	3.0	2.7	2.6	2.6	2.4	2.5
Capital transfers received	:	:	0.3	0.3	0.3	0.3	0.3	0.4	0.3
Total public revenues	**35.2**	**35.8**	**40.1**	**39.8**	**40.0**	**41.2**	**41.4**	**42.1**	**41.6**
Total current expenditures	40.2	40.0	41.5	40.8	39.2	38.2	37.8	37.8	37.9
Government consumption expenditure	21.6	21.3	19.8	19.4	18.4	18.2	18.5	18.7	19.1
Of which compensation of employees	10.7	9.1	8.8	8.3	7.8	7.4	7.5	7.5	7.7
Social transfers other than in kind	13.8	14.7	15.4	14.9	14.4	13.7	13.5	13.3	13.2
Interest payments	2.8	3.2	3.7	3.7	3.7	3.6	3.0	2.7	2.3
Subsidies	1.1	1.1	0.7	0.8	0.6	0.5	0.6	0.6	0.6
Other current expenditure	:	:	1.9	2.0	2.0	2.2	2.2	2.5	2.8
Gross fixed capital formation	2.0	2.0	1.9	1.5	1.2	1.2	1.1	1.2	1.6
Other capital expenditure	:	:	1.2	0.9	0.7	0.6	0.6	−1.9	0.5
Total public expenditures	**43.0**	**42.5**	**45.8**	**44.2**	**42.0**	**40.7**	**40.1**	**37.7**	**40.6**
Tax burden	31.4	32.0	36.8	36.5	36.9	38.3	38.5	39.3	38.7
Budget balance	**−7.8**	**−6.7**	**−5.8**	**−4.4**	**−2.0**	**0.4**	**1.3**	**4.3**	**1.0**
Cyclically adjusted budget balance	−6.5	−6.3	−5.5	−4.1	−2.2	0.3	1.3	1.8	0.9
Consolidated gross public debt	47.9	49.8	52.1	52.7	51.1	48.1	45.7	42.9	38.3

Source: EC, 2002.

equality of income, but rather as equality in terms of social inclusion (Giddens, 1999). This, they affirm, is best achieved through strong public investment in public education, in new technologies and in infrastructures for the poorest areas.

Italy: high fragmentation of decision-making and revenue-based adjustment, 1991–97

In contrast to the United Kingdom, Italy is a country characterized by an extreme fragmentation of decision-making in the budget process. This is mainly the result of the extreme proportionality of its electoral system which results in the parliamentary representation of many small parties, and, therefore, the survival of minority parties. Also, Italy's budgetary process has traditionally lacked transparency. For example, there is no single document describing the budget, but a set of documents with different accounting bases that are issued throughout the year, and that describe different items of revenues and expenditures. In addition, there is no link between the accounts in those documents and the national accounts, and government loans to non-government entities are not included in those budgetary documents. Finally, at the stage of budget formulation, three ministries (the Treasury, Budget, and Finance) are involved, which diffuses responsibility at this stage. In addition, the Treasury, which used to have a higher responsibility at the implementation stage, could not block expenditures if they were already approved by the budget, something which gave it little flexibility to correct any deviation from the forecasts (De Haan, Moessen, and Volkerink, 1999).

As a consequence of this institutional structure, Italy has traditionally been among the worst fiscal performers in Europe. In fact, at the beginning of the 1990s, Italy was the country that caused the most concern among Europe's policy-makers that were designing convergence in fiscal policies as a previous step towards monetary union. Italy's debt level above annual GDP and a fiscal deficit in 1990 of −11 per cent seemed to require tremendous and sustained efforts to meet the Maastricht convergence criteria.

The consolidation episode in Italy during the 1990s was continuous and uninterrupted, although the strongest part of the adjustment took place between 1991 and 1997. During this period three phases can be identified.

The first phase lasted from 1990 to 1993, a period which was particularly volatile in political terms, since each year witnessed a new prime minister: the Christian Democrat Giulio Andreotti in 1990–91, the Socialist Giuliano Amato in 1992, and the independent Carlo Azeglio Ciampi from April 1993 to May 1994. During these years, the strategy of adjustment was strongly based on temporary measures on the revenue side, since they were enacted through supplementary emergency budgets when the actual budget deviated substantially from the forecast budget. For example, in 1991 the government promoted advanced tax payments on imputed capital gains and raised the withholding tax on saving deposits with maturity of less than one year. In addition, higher indirect taxes and social security contributions were also imposed (OECD Economic Survey, 1992). During 1992 and 1993, excise duties on tobacco and oil products were raised, VAT rates were harmonized with EU rules, and social contributions were raised once again to provide local health care institutions with more resources and to reduce intergovernmental transfers (Banca d'Italia Economic Bulletin, 1993: 45). Direct taxation was also increased. The government enacted a compulsory revaluation of corporate property, a tax amnesty, and one-off taxes on real estate and bank deposits. 'More importantly, the personal tax rate on all income brackets except the first and second one increased one percentage point' (Von Hagen, Hallett and Strauch, 2001: 100). This happened in 1992, and again in 1993 – personal income tax was revised upwards and the income tax brackets from 1989 were reintroduced. The only measures on the spending side were those related to public sector pay, through the freezing of public sector hiring, and a timid initial reform of the pension system which included the gradual rise of the compulsory retirement age and the enlargement of the reference period for the calculation of pensions (OECD Economic Survey, 1992: 46).

A second phase started in 1994. In that year there was a diversion from the fiscal policy of previous years, and Berlusconi's government largely avoided any renewal of temporary taxes. In fact, in an attempt to revive economic activity, a tax exemption for reinvested corporate profits was introduced, taxation on imputed rents was reduced, and lower advances of income tax payments were approved (Banca d'Italia Economic Bulletin, 1995: 38). These liberal measures on the revenue side were coupled with important spending cuts: the government reclassified drugs that were covered by the public system, 'seniority pensions for public employees having less than 35 years of service were cut, the automatic adjustment for disability pensions suspended, and the commencement date for new pensions under the general scheme for the private sector postponed' (Von Hagen, Hallett and Strauch, 2001: 101). Reform of the pensions and health systems continued during 1995, under the technocratic government of Lamberto Dini. An encompassing pension reform was enacted in 1995, while a strong reduction of local health care units was supposed to enforce a long-run rationalization of health expenditures. In addition, prices paid to retailers were renegotiated downwards and a new reclassification of 'free' pharmaceutical products was issued. These measures were reinforced a third time by the new socialist government of Romano Prodi in 1997, who accelerated the increase in the early retirement age, brought forward the harmonization of public and private pension schemes, increased the pension contributions of the self-employed, put forward measures to reduce the overcapacity in hospitals, reduced again the profit margins of pharmacists, and provided guidelines for diagnostic and ambulatory standards (OECD Economic Survey, 1997: 61–3).

A third phase of new temporary revenue-side measures took place between 1996, 1997 and 1998 under both the socialist Prodi's and Amato's consecutive coalition governments. For example, in 1996 some tax reductions were removed, higher property taxes and social security contributions were enacted, and a one per cent increase in the corporate tax rate was approved. The VAT tax rate was also raised from 9 per cent to 10 per cent and from 13 per cent to 16 per cent, respectively (OECD Economic Survey, 1996: 43–4; Banca d'Italia Economic Bulletin, 1996: 38). In 1997, the most important measure was the introduction of the special 'Euro-tax', a one-year progressive income tax, the rate ranging from 1.5 per cent for employees with a minimum annual salary of ITL 23.4 million to 3.5 per cent on incomes over ITL 100 million (OECD Economic Survey, 1997: 65). This measure was also accompanied by new measures against tax evasion and new taxes on lotteries, drugs and tobacco (OECD Economic Survey, 1997: 63). Finally, in 1998, the structure of revenues was changed again by a broad-based tax reform.[31] The most important features of the reform were the following:

> first, the introduction of a new regional tax on production activities with the abolition of a number of excise duties, capital taxes and health contributions; second, the revision of the personal income tax; third the reorganization rules governing the taxation of capital gains; fourth the introduction of a two-tier system for corporate taxation; fifth, the change of the VAT tax system (see OECD Economic Survey, 1999: 68–70; Banca d'Italia Economic Bulletin, 1998). Overall, the tax reform was designed to rationalize and simplify the tax system and to increase the fiscal autonomy of the lower levels of government. (Von Hagen, Hallett and Strauch, 2001: 103)

In conclusion, the episode of fiscal adjustment in Italy during the 1990s relied more on revenue-based measures than on spending cuts. As Table 5.8 shows, total public revenues grew almost 6 percentage points, from 42.8 per cent of GDP in 1991 to 48.4 per cent of GDP in 1997, while total public expenditures fell by only 2.7 percentage points – from 53.8 per cent of GDP in 1991 to 51.1 per cent of GDP in 1997. On the revenue side, all items were increased during that period by around 1 per cent and 1.7 per cent percentage points, while on the expenditure side social transfers, the government wage bill, and public investment were cut by 1 percentage point during the adjustment episode, while interest payments fell only by 0.6 per cent of GDP.

However, the above-mentioned trends hide some interesting particularities, especially regarding the possibility of identifying small pieces of evidence of partisan fiscal behaviour, in the midst of the general chaos of Italian public finances during the 1990s. For example, there was an important retrenchment of social transfers between 1994 and 1996, which fell by 3 percentage points. On the contrary, during the subsequent Prodi's government, public

Table 5.8 Fiscal policy in Italy, 1990–2000

		Fiscal adjustment episode									
	1990	*1991*	*1992*	*1993*	*1994*	*1995*	*1996*	*1997*	*1998*	*1999*	*2000*
Total current resources	42.8	43.8	44.5	47.7	45.5	44.8	45.5	47.2	45.8	46.3	45.5
Taxes on production and imports	11.3	11.8	11.8	12.7	12.3	12.1	11.8	12.4	15.3	15.2	15.1
Current taxes on income and wealth	14.3	14.4	14.6	16.0	14.8	14.8	15.4	16.1	14.4	15.1	14.6
Social contributions	14.3	14.6	14.9	15.4	14.8	14.8	15.0	15.3	12.8	12.8	12.7
Other current resources	2.9	3.0	3.3	3.6	3.6	3.1	3.2	3.2	3.2	3.2	3.0
Capital transfers received	:	:	:	:	:	0.9	0.4	1.0	0.7	0.5	0.4
Total public revenues	**42.8**	**43.8**	**44.5**	**47.7**	**45.5**	**45.8**	**46.1**	**48.4**	**46.8**	**47.1**	**46.1**
Total current expenditures	48.5	49.5	51.6	53.1	51.0	48.6	49.2	47.4	45.6	44.7	43.8
Government consumption expenditure	17.4	17.4	17.5	17.5	17.0	17.9	18.1	18.2	17.9	18.1	18.0
Of which compensation of employees	12.6	12.6	12.5	12.4	11.9	11.2	11.5	11.6	10.7	10.7	10.5
Social transfers other than in kind	18.3	18.4	19.5	19.7	19.7	16.7	16.9	17.3	17.0	17.2	16.7
Interest payments	9.4	10.1	11.4	12.0	10.9	11.5	11.5	9.4	8.0	6.7	6.5
Subsidies	2.5	2.6	2.3	2.7	2.4	1.5	1.5	1.2	1.3	1.2	1.2
Other current expenditure	:	:	:	:	:	1.1	1.3	1.3	1.3	1.4	1.4
Gross fixed capital formation	3.3	3.2	3.0	2.6	2.3	2.1	2.2	2.2	2.4	2.5	2.4
Other capital expenditure	:	:	:	:	:	2.5	1.6	1.3	1.4	1.4	0.1
Total public expenditures	**53.8**	**53.8**	**54.0**	**57.1**	**54.6**	**53.4**	**53.2**	**51.1**	**49.6**	**48.9**	**46.5**
Tax burden	40.0	40.9	41.5	44.2	42.1	42.3	42.9	44.4	43.2	43.5	43.0
Budget balance	**−11.0**	**−10.0**	**−9.5**	**−9.4**	**−9.1**	**−7.6**	**−7.1**	**−2.7**	**−2.8**	**−1.8**	**−0.3**
Cyclically adjusted budget balance	−11.9	−10.7	−9.8	−8.6	−8.5	−7.5	−6.7	−2.4	−2.5	−1.2	−1.3
Conslidated gross public debt	97.3	100.7	107.7	118.2	123.9	123.3	122.1	120.1	116.2	114.5	110.3

Source: EC, 2002.

investments stopped falling and were maintained at the level of 2.2 per cent of GDP during the latest part of the consolidation.

Finally, in 1998–99, still under the leftist coalition of L'Olivo, the primary balance deteriorated again, while transfers and wage payments continued to fall, but 'purchases started to grow and public investment expanded modestly' (Von Hagen, Hallett and Strauch, 2001: 104).

This latter fiscal policy strategy under Prodi's government has a very strong resemblance to the typical leftist strategy of fiscal adjustment depicted in Chapter 4, according to which left-wing governments, if forced to adjust, prefer to increase revenues and maintain expenditure; and if forced to reduce expenditures too, they prefer to keep public investment in order to articulate supply-side policies of physical and human capital formation, even at the expense of social transfers or public employment. In addition, the spending cuts introduced by Berlusconi's cabinet in 1994 and 1995, which resumed again after he was re-elected in 2001, might be also interpreted as further evidence of the partisanship hypothesis starting to play a role in explaining part of fiscal policy in Italy. Nevertheless, if this partisanship hypothesis really started to play any role at all in the second half of the 1990s, it was due to a previous and more important process of institutional transformation that modified deeply the budgetary process in Italy, reducing its degree of fragmentation.

The institutional change in Italian public finances started in 1992, and its main objectives, were: (1) to re-establish fiscal responsibility at the local level, reducing the high degree of vertical imbalance of the public finance system; and (2) to improve the budgetary process at the federal level (Bordignon, 2000).

At the local level, in 1992 and 1994 policy measures were taken to end the practice of local governments' overspending, and demanding additional funds to the national government under the threat of a likely collapse of local public services such as health and education. The reforms of 1992 limited the responsibility of the central government in these areas, to the extent that it was only left with the responsibility for setting and financing minimum national standards, leaving the regions with the responsibility of financing any cost beyond those standards. In 1995, this initiative was complemented by a new regulation that abolished conditional and unconditional grants from the national government to the regions. In return, the regions obtained a larger share of tax collections, and the national government introduced a system of redistribution to reduce inequalities among the regions. Finally, in order to increase the transparency and accountability of local governments, the national government reduced the level of managerial intervention at the local level, and forced some changes in the municipalities to increase politicians' accountability in local elections.

At the national level, the main reforms took place in 1994, and focused on strengthening the role of the parliament in the budgetary process in order to increase transparency; strengthening the role of the Treasury minister; and providing the conditions for more flexibility during the implementation of the budget (see Table 5.9).

These changes were accompanied by a crucial modification of the electoral system, away from pure proportional representation. Since the 1994 elections, three-quarters of the seats in the Senate and one-quarter of the seats in the Chamber of Deputies are determined according to plurality votes. Taking into account that both chambers have the same legislative and veto powers in the process of budget approval, the change in the electoral law has been very important in reducing the fragmentation of decision-making. However, the intended shift towards a more bipolar party system only occurred in the 1996 elections:

> Under the Prodi government, new legislation was passed that moved the budget process in the direction of centralization under the delegation approach. The former Budget ministry was incorporated in the Treasury, which now has a leading role in the budget process. The Treasury was also given the authority to block expenditures, thus reducing the power of the spending ministries during the implementation phase of the budget. (Von Hagen, Hallett and Strauch, 2001: 47)

Finally, another very important change took place in 1997 since when the parliament no longer approves a budget in which expenditure used to be

Table 5.9 Changes in budgetary procedures in the 1990s[32]

	Belgium		*Ireland*		***Italy***		*Sweden*	
Aspect	*Old*[a]	*New**	*Old*	*New*	***Old***	***New***	*Old*	*New*
Position of finance ministry	1.25	3.25	0.25	3.25	**0.75**	**0.95**	1.00	1.75
Position of legislature	0.80	1.60	1.60	3.00	**1.20**	**2.80**	1.60	3.20
Constraints	0.00	3.00	2.50	3.00	**2.50**	**2.50**	0.50	4.00
Transparency	2.00	3.13	1.00	1.53	**1.00**	**0.80**	1.00	3.20
Flexibility in execution	1.80	2.92	3.00	2.67	**0.25**	**1.58**	1.68	2.02
Relationship with other parts of gov't	1.33	1.33	0.00	3.33	**1.33**	**2.66**	0.00	1.33
Total	7.18	15.23	8.35	16.78	**7.03**	**11.29**	0.78	15.5

Notes:
1. [a]Old refers to classification in Von Hagen (1992).
2. *New refers to the revision of these indexes in 1999 by the mentioned authors.

Source: De Haan, Moessen, and Volkerink (1999: 275).

organized into 6,000 items; now the budget is organized according to 'functional targets' which indicate the main political decisions, and according to 'base units' which indicate resources for the responsibility centres of state administration (de Haan, Moessen and Volkerink, 1999).

Finally, Italy qualified for stage 3 of EMU, through the combined action of two institutional factors that succeeded in curbing down the endemic fragmentation of decision-making in Italian politics: the reform of the Italian budgetary process, and the external pressure of the Maastricht criteria.

When Prodi's government realized that Italy could join the euro in 1999 by combining all the previous years of slow but constant fiscal adjustment, and the internal institutional reforms mentioned above, it became determined to join with the first group and pledged to resign in case of failure. This decision was taken after Italy realized that it could not count on Spain to relax the criteria following a bilateral meeting between Aznar and Prodi in Valencia (23–24 September 1996) (Chiorazzo and Spaventa, 1999). It was then that Prodi confronted the possibility of Italy being left out the group of core countries, and when he decided to use the 'national pride' argument to ask Italians for a new budgetary effort. In this respect, the Maastricht criteria, as an external institutional constraint, had a significant effect in Italy (and also in Belgium, Finland, and Spain). A sustained fiscal adjustment was implemented in Italy only because a domestic institutional reform to reduce political fragmentation had previously taken place, but certainly, the external constraint played a crucial role during the last year of hard but uncontested measures taken by the government.[33]

Proximity of elections: France vs Germany

If in the previous section the cases of the United Kingdom and Italy served to illustrate how the fragmentation of decision-making can influence the strategy of adjustment and distort or enhance the influence of cabinet ideology as the main predictor of fiscal policy, in this section the French and German cases of the 1990s will be presented as clear examples of how the proximity of elections can reverse the influence that both ideology and fragmentation of decision-making normally have during non-election years.

There are numerous examples of alterations in fiscal policy having been caused by the proximity of elections. These alterations take different forms. The most common alteration usually takes the form of expansionary fiscal policy occurring prior to the election, in order to accelerate the rate of economic growth and increase the chances of re-election. Consequently, when elections come and the country had plans to start a fiscal adjustment, these plans were postponed. Or if the country was already in the middle of a fiscal consolidation, the probability of ending this episode of adjustment increases rapidly as the election gets closer (see Chapter 3).

A case that combines both of these aspects was the case of Spain in 1993. The socialist government of Felipe González submitted its first Convergence

Programme to the European Commission in 1992, when the deficit stood at 4 per cent of GDP. The 'promised' path of adjustment in April 1992 established that the deficit should fall continuously over the following four years to reach 1 per cent of GDP in 1996. But the predictions of that first Convergence Programme relied on extremely optimistic scenarios of 3 per cent annual GDP growth. The reality turned out to be very different, and the economic slowdown of 1991–92 indicated that if a reduction of the deficit were to take place, hard measures needed to be taken on the expenditure side. However, the damaging effect of the first publicly known cases of corruption, and the growing voter support for the conservative Popular Party, placed the socialist government in a position from which it was likely to lose an election for the first time in eleven years. As a consequence, González decided to use the 'fear of dismantling the welfare state' as the core of his campaign to convince the electorate that he was the only political option that would defend this system from the neoliberal intentions he attributed to 'the right'. Therefore, measures to maintain public expenditures and increase social transfers were enacted despite what was promised in the first Convergence Programme; the deficit reached 6.7 per cent of GDP by the end of 1993, and the necessary fiscal consolidation had to wait until 1994–95. González, however, was re-elected to serve his fourth term in office.

Nevertheless, sometimes fiscal consolidation cannot be avoided or postponed, and then the government decides to alter the electoral calendar, rather than altering fiscal policy plans. This is what happened in France in 1997, when President Chirac dissolved the parliament and called an early election to avoid having these elections in 1998 immediately after all of the hard budget measures needed to qualify for the third stage of EMU in 1999 had taken place.

However, sometimes elections cannot be postponed and nor can sound fiscal policy be avoided. In such circumstances governments tend either to implement the fiscal adjustment even if it coincides with elections, or they try to weaken fiscal institutions due to electoral reasons. This latter case is the German case during the 1990s.

Both, Germany and France have fiscal institutions that use the 'delegation approach' to maintain a high degree of fiscal balance. Both countries also had conservative governments in power in the mid-1990s. And both countries faced elections in 1997, the last year to meet the 3 per cent deficit limit (Willett, 1999: 55). The difference between both cases lies, however, on the point of departure. While France maintained important fiscal deficits during the 1980s and followed an expansionary fiscal policy between 1991 and 1994 that meant that the country had a deficit of 5.6 per cent of GDP in 1994, Germany started the decade with no apparent problems in fulfilling any of the criteria, but ended up coming very close to being left out of the qualifying group in 1997. Although the partisanship hypothesis would have predicted clear expenditure-based adjustments taking place in both countries (even more so given the low degree of fragmentation in decision-making present in both cases), the proximity of elections pushed France into a late revenue-based strategy, and sent Germany into an artificial 'freezing effort' accompanied by a weakening of its fiscal institutions that was behind the persistent difficulties to perform its fiscal obligations since 2002.

France: early elections and revenue-based adjustment, 1995–97

At the beginning of the 1990s, the budget deficit in France stood at 2 per cent of GDP and the accumulated debt level represented 40 per cent of GDP. Thereafter, the deficit quickly deteriorated to 4.3 per cent in 1992 and 5.6 per cent in 1993, essentially as a result of the economic recession that occurred in Europe at the start of the decade.

At that time, fiscal policy consisted of a number of measures that pulled in different directions. On the one hand, spending caps on ambulatory care expenditures, direct payments by patients, and general guidelines for savings in hospitals were introduced in 1992, together with a pension reform and new measures to tighten unemployment compensation, in 1993. On the other hand, these measures were offset by other expansionary initiatives, such as new labour market policies in 1992, new programmes to subsidize agriculture, small and medium-sized industry enterprises, and extraordinary capital spending in state-owned enterprises. The revenue side also presented a combination of offsetting initiatives. Corporate taxes and the top VAT rate were cut in 1992, while social security contributions were raised in 1993.

This cross-combination of policies remained intact during 1994, although the remarkable enlargement of subsidies and transfers to households ended up by placing French public finances on a path which was incompatible with the Maastricht criteria. Many initiatives were then taken on both sides of the budget to reduce the deficit, being the increase in revenues the dominant strategy until 1996. In this respect, a temporary increase in wealth and corporate taxes (10 per cent surcharge) was imposed. In addition, excise duties on tobacco and petrol were raised. A two-point rise in VAT (from 18.6 per cent to 20.6 per cent) became effective from August 1995, while employers' social contributions were raised 3.8 points in order to balance the accounts of the local authorities' pension funds (*Banque de France Bulletin Digest*, 2/95).

Finally, some emergency measures were taken to comply with the 3 per cent reference value of the Maastricht criteria: 'a 5 per cent increase (from 36.6 to 41.6 per cent) in corporate tax levied on companies with a turnover above FFr 50 Million was imposed for two years. This tax hike affected also certain long-term capital gains which were included in the tax base and, therefore, were subjected to a tax increase from a reduced rate of 19 per cent to 41.6 per cent' (Von Hagen, Hallett and Strauch, 2001: 88). Furthermore, the domestic tax on oil products increased, and a 1 per cent rise in the social security surcharge was approved to offset the 1.3 per cent cut in employees' health contributions (*Banque de France Bulletin Digest,* 11/96; OECD Economic Survey, 1997: 51).

As a result of the strategy depicted above, France maintained the level of its public expenditures at 55 per cent of GDP, and increased the share of public revenues in terms of GDP by 3.5 per cent between 1994 and 1997, until they reached 52 per cent of GDP (see Table 5.10).

This revenue-based strategy of adjustment is directly related to the difficulties that the Juppé government encountered in introducing its numerous plans for welfare reform with the aim of reducing public expenditures to allow for important tax cuts that could stimulate the French economy and accelerate job creation.

The failure of the partisanship hypothesis to explain the strategy of fiscal adjustment pursued by France between 1995 and 1997 is related to the widespread rejection in French society of the liberal measures promoted by the conservative government of Chirac and Juppé, and most importantly with the fear that the government had of implementing hard unpopular measures when elections were imminent.

Their fears were not without foundation. On 7 November 1995 Alain Juppé was reappointed as prime minister by President Chirac. Juppé's first announcement after the cabinet reshuffle was that the 'new team's main tasks would be to restore order to the government's finances, so as to open the way for lower interest rates and an easing of the tax burden. Of particular importance, he said, were reform of the social security system, government administration and taxation, and the implementation of a policy of urban renewal aimed at social integration' (EIU France Country Report, 1996, 1/4: 9). Eight days later, the social security reforms were made public, and on 24 November, nationwide strikes of public sector workers and students erupted, causing four weeks of economic havoc.

Although the massive demonstrations were motivated by a range of different factors, ranging from general discontent with the inability of the government to maintain Chirac's presidential promises of employment creation,[34] to cuts in education spending[35] and the labour conditions of workers in the public transportation system, the social explosion was very much directed against the Juppé government crusade for public finance deficit reduction and the social security package.

In the intensity of the protests there was also an element of personal rivalry on the part of the trade union leader of Force Ouvrière (FO), Marc Blondel, who promoted the most intense strikes in the government administration and public service sectors, where its union had traditionally have the strongest representation. These protests entailed a direct response to the unilateral initiative of the Juppé government to freeze the civil service pay-scale announced for 1996, to tighten the public sector pension schemes,

Table 5.10 Fiscal policy in France, 1993–2001

			Fiscal adjustment episode						
	1993	*1994*	*1995*	*1996*	*1997*	*1998*	*1999*	*2000*	*2001*
Total current resources	**48.4**	**48.3**	**48.1**	**49.7**	**49.6**	**49.6**	**50.4**	**50.2**	**49.8**
Taxes on production and imports	14.3	14.7	15.4	16.1	16.0	16.0	16.1	15.7	15.4
Current taxes on income and wealth	9.0	9.2	8.5	8.9	9.5	11.7	12.2	12.3	12.1
Social contributions	21.1	20.7	20.5	20.7	20.3	18.2	18.4	18.5	18.5
Other current resources	4.1	3.7	3.7	4.0	3.9	3.7	3.6	3.7	3.7
Capital transfers received	:	:	0.4	0.3	0.8	1.2	1.4	1.5	1.5
Total public revenues	**48.4**	**48.3**	**49.7**	**51.4**	**51.9**	**51.3**	**52.1**	**51.9**	**51.4**
Total current expenditures	50.7	50.4	49.2	50.0	49.8	48.6	48.3	47.9	47.3
Government consumption expenditure	19.4	19.2	23.9	24.2	24.2	23.5	23.7	23.5	23.3
Of which compensation of employees	14.0	14.0	13.7	13.9	13.8	13.7	13.7	13.5	13.2
Social transfers other than in kind	23.1	22.9	18.5	18.7	18.8	18.4	18.3	18.1	17.8
Interest payments	3.3	3.5	3.8	3.9	3.7	3.6	3.4	3.3	3.2
Subsidies	2.4	2.3	1.5	1.5	1.5	1.4	1.3	1.3	1.3
Other current expenditure	:	:	1.6	1.7	1.6	1.7	1.7	1.7	1.6
Gross fixed capital formation	3.1	3.1	3.3	3.2	3.0	2.9	2.9	3.0	3.0
Other capital expenditure	:	:	1.5	0.9	0.8	2.1	2.2	2.1	1.5
Total public expenditures	**54.1**	**54.0**	**55.2**	**55.5**	**55.0**	**54.0**	**53.7**	**53.2**	**51.9**
Tax burden	45.6	45.9	45.2	46.4	46.5	46.5	47.3	47.0	46.6
Budget balance	**−5.6**	**−5.6**	**−5.5**	**−4.1**	**−3.0**	**−2.7**	**−1.6**	**−1.3**	**−0.6**
Cyclically adjusted budget balance	−5.2	−5.4	−5.1	−3.3	−2.2	−2.2	−1.3	−1.3	−1.2
Consolidated gross public debt	46.1	49.6	54.0	57.1	59.3	59.7	58.8	58.0	56.9

Source: EC, 2002.

and to launch health care reforms directly affecting public workers, without any previous consultation with the union, as had traditionally been the case (Howarth, 2000).

In view of the level of social unrest created by the announced initiatives, the government and the presidency launched a joint campaign to explain to the public opinion, through a series of media interviews, the importance of public deficit reduction as a precondition for lower interest rates, sustained growth, and further employment creation. This was also interpreted as an attempt to detach the necessary reforms to the French welfare system from the process of European Monetary Union.

During 1996, the introduction of the pension reforms continued. For the Juppé government it was a crucial question that could not be postponed once again, as the government of Bérégovoy in 1992 and the Balladur government had done for electoral considerations (Reland, 1998: 99). It was finally decided that the repayment of social security debt should be financed through a special tax called the social debt repayment (RDS) levy, which was imposed in 1996 at a rate of 0.5 per cent on all incomes. In addition, the government wage bill was frozen once again, but this time not by means of a real freeze in public salaries, but by an actual cut in public employment largely resulting from the non-replacement of posts vacated through normal retirement.

As a consequence, social tensions remained. In January 1997, the French president, Jacques Chirac, exhibited only 30–35 per cent of electoral support, while its prime minister had only 25–27 per cent. However, polls still suggested that they would be most likely victorious if elections were to be held then.[36] Suddenly on 21 April 1997, Chirac announced the dissolution of the National Assembly, nearly a year ahead of the end of its five-year normal term. He told the French public that 'the government was in need of a new mandate in view of the difficult, but important, challenges that laid ahead, including the introduction of further reforms of the country's public finances (providing for major cuts in both taxes and expenditures); the creation of a more favourable climate for business and employment creation; and, above all, additional progress in European integration' (EIU France Country Report, 1997, 2/4: 11). However, the true reason for this early call was one of political calculation: Chirac was convinced that it would be easier to maintain the conservative majority and avoid a third cohabitation,[37] if elections did not coincide with the strongest measures that remained ahead, and if it took the opposition by surprise, which at the time was very divided regarding the austerity measures attached to EMU and was willing to join the government later if this meant a slower rhythm of reforms.

But Chirac's gamble failed, despite a last-minute attempt to regain the leadership in the polls (which the government kept until the first round of the legislative elections on 25 May) consisting in forcing Juppé to renounce publicly before the second round any ambition of staying as prime minister, and signalling the popular president of the National Assembly, Philippe Séguin, as the next prime minister in the event of the right maintaining power. Lionel Jospin and his leftist allies won 320 seats in the 577-member National Assembly, formed a new government before the summer, and France finally met the 3 per cent deficit criteria thanks to the controversial inclusion as a budget receipt of a one-off payment to the State by France Télécom, linked to the subsequent partial privatization, which was estimated as the equivalent of 0.45 per cent of GDP. The European Commission permitted this payment, and it certainly allowed France to qualify among the first group of countries joining the euro.

A posteriori, most French political analysts agreed that the surprising victory of Lionel Jospin was more a punishment inflicted to Chirac for not having complied with his 1995 electoral promises of a radical shift in economic policy to stimulate the economy, than a strong preference for a socialist government.[38] Nevertheless, it must also be noticed that Jospin ran the election campaign on a platform of socialist-communists that was purposely ambiguous regarding the reforms entailed by the Maastricht criteria. In fact, Jospin advocated the inclusion of the unemployment rate among the convergence criteria, in order to create an economic government that would serve as counterweight to the monetarist European Central Bank, and initially admitted that a relaxation of the criteria or a postponement of the entry date were acceptable measures if this served to bring the needed stimulus to the French economy. However, once in power, Jospin became satisfied on the European front with the inclusion of an employment chapter in the Treaty of Amsterdam of 1997 and the inclusion of all small candidates and Italy in the euro group. In the domestic arena, Lionel Jospin, during his first year in power, left untouched the social security reforms launched by his predecessor Alain Juppé, and postponed the promised downward revision of the VAT. Because the economy started to grow, public finance worries eased and the new government immediately focused on innovative social policies (such as raising the minimum wage by 4 per cent), and active labour market policies to reduce unemployment (the most important of which was the passage of the law introducing the week of 35 working hours), which began in 2000.

All in all, the French case illustrates that if elections are close and the government cannot postpone a necessary fiscal consolidation (because the EMU timetable was fixed), then politicians will opt to alter the electoral calendar in order to avoid campaigning for re-election in an adjustment year. In this case, the manipulation was blatant: it displeased the French electorate, who punished the incumbent government for not having complied with its previous electoral promises. As such, this latter aspect is to be borne in mind for Chapter 7, when the political consequences of fiscal adjustments will be analysed.

Germany: elections, weakening institutions and non-adjustment, 1990–97

On Wednesday 30 January 2002, Germany received an unprecedented warning from the European Commission about the size of its budget deficit. This warning started a process that ended up with the Commission denouncing the Council at the Court of Justice for not applying the rules of the Stability and Growth Pact, an event that was decisive for the reforms of the Pact that was approved in March 2005. As a result of the economic downturn Germany's deficit had risen to 2.7 per cent of GDP in 2001, fairly close to the maximum of 3 per cent laid down in the Stability Pact (a set of budgetary rules that had been promoted by Germany itself to guarantee sound budgetary politics in the countries joining the euro). How could the strongest advocate of fiscal discipline be the first one in receiving a warning for getting extremely close to the limit in 2001, and finally breaking it at the end of 2002?[39]

The explanation of this paradox is very much related to the weakening of the German budgetary institutions driven by political considerations of the Kohl government in the aftermath of German reunification, as explained by Von Hagen and Strauch (1999). As such, the German case exemplifies a government which, unable to modify the electoral calendar or the fiscal austerity that its institutions forced it to follow, decided to weaken those same institutions in order to implement an expansionary fiscal policy directly oriented towards guaranteeing its re-election. As a consequence, when the time to evaluate the fiscal accounts came, Germany found itself among the non-complying countries in 1996. Then, with the German fiscal institutions badly damaged, and new elections imminent, the same conservative government of Helmut Kohl resorted to a set of revenue-based adjustment measures that had only temporary effects on the budget, allowing Germany to qualify for the third stage of EMU, but weakening the capacity of future German governments to maintain fiscal discipline.

The process of German reunification between 1989 and 1991 was indeed an exogenous and unexpected shock to German fiscal policy, and one which had a strong impact on Germany's public finances. As an example, in only two years reunification transformed a structural surplus of 0.4 per cent of GDP in 1989 into a deficit of −5.9 per cent of GDP in 1991, and a debt level of 38 per cent of GDP in 1989 into a debt level of 57.1 per cent of GDP in 1995 (see Table 5.11).

To most observers, German reunification was a classical case of tax-smoothing. According to this view, Germany was right to finance the real investment necessary to rebuild the East German economy with additional public debt:

> But this view is inconsistent with the nature of the public transfers actually paid to former East Germany since unification, which predominantly

> served to finance consumption, [and were] the outcome of a series of political choices based on short run strategic considerations that led to the deterioration of public budgeting and budgetary institutions in Germany. (Von Hagen and Strauch, 1999: 70–1)

The first political reunification measures taken by the Kohl government had important fiscal consequences. The most important of these measures was the determination of the conversion rate between the West and East Deutsche Marks. Although most economists agreed that the proper conversion should have been 1 West DM per 4 East DM, the government established a conversion rate of 1 : 2 for most bank accounts, but for prices, pensions and wages, the conversion rate was 1 : 1 (Deutsche Bundesbank Annual Report, 1990). Together with this decision, the Kohl government also decided the full extension of West Germany's labour market institutions. Both measures had important fiscal consequences, since the higher rate of conversion resulted in higher pensions, and the extension of the long and high Western unemployment insurance resulted in higher pressures on the social security system.

The decision to transplant labour market conditions to the East also had very important effects on East Germany's unemployment rate. Because Western trade unions and employers soon extended their wage bargaining process to the East, with the intention of dissolving any possibility of low-wage/low-price competition from these regions, real wages grew in the East at a much faster rate than productivity, resulting in massive unemployment during the 1990s. 'Instead of creating jobs in the East, the adjustment process triggered huge social transfers flowing from West to East Germany' (Von Hagen and Strauch, 1999: 75).

These massive transfers, the largest share of them being transfers to private households, were mainly financed by the general government. While total gross transfers from the West to the East rose from DM 139 billion in 1991 to DM 189 billion in 1997, local governments did not transfer to their East counterparts more than DM 14 billion in the whole process (Deutsche Bundesbank Annual Report, 1998). In contrast, over the same period, public investment in East Germany financed by West Germany only rose from DM 22 billion to DM 33 billion, and never exceeded one-fifth of social transfers. 'This is a clear refutation of the tax smoothing interpretation of German fiscal policy after unification' (Von Hagen and Strauch, 1999: 80).

The financing of all of these expenditures came largely from government borrowing, as they were thought to be temporary measures. At last, the reunification process was conceived as an event that would be self-financing in the medium and long term. However, as early as in 1992–93, it became clear that the reunification would require long-term permanent transfers, mostly as a result of the high unemployment rate triggered by the labour market initiatives of 1989 and 1990.[40]

Table 5.11 Fiscal policy in France, 1993–2001

					Fiscal adjustment episode						
	1991	*1992*	*1993*	*1994*	*1995*	*1996*	*1997*	*1998*	*1999*	*2000*	*2001*
Total current resources	**43.5**	**44.9**	**45.3**	**45.9**	**44.8**	**45.7**	**45.4**	**45.5**	**46.1**	**46.0**	**44.6**
Taxes on production and imports	12.2	12.4	12.7	13.1	11.4	11.4	11.4	11.6	12.2	12.0	12.1
Current taxes on income and wealth	11.3	11.6	11.2	10.8	11.1	11.5	11.2	11.5	12.0	12.5	11.4
Social contributions	17.5	17.8	18.4	18.9	18.8	19.4	19.6	19.2	18.9	18.7	18.3
Other current resources	2.6	3.1	3.0	3.0	3.5	3.4	3.2	3.2	3.1	2.9	2.8
Capital transfers received	:	:	:	:	0.5	0.4	0.4	0.5	0.4	0.4	0.4
Total public revenues	**43.5**	**44.9**	**45.3**	**45.9**	**46.1**	**46.8**	**46.5**	**46.6**	**47.2**	**47.0**	**45.9**
Total current expenditures	42.3	43.4	44.8	44.9	44.9	46.2	45.5	44.8	44.8	44.3	43.8
Government consumption expenditure	18.9	19.5	19.6	19.4	19.8	19.9	19.5	19.1	19.0	18.9	18.7
Of which compensation of employees	10.1	10.4	10.6	10.3	9.0	8.9	8.7	8.4	8.3	8.1	7.9
Social transfers other than in kind	16.6	17.3	18.4	18.6	18.1	19.3	19.3	18.9	18.9	18.7	18.5
Interest payments	2.6	3.2	3.2	3.3	3.7	3.7	3.6	3.6	3.5	3.3	3.2
Subsidies	2.4	2.1	2.1	2.1	2.1	2.0	1.8	1.8	1.7	1.7	1.6
Other current expenditure	:	:	:	:	1.2	1.3	1.4	1.4	1.6	1.7	1.7
Gross fixed capital formation	2.6	2.8	2.7	2.5	2.3	2.1	1.9	1.8	1.8	1.8	1.8
Other capital expenditure	:	:	:	:	1.6	1.2	1.2	1.3	1.3	−1.1	1.2
Total public expenditures	**46.8**	**47.6**	**48.8**	**48.4**	**49.6**	**50.3**	**49.2**	**48.6**	**48.6**	**45.6**	**47.6**
Tax burden	40.8	41.5	42.0	42.5	42.2	43.1	43.0	42.9	43.7	43.8	42.3
Budget balance	**−3.2**	**−2.8**	**−3.5**	**−2.6**	**−3.5**	**−3.4**	**−2.7**	**−2.1**	**−1.4**	**−1.5**	**−2.6**
Cyclically adjusted budget balance	−5.9	−4.7	−3.8	−3.0	−3.7	−3.1	−2.1	−1.5	−0.7	−0.8	−1.9
Consolidated gross public debt	40.4	43.1	47.2	49.5	57.1	59.8	60.9	60.7	61.1	60.3	61.7

Source: EC, 2002.

This is why, from 1993 onwards, the Kohl government, unable to mobilize the political strength to cut spending and facing new elections in 1994, engaged in a series of revenue-raising measures that affected almost all taxes and revenue sources. As Table 5.11 reports, total public revenues rose by 1.3 per cent of GDP between 1993 and 1998, while total public expenditures fell only by 0.2 per cent during the same period. Some of the most important measures on the revenue side were: the increase in the mineral oil tax in 1994, the reintroduction of the 'solidarity surcharge' in 1995,[41] the increase in VAT from 12 per cent to 15 per cent, and the doubling of the wealth tax from 0.5 per cent to 1 per cent for most assets.[42] This overall revenue-based adjustment, switched, however, to an expenditure-based strategy in 1997, when public expenditures were cut by 0.8 per cent, mostly those coming from the government's wage bill (0.3 per cent), public transfers (0.4 per cent), and public investment (0.1 per cent).

However, in spite of these numerous budgetary initiatives, slow rates of economic growth made it increasingly difficult to match revenue forecasts and actual revenues (SVR, 1997). As a consequence, Germany was close to fail the 'Maastricht exam'. Only the consecutive exercise by Theo Waigel of the finance minister's prerogative to block expenditures in March 1995 and June 1997, made Germany's qualification possible. This qualification happened, however, after the German government attempted to force the Bundesbank to revalue its gold reserves against accounting conventions in May 1997, and cash in the resulting profits. In addition, the German government used unreported budget gimmicks that accounted for about 0.4 per cent of GDP (DIW, 1998), what summed to the official 2.7 per cent budget deficit recognized by the European Commission in 1998, would have caused a violation of the deficit criterion by Germany.

Throughout this process, political decisions in Germany were heavily influenced by electoral considerations. In a general climate of uncertainty about the economic impact of reunification, and fearing massive migrations from the East into the West, Kohl's government moved quickly to grant all types of benefits to the new Eastern German citizens. These measures were also full of electoral motivations. Earlier in 1989, electoral expectations for the governing coalition had looked rather bleak, with the CDU-CSU lagging behind the SPD in opinion polls from Fall 1989 (Schwin, 1997). Active policy initiatives returned the governing coalition to a leadership position in setting the German political agenda, a position that had been lost to the SPD in the two years previous to the fall of the Berlin Wall. The conversion rate of 1 : 1, the extension of all labour benefits, and the massive transfers to East Germany must be understood against this background. Even more if one takes into account the strong incentives that the West German government faced to please a new East German electorate that would eventually vote in the 1990 federal elections.

To do this, the Kohl's government resorted to a series of political initiatives aimed at circumventing the strict provisions of the German budgetary process. The most important of these initiatives was the increased use of special funds by the federal government to finance reunification. The fact that these special funds do not appear in the budget meant that their use was not scrutinized by the powerful budget committee in the Parliament, and the government could then escape from legislative control. Another important initiative was the increased use of tax expenditures. 'While the budgetary effect of tax expenditures is the same as that of explicit subsidy payments, they are harder to control in the budget process, because they do not appear as an expense in the budget law' (Von Hagen and Strauch, 1999: 88).

In addition, Kohl decided to weaken the otherwise strong institutional budgetary powers of the finance minister, either by assuming some of its duties, or by transferring also some powers to other offices strongly involved in the re-unification process, such as the Treuhand.[43]

A third indication of the institutional deterioration of the budget process was the proliferation of budget freezes, last-minute revisions of budget proposals, and multiple 'ad hoc' fiscal measures. These measures generally took the form of amendments to the budget, and/or direct compensation of pressure groups who complained of being particularly affected by the reunification process. It was said at the time that the Chancellery was so ready to gather support for the reunification project, that it used to compensate those with 'particularly affected interests' with sums of up to DM 1 billion (Von Hagen and Strauch, 1999).

As a result, while German governments had only resorted to supplementary budgets four times between 1952 and 1980, between 1990 and 1997 Kohl's government presented seven supplementary budgets (Sturm, 1998). 'Disastrous financial decisions taken out of electoral opportunism were never reversed or replaced by a more long-term orientated financial strategy. The 1990s, therefore left Germany with a large fiscal problem that still awaits a sustainable solution' (Von Hagen and Strauch, 1999: 90).

The solution to this problem, however, seems very difficult. During the 1990s, German fiscal institutions were circumvented unofficially, meaning that there was no specific legal reform of these institutions, and, therefore, no legislative initiative can restore their previous power. It is the task of politicians to return to old practices, which mostly relied on the mutual agreement among the main German political actors to abide by these institutional rules. However, once one party in the contract has succumbed to the temptation of electoral manipulation of the budget process, the incentives for the political opponent to keep its word and stick to the rules diminish.

5.3 Conclusion

This chapter has used several concrete case studies to illustrate the type of constraints that political and institutional factors impose on fiscal policy formulation. The strong effect that the ideology of the party in government, the fragmentation of decision-making, and the proximity of elections have on fiscal adjustment strategies has already been highlighted in Chapters 3 and 4. However, one of the disadvantages of arriving at substantive conclusions by means of statistical analysis is that the story lacks the richness of concrete historical examples. The purpose of this chapter was precisely this: to provide the book with some historical background against which statistical results could be contrasted. Given its historical salience, the chapter tells the story of the Maastricht Treaty and the fiscal efforts made by all member states to qualify for the third stage of EMU, underscoring the political dimensions of the process.

This is why the chapter started by answering some of the more puzzling questions that arose from the results obtained in chapters 3 and 4. Questions such as why did European countries tie their own hands in the first place by establishing the Maastricht convergence criteria, if domestic constraints played such an important role?; and why did social democratic parties, traditionally associated with policies of economic management within national boundaries, embrace monetary union so enthusiastically?, have been the subject of the first part of this chapter.

Although answered from different perspectives, the response to the first question posed in the chapter was a response in terms of foreign politics, whereby the move to EMU was a combination of French and Italian desires to rebalance power in the EMS, and the German acceptance of these new conditions in exchange for an approval of German reunification. In a similar way, the main reason why social democratic parties across Europe embraced monetary union had to do with two factors: their conviction of the merits of economic stability, and the normal support that opposition parties tend to give to their governments in issues related to foreign policy and the national interest.

However, this pre-eminence of foreign policy motivations in the period leading up to the signing of the Treaty of Maastricht does not imply that domestic political constraints played no role in the subsequent period of fiscal adjustment. Once countries agreed on the convergence criteria, each found its own way to fulfil them. It was precisely during the formation of these interim decisions that factors such as the ideology of the party in government, the fragmentation of decision-making and the proximity of elections, again played a role in the 1990s. The cases of Portugal and Spain (in terms of ideology), the UK and Italy (with respect to institutional fragmentation), and France and Germany (regarding the influence of elections), all illustrate, in different ways, the influence that one or more of these factors had on the formulation of alternative fiscal adjustment strategies during the 1990s.

Overall, revenue-based or expenditure-based strategies of adjustment are important not only for the role that they assign to the state in the economy, but also (and mainly) because they may have different economic and political consequences for the countries and governments which implement them. The final two chapters of the book deal precisely with these aspects, since Chapter 6 investigates the economic consequences of different adjustment strategies, and Chapter 7 analyses the political ones.

6
The Economic Consequences of Fiscal Adjustments

> 'Large fiscal adjustments that are expenditure-based and are accompanied by wage moderation and devaluation, are expansionary.'
>
> Alesina and Ardagna, 1998: 516

> 'Large changes in the distribution of income have taken place within many European nations, with most finding a higher level of inequality in the mid-to-late 1990s than in the 1980s.'
>
> Smeeding, 2000: 2

A central concern when considering the political economy of fiscal adjustments is whether or not these adjustments have any economic consequences.

The first part of this book has analysed the economic and political factors that determine the timing, the duration, and the composition of adjustment episodes. Nevertheless, it seems reasonable to expect that different strategies of adjustment (in their length and their composition) can have different economic and political consequences. This chapter will deal with the economic consequences of fiscal adjustments, while Chapter 7 will analyse the political ones.*

To analyse the economic impact that different types of fiscal consolidations have, implies in itself a primarily empirical question, given that theoretical predictions are varied and sometimes even contradictory. For example, while standard Keynesian theory predicts that a fiscal adjustment will reduce the level of output, supply-side theorists sustain the opposite. In their view, if tax cuts and decreasing interest rates accompany the fiscal adjustment, consolidations can have a crowding-in effect of private investment and consumption that might eventually overcome the loss in economic presence of the public sector and have overall expansionary effects.

Although the empirical literature on the effects of fiscal policy on economic activity in advanced economies expands from macroeconomic models that estimate the sign of fiscal multipliers to simulations that try to test the Ricardian equivalence, the most popular strand of this empirical literature is the one that draws lessons by looking across episodes of fiscal consolidations, with a special emphasis on identifying expansionary fiscal adjustments. As can be seen in Appendix 5 at the end of this volume, although the country examples that are identified differ between studies, most of them identify expansionary fiscal contractions and confirm the original Giavazzi and Pagano (1990) finding, namely that Denmark (1983–86) and Ireland (1987–89) are the clearest instances of expansionary fiscal contractions.

These works have always focused on the effects of fiscal adjustments on economic output and on its rate of growth, but they have systematically ignored the possible impact that budget cuts could have on the distribution of that output. Since fiscal consolidations are more likely to be expansionary when there are important reductions in the most rigid budget items (public wages and social transfers), it is reasonable to expect that these adjustments could also increase income inequalities. If this were true, there could be a trade-off between growth and equality that any government willing to undertake a fiscal consolidation would have to confront.

Such a hypothesis (of the existence of a trade-off mediated by fiscal adjustments) has never been tested before. The main purpose of this chapter is thus to do that, using fresh empirical data from the recent experience of fiscal consolidations in Europe.[1]

The chapter combines different methodologies used by previous empirical works on the topic, and applies them to a different sample and to a new set of economic variables.[2] Besides the updated time-frame and the focus on EU countries, this chapter introduces a major innovation with respect to previous studies: by focusing on the effects that different budgetary compositions have on the distribution of income after fiscal adjustment episodes, the chapter presents very strong empirical evidence pointing to the existence of a trade-off between growth and equality mediated by fiscal consolidations. While expenditure-based adjustments perform better in terms of subsequent economic growth than do revenue-based adjustments, the latter are less harmful in terms of income distribution.

Section 6.1 reviews the theoretical and empirical literature related to the effects of fiscal policy and fiscal adjustments on economic growth and income distribution. Section 6.2 deals with the research design and the formulation of the empirical hypotheses to be tested in this chapter, and sections 6.3 and 6.4 present the main empirical results using alternative but complementary techniques. Section 6.5 summarizes the main findings and conclusions.

6.1 Fiscal policy and the macroeconomy

The effects of fiscal policy on the macroeconomy have been the subject of long and fruitful debate. An understanding of the different theoretical contributions to this issue is crucial in order to comprehend the possible economic impact of fiscal adjustments, and the channels through which fiscal variables influence the economy. The following theoretical revision extends the brief analysis that was presented in Chapter 2, and then in Chapter 4, with the purpose of providing more detailed explanations that contribute to this understanding.

Demand-side effects on growth of fiscal policy: Keynesian effects

A natural place to start a review of the theoretical literature on the demand-side effects of fiscal policy is with the Keynesian approach. The simplest Keynesian model assumes price rigidity and slack in productive capacity, so that output is determined by aggregate demand. In this model, a fiscal expansion has a multiplier effect on aggregate demand and output. The Keynesian multiplier exceeds one, it increases with the responsiveness of consumption to current income, and it is larger for a spending increase than for a tax cut. If a spending increase is matched by a tax increase, the resulting 'balanced budget multiplier' is exactly one.

Extensions of the simplest Keynesian model allow for crowding-out through induced changes in interest rates and the exchange rate. This is additional to the crowding-out which occurs to the extent that the government provides goods and services that substitute those provided by the private sector, and insofar as part of any increase in domestic demand in an open economy is met from imports. The extent of crowding-out affects the size of fiscal multipliers but does not change their sign. In the standard IS-LM model, private investment depends negatively on interest rates, and therefore a fiscal expansion paid for by increased borrowing that leads to higher interest rates reduces investment. In the open economy IS-LM (Mundell–Fleming) model, there can also be crowding-out through the exchange rate. Higher interest rates attract capital inflows which raise the exchange rate, and the resulting deterioration in the external current account offsets the increase in domestic demand deriving from a fiscal expansion.

Crowding-out through interest rates and the exchange rate is influenced by certain features of the IS-LM framework such as: (1) the determinants of private investment (crowding-out is likely to be greater if investment is fairly sensitive to interest rates); (2) money demand and monetary policy (the tendency for interest rates to rise in response to a fiscal expansion could be offset by a monetary expansion; (3) openness and the exchange rate regime (with perfect capital mobility and flexible exchange rates and perfect capital mobility, there is a complete crowding-out and so fiscal policy is ineffective).

The extent of crowding-out is also affected by price flexibility. Neo-Keynesian models allow for price flexibility, although nominal rigidities remain if prices do not adjust completely to clear markets. Price flexibility, even if it is limited in the short term, will tend to narrow the range of values taken by fiscal multipliers, and will, in particular, limit the influence of the exchange-rate regime. In an open economy with a flexible exchange rate, the extent of crowding-out depends upon the response of domestic prices to changes in the exchange rate. In particular, if domestic prices move with the exchange rate, crowding-out will be less than with price rigidity, since appreciation of the exchange rate will lower prices. With a fixed exchange rate, the current account will deteriorate in response to price increases via a real appreciation of the exchange rate, and there will be more crowding-out than with price rigidity.

In addition, changes in interest rates, the exchange rate, and prices can influence crowding-out via wealth effects on aggregate demand. This will be the case in particular if consumption depends upon current financial wealth. An increase in interest rates will generally reduce the nominal value of financial assets, as will an appreciation of the exchange rate in the case of foreign-currency-denominated assets. For households and firms that are net creditors these wealth effects will reinforce the crowding-out effects through interest rates and exchange rates described above, and will reduce fiscal multipliers further. The impact of higher prices is more ambiguous, since they can have opposite effects on nominal and real wealth.

Finally, dynamic effects of fiscal policy have to be considered (Auerbach and Kotlikoff, 1987). If crowding-out takes longer to manifest than the direct impact effect of a fiscal expansion, fiscal multipliers are likely to be relatively large in the short term but then to decline over time. In particular, the wage-price loop, which determines the rapidity of wage increases in response to a fiscal expansion, and the responsiveness of trade volumes to changes in the domestic currency price of imports and exports, will influence the size of short-term fiscal multipliers.

Demand-side effects on growth of fiscal policy: non-Keynesian effects

Non-Keynesian effects of fiscal policy emerge from new classical models which address the well-known shortcomings of the Keynesian approach, and in particular its lack of microeconomic foundations. While new classical models place considerable emphasis on the supply-side effects of fiscal policy, the focus here is on the features of some new classical models (that is, those that do not assume full market clearing) with demand-side implications. An important consequence of non-Keynesian effects is that they can lead to negative fiscal multipliers, which at last could make fiscal adjustments have an expansionary effect of economic activity, instead of their traditional recessionary impact.

While some variants of the Keynesian approach recognize the role of expectations (for example, on consumption in life cycle and permanent income models), they typically rely on adaptive expectations. By comparison, rational expectations tend to bring forward adjustments in variables that would occur more progressively with adaptive expectations. Thus the longer-term effects of fiscal policy will matter even in the short term, and in this connection the distinction between temporary and permanent policy changes is important. For example, while a temporary fiscal expansion that has no long-term effects will not influence expectations, a permanent fiscal expansion can add to crowding-out (possibly to an extent that fiscal multipliers turn negative) because households and firms will expect that an initial increase in interest rates and appreciation of the exchange rate will persist and could even become larger (Krugman and Obstfeld, 1987). The opposite effect applies then for a fiscal adjustment that is perceived as permanent. As will be shown later, empirical evidence suggests that a crowding-in following the episodes of fiscal adjustment in the European Union occurred as a result of the perception by private agents that consolidations required to join EMU would be permanent.

The Keynesian approach is based on an assumption that consumption is related to current income. If consumers are Ricardian, in the sense that they are forward-looking, and are fully aware of the government's intertemporal budget constraint, they will anticipate that a tax cut today, financed by higher debt, will result in higher taxes being imposed on themselves and/or their children in the future. Permanent income is therefore unaffected, and in the absence of liquidity constraints and with perfect capital markets, consumption will not change (Barro, 1974). Thus, there is Ricardian equivalence between taxes and debt. Ricardian equivalence implies that a reduction in government saving resulting from a tax cut is fully offset by higher private saving and bequests, and that therefore aggregate demand is not affected. The fiscal multiplier is zero in this case. Nevertheless, if taxes are not lump-sum but progressive, financing the deficit through tax increases or debt will not have the same impact. Finally, it is important to note that Ricardian equivalence is based on strong assumptions. Thus short time horizons, less than perfect foresight, partial liquidity constraints, imperfect capital markets, and non-altruistic desire to pass some of the current fiscal burden to future generations can re-establish a stronger link between fiscal policy and consumption. Consequently, the practical significance of Ricardian equivalence is problematic, at least in its perfect form.

Finally, another, perhaps more important, channel through which debt accumulation may affect the fiscal multiplier relates to risk premia on interest rates. As government debt builds up with fiscal expansion(s), risk premia that reflect the mounting risk of default or increasing inflation risk will reinforce crowding-out effects through interest rates (Miller, Skidelsky and Weller, 1990). Under such circumstances, a temporary fiscal expansion will be more effective than a permanent one, because it poses less risk of undermining debt sustainability. In this context, policy credibility is crucial. If there is little faith in the government's ability to reverse a temporary spending increase or tax cut because it lacks a track record of fiscal prudence, and the expectation is that a fiscal expansion which is announced to be temporary will in fact turn out to be permanent, then interest rate will most likely reflect risk premia. Sizable risk premia represent perhaps the clearest reason that fiscal multipliers could turn negative, because private spending responds positively to a credible commitment to debt reduction and a lowering of risk premia. This is one of the main explanations for expansionary fiscal contractions given by Giavazzi and Pagano (1990) and Alesina and Perotti (1997a). As this chapter will also show, it was in those countries that started fiscal adjustments in conditions of fiscal stress and subsequently with high risk premia that decisive cuts in welfare spending sent a signal of credible commitment to deficit reduction and produced a crowding-in effect that resulted in non-Keynesian effects and expansionary fiscal adjustments.

Supply-side effects on growth of fiscal policy

The analysis of the stabilization role of fiscal policy traditionally focuses on its demand-side effects, while supply-side effects are seen as more important over the longer term. However, the distinction between short-term demand-side concerns and longer-term supply-side issues may not be as clear. If the economy is operating at full capacity and productive capacity cannot be increased in the short term, a fiscal expansion (which may be undertaken on the assumption that there is excess capacity or for political reasons) has to be crowded-out. Only policies that promote supply-side responses can address capacity constraints, and their impact is primarily longer-term in nature. However, supply-side effects of fiscal policy can have short-term demand-side consequences because of expectations that longer-term growth will be higher. If a fiscal adjustment is imparted through tax increases and spending cuts that are good for the supply side, this will tend to decrease fiscal multipliers, and the adjustment will be expansionary.

In assessing the long-term impact of fiscal policy, attention should thus be paid to the way in which changes to labour income taxes affect the supply of labour, and changes to capital taxes affect saving and investment. The location of internationally mobile labour and capital can also be affected. In the final analysis, however, the impact of tax changes on the supply of labour and capital, and thus on growth, is an empirical issue about which clear-cut conclusions have yet to be provided (Blundell and MacCurdy, 1999). Attention should be also paid to the way in which spending on public goods and other goods with positive externalities can lead to higher growth. As has already been explained in Chapter 2, this is demonstrated in models where the government invests in both physical and human capital (Murphy, Shleifer, and Vishny, 1989; Lucas, 1988), typically an option that social democratic parties have embraced since the late 1970s in Europe.

Changing the emphasis, some attention has been given to the way in which labour market characteristics might influence whether or not changes in taxes and spending can have non-Keynesian effects through supply-side channels. In particular, Alesina and Perotti (1997a) note that increases in labour income taxes can have a significant negative supply-side impact in unionized, imperfectly competitive labour markets where before-tax wages, and hence labour costs, also increase to reflect the higher taxes. However, they argue that an agreement on wage moderation with trade unions could limit the increase in before-tax wages, or inflationary pressures during a fiscal contraction accompanied by a sharp devaluation, thus reducing the fiscal multiplier and possibly contributing to non-Keynesian effects. Such an agreement is more likely with highly centralized unions. Lane and Perotti (1996) also argue that reductions in government employment (which reduce labour demand, weaken unions, lower wages, and thus increase profitability) can be a source of non-Keynesian effects.

At this point, a final word should be said about new classical models. The distinctive feature of fully-fledged new classical models is that prices clear markets, so that fluctuations in output are the result of supply-side shocks and not of changes in aggregate demand. One implication of new classical models, first highlighted by Lucas (1975) and Sargent and Wallace (1975), is that fully anticipated policies affecting aggregate demand (but not aggregate supply) have no effect on growth either in the short term or the longer term. Only unanticipated policies (which reflect either surprises by the government or imperfect information) have an effect, which emerges entirely on the supply side. This does not mean that these models are silent on fiscal policy. However, they focus on the design of optimal fiscal policy, as distinct from the impact of fiscal policy on economic activity (see Lucas and Stokey, 1983; and Chari and Kehoe, 1998).

Despite all these new theoretical approaches explaining both the demand- and supply-side mechanisms that may be behind the non-Keynesian effects of fiscal adjustments, the characteristics of expansionary fiscal consolidations are not completely clear. The description of these characteristics has remained a matter for empirical work. Some studies, such as Cour, Dubois, Mahfouz and Pisani-Ferry (1996), Giavazzi and Pagano (1996), and Giavazzi, Japelli and Pagano (2000) find that large consolidations are most effective in increasing growth. While Alesina and Perotti (1997) and subsequent studies by the same authors emphasize instead the composition of the adjustment, and in particular the gains from cutting transfers and other forms of unproductive spending, McDermott and Wescott (1996) conclude that both the size and the composition of fiscal consolidations are important, which is precisely what this chapter finds too.

Initial fiscal conditions and the other economic policies that accompany fiscal consolidation may also play a role. While some studies find no evidence that these things are important, other works affirm that the initial level of debt, a currency depreciation preceding the consolidation, wage restraint, and accompanying structural reforms, are all crucial factors that can make fiscal consolidations expansionary or contractionary.[3]

The effects of fiscal policy on income distribution

The theoretical and empirical literature that links fiscal policy to growth is abundant, but it is almost non-existent with regard to fiscal policy and income distribution.[4] Nonetheless, the idea that a trade-off could exist between policies that promote economic growth and those that promote fairer income distribution is an old hypothesis, that still seems to hold pretty well today when fiscal policy is under discussion.

The reasoning behind this trade-off is that if the state is going to intervene to redistribute income, it will impose taxes that will distort the sound functioning of efficient markets, which will in turn discourage private investment and have a decisive negative impact on productivity and economic growth (Przeworski, 1986; Boix, 1996). Therefore public transfers of income and capital from the richer strata to the poorer strata of any economy would only be sustainable in the long run as long as the associated taxes do not damage domestic productivity and the capital's net rate of return. If the productivity and the rate of return are positive and higher than in other countries with lower taxes, investors will still remain in the country.

Both conditions are necessary to maintain growth in the long run with considerable public spending. In fact, these are the conditions that have supported the generous welfare states in Europe until today.

The existence of this trade-off between growth and redistribution was widely accepted under the paradigm of neoclassical economics up to the point that socialist governments in the 1920s were willing to abandon redistributive policies if they harmed the medium-term rate of economic growth (Boix, 1996). The substitution of this paradigm by the Keynesian one offered a way to escape that zero-sum game. Keynesian economics affirmed that economic growth was less a matter of supply conditions, and more a matter of aggregate demand. By stimulating aggregate demand, output would grow, and full employment could be reached, without very strong costs in terms of inflation. The combination of full employment policies and public spending expansion to stimulate domestic consumption, offered a combination of policies that were positive for both growth and equality.

Once these policies proved no longer applicable in the 1970s, basically because of the induced rigidities that they had generated in the aggregate supply, the neoclassical paradigm came to dominate the landscape of economic ideas once again. EMU was conceived under its direct influence and, as the empirical evidence in this chapter will show, it has coincided with a rebirth of the old trade-off.

With aggregate demand locked by means of a supranationalized monetary policy and the 3 per cent deficit limit to fiscal policy, economic growth has become once again a question of supply-side economics. For social democratic governments this means intervening in the provision of human and physical capital. For more conservative governments this means lowering the taxes that are a disincentive to private investment, and reducing labour costs. In this framework again, direct transfers of income to the worse off (the very basis of the welfare state) are considerably restricted by how much they damage the rate of return on capital, and how much they affect productivity.

When too much social spending reduces both, economic growth will be negatively affected and redistribution policies will be unsustainable. In such circumstances, expenditure-based fiscal adjustments that arrive in moments when budget deficits are harming productivity and private investment, are likely to increase economic growth (via positive supply-side effects associated to a crowding-in of private investment and consumption). However, this will be achieved at the cost of increasing income inequality.

Only the IMF and the World Bank have systematically studied the effect of stabilization policies (that include serious fiscal adjustments) in developing countries on both growth and equality.

Their studies have almost always concluded that successful stabilization experiences have increased economic growth and have reduced inequalities, normally as a 'collateral effect' of the general economic stabilization, and sometimes also helped by World Bank's poverty reduction programmes (Tanzi, Chu, and Gupta, 1999). Nevertheless, the story for industrial countries seems to be somewhat different. Among the very few studies that have addressed the equity dimension of fiscal adjustments in advanced economies is the work by Ford (1998) and Smeeding (1997, 2000), who find that recent fiscal consolidations in OECD countries have run in parallel with widening distribution of incomes and poverty increases. Whether such findings can be confirmed or refuted through a systematic empirical analysis is the subject of the rest of the chapter.

6.2 The 'economic trade-off hypothesis'

What the rest of the chapter will test is what we referred to in Chapters 1 and 2 as the '*economic trade-off hypothesis*'. This hypothesis stated that fiscal adjustments do not have the same impact on growth and income distribution, especially if these adjustments have relied on spending cuts. In fact, this '*economic trade-off hypothesis*' can be split into two complementary hypotheses.

- *Hypothesis regarding the economic consequences of fiscal adjustments*: H_0 (null hypothesis): the effect of fiscal adjustments on growth and income distribution are not the same (having an opposite sign); H_1 (alternative hypothesis): these effects are the same on both growth and income distribution
- *Hypothesis regarding the effect of different fiscal adjustment strategies*: H_0 (null hypothesis): expenditure-based and revenue-based fiscal adjustments have different results in terms of economic growth and income distribution; H_1 (alternative hypothesis): expenditure-based and revenue-based adjustments have the same effects on both variables.

In order to test these hypotheses, this chapter applies two simple but complementary analyses:

- **Means analysis:** This methodology selects a sample of adjustment episodes and looks at the evolution of economic growth and income distribution (plus another set of economic indicators) in the aftermath of each episode. To put it in context, average figures for all episodes in the sample are compared in the periods immediately preceding and following the adjustment episodes.[5]

- **Parametric estimation**: This second methodological approach is based on bilateral correlations and linear regressions of the main variables, using all datapoints in the sample. For the regression analysis, the chapter takes GDP growth rate as the dependent variable and includes the annual change of the (primary) budget balance among a wider set of independent variables and controls. In order to test the trade-off hypothesis, this chapter also estimates a model for the determinants of income distribution, including an indicator of the composition of fiscal adjustments among the set of independent variables. Because this is a chapter about the immediate economic consequences of fiscal consolidations, both parametric models are conceived to capture short-run interactions and causality between the main variables, and do not focus on long-term dynamics that are difficult to attribute to the effect of isolated fiscal adjustments.

Both methodologies complement each other. While the analysis of means deals with episodes of fiscal adjustment of more than one year, the parametric analysis does not introduce any criteria for the selection of these episodes and simply links annual changes in the budget balance between year $t-1$ and year t to the observed variations in the rate of growth or the inequality indexes in the same year or in subsequent years ($t+1$, $t+2$, ..., $t+n$). In addition, while the means analysis allows for a comprehensive description of the contemporaneous evolution of a wider set of economic variables, the parametric analysis is restricted to studying the determinants of growth and income distribution determinants. Most importantly, the parametric analysis tests for relationships of causality, which can only be stated tentatively using the analysis of means or bilateral correlations.

A final word should be said about the research design before reporting the results obtained from the application of both analyses. This chapter is not about the effect of income distribution on growth,[6] but about the effects of fiscal adjustments on economic growth and income distribution. The chapter does not try to establish any causality between the evolution of economic growth and the previous or simultaneous evolution of income distribution. Instead, this chapter tests the parallel effect that fiscal adjustments may have on growth and on income distribution. This is the reason why the parametric analysis does not estimate a model for the interaction between growth and income distribution, but does estimate a separate model for the determinants of each.

6.3 The economic impact of fiscal adjustments: means analysis

From the 615 observations of the panel of 15 EU member states between 1960 and 2000, this section will work with the sub-sample of 53 consolidation episodes already used in Chapter 4. Remember, that episodes were then selected according to the following criterion: fiscal adjustment episodes are those years in which the cyclically adjusted primary budget balance (CAPBB) improved by at least 1.5 per cent of GDP one year and were followed by a positive figure in the subsequent or preceding year; or when the CAPBB improved at least 1.25 per cent of GDP during two consecutive years.[7] Using this standard definition to select fiscal adjustment episodes resulted in a sample of 53 cases that could be divided into 28 revenue-based adjustments and 25 expenditure-based adjustments.[8]

The means analysis consists of looking at the average values of a wide range of economic variables two years before adjustment, during the adjustment episode, and two years after the adjustment. The main reason for looking only at two-year intervals before and after consolidation episodes is that, in the longer term, the relationship between fiscal adjustments and other economic variables is more difficult to identify, since the latter may reflect the impact of many other factors (Alesina and Ardagna, 1998). Also, in the section that focuses on the 1990s (a decade that concentrates 18 of the 53 episodes), the two-year interval is motivated by the need to keep as many data points as possible to perform the analysis.

Results for the whole sample, 1960–2000

Results in Table 6.1 show that revenue-based adjustments typically increase revenues from direct taxes to maintain public spending in public transfers, public wages and public investment. On the contrary, expenditure-based adjustments rely mostly on cuts in transfers, wages and investment, and only increase direct taxes marginally during the adjustment. This slight increase in revenues coming from direct taxation is, however, immediately reversed, once the adjustment comes to an end.

It is important to note that expenditure-based adjustments take place when the initial fiscal conditions in terms of public deficit and debt are very deteriorated.[9] The debt to GDP ratio, the level of expenditures and the overall budget deficit are systematically higher in the two years previous to expenditure-based adjustments. This implies that governments facing strong fiscal imbalances are more likely to undertake a fiscal adjustment based on spending cuts.

The amelioration of the debt-to-GDP ratio, the reduction of total expenditures, and the improvement of the budget balance is remarkable after expenditure-based adjustments, while it is more moderate after revenue-based ones. In the latter cases, once the budget deficit is under control and the consolidation episode comes to an end, the increase in revenues that made the adjustment possible is then used to finance further increases in public transfers, wages and investment. As shown in Chapter 4, these two different strategies could be generally associated with governments that have opposite economic preferences regarding the role of the public sector in the economy.

Table 6.1 Initial fiscal conditions, budget composition and fiscal adjustment strategies, 1960–2000

	Non-Adjustment	Adjustment					
		Revenue-based			Expenditure-based		
Fiscal policy		*Before*	*During*	*After*	*Before*	*During*	*After*
Debt ratio	47.44	55.05	61.60	60.37	59.62	69.26	65.11
	(28.64)	(33.47)	(35.25)	(38.98)	(25.86)	(24.22)	(25.05)
Δ Debt ratio	0.87	2.32	2.34	1.03	4.36	1.67	0.04
	(4.03)	(3.70)	(3.65)	(4.08)	(6.11)	(4.81)	(4.95)
Budget balance	−1.60	−4.41	−3.41	−2.95	−6.34	−4.11	−3.33
	(3.72)	(5.12)	(4.87)	(5.16)	(4.77)	(3.91)	(5.13)
Δ Budget balance	−0.29	−0.99	0.96	−0.32	−1.03	1.53	0.19
	(1.49)	(1.89)	(1.31)	(1.63)	(2.19)	(1.62)	(1.57)
Total revenues	39.19	40.89	43.22	44.89	46.18	46.48	44.09
	(9.67)	(7.71)	(6.83)	(7.53)	(9.98)	(9.77)	(10.08)
Δ Total revenues	0.36	0.58	1.41	−0.08	0.22	0.78	−0.42
	(1.22)	(1.82)	(1.10)	(1.41)	(1.27)	(1.22)	(1.14)
Total direct taxes	12.10	12.60	13.59	14.04	13.24	14.07	13.27
	(5.72)	(5.04)	(4.41)	(5.32)	(7.02)	(6.66)	(6.67)
Δ T. direct taxes	0.20	0.17	0.56	0.01	−0.03	0.31	−0.23
	(1.24)	(0.87)	(0.88)	(0.95)	(0.73)	(0.87)	(0.82)
Total expenditures	41.08	45.34	46.50	47.75	52.30	51.59	48.12
	(10.43)	(7.56)	(7.05)	(7.08)	(8.50)	(8.46)	(7.27)
Δ Total expenditures	0.68	1.41	0.41	0.05	1.46	−0.81	−0.18
	(1.88)	(2.57)	(1.32)	(1.67)	(2.62)	(1.78)	(1.65)
Total transfers	14.60	15.75	16.46	16.23	17.75	17.25	16.46
	(5.02)	(5.54)	(5.50)	(4.49)	(4.90)	(4.85)	(4.31)
Δ T. transfers	0.33	0.43	0.42	0.22	0.40	−0.34	−0.28
	(1.40)	(1.32)	(0.57)	(1.35)	(1.11)	(1.52)	(1.66)
Total public wages	11.26	11.28	11.28	11.63	12.67	12.37	11.68
	(2.84)	(2.00)	(1.95)	(2.45)	(3.44)	(3.35)	(2.75)
Δ T. public wages	0.23	0.13	0.06	0.03	0.13	−0.29	0.04
	(1.03)	(0.52)	(0.43)	(0.47)	(0.54)	(0.41)	(0.43)
Total pub. investment	3.33	3.54	3.28	3.42	3.48	2.82	2.72
	(1.02)	(1.26)	(1.20)	(1.08)	(1.09)	(0.92)	(1.08)
Δ T. pub investment	0.06	0.06	−0.10	0.03	−0.01	−0.24	0.02
	(0.51)	(0.47)	(0.28)	(0.34)	(0.54)	(0.35)	(0.33)

Source: Own elaboration using data from AMECO (2003).

However, these different strategies may not be neutral (Garcia and Hénin, 1999), meaning that they may not have the same economic results.

As shown in Table 6.2, GDP growth, unemployment, inflation, and inequality[10] behave very differently depending on the type of adjustment implemented. Starting with initial conditions, it is worth noting that GDP growth is lower before expenditure-based adjustments than before revenue-based ones, and both are smaller than during years of non-adjustment. The same happens with unemployment and inflation rates. This means that

Table 6.2 Macroeconomic outcomes of fiscal adjustments, 1960–2000

	Non-Adjustment	*Adjustment*					
		Revenue-based			*Expenditure-based*		
Macroeconomic outcomes		*Before*	*During*	*After*	*Before*	*During*	*After*
Real GDP growth	3.72	2.19	1.61	3.16	1.73	2.46	3.36
	(2.75)	(2.18)	(1.84)	(2.39)	(3.08)	(1.94)	(2.19)
Δ Real GDP growth	−0.11	−0.50	−0.11	0.50	−0.19	0.50	0.56
	(2.96)	(2.63)	(2.29)	(2.82)	(2.83)	(2.19)	(2.10)
Unemployment rate	5.32	6.14	7.02	6.96	8.76	9.08	8.41
	(4.15)	(3.20)	(3.35)	(3.48)	(5.48)	(4.85)	(4.65)
Δ Unemployment rate	0.08	0.25	0.55	−0.02	0.63	0.04	−0.45
	(0.90)	(0.70)	(1.04)	(0.68)	(1.47)	(1.15)	(0.88)
Price index	73.33	91.76	116.56	128.86	117.89	133.50	120.93
	(64.86)	(64.47)	(106.23)	(113.35)	(72.94)	(46.56)	(61.91)
Δ Prices	3.71	6.80	7.03	6.70	9.36	7.53	6.75
	(4.43)	(7.93)	(7.34)	(8.94)	(9.84)	(7.92)	(9.02)
Gini coefficient	34.55	29.86	30.90	31.51	30.84	33.31	34.15
	(7.09)	(6.04)	(5.56)	(5.19)	(5.22)	(4.46)	(3.60)
Δ Gini coefficient	−0.12	0.04	0.10	0.19	0.03	0.31	0.47
	(1.34)	(0.93)	(1.15)	(1.32)	(1.30)	(1.23)	(1.22)
Theil index (c=1)	32.64	31.23	32.33	33.87	31.98	33.76	35.45
	(8.01)	(5.99)	(5.22)	(5.43)	(4.98)	(4.87)	(4.54)
Δ Theil index	0.15	0.05	0.14	0.21	0.09	0.42	0.58
	(1.08)	(1.19)	(1.01)	(1.02)	(1.10)	(1.07)	(1.00)
Ratio D9/D1	2.63	2.67	2.88	2.93	2.72	2.94	3.02
	(0.66)	(0.45)	(0.67)	(0.55)	(0.71)	(0.66)	(0.54)
Δ Ratio D9/D1	0.03	0.02	0.04	0.06	0.03	0.07	0.11
	(0.11)	(0.06)	(0.22)	(0.11)	(0.15)	(0.10)	(0.18)

Source: Own elaboration using data from AMECO (2003).

governments decide to undertake expenditure-based adjustments when domestic macroeconomic conditions have worsened considerably, probably because it is only then that public opinion is willing to accept the welfare cuts associated with expenditure-based adjustments. As an example, the average unemployment rate before expenditure-based adjustments is 2.5 percentage points higher than before revenue-based ones. For inflation rate and GDP growth, these differences are around 3 per cent and 0.5 per cent, higher and lower respectively.

Increased growth follows after both revenue-based and expenditure-based consolidations. However, during revenue-based consolidations there is a typical Keynesian temporary recession that increases unemployment, and reduces the growth rate, while the opposite happens during expenditure-based adjustments. During and after the latter, growth increases and unemployment is reduced. In the same way, inflation remains constant during and after revenue-based consolidations, but decreases considerably in cases of expenditure-based adjustments.

If expenditure-based adjustments perform better than revenue-based ones in terms of growth, unemployment and inflation, they also have higher costs in terms of income inequality than do revenue-based ones.

As Table 6.2 shows, all indexes show that inequality increases during and after both types of fiscal adjustments, but it is during and after expenditure-based adjustments when these inequality indexes grow more, indicating a worsening in income distribution. These results confirm the latest contributions in this area, which pointed toward important increases in income inequality by the end of the 1990s, regardless of the type of index employed to measure income distribution.[11]

So far, the empirical evidence presented in Tables 6.1 and 6.2 supports the argument that expansionary fiscal adjustments occur primarily when initial fiscal and economic conditions have worsened considerably, and when the adjustment takes place on the spending side.[12] These expenditure-based adjustments, although they can be expansionary and increase economic growth, have important costs in terms of increased income inequality.

It remains unclear, however, whether the budget's composition and initial economic conditions are the only factors behind expansionary fiscal adjustments; it may be the case that the size of the adjustment[13] and the accompanying monetary conditions can also play a role in generating economic expansion. Furthermore, it remains to be clarified whether these expansionary fiscal adjustments work primarily through supply-side or demand-side mechanisms.

With regard to the size of the adjustment, it may actually be a factor generating expansionary fiscal consolidations, since the differences between the figures for the budget balance 'after' and 'before' the adjustment are bigger in the case of expenditure-based expansionary fiscal adjustments than for revenue-based ones. Nevertheless, this effect does not seem to be very important because the differences are small in comparison: expenditure-based adjustments reduce the budget deficit by 2 average percentage points, while revenue-based adjustments reduce the budget deficit by 1.5 percentage points.

The question of accompanying monetary conditions does seem to play a role too, but again a very limited one. As shown in Table 6.3, a nominal devaluation (increase in the exchange rate) accompanies both types of fiscal adjustments. This devaluation is, however, maintained after expenditure-based consolidations but reversed after revenue-based ones. With respect to short-term real interest rates, there seems to be no difference in their behaviour across types of adjustment, since they remain more or less constant before and during the adjustment, and they only fall after expenditure-based ones, reflecting the lower risk premia.

Table 6.3 Monetary policy and fiscal adjustments, 1960–2000

	Non-Adjustment	*Adjustment*					
		Revenue based			*Expenditure based*		
Monetary policy		*Before*	*During*	*After*	*Before*	*During*	*After*
Real interest rate (ShTerm)	1.85	3.02	3.11	3.11	3.04	2.95	2.62
	(3.73)	(4.64)	(3.61)	(3.60)	(4.71)	(2.83)	(3.44)
Δ Real interest rate	0.07	−0.44	−0.11	0.41	0.30	−0.17	−0.02
	(2.63)	(3.83)	(2.15)	(1.99)	(2.52)	(2.53)	(2.31)
Real exchange rate	99.06	101.18	102.75	101.11	97.19	97.89	96.62
	(15.51)	(14.56)	(15.22)	(12.92)	(12.41)	(12.98)	(13.66)
Δ Real exchange rate	−0.07	−0.27	0.50	−0.69	−0.12	0.64	0.87
	(5.02)	(5.32)	(7.56)	(4.63)	(6.84)	(6.12)	(4.37)

Source: Own elaboration using data from AMECO (2003).

The story of expansionary fiscal adjustments, therefore, seems to be based more on the composition of the budget than on the size of the budget cut or the simultaneous expansion of monetary conditions. It is true that monetary policy was slightly more relaxed around expenditure-based expansionary adjustments, but this may also reflect the fact that almost all expenditure-based fiscal consolidations that took place in the 1990s started right after the devaluations of 1992–93.

With the description of the macroeconomic results that different types of fiscal adjustments bring about, and the type of initial and accompanying fiscal and monetary conditions influencing those final outcomes having been made clear, the last step in this analysis is to investigate the channels through which expansionary fiscal adjustments work. As can be observed in Table 6.4, economic expansion after expenditure-based fiscal consolidations is mediated by a remarkable crowding-in of the private sector in the form of increasing consumption and a private investment boom.

This crowding-in is also present in revenue-based adjustments but is much less significant.[14] This important crowding-in of the private sector in expansionary expenditure-based consolidations is accompanied by higher profits and lower labour costs, which are eventually translated into an improved trade balance. The argument behind the reduction in labour costs that improves the budget balance that increases profits and investment, thus contributing to an increase in the level of output is as follows: during expenditure-based adjustments, the government wage bill is reduced and there are no increases in direct taxes (that principally rely on the labour factor). Both measures have the effect of reducing labour costs directly and indirectly by undermining the bargaining power of labour unions.

Table 6.4 Microeconomic outcomes, trade policy outcomes, and fiscal adjustments, 1960–2000

	Non-Adjustment	Adjustment					
		Revenue based			Expenditure based		
Microeconomic outcomes		Before	During	After	Before	During	After
Private consumption	57.80	57.93	58.32	58.09	57.95	58.39	58.97
	(6.34)	(6.02)	(6.00)	(6.54)	(6.55)	(5.95)	(6.74)
Δ Private consumption	−0.09	−0.07	0.19	0.03	−0.02	0.23	0.37
	(1.16)	(1.36)	(1.27)	(0.85)	(1.02)	(1.18)	(1.02)
Private investment	18.66	17.63	18.22	18.01	17.35	18.16	19.26
	(3.09)	(3.58)	(3.11)	(2.34)	(3.59)	(3.13)	(2.54)
Δ Private investment	0.02	−0.03	0.49	−0.40	0.05	0.55	0.76
	(1.40)	(1.56)	(1.19)	(1.77)	(1.94)	(1.11)	(1.58)
Non-residential construction	15.56	15.03	15.24	15.49	15.47	15.88	16.02
	(2.98)	(3.88)	(3.01)	(3.85)	(3.21)	(3.85)	(2.67)
Δ Non-residential construction	0.14	0.09	0.12	0.13	0.10	0.13	0.16
	(0.99)	(1.10)	(1.03)	(1.32)	(1.59)	(1.16)	(1.08)
Equipment	21.86	21.56	21.77	21.93	21.90	21.99	22.31
	(3.78)	(3.96)	(3.24)	(3.65)	(3.22)	(3.12)	(3.89)
Δ Equipment	0.08	0.05	0.05	0.06	0.07	0.09	0.12
	(0.11)	(0.17)	(0.23)	(0.56)	(0.22)	(0.31)	(0.64)
Labour costs index	107.08	108.88	108.02	105.43	108.20	104.86	101.83
	(8.28)	(8.07)	(7.45)	(6.85)	(7.50)	(5.85)	(6.77)
Δ Labour costs	−0.13	0.48	−0.49	−1.39	−0.98	−1.85	−1.54
	(2.98)	(4.25)	(2.32)	(2.19)	(2.69)	(2.26)	(2.08)
Profits share	31.84	31.77	31.06	31.88	31.10	32.31	32.92
	(4.25)	(4.13)	(3.21)	(4.66)	(3.59)	(4.11)	(4.22)
Δ Profits share	0.04	0.05	0.02	0.09	0.03	0.72	0.31
	(1.10)	(0.98)	(1.04)	(1.17)	(1.33)	(1.49)	(1.11)
Trade policy outcomes							
Imports	29.60	35.99	35.50	36.60	36.34	35.86	37.44
	(22.28)	(27.47)	(25.15)	(31.70)	(26.77)	(17.67)	(21.29)
Δ Imports	0.80	0.47	0.33	1.54	0.74	0.94	1.10
	(1.71)	(1.84)	(1.83)	(2.08)	(2.53)	(1.32)	(1.57)
Exports	21.46	24.06	24.13	26.01	25.80	28.51	29.08
	(14.53)	(13.83)	(13.17)	(14.83)	(16.87)	(13.32)	(16.26)
Δ Exports	0.65	0.34	0.61	0.77	0.87	1.08	1.15
	(1.33)	(1.83)	(1.25)	(1.88)	(1.87)	(1.26)	(1.42)
Trade balance	−0.36	−1.41	−0.25	−0.30	−1.77	0.67	0.68
	(5.11)	(6.54)	(5.01)	(5.33)	(6.81)	(5.27)	(5.33)
Δ Trade balance	−0.08	−0.20	−0.02	−0.11	0.31	0.95	0.20
	(2.00)	(3.68)	(2.14)	(1.91)	(2.22)	(1.82)	(1.72)

Source: Own elaboration using data from AMECO (2003)

The truth is that this mechanism of diminishing labour costs that trigger expansionary fiscal adjustments should not be linked exclusively to expenditure-based fiscal adjustments. In fact, this mechanism would also work for revenue-based fiscal adjustments as well, if trade unions internalized the government's budget constraint, or if they did not ask for an increase in real salaries when taxes grew. This only happens in countries such as the United States or Canada, where trade unions are very weak, or in countries such as in Scandinavia, where the high degree of corporatism and a centralized wage bargaining process have traditionally made trade unions assume the government's budget constraint. Such labour market institutions allow these governments to balance their budgets via revenues without damaging labour costs, domestic productivity and economic growth (Alesina and Ardagna, 1998; Alesina, Perotti and Tavares 1998; Garrett 1998, and Esping-Andersen, 1999). In other countries, trade unions are strong enough to protest and demand higher salaries, but not enough to be able to control all wage demands across different sectors of the economy.[15]

Summing up, what the empirical evidence of this section reveals can be regrouped into three sets of conclusions:

(1) In the short run, the composition of fiscal adjustments is a crucial factor determining the economic consequences of consolidation episodes. Expenditure-based adjustments normally take place in situations of fiscal stress, with low GDP growth, high debt levels, strong budget deficits and poor initial economic performance. When these consolidations succeed in reducing the most rigid budget items, namely public transfers and public wages, they are expansionary. Their economic effects are to increase GDP growth and reduce inflation and unemployment rates, but they do so at the cost of increasing income inequality more than revenue-based adjustments do. Note that these results are important for two strands of the economic literature: that on the growth-equality trade-off, and that related to growth theory.

(2) When fiscal adjustments are expansionary, non-Keynesian effects work through both demand-side and supply-side mechanisms.
   (a) With respect to demand-side mechanisms, this section has provided evidence of the existence of *wealth effects*, given that a cut in public consumption that is perceived as permanent increases private consumption, because households discount future higher levels of disposable income as a result of the expected reduction in taxes;
   (b) There are also *credibility effects* that benefit both private consumption and private investment. When debt is high, interest rates are high and any deficit reduction, mostly if it is based on spending cuts, reduces the risk premia and therefore interest rates, facilitating the crowding-in of private consumption and investment,[16]
   (c) And with respect to the supply side, the reduction in the government wage bill in imperfectly unionized labour markets proves crucial to reduce labour costs, to increase business profits, and to improve the trade balance, thus contributing to economic expansion.

(3) Finally, the choice that governments planning to undertake a fiscal adjustment face seems to lie between two extremes: one option is to

undertake a revenue-based adjustment that may not be so expansionary but that will prevent income inequality from rising dramatically; an alternative option is to pursue an expenditure-based strategy that may be expansionary but at the cost of substantially increased inequalities. As shown in Chapters 3 and 4, this decision is heavily influenced by the unemployment rate, by the structural budget balance in previous years, by the electoral calendar, by cabinet fragmentation and, most importantly, by the ideology of the party in government.

Results for the 1990s

During the 1990s, the story of expansionary fiscal adjustments depicted in the previous section applies almost exactly. Revenue-based adjustments and expenditure-based ones had characteristics similar to those in previous decades. Likewise, they also had opposite economic consequences, in the short run. While expenditure-based adjustments in the 1990s showed better chances of increasing economic growth, revenue-based ones proved less likely to increase income inequality (see Table 6.5).

The driving forces leading to expansionary fiscal adjustments during the 1990s were also a mix of supply-side and demand-side mechanisms of wealth effects, investment boom and credibility effects. The process of strong deficit reduction in Europe and the downward convergence of interest rates maintained inflation at historically low levels, and this curbed unit labour costs downward following expenditure-based adjustments. The trade balance improved, and private investment and consumption boomed, increasing GDP growth rate in the EU.[17]

6.4 The economic impact of fiscal adjustments: parametric analysis during the 1990s

Although the means analysis in the previous section already seems to confirm the '*economic trade-off hypothesis*' (in its two formulations), the statistical robustness of an averages-based analysis needs to be enhanced with complementary techniques that establish correlations among variables and directions of causality.

Simple Spearman-correlations between the two major measures of fiscal policy (the annual change in the primary budget balance, corrected and non-corrected for the economic cycle), and the four measures of economic policy outcomes (GDP growth rate, unemployment rate, inflation rate and the Gini coefficient) are reported in Table 6.6.

As expected, the main correlations among important variables are statistically significant: economic growth is negatively associated with fiscal adjustments, specially if they are strong. Nevertheless, economic growth is positively correlated with better budget quality,[18] which seems to confirm a relationship between adjustments based on spending cuts and economic

Table 6.5 Macroeconomic outcomes of fiscal adjustments, 1990–2000

	Non-Adjustment	*Adjustment*					
		Revenue-based			*Expenditure-based*		
Macroeconomic outcomes		*Before*	*During*	*After*	*Before*	*During*	*After*
Real GDP growth	2.85	1.96	2.26	2.66	1.74	2.56	3.61
	(2.55)	(1.65)	(2.00)	(1.50)	(4.04)	(1.93)	(2.36)
Δ Real GDP growth	−0.02	0.03	−0.04	0.25	0.42	0.13	0.30
	(2.26)	(2.70)	(1.76)	(2.37)	(3.13)	(1.72)	(1.88)
Unemployment rate	8.45	8.24	8.42	9.10	9.35	8.84	8.82
	(4.62)	(3.07)	(2.65)	(2.83)	(5.70)	(5.01)	(4.76)
Δ Unemployment rate	−0.08	0.21	0.21	−0.09	0.55	−0.08	−0.67
	(1.25)	(0.62)	(0.76)	(0.73)	(1.94)	(1.25)	(0.97)
Price index	157.51	155.88	193.75	212.96	172.81	170.31	162.85
	(66.91)	(81.23)	(129.72)	(139.47)	(79.55)	(43.54)	(73.19)
Δ Prices index	5.54	8.14	8.48	8.80	10.67	6.94	6.29
	(6.70)	(12.31)	(10.44)	(12.60)	(14.27)	(11.33)	(11.97)
Gini coefficient	32.40	30.60	31.08	31.41	29.30	30.28	34.64
	(4.22)	(3.38)	(3.73)	(3.97)	(3.10)	(3.68)	(2.63)
Δ Gini coefficient	−0.21	0.03	0.07	0.10	0.05	0.24	0.65
	(0.95)	(0.82)	(1.10)	(1.12)	(0.99)	(1.49)	(0.72)
Theil index(c=1)	32.55	31.24	32.13	33.76	31.89	32.99	35.66
	(3.98)	(4.01)	(4.29)	(3.76)	(3.76)	(3.86)	(2.98)
Δ Theil index	0.11	0.03	0.12	0.19	0.18	0.33	0.57
	(0.23)	(0.56)	(0.65)	(0.31)	(0.48)	(0.51)	(0.84)
Ratio D9/D1	2.59	2.63	2.79	2.86	2.59	2.91	2.99
	(0.81)	(1.10)	(0.27)	(0.76)	(0.93)	(0.75)	(1.01)
Δ RatioD9/D1	0.05	0.07	0.06	0.10	0.06	0.09	0.15
	(0.18)	(0.09)	(0.07)	(0.08)	(0.21)	(0.17)	(0.09)

Source: Own elaboration using data from AMECO (2003)

Table 6.6 Bilateral correlations: fiscal policy and macroeconomic outcomes, 1960–2000

	Δ Primary budget balance	*Δ Cyclically adjusted primary budget balance (CAPBB)*	*Budget quality*	*Strength of fiscal adjustment*
Δ Primary budget balance	1			
Δ CAPB	0.77***	1		
Budget quality	0.16***	0.15***	1	
Strength of adjustment	0.74***	0.93***	0.22***	1
Δ Real GDP growth	0.14***	−0.17***	0.10***	−0.13***
Δ Unemployment rate	−0.24***	0.04	−0.06	−0.06
Δ Price index	0.03	0.12***	−0.12***	0.04
Δ Gini coefficient	0.18***	0.24***	0.16***	0.21***

Notes: * significant at 10%; ** significant at 5%; *** significant at 1%

growth. Unemployment is negatively associated with improvements in the budget balance, since higher unemployment means less public revenue and more expenditure. By contrast, prices are positively associated with improvements in the budget balance, meaning that monetary easing and fiscal adjustment work together. Finally, income inequality measured by the Gini coefficient is positively associated with improvements in the budget balance.

With these correlations in hand, it is confirmed that most variables that apparently moved simultaneously in the means analysis are in fact significantly correlated. Nevertheless, correlations can hide possible endogeneity problems because they do not establish the direction of the relationships. For this purpose, the regression analysis set in the next two sub-sections is needed.

Results for growth

To build a comprehensive statistical model for the determinants of economic growth is beyond the purpose of this section. There is a long tradition of econometric studies that analyse the long-term impact of fiscal policy on growth,[19] but what this section aims to do is simply to test whether there is a statistically significant positive relationship between fiscal adjustments and short-term increases in output, as initially indicated in previous sections.

Given that the objective for this section is very concrete, the statistical model is simple. This model takes into account the interaction between fiscal and monetary policy as the short-term determinants of output, as well as the relationships between output and monetary and fiscal policies. The purpose of this design is to check the existing endogeneity between output, fiscal policy and monetary policy. The analysis of the monetary stance is not of particular interest for this chapter, but must be included as part of the policy mix and because it performs a crucial role in determining output in the short run.

Thus, this section estimates the following model for the interaction between fiscal policy, real output and monetary conditions, in a system of three endogenous variables:[20]

$$\Delta Y_t = y(\Delta Y_{t-1}, \Delta F_{t-1}, \Delta Q_{t-1}, \Delta M_{t-1}, \Delta GAP_t) \tag{6.1}$$

$$M_t = m(M_{t-1}, \Delta F_t, i_{t-1} \Delta Y_t, \Delta F_{t-1}) \tag{6.2}$$

$$\Delta F_t = f(\Delta F_{t-1}, M_{t-1}, Y_t, \Delta Y_{t-1}, DEBT_t, dummies) \tag{6.3}$$

The GDP growth equation (6.1) is characterized by output being dependent only on its lag, lagged change in the cyclically adjusted primary budget balance, lagged monetary policies, lagged change in the quality of the budget, lagged output growth, and the change in the EU-15 output gap.[21] The monetary policy equation (6.2) has the real monetary conditions index[22] depending on its own lag, the change in the cyclically adjusted primary budget balance, and its lag, output growth, and the long-term interest rate lag. Finally, the fiscal policy equation (6.3) describes the change in the cyclically adjusted primary budget balance as a function of its own lag, lagged monetary conditions, current and lagged domestic output growth, and the debt-GDP ratio.

This model is estimated using a three-stage least squares estimator in order to take into account any cross correlation between the various residuals that may reflect some of the behaviour of the variables that had to be omitted from the panel estimation. Robust standard errors were estimated to account for heteroscedasticity and any remaining serial correlation.

As results in Table 6.7 show, during the 1970s and the 1980s, GDP growth was positively affected strongly by its own lag and by the surrounding cyclical conditions in the EU. It was negatively affected by monetary and fiscal contractions, although the coefficient for the change in the fiscal stance is not statistically significant. These effects were all reinforced in the 1990s. GDP growth became even more dependent on its lag and on the average EU output gap, reflecting the growing interdependence of European economies. It was also more negatively affected by monetary contractions, meaning that devaluations and/or falling interest rates had a bigger positive impact in increasing growth during the 1990s than before. What is most striking is that the impact of fiscal consolidations on growth became much less negative during the 1990s. Also, the positive impact of budget quality on growth before 1990 was reinforced in the following decade. These two results confirm that non-Keynesian effects of expenditure-based fiscal consolidations applied even better during the 1990s than in previous decades.

Table 6.7. The effects of fiscal adjustments on economic growth

Growth equation *Dep. variable: real GDP growth*	*Real GDP growth (1970–89)*	*Real GDP growth (1990–2000)*
Real GDP growth $t-1$	0.253***	0.562***
	(3.76)	(6.79)
Monetary Conditions Index $t-1$	−0.242**	−0.489***
	(1.91)	(2.88)
Δ Output gap (EU-15)	0.677***	0.793***
	(8.01)	(3.55)
Δ Cyclic. adj. primary budget balance $t-1$	−0.101	−0.078
	(1.40)	(0.57)
Budget quality $t-1$	0.088*	0.112**
	(1.89)	(2.23)
Constant	1.885***	1.655***
	(6.73)	(3.70)
Observations	297	163
Adj. R-squared	0.31	0.46
LR Chi 2(7)	72.66	110.71
Prob>Chi 2	0.000	0.000

Continued

Table 6.7. Continued

Monetary policy equation Dep. variable: Monetary Conditions Index	***Monetary Conditions Index (1970–89)***	***Monetary Conditions Index (1990–2000)***
Monetary Conditions Index $t-1$	0.653***	0.612***
	(8.67)	(7.27)
Δ Cyclic. adj. primary budget balance	0.267***	0.201***
	(3.11)	(2.96)
Δ Cyclic. adj. primary budget balance $t-1$	0.187***	0.098***
	(3.77)	(3.02)
Real GDP growth	−0.101	−0.112*
	(1.57)	(1.77)
Long-term interest rate $t-1$	0.045	0.063*
	(1.66)	(1.86)
Constant	−0.766	−0.702
	(1.65)	(1.77)
Observations	296	162
Adj. R-squared	0.26	0.29
LR Chi 2(7)	132.12	131.14
Prob>Chi 2	0.000	0.000

Fiscal policy equation Dep.variable: Δ cyclically adjusted Primary budget balance (CAPBB)	***Δ CAPBB (1970–89)***	***Δ CAPBB (1990–2000)***
Δ CAPBB $t-1$	−0.312***	0.009
	(4.76)	(0.04)
Monetary Conditions Index $t-1$	−0.311***	−0.134
	(3.24)	(1.22)
Real GDP growth	0.165***	0.321
	(1.98)	(1.23)
Real GDP growth $t-1$	0.087*	0.146
	(1.64)	(1.38)
Debt-to-GDP ratio	0.078***	0.098***
	(5.76)	(3.01)
Constant	−2.786***	5.122***
	(2.01)	(4.76)
Observations	297	163
Adj. R-squared	0.37	0.29
LR Chi 2(7)	82.46	82.91
Prob > Chi 2	0.000	0.000

Note: Absolute value of t-statistics in parentheses

* significant at 10 per cent; ** significant at 5 per cent; *** significant at 1 per cent.

Results for income distribution

The purpose of this final section is to perform a parametric estimate of the determinants of income distribution in Europe. Results should help us confirm or reject the initial evidence from previous sections, according to which fiscal adjustments worsen income distribution, mostly if they are expenditure-based.

There are various potential determinants of income distribution, but since the purpose of this exercise is limited to the effect of fiscal policies on inequality, the equation below includes only the basic factors:[23]

$$\Delta I_t = i(\Delta I_{t-1}, \Delta F_{t-1}, \Delta Q_{t-1}, DT_{t-1}, SS_{t-1}, Educ_{t-1}, dummies) \qquad (6.4)$$

In the expression above, the change in the income distribution (measured by the Gini and the Theil indexes) depends on its lag, on the lagged change of the cyclically adjusted budget balance, the lagged change in budget quality, the lagged share of direct taxes to GDP, the lagged share of social spending to GDP and the lagged share of people enrolled in secondary education.

The lagged change in the budget balance and budget quality should capture the effects of fiscal adjustments on income distribution. In addition, the inclusion of the share of direct taxes and the share of social spending in the equation attempts to account for the different degrees of welfare state development in different member states: more developed welfare states use higher social spending and higher direct taxation to redistribute income, which should be reflected in the evolution of the Gini and Theil indexes. The share of social spending also serves to capture the effect that globalization may have had on income distribution. According to some authors,[24] recent economic globalization may be responsible for increased income inequalities in the 1990s, because this process has imposed cuts in welfare spending as a means of gaining external competitiveness. A quick look at the evolution of social spending and income distribution in Europe during the Maastricht years (1993–97) seems to support such a hypothesis.

Some cases in Table 6.8 are especially relevant in this respect (e.g. Finland, Austria, Italy, the United Kingdom and Spain). In all those countries, strong reductions in social spending were accompanied by notable increases in income inequality. There are some cases, however, which did not follow the same pattern. France and Germany, for example, are two cases where income inequality increased in spite of moderate increases in transfers. While the German case is obviously explained by the process of German unification, the French case remains unclear. Something similar, albeit in the opposite direction, happened with Denmark, the only country where inequalities were significantly reduced during the 1990s despite a serious retrenchment in public transfers.

Equation (6.4) is estimated by Ordinary Least Squares with panel-corrected standard errors to deal with panel heteroscedasticity, spatial and serial correlation.[25]

Results reported in Table 6.9 show that ameliorations in the budget balance and the quality of the budget increase both the Gini and the Theil indexes. The strongly significant impact of the latter is very important

Table 6.8. Changes in social spending and income distribution, 1993–97 (per cent of GDP)

	Δ Gini coefficient	*All transfers (total change)*	*Major transfers (disaggregated change)*		
			Δ Transfers (16–65) (*)	*Δ Disability*	*Δ Unemployment*
Austria	1.1	−0.6	0.3	0.4	−0.1
Belgium	0.4	−1.2	−0.7	−0.3	−0.4
Denmark	−1.6	−1.1	−2.1	0.1	−2.0
Finland	1.4	−4.3	−2.5	−0.9	−1.6
France	0.1	0.2	−0.3	−0.1	−0.3
Germany	0.2	0.6	−0.1	0.1	−0.3
Greece	−0.2	0.7	−0.1	−0.1	0.0
Ireland	0.4	−2.3	−0.6	0.0	−0.7
Italy	1.5	−0.9	−0.4	−0.2	−0.2
Luxembourg	−0.2				
The Netherlands	0.5	−2.9	−1.2	−0.7	0.2
Portugal	−0.2	0.7	−0.1	−0.2	0.0
Spain	0.6	−2.3	−2.3	−0.1	−2.2
Sweden	0.4	−3.5	−1.2	−0.4	−0.6
UK	0.9	−1.3	−0.8	0.0	−0.8
EU−15	0.3	−0.4 (^)	−0.6	−0.1	−0.5

Source: Own elaboration. Data on social spending from EC (2001: 25). Data on Income Inequality from Smeeding (2000) and WIID (2000).

Notes: Figures show changes between 1993 and 1997, all measured in terms of GDP, except the change in income inequality measured by the Gini coefficient.

(*) Transfers to working-age people. Includes unemployment, plus disability benefits, plus social assistance.

(^) Weighted by Real GDP share in 1997, excluding Luxembourg.

because the 'quality' variable is a proxy for expenditure-based adjustments. Better quality budgets are those in which cuts in primary spending contribute most to the fiscal consolidation, and are significantly associated with a widening in the distribution of income. These results are consistent with the negative impact of lower shares of social spending on inequality, and confirm that fiscal adjustments have opposite effects in terms of growth and income distribution, especially if they are based on spending cuts. That opposite effect becomes graphically very clear in Figure 6.1, where economic growth and income distribution (measured by the Gini coefficient) are plotted against the change in the primary budget balance. As can be observed, the more consolidations rely on spending cuts, the more unequal the distribution of income.

Finally, the other variables included in equation (6.4) show the expected signs, but are not statistically significant. In this respect, the share of direct taxes and the education level are all positively associated with ameliorations in the distribution of income, but do not have a significant impact.

Table 6.9 The effects of fiscal adjustments on income distribution

Income distribution equation ***Dep. variable: change in Gini coefficient***	***Gini coefficient (1970–89)***	***Gini coefficient (1990–2000)***
Δ Gini coefficient $t-1$	0.134***	0.142***
	(3.31)	(3.56)
Δ Cyclic. adj. primary budget balance $t-1$	0.253***	0.133**
	(1.98)	(1.88)
Δ Budget quality $t-1$	0.432***	0.431***
	(4.59)	(4.37)
Direct Taxes (%GDP) $t-1$	−0.078	−0.099
	(1.43)	(1.36)
Social Spending (%GDP) $t-1$	−0.101*	−0.099*
	(1.81)	(1.88)
Secondary education enrolment $t-1$	−0.276	−0.241
	(1.68)	(1.40)
Constant	1.122***	1.426**
	(2.21)	(1.89)
Observations	297	163
Adj. R-squared	0.35	0.32
LR Chi 2(7)	85.32	98.72
Prob>Chi 2	0.000	0.000

Income distribution equation ***Dep. variable: change in Theil coefficient***	***Theil index (1970–89)***	***Theil index (1990–2000)***
Δ Theil index $t-1$	0.112***	0.134***
	(3.11)	(3.28)
Δ Cyclic. adj. primary budget balance $t-1$	0.204***	0.132**
	(2.01)	(1.86)
Δ Budget quality t−1	0.366***	0.402***
	(4.14)	(4.02)
Direct taxes (%GDP) $t-1$	−0.086	−0.108
	(1.34)	(1.23)
Social spending (%GDP) $t-1$	−0.096*	−0.098*
	(1.92)	(1.92)
Secondary education enrolment $t-1$	−0.212	−0.202
	(1.58)	(1.38)
Observations	1.022***	1.126**
	(2.11)	(1.39)
Adj. R-squared	297	163
LR Chi 2(7)	0.36	0.31
Prob>Chi 2	88.12	96.15
	0.000	0.000

Notes: Absolute value of t-statistics in parentheses

* significant at 10 per cent; ** significant at 5 per cent; *** significant at 1 per cent.

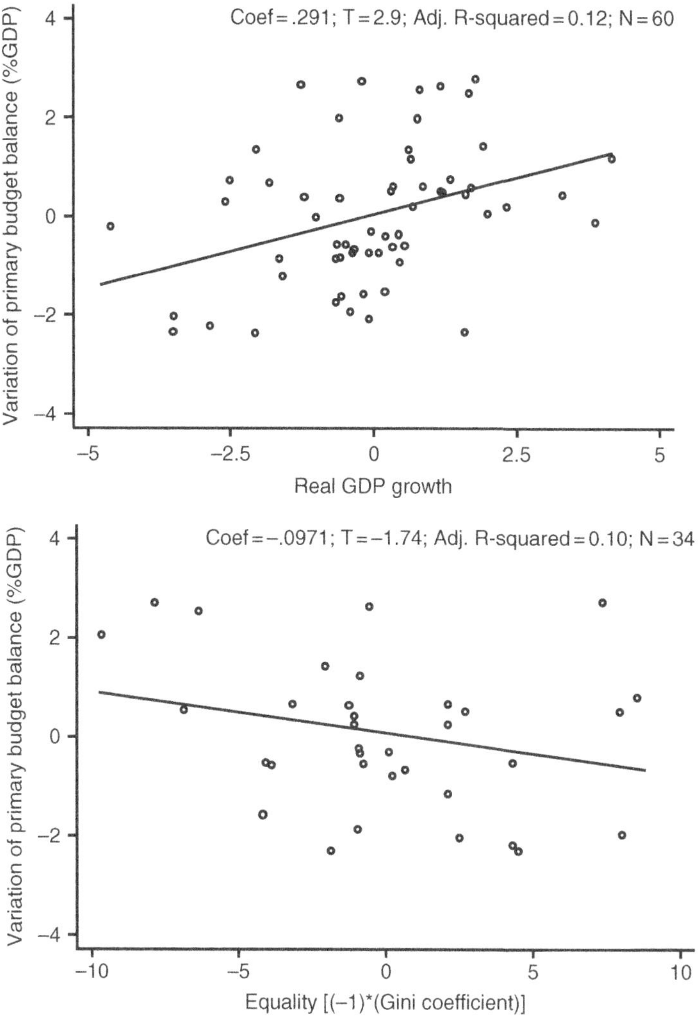

Figure 6.1 Fiscal adjustments, and the trade-off between growth and equality, 1960–2000

6.5 Conclusion

The clearest and most comprehensive way to conclude this chapter and to summarize all of the empirical evidence presented to date is to affirm that different strategies of fiscal adjustment bring about different economic consequences.

Expenditure-based adjustments that are preceded by bad economic and fiscal initial conditions, that are accompanied by a devaluation, and that succeed in cutting the least productive expenditures of the budget, are likely to have anti-Keynesian effects and to be expansionary. Nevertheless, they do so at the expense of increasing income inequality. The opposite is true in the case of revenue-based consolidations.

In order for expansionary fiscal adjustments to take place, demand-side effects in the form of crowding-in of the private sector, as well as supply-side effects in the form of lower labour costs and increased investment, usually take place simultaneously. Expenditure-based adjustments indicate to private agents that the government is committed to a sustained fiscal effort, and this produces a credibility effect that is crucial for expansionary fiscal adjustments to take place.

The 1990s epitomize the story of expansionary fiscal consolidations, since the process of fiscal adjustment imposed by the Maastricht criteria arrived at a moment of particularly acute fiscal stress for public finances across Europe. However, the negative side of the strongest episode of fiscal adjustment in Europe since the mid-1970s has been the progressive widening of income distribution and the increase in inequalities that reached its highest level in the 1990s.

The reactions of public opinion to the formulation of the different strategies described in Chapter 4, and to the divergent economic consequences that they have brought about as shown in this chapter, are crucial to close the circle and understand what (if any) political price governments pay for implementing different fiscal adjustments that have different economic impacts. This is the task undertaken in Chapter 7.

7
The Political Consequences of Fiscal Adjustments

> 'Governments do not seem to be systematically punished at the ballot box for engaging in fiscal adjustments.'
>
> Alesina, Perotti and Tavares, 1998: 241

Equally important as the economic consequences brought about by fiscal adjustments is the question of whether or not these adjustments have any political consequence for the cabinets that implement these policies.*

Evidence from Chapters 3 and 4 respectively showed that the probability of ending a fiscal adjustment increased when elections were imminent. It also showed that taxes decreased, and public transfers and consumption increased, when governments felt the pressure of once again facing their electorates. This evidence suggested that politicians believe that voters dislike fiscal adjustments and will not re-elect them in the aftermath of fiscal consolidations. Are politicians right in acting according to these assumptions?

Evidence from the only study that has indirectly[1] tested if this belief is correct or not in western democracies concludes that the probability of government termination after fiscal adjustments is no higher than the average.[2] In their words: 'governments do not seem to be systematically punished at the ballot box for engaging in fiscal adjustments' (Alesina, Perotti and Tavares, 1998: 241).[3]

If voters do not care about fiscal adjustments but politicians are making their fiscal decisions dependent upon the proximity of elections (assuming that the public prefers less taxes and more transfers) then the evidence from previous chapters showing certain degree of responsiveness on the part of the rulers with respect to the fiscal preferences of the ruled, should be reassessed.

Is it really the case that the probability of re-election is unaffected by the budget balance? Are politicians truly misinformed about voters' preferences when they consider the electoral calendar before deciding on the timing, the duration, and the composition of fiscal adjustments? If European voters really do not punish national politicians for undertaking fiscal adjustments, are they blaming anyone else – maybe Brussels?

It is the purpose of this chapter to answer these three crucial questions. Accordingly, this chapter also reports three main findings: (1) by considering the probability of re-election, instead of looking at the probability of government termination, some of the conclusions drawn from previous work on the topic can be rejected; (2) the composition of the budget is an important factor driving the political consequences of fiscal adjustments; (3) the traditional voters' aversion to expenditure-based fiscal adjustments decreased during the 1990s, most likely as a result of the broad information campaigns supporting fiscal adjustments, associated to the process of economic and monetary union in Europe.

Therefore, this chapter provides systematic direct empirical evidence of the negative impact that expenditure-based fiscal adjustments have on the probability of re-election. Not only the probability of re-election decreases during years of fiscal adjustment, but also if these adjustments have taken place on the expenditure side of the public budget, the probability of losing the next election is even higher. These results are perfectly consistent with the previous findings of this book, according to which the proximity of elections is an important factor explaining the timing, the duration, and composition of fiscal adjustments.

Nevertheless, when time is taken into account, it is striking to observe that this adverse effect of expenditure-based adjustments on the probability of re-election, which was very strong between 1960 and 1992, came to an end during the post-Maastricht years.

This calls for an explanation which is offered at the end of the chapter based on two related aspects: first, the steadfast commitment of European and national authorities to stick to the conditions of the Maastricht convergence criteria made European voters assume fiscal adjustments as something 'imposed from Brussels' that was going to happen anyway; and, second, the strong national coalitions between government and opposition that crystallized after 1994 offered European electorates no visible political alternative on fiscal policy issues. These two factors, together with an unprecedented Europe-wide campaign underscoring the future economic prosperity that these adjustments would generate, succeeded in changing the traditional negative electoral response that public opinion previously had towards fiscal adjustments.

Despite the high probability of 'demonizing' Brussels for imposing such adjustments, this possibility only temporarily materialized, and this change in public attitudes towards fiscal consolidations was achieved without any major impact on the medium-term public support for the European integration project.

The chapter proceeds as follows: section 7.1 reviews the literature on political accountability and economic voting that is relevant to justify the main hypotheses that will be tested throughout the rest of the chapter. Section 7.2 elaborates on the research design following on these hypotheses and on the statistical model. Sections 7.3 and 7.4 test the model and report the main results. Finally, section 7.5 summarizes the main findings and concludes.

7.1 Economic policy, fiscal adjustments and elections

In its simplest form, the fundamental contention in the literature on economic voting is that voters tend to reward incumbents when the economy is sound and punish them when it is not. Citizens assess past performance rather than looking at economic promises (Key, 1966; Fiorina, 1981; Norpoth, Lewis-Beck and Lafay 1991). The effect of economic performance on government tenure has been widely studied, with unclear and even contradictory results. There is a wealth of evidence confirming that short-term economic conditions influence electoral outcomes in the United States (Tufte, 1978; Erikson, 1989; Kramer, 1983; Markus, 1988) although the strength of the relationship appears to be weaker in other democracies (Lancaster and Lewis-Beck, 1986; Rattinger, 1991; Sanders, Ward and Marsh 1991). While most agree that economics matter for the election outcome (Paldam, 1991), the relative effect is by no means constant in all countries, and there is no agreement as to what explains such differences (Lewis-Beck, 1988).[4]

In relation to fiscal policy issues, this literature has traditionally assumed that voters dislike taxes and prefer government outlays concerning public health, education, unemployment benefits and pensions. These assumptions are the basis for the literature on political business cycles (Nordhaus, 1989) according to which politicians undertake fiscal expansions just before elections take place in order artificially to accelerate the economy and the rate of job creation because they expect to be rewarded at the polls if the economy is doing well when the election arrives. Consequently, the basis for believing that voters dislike fiscal adjustments relies on two explanations: fiscal adjustments imply raising revenues and/or the reduction of government outlays which, in a Keynesian framework, is likely to cause a temporary economic recession and a loss of jobs. Because neither of these options is desirable for voters, governments expect to be punished at the ballot box if they undertake a fiscal adjustment just before an election takes place.

As Chapters 3 and 4 have demonstrated, the last forty years offered consistent evidence that policy-makers acted according to this expectation. The proximity of elections systematically decreased the probability of starting consolidations, shortened their duration and also affected their composition. Although this evidence demonstrates that policy-makers discount the expected reaction of the electorate to these measures, we know very little about whether the electorate has actually used its vote to make the government accountable for having pursued unpopular fiscal policies. In democratic politics, the only way to punish governments is to abandon the incumbent government at the polls (Cheibub and Przeworski, 1998; Maravall, 1998).

Only Alesina, Perotti and Tavares (1998) have, to my knowledge, studied the political consequences of fiscal adjustments in advanced democracies. Their research design does not, however, directly explore the electoral costs of such adjustments. They prefer to study instead whether fiscal adjustments increase the probability of government termination or whether these decisions affect the popularity of the incumbent cabinet. In my opinion, this indirect approach generates misleading results. Since the authors do not find any significant statistical relationship between fiscal adjustments and government terminations or popularity losses, they interpret that fiscal adjustments are politically costless.

The first and most important problem in the research design of Alesina, Perotti and Tavares (1998) arises from the definition of the dependent variables. The problem with government termination as the first dependent variable is that governments can end and change due to a multiplicity of reasons that are totally independent of the electorate's reaction to fiscal adjustments. This is the case, for example, when governments end as a result of coalition rearrangements, or due to a voluntary resignation of the prime minister. In both cases, the electorate does not intervene in the process, which makes it very difficult to establish any link between fiscal adjustments measures and their political consequences. Acknowledging this shortcoming, the authors also test the relationship between fiscal policy and government popularity, measured as intention to vote for the government if the election was held tomorrow. Although this variable captures much better the reaction of the electorate, it retains a margin of error because what really matters in making the government accountable for past actions is the actual vote on the election day rather than the intentional vote declared to an opinion pollster (Obstfeld and Eichengreen, 1998).

A second problem is the potentially reversed causality between the probability of government termination and fiscal adjustments. Alesina *et al.* (1998) test whether fiscal adjustments increase the probability of government termination, assuming that the causality runs from fiscal policy to government tenure. Nonetheless, it is equally plausible that causality runs in the opposite direction, from government tenure to fiscal policy decisions. In fact, it is very likely that long-lasting governments (those with a lower probability of termination) assume more easily the political risk of launching a fiscal adjustment, counting on the room of manoeuvre that their past strength and stability grants them.

Finally, a third problem in the model of Alesina, Perotti and Tavares (1998) is multicollinearity, resulting from the simultaneous inclusion as regressors of the two main indicators of political fragmentation (majority status in the parliament and coalition size), and a measure of fiscal adjustment. The former indicators of fragmentation are the most robust predictors of government tenure, but they are also predictors of fiscal policy. This causes multicollinearity between independent variables and makes 'the effect of the latter (fiscal variables) difficult to pin down' (Obstfeld and Eichengreen, 1998: 260).

Maybe due to these important problems, Alesina, Perotti and Tavares (1998) arrive at such paradoxical conclusions that leave the reader wondering: if fiscal adjustments are economically beneficial and politically costless, why then would politicians be so reluctant to implement them? The authors never raise this obvious question nor do they address the statistical problems of their study. The only partial answer that they provide to the paradox is that successful fiscal adjustments rely on spending cuts in the most rigid items of the budget that are strongly opposed by the recipients of public outlays and by public employees. Although Alesina, Perotti and Tavares (1998) do not go much further, they implicitly admit with this statement a potential connection between public discontent and a future electoral punishment for the government. If this connection did not exist, governments would never refrain from implementing adjustments, regardless of the public opposition that they could confront.

Taking into account all the problematic aspects, this chapter proposes a different and more direct approach which consists of exploring the relationship between fiscal adjustments and the probability of prime ministerial re-election. I focus exclusively on the electoral dimension of these potential political consequences by using the probability of re-election as their main indicator.

7.2 The 'fiscal voting hypothesis'

This section introduces the main assumptions and hypotheses. It also presents the statistical model that will be estimated to reject or accept these conjectures.

Main hypotheses

This chapter draws on three basic assumptions: first, politicians are pure office-seekers and, thus their main preoccupation when formulating public policies is the relative impact that these policies may have on their chances of winning re-election. Second, voters prefer economic growth and employment to recessions, and they also dislike taxes and like government outlays. This assumption is based on the existence of a common-pool resource situation, whereby every voter demands more outlays because the associated cost will be shared with more tax payers. Third, both policy-makers and voters have perfect information about the preferences and actions of each other, which assures that voters will be capable of attributing responsibility for government actions. Under these assumptions, the main hypotheses that this chapter tests are the following:

The 'fiscal voting' hypothesis The main hypothesis of this chapter (and the fourth principal hypothesis of this book as explained in Chapter 1) is that fiscal adjustments will decrease the chances of being re-elected if the electorate considers that governments are responsible for such measures. Fiscal adjustments imply taking decisions (increasing revenues, cutting expenditures, or a mix of both) that the electorate dislikes. The alternative hypothesis would be that the public is fiscally conservative and does not punish governments that consolidate the budget, as Alesina, Perotti and Tavares (1998) affirm.

The 'economic voting' hypothesis Complementarily to the previous hypothesis and based on economic voting literature, this second hypothesis that will be tested in this chapter says that the electorate is expected to reward governments when the economy is doing well, when prices are under control, and when there are new jobs being created. In addition, this chapter will also test the hypothesis that the electorate in Europe rewards a fair distribution of economic prosperity.

The 'Europeanization' hypothesis Finally, the chapter considers the possibility that voters could have stopped punishing governments for fiscal adjustments in Europe not because they turned fiscally conservative but because they considered that these policies were being imposed from European institutions. If this were the case, voters could have stopped punishing national governments just because they transferred the responsibility for fiscal adjustments to the European level. Since it was the project of Monetary Union that motivated European authorities to insist on fiscal discipline, it is reasonable to expect that public support for monetary union decreased as the number and scope of budget cuts increased across Europe.

The statistical model

To start with the analysis of the 'economic' and the 'fiscal voting' hypotheses, this chapter uses a baseline probit model where the probability of re-election is a function of the change in the budget balance, the change in a set of economic factors, and the present values of different political and social accompanying conditions. Equation (7.1) summarizes this model:

$$REELEC_{t,t} = \alpha_0 + \alpha_1 \Delta BBAL_{i,t} + \beta_1 \Sigma \Delta ECON_{i,t} + \beta_2 \Sigma POLIT_{i,t} + \beta_3 SOCIAL_{i,t} + \beta_4 DECFADJ_{i,t} + C_i + \varepsilon_{i,t} \tag{7.1}$$

The dependent variable ($REELEC_{i,t}$) takes two different forms: *re-election* and *government termination*. The purpose of considering these two alternative dependent variables is to make this chapter's results comparable to those of Alesina *et al.* (1998). Note, however, that they used a sample of 19 OECD countries between 1965 and 1995, while this chapter uses a sample of 15 EU member states between 1960 and 2000.

These variables are constructed as follows. First, I create a dummy variable called government termination, which takes value 1 when a government ends regardless of the reason,[5] and 0 otherwise. I calculate the duration of each government by counting the number of years between two consecutive terminations. In order to keep the correspondence between fiscal policies and government changes that occurred as a response to those policies, I have considered, in line with Alesina, Perotti and Tavares (1998), that government terminations that occur between 1 July of year *t* and 30 June of year *t+1* fall into calendar year *t*.

Second, from the sample of general elections that occurred during the period of study, I create a dummy variable called re-election which takes value 1 when the same prime minister was reappointed, and takes value 0 in all other cases. Here, I depart from Alesina, Perotti and Tavares (1998: 220), who 'use the sample of changes irrespective of whether a transition to a new cabinet occurs by means of elections, cabinet reshuffling or other procedures'. As the following section will show, taking this difference into account is crucial to rejecting their conclusion that fiscal adjustments do not have major political consequences.[6]

Government terminations may lead to changes in the prime minister and/or changes in the ideological orientation of the cabinet. These are dummy variables, equal to 1 when each type of change occurs. But the two sets are not the same. For example, the replacement of J. Santer by J.C. Juncker, when the former abandoned the Luxembourgois government to become President of the European Commission in 1994, is classified as a prime minister change but not as an ideological change. Changes in prime minister are more frequent than changes in ideology, because often the leadership of a major coalition party changes, and hence also the prime minister, although the ideological status of the cabinet remains unchanged.

When an ideological change occurs, this change may replace a leftist government by a centrist or rightist government, or replace a rightist government by a centrist or leftist one. The first set of cases is labelled as change to the left, and the second set of cases, as change to the right. Note that if the initial government was a centrist government and it was replaced by a leftist government, the case would be labelled as a change to the left, while if it was replaced by a rightist government, the case would be labelled as a change to the right.

Table 7.1 shows the relative frequency of positive values for the dummy variables defined above in the full sample and for each country. Out of a total of 574 observations,[7] 266 are government terminations. Of them, 101 are ideology changes (55 to the left, and 46 to the right) and 118 are changes in prime minister. Of all government changes, 129 were mediated by elections.

The picture by country is very illustrative of some major tendencies. Finland, Italy and Belgium are the countries with the lowest government durations, lowest probability of re-election, and highest number of government terminations. With a probability of government termination of 80 per cent, a probability of re-election of only 28 per cent, and an average government duration of only 1.22 years, the extreme case is Italy. As Pasquino (1994: 25) observed, in Italy, 'governing parties seemed to expropriate the voters of the political influence by making and unmaking governments at all levels with very little respect for electoral results.'[8]

The most stable governments in Europe are those in Luxembourg (2.7 years), the United Kingdom (2.5 years), Austria (2.09 years) and Spain (2.08 years), while the countries with the highest probabilities of re-election are

Germany (80 per cent), Spain (71 per cent), Portugal (66 per cent) and Austria (60 per cent). The probabilities of re-election are strikingly high in these countries, which makes one wonder about the possible influence that past authoritarian regimes may have had on the political culture of those countries.

With respect to ideological volatility, Portugal, the Netherlands, and Belgium show the highest scores around 60 per cent, while Germany and Austria remain at a very low 20 per cent probability that there is a change in the ideological complexion of the cabinet, whenever there is a change in the cabinet.

Finally, Portugal, the Netherlands, and Greece experienced the highest number of changes toward more leftist governments, and Luxembourg and Ireland toward more rightist ones.

According to the model specified in equation (7.1), the observed variation in the dependent variables can be explained by a set of fiscal, economic, and political independent variables or regressors. The vector of *fiscal regressors* ($\Delta BBAL_{I,t}$) includes two variables that capture the fiscal policy stance: the change in the budget balance and the change in the cyclically adjusted primary budget balance (both as a percentage of GDP). It is important to include both definitions because public opinion tends to follow more easily

Table 7.1 Frequency of government termination and cabinet changes: by country, 1960–2000

	Gov't duration	*Gov't termination*	*Ideology changes*	*Ideology ch. left*	*Ideology ch. right*	*Pr. minist. changes*	*Re-election*
Austria	2.09	0.36	0.20	6.67	13.33	0.53	0.60
Belgium	1.92	0.46	0.47	26.32	21.05	0.42	0.28
Denmark	1.75	0.51	0.30	15.00	15.00	0.60	0.66
Finland	1.56	0.58	0.42	20.83	20.83	0.25	0.10
France	1.41	0.63	0.34	19.23	15.38	0.42	0.30
Germany	1.90	0.43	0.16	11.11	5.56	0.72	0.80
Greece	2.01	0.48	0.50	33.33	16.67	0.29	0.50
Ireland	1.95	0.36	0.46	20.00	26.70	0.33	0.57
Italy	1.22	0.80	0.37	15.63	21.88	0.36	0.28
Luxembourg	2.70	0.24	0.50	20.00	30.00	0.60	0.57
Netherlands	2.17	0.36	0.66	33.33	33.33	0.40	0.33
Portugal	1.84	0.48	0.60	40.00	20.00	0.41	0.66
Spain	2.08	0.37	0.33	22.22	11.11	0.55	0.71
Sweden	1.78	0.46	0.36	21.05	15.79	0.52	0.61
United Kingdom	2.50	0.34	0.35	21.43	14.29	0.42	0.50
All Countries	1.90	0.46	0.39	21.32	17.83	0.44	0.49
Observations	574	266	101	55	46	178	129

Note: The 266 terminations of government motivated 100 changes of ideology, 117 changes of prime minister and 49 continuations of cabinet composition. Out of these 217 changes, only 129 occurred by means of elections (of which 63 were re-election of the prime minister).

Source: Own elaboration.

the evolution of the budget balance, while politicians and economic authorities prefer instead to focus on the cyclically adjusted primary balance. Any amelioration in both fiscal variables is expected to be negatively associated with the probability of the prime minister's re-election.

The vector of *economic regressors* ($\Sigma\Delta ECON_{I,t}$) includes four macroeconomic indicators: real GDP growth, changes in the price level (inflation), the unemployment rate, and in income inequality (measured by the annual change in the Gini coefficient). As mentioned above, these variables allow testing for the possible presence of economic voting. Note that almost no empirical studies on the effect of fiscal adjustments on income inequality exist. Nevertheless, as Chapter 6 has already shown, fiscal consolidations have a variety of economic consequences on most macroeconomic aggregates, including economic growth and income distribution. Therefore, a proper exploration of any type of economic voting pattern justifies the inclusion of these four macroeconomic variables. In all cases, higher rates of economic growth, lower rates of unemployment, lower inflation and a lower level of income inequality are expected to be positively associated with the probability of prime ministerial re-election.

The vector of *political regressors* ($\Sigma POLIT_{I,t}$) includes three variables that attempt to capture additional factors not included among the main hypotheses formulated in this chapter but which are likely to affect the chances of government survival. The first one is the number of years in power (government duration). The second one is the parliamentary status of the government (whether it is supported by a majority or a minority in parliament). The third one is the number of parties that form the government (coalition size). The reason for including government duration among the explanatory variables is to control for the likely presence of anti-incumbent forces. In addition, with office and power come scandals and corruption that tarnish any administration. Incumbent status is generally associated with an erosion of electoral support. Therefore, long-lasting governments are expected to have an increased probability of government termination and to feature a decreased probability of re-election compared to short incumbencies. For the same reasons, a majority in Parliament is expected to reduce the chances of re-election. Furthermore, bigger coalitions are typically associated with internal fights and thus are also expected to increase the likelihood of government termination and to reduce the chances of electoral success.

Moreover, the equation includes a variable that proxies public discontent with the most controversial adjustment initiatives. Such public discontent tends to be more acute among the net recipients of public outlays (typically the least well-off), and generally ends in strikes and demonstrations against welfare cuts across Europe. The social unrest variable ($SOCIAL_{i,t}$) is an interaction between the variable that measures the variation in income inequality and a variable that measures the total number of working days lost per year due to strikes.

To allow for important institutional differences in the 15 EU member states, the equation includes *Country dummies* (C_i).

There is no reason to think that temporal dynamics have had any effect on the probability of re-election, but time may have played a role in the frequency and composition of fiscal adjustments. In order to control for these temporal dynamics, the equation includes four interaction terms between four decade dummies and the budget balance variables ($DECFADJ_{i,t}$). These four decade dummies are the following: *1960s* (1963–72); *1970s* (1973–82); *1980s* (1983–92); *1990s* or *Post-Maastricht* (1993–2000). There are three reasons to select these intervals: (1) four countries in the sample have missing data between 1960 and 1962; (2) no fiscal adjustment took place in those two years in any EU country; (3) there is a substantive interest in having a single dummy variable that covers all the post-Maastricht years.

7.3 The electoral consequences of fiscal adjustments – estimation results

This section estimates the statistical model using the complete panel of economic and political data for the fifteen EU member states between 1960 and 2000 that has served as the basis for the empirical estimations throughout the book. In the first part of the analysis, all years of the panel are included for the probit estimations. This means that adjustment and non-adjustment years are included together in the same data set.[9] Therefore, 615 data points are used in the analysis of the first sub-sections which estimate the effect that fiscal adjustments have on the chances of re-election. The same applies for the second sub-section which adds some variables to the equation to deal with the composition of these adjustments. Afterwards, the third sub-section replicates the analysis but only for fiscal adjustment episodes that may include several years. The purpose of that additional analysis is to test whether results are robust to a different definition of fiscal adjustment which considers as fiscal adjustments only those improvements in the budget balance that last for more than one year and not only for one year as assumed in the first and the second sub-section.

The budget balance and re-election

The expected negative effect of fiscal policy variables on the probability of re-election is confirmed in the results presented in Table 7.2.

As we observe in the first two columns from model 1 and model 2, the 'fiscal voting' hypothesis, which affirms that fiscal adjustments have electoral costs, is corroborated. Positive annual variations of the budget balance (fiscal adjustments) clearly reduce the probability of a prime minister's re-election. These results hold for both indicators of fiscal policy. Nevertheless, as the interaction term in the third row of Table 7.2 shows, fiscal adjustments that occurred during the post-Maastricht years stopped having a negative effect

Table 7.2 Budget balance and re-election, 1960–2000: probit estimates – sample of adjustment and non-adjustment years

	Prob. re-election^a_t		*Prob. gov't termination*^a_t	
	Model 1	*Model 2*	*Model 3*	*Model 4*
Δ Budget balance$_{t,\,t-1}$	−0.323**		−0.081	
	(−2.07)		(−1.07)	
Δ C.A.P. Budget balance$^b_{t,\,t-1}$		−0.341**		−0.111
		(−1.99)		(−1.24)
Δ Budget balance$_{t,\,t-1}$* post-Maastricht	0.101*		−0.011	
	(1.87)		(−0.22)	
Δ C.A.P. Budget balance$_{t,\,t-1}$* post-Maastricht		0.107*		−0.394
		(1.85)		(−0.81)
Δ Real GDP$_{t,\,t-1}$	0.044**	0.036**	−0.009	−0.014
	(1.98)	(1.96)	(−0.19)	(−0.49)
Δ Price index$_{t,\,t-1}$	−0.106	−0.082	0.134**	0.129**
	(−0.99)	(−0.65)	(2.48)	(2.17)
Δ Unemployment rate$_{t,\,t-1}$	−0.314*	−0.177*	0.031	0.021
	(−1.83)	(−1.86)	(0.26)	(0.29)
Δ Inequality index$_{t,\,t-1}$	−0.526**	−0.640**	0.123	0.117
	(−2.32)	(−2.49)	(1.17)	(0.99)
Government duration$_t$	−0.867***	−0.924***	0.526***	0.526***
	(4.45)	(4.22)	(4.28)	(4.23)
Majority in parliament$_t$	−1.825**	−1.175	−0.343	−0.288
	(−2.22)	(1.22)	(−0.89)	(−0.73)
Coalition size$_t$	−0.249	−0.255*	0.091	0.106
	(−0.85)	(1.89)	(0.61)	(0.70)
Social unrest$_t$	−1.393	−1.79**	0.522	0.533
	(−1.52)	(−1.95)	(1.32)	(1.34)
Constant	−6.964**	−1.226	−1.405	−0.482
	(−4.04)	(−0.89)	(−1.37)	(−0.54)
Observations	175	165	595	585
Pseudo R-squared	0.39	0.42	0.19	0.20

Note: Absolute value of z-statistics in parentheses.
** significant at 10 per cent; ** significant at 5 per cent; *** significant at 1 per cent.*
[a] Coefficients for Austria, Belgium, Denmark, France, Germany, Netherlands, Spain and Sweden were significantly different from 0 in the regression on the probability of re-election. Also, coefficients for Austria, Belgium, Denmark, France, Germany, Ireland, Netherlands, Portugal, Spain and Sweden were significantly different from 0 in the regression on the probability of government termination.

[b] Only the interaction term for ΔBudget balance * post-Maastricht is included in the table. The other interaction terms for previous decades were statistically insignificant but had a negative sign for the regression on the probability of re-election, and a positive sign for the regressions on the probability of government termination.

on the probability of re-election. Note that the positive coefficient of the interaction variable (Δ budget balance * post-Maastricht) not only shows that fiscal adjustments stopped leading to electoral punishment during most of the 1990s, but it also points out the existence of positive electoral effects for undertaking such adjustments before the advent of the euro. This result will be explored in further detail later in the chapter.

Results for the regressions on government termination, calculated in model 3 and model 4, are very similar to those presented by Alesina *et al.* (1998) using a different sample. As they also find, there is no relationship between the probability of government termination and the amelioration of the budget balance, regardless of the type of indicator and the decade in which the consolidation occurs.

With respect to the 'economic voting' hypothesis, Table 7.2 shows that the impact of economic variables on the probability of re-election is important in the case of economic growth, unemployment and inequality. However, it is statistically insignificant for inflation rates.[10] Higher rates of economic growth increase the probability of prime ministerial re-election, while increases in the unemployment rate or in the inequality index reduce the chances of winning office again. These results are similar to those reported by Paldam (1991), Cheibub and Przeworski (1998) and Brender and Drazen (2005)[11] who found a moderate positive electoral effect of economic growth and unemployment reduction on the chances of remaining in office.

Political variables also show the expected signs. Longer government duration decreases the probability of a prime minister's re-election and increases the probability of government termination. Parliamentary majorities decrease the probability of re-election, and larger coalitions make government survival increasingly difficult. Social unrest does not have any effect on the probability of government termination, but it does play a moderate role in the probability of prime ministerial re-election. Fiscal adjustments that increase inequality and generate social mobilization are likely to become an electoral burden. This is probably why politicians are reluctant to implement such adjustments as often as economists recommend them.

The budget's composition and re-election

Previous results are confirmed when the analysis is extended to take into account the electoral effect of the budget's composition. As Table 7.3 shows, the probability of a prime minister's re-election increases when total expenditures (as percentage of GDP) grow (model 2).

The same is true for the share of social transfers (model 3) and public wages (model 4) although their statistical significance is weaker. Finally, it is worth noting that the inability of voters to reward or punish the quality of the budget (model 1) signals a limit to accountability for fiscal policy decisions, and demonstrates how difficult it is for voters to understand the details of budgetary policies.[12]

Table 7.3 Budget composition and re-election, 1960–2000: Probit estimates – sample of adjustment and non-adjustment years

	Probability of Re-election$^{a}_{t}$			
	Model 1	*Model 2*	*Model 3*	*Model 4*
Δ Budget balance$_{t,\,t-1}$* post-Maastricht[b]	−0.311** (−1.96)	−0.336* (1.85)	0.328** (1.97)	0.341* (1.88)
Δ Real GDP$_{t,\,t-1}$	0.045** (1.99)	0.047** (1.98)	0.048** (1.98)	0.046* (1.80)
Δ Price index$_{t,\,t-1}$	−0.158 (−0.76)	−0.101 (−0.87)	−0.091 (−0.79)	−0.123 (−0.96)
Δ Unemployment rate$_{t,\,t-1}$	−0.140 (−0.71)	−0.143 (−0.72)	−0.151 (−0.77)	−0.165 (−0.82)
Δ Inequality index$_{t,\,t-1}$	−0.620** (2.44)	−0.634** (2.47)	−0.636** (−2.47)	−0.616** (−2.48)
Government duration$_t$	−0.881*** (−4.40)	−0.878*** (−4.34)	−0.882*** (−4.38)	−0.894*** (−4.39)
Majority in parliament$_t$	−0.900 (−1.04)	−0.810 (−0.92)	−0.878 (−1.01)	−0.743 (−0.85)
Coalition size$_t$	−0.291 (−0.85)	−0.292 (−0.87)	−0.288 (−0.84)	−0.332 (−0.99)
Social unrest $_t$	1.834** (1.99)	1.932** (2.05)	1.894** (2.02)	1.956** (2.02)
Quality of budget$_t$	0.005 (0.02)			
Total public expenditures (GDP)$_t$		0.025** (2.70)		
Social transfers (GDP)$_t$			0.042 (1.51)	
Public wages (GDP)$_t$				0.156* (1.85)
Constant	−0.971 (−0.74)	−1.915 (−0.99)	−1.525 (−0.88)	−2.422 (−1.11)
Observations	163	165	165	165
Pseudo R-squared	0.41	0.40	0.41	0.42

Notes: *Absolute value of z-statistics in parentheses*
* significant at 10 per cent; ** significant at 5 per cent; *** significant at 1 per cent
[a] Coefficients for Austria, Belgium, Denmark, France, Germany, Netherlands, Spain and Sweden were significantly different from zero in the regression on the probability of re-election.
[b] Only the interaction term ΔBudget Balance*Post-Maastricht is included in the table. The other interaction terms for previous decades were statistically insignificant but had a negative sign for the regression on the probability of re-election, and a positive sign for the regressions on the probability of government termination.

Sensitivity analysis: adjustment episodes

Finally, the main results from the previous two sub-sections must be tested against an alternative research design. Up to now, the chapter has performed all its analyses on a sample of 40 years and 15 countries, where both adjustment and non-adjustment years entered together in the regressions. Every year, in which the budget balance improved, we observed that the probability of re-election decreased. The advantage of this research design is that it combines the *factual* cases (the adjustment years) and the *counterfactual* ones (the non-adjustment years), and thus avoids a likely problem of selection bias which is very common in the related literature. Such an approach allows us to extract general conclusions regarding the effect that changes in any independent variable have on the probability of re-election.

Nevertheless, it could be argued that the previous approach does not take into account the multi-annual dimension of budgetary consolidations. Since governments typically design their adjustment strategies with a medium-term perspective, the most relevant works in the literature have based their studies around a set of adjustment episodes. The criteria for selecting these episodes are very standard, and aim at selecting groups of years during which strong fiscal adjustments occurred, and where the government's intention to consolidate the budget could be easily identified. Therefore, for this sensitivity analysis, we use again here the sample of 53 adjustment episodes already used in previous chapters of the book.[13] Recall from Chapter 3 that the average duration of these episodes was 2 years. From a total of 53 episodes of strong fiscal consolidation between 1960–2000, 18 of these episodes occurred during the 1990s. This means that 34 per cent of the cases occurred in the last decade. All adjustments that experienced a government change in the middle of the episode were split into two cases. This was the only way to attribute each different episode to a single government which could be punished or rewarded for the type of policy it followed during the consolidation episode. As a consequence, the re-election variable here was defined as taking the value of 1 whenever the prime minister who pursued the consolidation was re-elected in the first election following the end of the adjustment episode, and 0 otherwise.

The question is whether the first two hypotheses of this chapter also hold when they are tested on a new and restricted sample of adjustment episodes. It is not possible to test whether fiscal adjustments have any electoral cost using this restricted sample of adjustment episodes. Since all data points in this new sample correspond to strong consolidations performed by different governments, the emphasis should rely on the question of whether different types of adjustment episodes (in terms of duration and composition) have had a different impact on the probability of re-election after the adjustment has come to an end.

As Table 7.4 shows, the results of the probit regressions for this new sample of adjustment episodes partially confirm previous findings.

Table 7.4 Budget composition and re-election, 1960–2000: sensitivity analysis; probit estimates – sample of adjustment episodes

	Probability of re-election		
	1960–2000	*Pre-Maastricht 1960–1992*	*Post-Maastricht 1993–2000*[a]
Δ Real GDP$_{t,\,t-1}$	0.186	0.027	0.048
	(1.18)	(0.13)	(1.08)
Δ Price Index$_{t,\,t-1}$	−0.027	−0.028	
	−(0.94)	−(0.36)	
Δ Unemployment Rate$_{t,\,t-1}$	−0.080	−0.057	
	(0.35)	(0.19)	
Δ Inequality Index$_{t,\,t-1}$	−0.176	−0.182	0.576
	(0.52)	(0.42)	(0.52)
Adjustment Duration$_t$	−0.231	−0.336	−2.227
	(1.03)	(1.14)	(1.38)
Majority Parliament$_t$	0.813	0.721	1.166
	(1.35)	(1.07)	(0.73)
Coalition Size$_t$	0.275	0.367	
	(1.48)	(1.55)	
Social Unrest$_t$	−0.021	−0.011	
	(−0.12)	(−0.49)	
Expenditure-based Adjustment$_t$	−0.838*	−1.492*	−2.710
	(1.69)	(1.84)	(1.34)
Constant	−1.743*	−1.306	−7.501
	(1.70)	(0.82)	(1.64)
Observations	51	36	15
Pseudo R-squared	0.19	0.28	0.38

Notes: Absolute value of z-statistics in parentheses.
** significant at 10 per cent; ** significant at 5 per cent; *** significant at 1 per cent.*

[a] Note that in order to avoid problems derived from lack of degrees of freedom, some independent variables have been excluded.

Although the evolution of economic and political variables during episodes of fiscal adjustment is no longer a statistically significant determinant of the probability of re-election, signs are however in the expected direction. As before, a majority in parliament increases the probability of re-election, while having a fragmented government diminishes it. The latter finding indicates that more parties are likely to run in the election and therefore the probabilities of re-election are lower. Furthermore, longer consolidations tend to reduce the probability of re-election, and higher levels of social mobilization reinforce this effect.

Finally, and most importantly, the statistical significance of the variable that labels expenditure-based consolidations confirms that voters are likely to stop voting for the incumbent government when the adjustment is based on spending cuts. However, the importance of this variable vanished during the post-Maastricht period. The following section explores why this is the case.

7.4 The post-Maastricht period

Growing tolerance towards fiscal adjustments

In order to explore the existence of a different voting pattern during the post-Maastricht years, Table 7.5 presents a comparison of re-election probabilities in three different samples: (1) the whole sample of adjustment and non-adjustment years; (2) the same sample but only for adjustment years; and (3) the sample of adjustment episodes lasting longer than one year.

As can be observed, during adjustment years and after adjustment episodes, the probability of re-election is lower than during non-adjustment years. This is the case for the four decades between 1960 and 2000. Nevertheless, it is surprising to observe that in the post-Maastricht years the probability of re-election after fiscal adjustment episodes is 53 per cent, very close to the average probability for the whole sample, and seven points higher than the probability of re-election after an adjustment episode during the 1960–92 period. This indicates an increasing tolerance of fiscal adjustments on the part of the electorate during the past decade precisely when the most important fiscal consolidations took place across Europe. This growing tolerance becomes very clear in Figure 7.1

The second interesting finding is that voters not only became more tolerant towards fiscal adjustments in general, but also towards those consolidations that relied on spending cuts. The probability of re-election after an expenditure-based adjustment remained at 30 per cent during the three decades of the period 1960–92. This probability increased 10 percentage

Table 7.5 Probability of re-election during/after fiscal adjustments

Average probability of re-election	*Whole sample 1960–2000*		*Pre-Maastricht 1960–92*		*Post-Maastricht 1993–2000*	
	Prob.	*Obs.*	*Prob.*	*Obs.*	*Prob.*	*Obs.*
(1) During ajust. and non-adjust. years	0.49	184	0.48	121	0.54	63
(2) During adjustment years	0.48	93	0.47	65	0.50	28
(3) After adjustment episodes	0.48	51	0.46	36	0.53	15
-Adjustments by leftist cabinets	0.41	28	0.28	18	0.66	10
-Adjustments by rightist cabinets	0.59	23	0.66	18	0.25	5
-Revenue-based adj. episodes	0.65	27	0.70	17	0.60	10
-Expenditure-based adj. episodes	0.35	24	0.30	18	0.40	6

Source: Own elaboration. Data from AMECO (EC, 2002) and Armingeon *et al*. (2000).

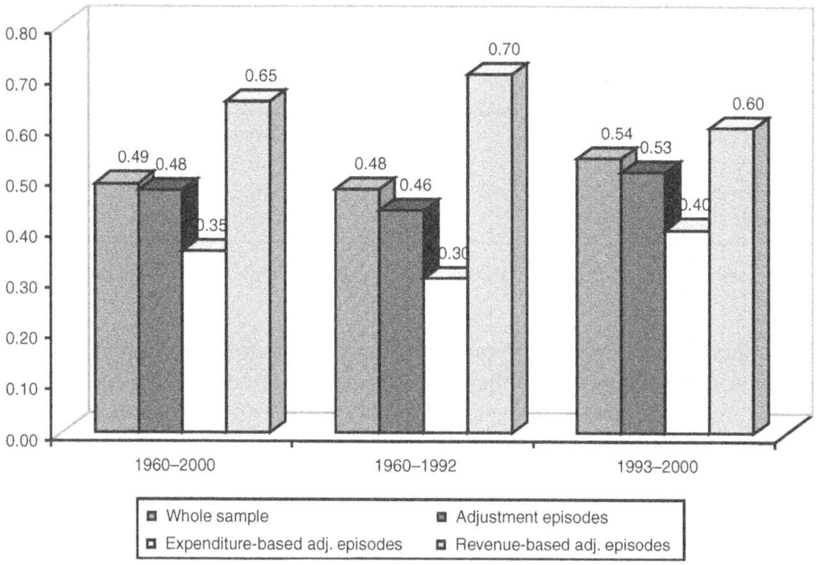

Figure 7.1 Probability of re-election during fiscal adjustments

points in only one decade, to reach a 40 per cent re-election probability during the 1990s.

These changes in the 1990s are corroborated when one looks at the bilateral correlation between probability of re-election and expenditure-based adjustment. As Table 7.6 shows, between 1960 and 1992 it seems as though after expenditure-based adjustments took place, it was more likely that there was a change towards more rightist governments.

This suggests that left voters punished leftist governments when they pursued expenditure-based adjustments by switching the sign of their vote, while rightist voters rewarded rightist governments that consolidated the budget by means of cuts in expenditures.

This effect of punishing leftist governments for undertaking fiscal consolidations, and rewarding rightist ones, does not hold during the post-Maastricht years, due to the fact that many leftist government implemented expenditure-based adjustments took place during the 1990s (see Table 7.7).

In fact, during that period, the probability of re-election was higher when a leftist cabinet had launched the adjustment than when a rightist government had done so. This may show that electorates across Europe voted for leftist governments while conscious that fiscal consolidations were a 'must' that any government was going to undertake anyway. Under such historical

Table 7.6 Correlations among type of adjustments and cabinet re-election variables

Type of adjustment (1 = expenditure-based; 0 = revenue-based)	*1960–2000*	*1960–92*	*1993–2000*
Re-election	−0.29 ***	−0.37 ***	−0.09
Ideology change	0.36 ***	0.39 ***	0.25
Ideology change to the left	0.11	0.20	−0.09
Ideology change to the right	0.32 ***	0.29 **	0.33

Notes: * significant at 10 per cent; ** significant at 5 per cent; *** significant at 1 per cent.

circumstances, the electorate may have even rewarded these leftist governments for sacrificing their policy preferences and taking the necessary measures to consolidate the budget and qualify for the third stage of EMU, for instance.

There are two alternative explanations for the observed change in the voting patterns during the post-Maastricht years. Either voters changed their initial aversion to fiscal adjustments, or they stopped considering national governments as being responsible for fiscal adjustments because they perceived that these measures were being imposed from Brussels. As the rest of the chapter will show, there is partial evidence to support both arguments.

Two factors explain the increase in tolerance of public opinion towards fiscal adjustments during the 1990s. The first is the strong commitment on the part of European officials and national governments to maintain the compromises signed in 1992 in Maastricht. The second factor that increased the electorate's tolerance is the unprecedented degree of campaigning of government officials in favour of undertaking any sacrifice necessary to qualify for the third stage of monetary union. In this respect, European politicians pursued a strategy of 'crafted talk' to change public opinion in order to offset the potential political costs of not following the preferences of average voters (Jacobs and Shapiro, 2000). They did so by reshaping their messages, insisting on the need to reduce budget deficits but in a way that was more appealing to national public opinions. Arguments such as 'unique historical opportunity', 'national pride', and 'the best for our country's future' were among those slogans preferred by politicians to convince their electorates that reforms were necessary.

In addition, the 1990s witnessed a fiscal policy consensus across Europe between national governments and oppositions to qualify for the third stage of EMU. As a consequence, the public did not perceive real fiscal policy alternatives in the opposition, which reduced the voters' tendency to make politicians responsive to their demands (Ferejohn, 1986). Occasionally, discrepancies arose about the rhythm of the fiscal consolidation efforts and their composition, mostly regarding pension reforms or cuts in unemployment benefits. But the electorate did not interpret these discrepancies as

Table 7.7 Fiscal adjustments and prime minister re-elections, 1993–2000

Country	*Adj. years*	*Adj. type*	*Re-election*	*Re-election year*	*Ideology change*	*Previous prime minister*	*New prime minister*
Austria	1995–97	Exp.-based	No	1999	Right	Vranitzky, F. (SPÖ)	Schüssel, W. (ÖVP)
Belgium	1992–94	Rev.-based	Yes	1995	None	Dehaene, J.-L. (CVP)	Dehaene, J.-L. (CVP)
Denmark	1993	Rev.-based	Yes	1994	None	Rasmussen, N. (SD)	Rasmussen, N (SD)
Denmark	1998–99	Exp.-based	No	2001	Right	Rasmussen, N. (SD)	Rasmussen, A.F. (CON)
Finland	1993–94	Exp.-based	No	1995	None	Aho, E. (KESK)	Lipponen, P. (SDP)
France	1996–97	Rev.-based	No	1997	Left	Juppé, A. (RPR)	Jospin, L. (PSF)
Greece	1991–92	Exp.-based	No	1993	Left	Mitsotakis, C. (ND)	Papandreou, A. (PASOK)
Greece	1995–98	Rev.-based	Yes	2000	None	Simitis, K. (PASOK)	Simitis, K. (PASOK)
Ireland	1999	Exp.-based	Yes	2002	None	Ahern, Bertie (FFail)	Ahern, Bertie (FFail)
Italy	1991–93	Rev.-based	No	1994	Right	Ciampi, C.A. (NONA)	Berlusconi, S. (Forza)
Italy	1999	Rev.-based	No	2001	Right	Amato, G. (Olivo)	Berlusconi, S. (Forza)
Luxembourg	1992–93	Rev.-based	Yes	1994	None	Santer, J. (CSP)	Juncker, J.C. (CSP)
Netherlands	1991–93	Rev.-based	No	1994	Right	Lubbers, R.F.M. (CDA)	Kok, W. (PvdA)
Netherlands	1995–96	Exp.-based	Yes	1998	None	Kok, W. (PvdA)	Kok, W. (PvdA)
Spain	1996–97	Exp.-based	Yes	2000	None	Aznar, J.M. (PP)	Aznar, J.M. (PP)
Sweden	1995–98	Exp.-based	Yes	1998	None	Persson, G. (SAP)	Persson, G. (SAP)
UK	1994–96	Exp.-based	No	1997	Left	Major, J. (CON)	Blair, T. (LAB)
UK	1997–99	Exp.-based	Yes	2001	None	Blair, T. (LAB)	Blair, T. (LAB)

clear signs of fiscal policy alternatives since main parties of the left and the right were committed to the fulfilment of the Maastricht criteria at any cost.

However, the fiscal policy consensus at national level may have really transformed voters' attitude towards fiscal adjustments. An alternative hypothesis to explain the economic voting phenomenon during the post-Maastricht years is that voters may have accepted the discourses of their different national politicians if they used Brussels as a scapegoat to justify their fiscal policy initiatives. If this hypothesis holds, the electorate has stopped punishing their governments for hard spending cuts, and has shifted the burden to the European sphere.

Blaming Brussels for budget cuts

There is one major difficulty when studying the possible 'Europeanization' of the accountability mechanism by which the electorate uses its vote to reward or to punish their national governments for their economic and fiscal policies. European citizens do not vote directly for the European executive every five years. Instead, they vote for local candidates for the European Parliament, and it is the Parliament that ratifies the President and the members of the European Commission. In addition, the European Commission's main role is to serve as the guardian of the Treaties, which are signed by member states at the end of long intergovernmental conferences.

Such a complex institutional set-up complicates the selection of a direct indicator to test the hypothesis that voters may have started to blame Brussels for fiscal adjustments in the 1990s. Those adjustments were driven by the necessity to comply with the provisions of the Maastricht Treaty to introduce the euro. Thus, it is plausible to assume that any possible 'Europeanization' in the attribution of responsibilities for hard fiscal consolidations should have affected support for the single currency. The evolution of this indicator can then be used to test the 'Europeanization hypothesis'.

Evidence from public opinion polls on the support for the European currency shows that there was a cost in public support when fiscal adjustments were stronger. As can be observed in Figure 7.1, the loss of popularity of the single currency project between 1995 and 1997 was remarkable – especially by the end of 1997 when the Maastricht deadline approached. In fact, most of the countries that made the strongest fiscal efforts during those two years (such as Belgium, Denmark, France, Greece, Portugal, Spain and the United Kingdom) rank among the group of countries in which support for the single currency remained stable or decreased between the end of 1995 and mid-1997 (Ahrendt, 1999).

The popularity losses were only temporary. In spring 1998, European support for the euro resumed. From that moment on, it remained at very high levels, along two phases. First, the support for the new currency followed a decreasing path between 1998 and 1999, probably reflecting the first problems that European citizens faced in the use of the new currency as a 'non-physical

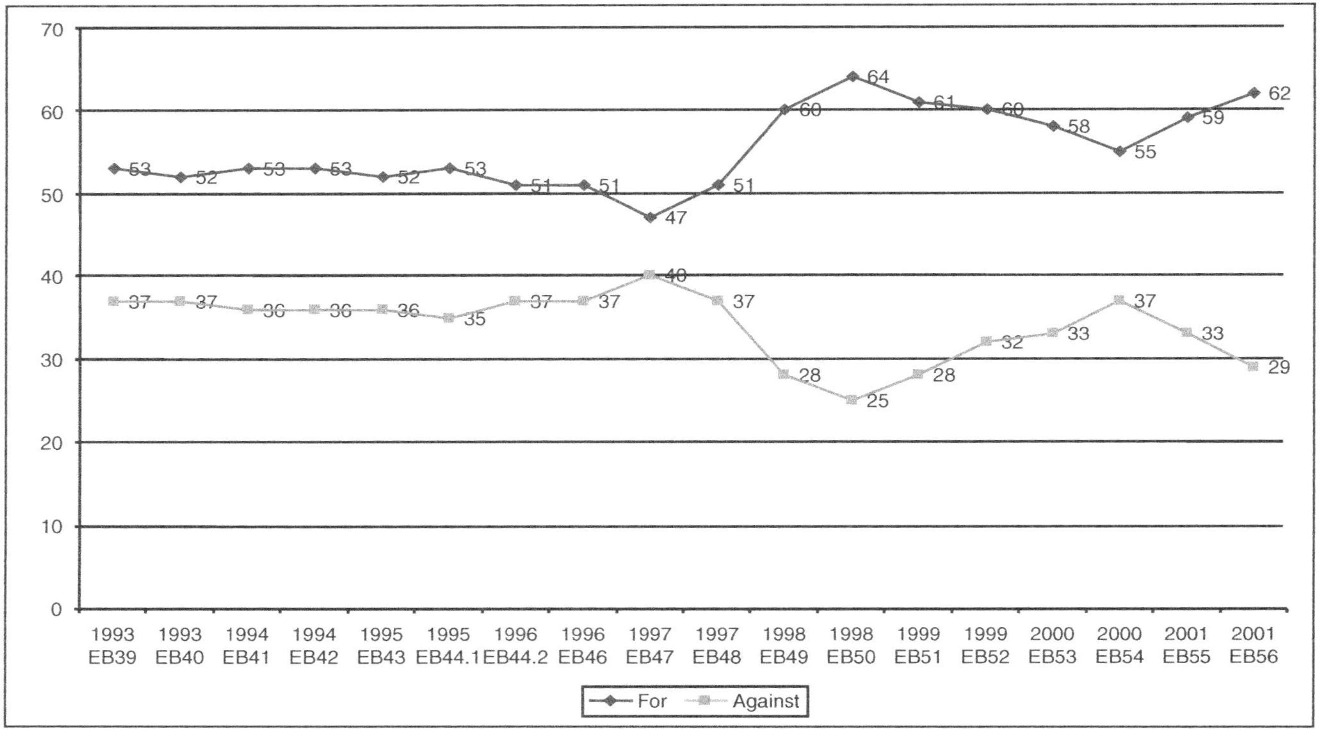

Figure 7.2 Support for the single currency, 1993–2001

currency' in 1999 (EC, 2001). But then, by the end of 2000, the tendency changed and support for the euro exploded in 2001.

Data from Eurobarometer 56 (EC, 2001) show a remarkable increase of 12 percentage points in the average confidence in the European Union and the European Commission within two years. It also shows 'vast majority support of the Union's policy initiatives' (EC, 2001: 5), while support for the single currency records its maximum, over 62 per cent.

The proliferation of media campaigns in the months immediately prior to the circulation of the physical currency in January 2002 may explain this impressive shift. These campaigns had two major objectives: first, to reassure public opinion in the EU-11 that all efforts made to join the euro would be compensated in every country by the associated economic benefits; and second, to reverse the low level of support among the elderly, the less educated, among women, and among manufacturers (groups that normally feel more insecure about their economic stability, who were more afraid of losing social benefits due to the convergence criteria).

Both information strategies proved very effective. The insistence on economic benefits strengthened the perception that the euro would be a vehicle for higher economic growth and lower inflation (EC, 1995) (see Figure 7.3).

Moreover, the strategy of aiming at more hostile social groups to the single currency succeeded in removing some long-standing reservations. For

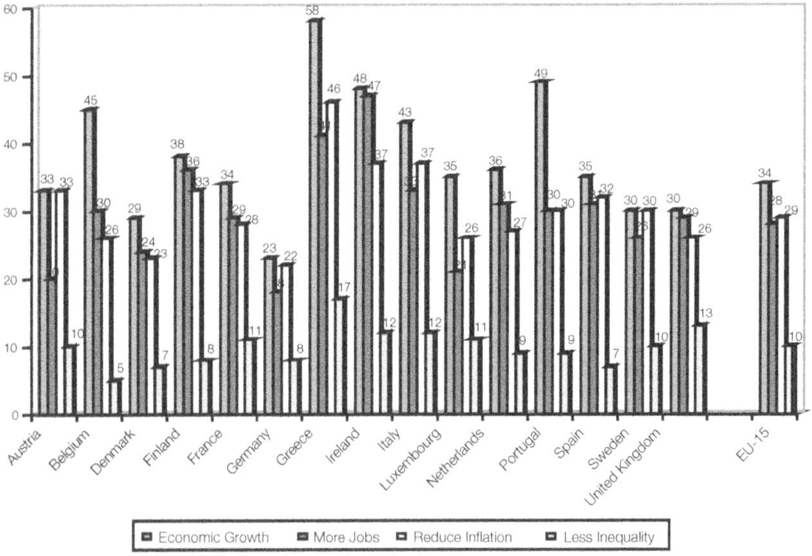

Figure 7.3 Expected consequences of the euro, 1995

Source: Own elaboration. *Sources of data*: Eurobarometer 44 (1995).

example, between 1995 and 1998, support for the single currency among women increased from 43 per cent to 56 per cent, among people who left school before 16 year of age from 44 per cent to 52 per cent, among retired people from 48 per cent to 56 per cent, among the unemployed from 47 per cent to 55 per cent, and among manual workers from 46 per cent to 54 per cent.

Summing up, from the evolution of public support for the single currency reported in Figure 7.2, we cannot conclude that the 'Europeanization' of responsibility for strong budget cuts seems the most plausible hypothesis to explain the observed change in voting patterns during the post-Maastricht period. Although the strongest loss in popularity of the single currency coincides with the period of strongest fiscal adjustments across Europe, support for the euro resumed immediately after. Such a development, together with the persistent growing tolerance of fiscal adjustments during the 1990s, supports the alternative hypothesis that information campaigns and internal political consensus succeeded in transforming voters' traditional aversion to fiscal adjustments.

These preliminary findings based on a simple graphical analysis must be corroborated by means of regression analysis. Consequently, Table 7.8 reports the results of estimating the following model:

$$NETSUPEURO_{i,t} = \alpha_0 + \alpha_1 \Delta BBAL_{i,t} + \beta_1 \Delta QUALITYADJ_{i,t} + \beta_2 \sum \Delta ECON_{i,t} + \varepsilon_{i,t} \tag{7.2}$$

where the dependent variable *NETSUPEURO* is the difference between people in favour of the single currency and those against it. (ΔBBAL is the primary budget balance, ΔQUALITYADJ is the contribution of primary expenditures to the amelioration of the budget, and ΔECON is the vector of the four economic indicators used in previous sections.) The regression analysis is performed by OLS on a panel of 15 EU member states between 1993 (the first year in which the question 'Are you against/in favour of the single currency?' was introduced in the Eurobarometer surveys) and 2001.

Table 7.8 shows that any amelioration in the budget balance (fiscal adjustment) reduced the net support for the single currency between 1993 and 2001. This effect was, however, particularly significant between 1995 and 1997, when the strongest adjustments took place. In fact, the quality of the budget became a significant predictor only in that period: better quality adjustments (i.e. those primarily based on spending cuts) considerably diminished the support for the single currency. The influence of economic variables on the net support for the single currency during the post-Maastricht period is remarkable as well. Economic growth and inflation increased support for the single currency, while variations in unemployment and inequality did not have statistically significant influence.

Table 7.8 Fiscal adjustments and net support for the euro in the post-Maastricht period

	Net support for the euro	
	1993–2001	*1995–1997*
Δ Primary budget balance$_{t,\,t-1}$	−2.67*	−3.431***
	(−1.74)	(−3.45)
Δ Quality of budget$_{t,\,t-1}$	0.352	−1.909**
	(1.23)	(−1.98)
Δ Real GDP$_{t,\,t}$−1	3.947**	1.009
	(2.29)	(0.37)
Δ Price index$_{t,\,t-1}$	1.137***	1.066*
	(2.83)	(1.69)
Δ Unemployment rate$_{t,\,t}$−1	3.137	1.798
	(1.37)	(0.30)
Δ Inequality index$_{t,\,t-1}$	3.386	1.853
	(1.45)	(0.45)
Constant	7.632*	16.14**
	(1.90)	(2.47)
Observations	112	45
Adj. R-squared	0.14	0.27
F-test	3.52	4.28
Prob > F	0.005	0.003

Notes: *Absolute value of t-statistics in parentheses.*

* *significant at 10 per cent;* ** *significant at 5 per cent;* *** *significant at 1 per cent.*

In conclusion, the regression analysis confirms that the change in voting patterns during the post-Maastricht period can only partially be attributed to a 'Europeanization' of responsibility for severe budget cuts. The tendency to stop punishing national governments for fiscal adjustments was partly caused by a parallel tendency to put the blame on Brussels, especially between 1995 and 1997, but was also the result of a real change in voters' attitudes towards fiscal adjustments. Most likely, this growing tolerance of fiscal discipline was heavily influenced by Europe-wide information and propaganda campaigns, as well as by the national fiscal consensus around the historic importance of the euro and the subsequent need to comply with the Maastricht deficit criteria.

7.5 Conclusion

Once the previous chapter on the economic consequences of fiscal adjustments had shown that different strategies of fiscal adjustment achieved opposite results in terms of economic growth and income distribution, the question about the possible reactions of the public opinion to these different strategies and results became even more salient.

This chapter has tackled this issue, testing three related hypotheses, all of them related to the likely political consequences that fiscal adjustments have for the governments that undertake them.

By considering the probability of prime minister re-election, instead of the probability of government termination, this chapter questions previous findings in the literature and provides strong empirical evidence to support the thesis that voters punish governments that implement expenditure-based fiscal adjustments. The composition of fiscal adjustments is an important determinant of their political consequences, since fiscal adjustments that reduce social spending and increase income inequalities are normally punished by voters.

Nevertheless, the costly electoral consequences traditionally associated with expenditure-based adjustments have been reversed during the 1990s, precisely when the most important consolidations have taken place. This suggests that voters have become more tolerant to expenditure-based adjustments during this decade, probably because they have seen no alternative in the political scenario regarding fiscal policy and the fulfilment of the Maastricht criteria.

Finally, the chapter shows that part of this process of not blaming national governments for what in other times would have been unpopular policies is related to the political campaigns that supranationalized political responsibilities and labelled Brussels as responsible for constraining national fiscal manoeuvrability. As a consequence, the single currency project suffered an important decline in popularity during the years of strongest fiscal effort, but this had only temporary effects, thanks to the impressive effectiveness of the compensating campaigns launched by the European institutions.

8
Conclusion

> 'Domestic economic and political conditions are crucial determinants of fiscal policy and fiscal adjustment strategies in Europe, despite the strict provisions of the Stability Pact. Factors such as the economic cycle, the debt burden, the fragmentation of the government, the proximity of elections, and the ideology of the cabinet have shaped in the last forty years the decisions that governments have taken relative to the timing, the duration and the composition of fiscal adjustments in the EU. By affecting these decisions, those factors have thus influenced decisively the economic and political consequences that these consolidations have generated.'
>
> Carlos Mulas Granados, 2006

The intention of this book was to explore the economic and political factors that affect the formulation of fiscal policies in the European Union, with a particular emphasis on understanding what explains that different countries followed different strategies of fiscal adjustment, when they all attempted to achieve the same aggregate fiscal outcomes, in the process towards monetary union.

The observed variation of fiscal policies and fiscal adjustment strategies among EU countries over the past forty years (Chapter 2) finds its roots in the different domestic economic and politico-institutional conditions faced by each country when confronted by the need to consolidate its budget. As a result of this original influence, these factors have also had a decisive impact on the strategy designed by national governments to re-equilibrate their public finances.

These strategies have varied in three dimensions: the timing, the duration (Chapter 3), and the composition (Chapter 4) of the adjustment episode.

Since only government cabinets are responsible for the design and the implementation of these strategies, all of the research has been especially focused on those factors that affect the cabinet in the moment of choosing between shorter or longer episodes of adjustment, based on raising revenues or spending cuts.

Among those factors, three were purely economic (the debt burden, the economic cycle, and the monetary conditions), and three were purely politico-institutional (the fragmentation of decision-making, the proximity of elections, and the ideology of the party in government).

While economic factors turned out to be more important determinants of the timing and duration of fiscal consolidations, political factors became crucial in understanding the budget's composition during adjustment episodes.

The book rests on the assumption that policy-makers formulate economic policies in order to achieve certain economic and political objectives. Consequently, fiscal policies are used as policy tools to achieve concrete economic policy goals in terms of growth, unemployment, prices, income distribution, and/or electoral results.

Only by understanding the consequences that fiscal adjustments bring about is it possible to compare if the initial objectives that motivated the strategic choice of the type of adjustment were fulfilled once the consolidation episode was over.

This circular relationship between causes and consequences of fiscal consolidations has shaped the structure and the conclusions of this book (see Figure 8.1).

Different choices regarding the timing, the duration or the composition of adjustment episodes bring about different economic (Chapter 6) and political

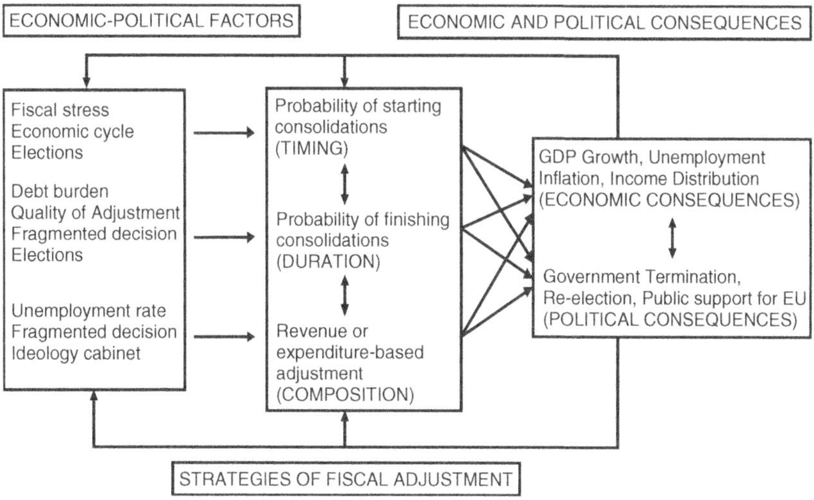

Figure 8.1 The book's conclusions: the inter-relation between the causes and consequences of fiscal adjustments

consequences (Chapter 7), in terms of growth, unemployment, prices, income distribution, and electoral support.

The importance of these different economic and political consequences lies in their backward impact:

1. In principle, these consequences generate a new set of economic and political realities that will affect the formulation of fiscal policies in the future;
2. In addition, these consequences feed back policy-makers' expectations and reshape both the initial factors affecting the strategic choice, and the choice itself.

This process of *expectations–design and implementation of fiscal adjustment strategies–economic policy outcomes–learning–and reshaping of initial expectations* gives a circular dimension to fiscal policy that has never been studied before in a comprehensive work.

The first contribution of this book is precisely its comprehensive and circular structure.

The second contribution of this book is that it has complemented traditional economic approaches to the analysis of fiscal policy with a politico-institutional perspective, and by doing so it has been able to answer some of the puzzles that economic theory had not yet been able to solve. These puzzles are those related to the continuous accumulation of debt in European economies after the Second World War, or the reasons why some countries under conditions of fiscal stress postpone or finish their consolidations unexpectedly. Furthermore, economic theory alone has not been able to account for the determinants of different adjustment strategies undertaken by different European countries over the past few decades. Only by complementing economic theory with politico-institutional approaches has this study been able to understand those fiscal phenomena and to answer these questions.

Such a combination of economic and politico-institutional approaches has enriched this book and has clearly contributed to the confirmation of the five principal hypotheses of this book; namely, the 'fiscal stress hypothesis' (to explain timing), the 'debt burden hypothesis' (to explain duration), the 'partisanship hypothesis' (to explain composition), the 'economic trade-off hypothesis' (to explain economic consequences) and the 'fiscal voting hypothesis' (to explain political consequences). It has also allowed the book to arrive at an interesting set of conclusions, the most important of which are the following:

1. The probability of starting fiscal consolidations is higher when the structural deficit is high, when the domestic economy is doing well with respect to the European economy and when elections have just passed.
2. The duration of fiscal consolidations is particularly dependent upon the accumulated fiscal effort, initial and accompanying economic conditions

(such as debt level and quality of the adjustment), and also on political determinants (such as the number of spending ministers in the cabinet). The higher the debt burden, the weaker the initial budget measures, the better the quality of the adjustment (based on cuts in unproductive expenditures), and the lower the fragmentation of the cabinet, the higher the probability that the consolidation will be of longer duration.

3. These results are sensitive to the definition of fiscal adjustment. When the definition is made more demanding, then political variables gain power as explanatory factors of duration of fiscal consolidations, while some economic factors lose that capacity. This means that the duration of stronger fiscal adjustments is very much dependent on the political commitment of governments undertaking them than on any other factor. This political commitment is always easier to maintain when the cabinet that sticks to that hard decision is a single-party cabinet, with ideologically homogeneous members, and if elections are not too close. Under such circumstances, the debt burden continues to be an important determinant of duration, but the strength of the adjustment and quality of the budget lose their initial predictive capacity.

4. The composition of the budget in general, and during adjustment episodes in particular, depends on the accumulated structural deficit, the rate of growth, the rate of unemployment, and on the three crucial politico-institutional variables of this book. In this respect, larger cabinets, larger coalitions, proximity of elections and more leftist governments are all associated with increases in public expenditures, especially in public transfers, and, thus, they are also associated to revenue-based strategies of adjustment. Evidence from the 1990s shows, however, that the effect of these variables has been reversed by the 'Maastricht rules', and in the case of leftist governments has forced them to prioritize their preferences. In doing so, leftist parties have preferred to increase revenues coming from direct taxation in order to finance increases in public consumption and public investments, even at the expense of public transfers. These policy choices seem to confirm the self-proclaimed social democratic commitment to supply-side policies of physical and human capital formation.

5. The economic consequences of revenue-based and expenditure-based fiscal adjustments are different. While revenue-based adjustments are not conducive to considerable increases in growth, they are also not particularly harmful to equality. By contrast, expenditure-based consolidations can be expansionary if they are preceded by difficult fiscal conditions, and if they reduce the most rigid items of the budget (transfers and public wages). These type of consolidations generate wealth and credibility effects that induce a crowding-in of private consumers and investors, and accelerate economic activity. But expenditure-based adjustments imply also higher costs in terms of increasing inequality than do revenue-based adjustments.

6. The political consequences of fiscal adjustments work in two directions:
   a. Fiscal adjustments reduce the probability of re-election. However, since this probability increases with economic growth, employment creation, and a fairer distribution of income, governments face two alternatives regarding their fiscal adjustment strategies: they can implement an expenditure-based adjustment hoping that higher growth will compensate the loss in popularity, or they can implement a revenue-based adjustment hoping that the maintenance of popular spending items, and a lower cost in terms of income distribution, will compensate the growth losses and will be enough to gain re-election.
   b. Fiscal adjustments reduce the popularity of those projects associated with spending cuts. For example, the public support for the EMU project worsened temporarily right in the midst of the consolidation effort between 1995 and 1997. Nevertheless, this support was quickly recovered by means of strong campaigns from national governments and the European Commission, insisting on the advantages of fiscal discipline in terms of future employment and growth.

This book has combined a systematic theoretical revision of the literature on the political economy of economic policy-making and fiscal adjustments with strong empirical evidence in order to support its main argument: that domestic economic and political conditions are still important determinants of fiscal policy and fiscal adjustment strategies in Europe, despite the standardizing provisions of the Stability Pact.

The combination of theoretical analysis with both quantitative and qualitative empirical evidence, in the form of systematic statistical analyses, and contemporaneous case studies, is the third contribution of this work. In this respect, the book has investigated the reasons behind the decision to surrender independent monetary policy and move towards monetary union, and the motivations of social democratic parties in Europe to support and promote this radical change in the economic policy framework (Chapter 5). By answering these questions regarding the origins of EMU and the Maastricht criteria, the book has illustrated its conclusions with six historical case studies of fiscal adjustment episodes in the run-up to EMU. The fact that these case studies examined very recent episodes of consolidation in the largest nations in Europe, increased the relevance of this chapter.

Spain and Portugal followed opposite strategies of fiscal adjustment from 1995 when their initial imbalances were almost identical, yet they reached very similar results in terms of fulfilment of the Maastricht criteria. This was the result, the book argues, of the different preferences of the parties in government, regarding the role of the state in the economy. While the socialist government of Antonio Guterres launched a revenue-based adjustment to protect public transfers, wages and investment, the conservative government of J.M. Aznar preferred to cut both public expenditures and revenues, in order to promote a crowding-in effect of the private sector in the economy. The results of both strategies were similar in the short run in terms of growth and qualification for stage 3 of EMU, but in the medium run, Spain has witnessed higher rates of growth than Portugal, and a better capacity to maintain a balanced budget.

Similar comparisons of opposite case studies served also to illustrate the effect of institutional fragmentation and elections on the consolidation strategy. Italy and the UK present opposite examples because of the degree of fragmentation of their budgetary processes. Only when budgetary reforms were introduced in Italy, sustainable measures could be implemented on the spending side of the budget. But these reforms are always difficult to undertake, even more so when they are close to elections. Under such circumstances, governments tend to postpone any decision to consolidate the budget, but, if this is not possible, politicians will try to alter the electoral calendar calling for early elections, as Chirac did in France in 1997. The extreme case of constrained decision occurs when fiscal adjustments cannot be avoided, the electoral calendar cannot be altered, and the government faces strong institutions guaranteeing fiscal discipline. In such cases, the government will try to circumvent those institutional rules in order to gain re-election, as Kohl did in Germany between 1990 and 1998.

If any, the main problem of this study is that its conclusions can only be generalized and exported to countries with economic, institutional and political structures similar to those found in the European Union member states. Unfortunately, outside the EU there are few countries with these characteristics.

Having acknowledged the spatial limitations of this book, let me finish with a last word on its temporal validity. While it is true that the current situation of economic globalization and economic policy convergence in Europe has constrained the capacity of national governments to formulate differentiated economic policies, this book has shown that these governments have found ways to do so in the arena of fiscal policy. And they have done so because domestic economic and political factors are still as influential for them as evident are the existing external rules and constraints.

Meanwhile the current fiscal framework in Europe does not move in the direction of a fully coordinated or even harmonized) fiscal policy that resembles the degree of supranationalization achieved in monetary policy, we can expect that the domestic economic and political factors highlighted by this book will continue to shape fiscal policy and fiscal consolidations in the future.

Appendix 1: Cyclically Adjusted Budget Balances: The Commission's Method[1]

For all its calculations, this book has used the AMECO database of the European Commission. In most cases the data used in the different empirical sections of this study were cyclically adjusted, following the EU Commission's method for discounting the effect of the economic cycle on the budget. Thus, the appendix presents here an analysis of this method.

The cyclical adjustment method used by the DG ECFIN of the European Commission is a simple and transparent method which provides a uniform framework for the calculation of cyclically-adjusted budget balances for each member state of the European Union. As the adjusted balance estimates are calculated mechanically, they do not require judgmental fine-tuning and can therefore be easily replicated.

The DG ECFIN method comprises three main steps. In the first step, the output gap is computed as the difference between the actual output and an estimated output trend. In the second step, the budget sensitivity to the output gap is computed. This allows us to compute the cyclical component of the budget. Finally, the cyclically-adjusted budget balance is obtained by deducting the cyclical component from the actual government budget balance.

1.1 First step: estimating trend GDP and output gaps

To obtain estimates for the output trend, the DG ECFIN cyclical adjustment method applies the Hodrick–Prescott (HP) filter to the actual output series. The HP filter minimizes the sum of squared deviations of actual output around its trend subject to a constraint on the variation of the growth rate of trend output. The filter applies weighted moving averages to the actual output series to obtain trend GDP estimates.

The HP filter calculates the trend as the solution to the following minimization problem:

$$\underset{\{y_t^T\}}{Min} \sum_{t=1}^{T} \left[(y_t - y_t^T)^2 + \lambda \left[(y_{t+1}^T - y_t^T) - (y_t^T - y_{t-1}^T) \right]^2 \right] \qquad \text{(A1.1)}$$

where the trend values y_t^T are chosen for each period such as to minimize (A1.1) for a given value of the smoothing parameter λ. The second part of the expression in square brackets determines the smoothness of the resulting trend component which depends on the value of λ. The minimization problem yields smoother trends as λ increases. For $\lambda \rightarrow \infty$ a linear trend would result. For $\lambda = 0$, the trend line would coincide with the actual series. There is no commonly agreed value for the smoothness parameter.

A lower bound for λ is usually 10, which implies that only cycles up to eight years would be retained fully in the cyclical component. The Commission services set a value for λ equal to 100 which is the 'industry standard'. This choice implies that cycles up to 15 years are passed and only cycles with a period larger than 20 years are fully eliminated.

However, the HP filter – in common with moving-average-based methods – is sensitive to the lack of information at the extremes of the series to be analysed. When the extremes of the series are approached, the filter becomes asymmetric as no observations are available at one side of the reference year. This is the so-called 'end-point bias'.[2] Thus the HP filter underestimates the length of the cycle close to the end point, if no corrective measures are taken. Since this phenomenon especially occurs for the last 3 or 4 observations, one possibility to correct for this bias is to extend the data set by adding GDP forecasts over a range of 3 to 5 years.

DG ECFIN tackles the end-point bias problem by adding GDP forecasts and mechanical time series projections of GDP. This ensures a symmetric filtering of the trend at the end of the series. This solution is consistent with the overall methodological approach followed by DG ECFIN as this univariate statistical procedure is mechanical, simple, can be easily reproduced and is applied with minimal judgemental intervention.

The output gap is calculated as the difference between the actual level of GDP in volume and that of trend GDP, expressed as a percentage of trend GDP.

1.2 Second step: estimation of revenue and expenditure sensitivities

In order to estimate the cyclical component of the budget, the value of the budget sensitivity of revenue and expenditure to the output gap is required. The sensitivity of tax revenue is obtained by multiplying the output gap with the marginal change of receipts with respect to GDP. The overall revenue elasticity is a weighted average of four revenue elasticities (personal income taxes, corporate taxes, social security contributions and indirect taxes), whereby the different components are weighted by the relative share of each category in total revenue over the period 1980–98. Elasticities for these specific tax categories, and also government unemployment expenditures, are those calculated and recently updated in OECD (1999a). A similar approach is followed in the case of government expenditure. Government transfers to households to cover costs related to unemployment are the only expenditure category which is assumed to react 'automatically' to cyclical fluctuations.

The total budget sensitivity to the output gap, which is given by the sum of the revenue and expenditure sensitivities, is around 0.5 in the euro area and the EU as a whole (Table A.1). This implies that if the output gap changes by one percentage point, the budget balance changes by 0.5 per cent of GDP. As shown in the table, the major determinant of the size of the budget sensitivity is the overall size of the government sector in the economy (which is around 50 per cent of GDP in the EU). The revenue sensitivity is more important than the expenditure sensitivity because most tax revenues fluctuate with growth while only unemployment expenditure, which forms only a small part of overall government expenditures, is assumed to respond to cyclical fluctuations. This implies that, in this approach, automatic stabilizers predominantly work on the revenue side.

Table A.1 Budget sensitivities used by the Commission services

	Budget revenue sensitivity to the output gap	*Budget expenditure sensitivity to the output gap*	*Total budget sensitivity to the output gap*
B	0.5	0.2	0.7
D	0.4	0.0	0.5
E	0.3	0.0	0.4
F	0.3	0.1	0.4
IRL	0.3	0.1	0.4
I	0.4	0.0	0.4
NL	0.4	0.4	0.8
A	0.3	0.0	0.3
P	0.3	0.1	0.3
FIN	0.5	0.2	0.7
EU-11	0.4	0.1	0.5
DK	0.5	0.3	0.9
EL	0.3	0.0	0.3
S	0.5	0.3	0.8
UK	0.4	0.1	0.5
EU-15	0.4	0.1	0.5

Source: EC (2000b).

1.3 Third step: calculation of cyclically adjusted budget balances

The application of the marginal sensitivity of revenue and expenditure ($\partial\, rev$ and $\partial\, exp$, respectively) to the output gap (*OG*) allows for the determination of the cyclical component) of the budget balance (*cc*). The cyclically adjusted budget balance is obtained by subtracting the cyclical component from the actual budget balance (*def*):

$$CAB_t = def_t - cc_t = def_t - (\varepsilon_{rev} + \varepsilon_{exp})^{*}OG_t \tag{A1.2}$$

In view of the simplifying assumption and usual estimation problems, the method only produces an approximate decomposition of the budget balance into a cyclical component and a structural component. Its results must therefore be interpreted with the necessary caution.

Appendix 2: Duration Models[3]

Duration analysis typically consists of: (1) a non-parametric analysis that focuses on the dependence of fiscal consolidation episodes on their accumulated duration; and (2) a parametric analysis that focuses of additional explanatory variables that can account for the observed variations in the duration of different consolidation episodes.

2.1 Non-parametric analysis

The non-parametric analysis of Chapter 3 uses the information contained in the *'Duration'* variable. Remember that this variable measures the time that passes between two years of fiscal expansion, or, in other words, between the beginning and the end of a fiscal consolidation.

Those econometric models developed to analyse this type of information are called duration models. If T is defined as the discrete random variable that measures the time that passes between the beginning of a fiscal consolidation until its transition to a non-consolidation period, the observations available consist of a series of data $(t_1, t_2, \ldots, t_n)$ which correspond to each of the observed durations of each consolidation period in my sample. The probability distribution of the duration variable can be specified by the cumulative distribution function:

$$F(t) = Pr\ (T<t) \tag{A2.1}$$

which indicates the probability that the random variable T is smaller than a certain value t. The corresponding probability function is then:

$$P(t) = Pr\ (T = t) \tag{A2.2}$$

But in duration models, two main functions are used to characterize the probability distribution of the duration variable:

(a) The survivor function, which is defined as:

$$S(t) = Pr\ (T \geq t) = 1 - F(t) \tag{A2.3}$$

and gives the probability that the duration of the fiscal consolidation (T)[4] is greater than or equal to t.

(b) The hazard function, which is defined as:

$$h(t) = Pr\ (T = t/T \geq t) \tag{A2.4}$$

and gives, for each duration, the probability of ending a consolidation episode, conditioned to the duration of the consolidation through that moment.

There exists a relation between both functions given by the following expression:

$$S(t) = \prod_{s=1/t}(1-h(s)) \tag{A2.5}$$

One of the advantages of the hazard function is that it allows us to characterize the dependence path of duration. Formally, there exists a positive duration dependence in t^* if $dh(t)/dt > 0$, in the moment $t = t^*$. This positive correlation implies that the probability that a fiscal consolidation ends in t, given that it has reached t, depends positively on the length of this consolidation period. Thus, the longer the period, the higher the conditional probability of entering into a fiscal expansion. Similarly, there exists negative duration dependence if $dh(t)/dt < 0$ in $t = t^*$. In this case, the longer the fiscal adjustment period, the lower the conditional probability of fiscal expansion.

The non-parametric analysis is used to estimate the unconditional hazard function which registers all the observations for which there is a change, that is, the relative frequency of observations with $T = t$. For this analysis of duration, the Kaplan–Meier estimate is widely used (Kaplan and Meier, 1958). The hazard function is calculated as follows:

$$\hat{h}(t) = \frac{d_t}{n_t} \tag{A2.6}$$

where dt represents the number of failures registered in moment t, and nt is the surviving population in moment t, before the change takes place. From the hazard function, it is possible to obtain the cumulative hazard function with a estimation procedure proposed by Nelson (1972) and Aalen (1978). It is given by the following expression:

$$\hat{H}(s) = \sum_{s=1}^{t}\hat{h}(s) \tag{A2.7}$$

The Kaplan–Meier survivor function for duration t is calculated as the product of one minus the existing risk until period t:

$$\hat{S}(t) = \prod_{j|t_j \leq t}\left(\frac{n_j - d_j}{n_j}\right) \tag{A2.8}$$

2.2 Parametric analysis

The non-parametric analysis is very limited because it does not take into account other variables that can influence the probability of ending a period of fiscal consolidation. In order to address the issue of other variables determining this probability, Chapter 3 also dedicates a section to the performance of a parametric analysis. In the literature, the model that has usually been used to characterize the hazard function is the *Model of Proportional Hazard* (PH), which assumes that the hazard function can be split as follows:

$$h(t,X) = h_0(t)^* g(X) \tag{A2.9}$$

where $h_0(t)$ is the baseline hazard function that captures the dependency of data to duration, and $g(x)$ is a function of individual variables. This function of explanatory variables is a negative function usually defined as $g(x) = \exp(X'\beta)$. Note that in this proportional specification, regressors intervene, re-escalating the conditional probability of abandoning the period of fiscal consolidation, not its own duration.

This model can be estimated firstly without imposing any specific functional form to the baseline hazard function, following the *Cox Model* (1972):[5]

$$h(t,X) = h_0(t)^* \exp(X'\beta) \qquad \text{(A2.10)}$$

Or an alternative estimation can be done by imposing one specific parametric form to the function $h_0(t)$. In this case, the models most commonly used are the *Weibull Model* and the *Exponential Model*. In the first one, $h_0(t) = pt^{p-1}$, where p is a parameter that has to be estimated. When $p = 1$, the *Weibull Model* is equal to the *Exponential Model*, where there exists no dependency on duration. On the other hand, when the parameter $p > 1$, there exists a positive dependency on duration, and a negative dependency when $p < 1$. Therefore, by estimating p, it is possible to test the hypothesis of duration dependency of fiscal consolidations.

A reasonable question to ask is: 'Given that there exist several possible parametric models, how should one be selected?' When parametric models are nested, the likelihood-ratios or the Wald tests can be used to discriminate between them. This can certainly be done in the case of Weibull versus Exponential. When models are not nested, however, these tests are unsuitable and the task of discriminating between models becomes difficult. A common approach to this problem is to use the Akaike Information Criterion (AIC). Akaike (1974) proposed penalizing each log likelihood to reflect the number of parameters being estimated in a particular model and then comparing them. For this purpose, the AIC can be defined as:

$$AIC = -2^*(log\ likelihood) + 2(c + q + 1) \qquad \text{(A2.11)}$$

where c is the number of model covariates (explanatory variables) and q is the number of model-specific auxiliary parameters. Although the best-fitting model is the one with the largest log likelihood, the preferred model is the one with the smallest AIC value.

Finally, there exists an additional method to test the power of each model, through graphic analysis of the Cox–Snell residuals (1968). These residuals are defined as follows:

$$\hat{e} = -\log S(t/x) \qquad \text{(A2.12)}$$

where $S(t/x)$ is the estimated probability of surviving to time t. If the fitted model is correct, these residuals, which are always positive, should have a standard censored exponential distribution with hazard ratio 1. The model's fit can be verified by calculating, based, for example, on the Kaplan–Meier survival estimates or the Aalen–Nelson estimator, an empirical estimate of the cumulative hazard function, using the Cox–Snell residuals (*cs*) as the time variable. If the model fits the data, then the plot of the cumulative hazard function versus *cs* should be a straight line with slope equal to unity and beginning at the origin.

As already shown in Chapter 3 (Figure 3.7), the *Weibull plot* satisfies the exponential requirement for most of the time, except in the part of larger residuals where the slope appears to exceed the unity. This confirms that the Weibull model should be my preferred model for the parametric analysis of duration of fiscal adjustment episodes.

Appendix 3: The Panel-Corrected Standard Errors Technique[6]

In pooled time-series research designs, annual time series from a cross-section of countries are stacked on top of one another and analysed jointly within the same data set. This implies a combination of time-series (temporal observations on a unit of analysis) with cross-sections (observations on a unit of analysis at a single time points). The current popularity of pooled time-series analysis stems from two great comparative advantages of this method. First, it produces a relatively large N and can therefore simultaneously test for the effect of a large number of independent variables. The number of cases is N × T, where N is the number of cross-sections and T is the number of time points. The second fundamental advantage of pooled time-series analysis is that it integrates both internal and external analysis, combining attention to both longitudinal and cross-sectional variation. It can therefore produce useful generalizations across both space and time.

Having said this, it is worth noting that any analysis of large pooled time series of cross-sections usually suffers from three related problems: panel heteroscedasticity, spatial correlation, and/or serial correlation.

The regression coefficients in panels of pooled time series can be estimated in several different ways, depending on the relative size of N with respect to T. James Stimson (1985: 929) developed an informal guide of pooled estimators for panel data (see table below).

In a situation like the one this book confronted in Chapter 4, where there was a temporally dominated panel of 15 countries over a 31-year period, and where between-unit effects were assumed to be taking place given the economic interrelations existing between European countries, the appropriate model prescribed in Table A.2 had to be a LSDV. In addition, in a panel like this (with countries of such different sizes such as Germany and Luxembourg) the presence of strong panel heteroscedasticity was also taken for granted. That is why, following the standard procedure for these situations, every regression of Chapter 4 included a set of country and year dummy variables.

In order to estimate these models, political economists have traditionally used the Feasible Generalized Least Squares (FGLS) estimator described by Parks and Kmenta (1986). This method consists of two sequential transformations, first eliminating serial correlation of the errors, and then eliminating contemporaneous correlation of the errors (what automatically corrects for any panel heteroskedasticity). Although the LSDV model estimated by Parks' FGLS performs well in large samples, regression coefficients in panels of pooled time series can be also estimated by OLS if one takes the appropriate additional measures to correct for panel heteroscedasticity, serial autocorrelation and spatial correlation. If this is carried out successfully, one could obtain more accurate estimations of all regression coefficients than using the Parks–Kmenta methodology.

Some years ago, Nathaniel Beck and Jonathan Katz (1995, 1996) presented an alternative method to the Parks–Kmenta (see Kmenta, 1986) one, based precisely on a OLS estimation of regression coefficients with a panel correction of standard errors. Their

Table A.2 Stimson's guide of pooled estimators for panel data

	No timewise autocorrelation in error	*Timewise autocorrelation present*
Cross-sectional dominance (N > T)		
No between-unit effects	—Ordinary Least Squares (OLS)	*
Between-unit effects (fixed)	—Least-Squares with Dummy Variables (LSDV)	*
(random)	—Error Components Model (GLSE)	
Time-serial dominance (T > N)		
No between-unit effects	—Ordinary Least Squares (OLS)	—GLS-ARMA
Between-unit effects	—Least-Squares Dummy Var. (LSDV)	—GLS-ARMA + Dummies

* No estimator developed specifically for this case.

method solved brilliantly all the problems mentioned above, and performed better in Monte Carlo analysis than the Parks–Kmenta method. In fact, Beck and Katz (1995: 634) showed that the 'Parks standard errors are likely to lead to extreme overconfidence for typical Time Series Cross Section data ... and may understate variability by between 50 per cent and 300 per cent in practical research situations'. Given the success of the new Panel Corrected Standard Errors technique, the Beck and Katz method became the most popular estimation technique among political economists working with temporarily dominated panels.

That is why Chapter 4 followed the Beck and Katz method for computing a heteroscedastic-consistent covariance matrix for pooled regression models. That covariance matrix estimate gave the Panel Corrected Standard Errors obtained as the square roots of the diagonal elements of the matrix:

$$Cov\,(b) = \left[\left[1/(X'X)\right]\left[X'(\Phi{*}It)X\right]\left[1/(X'X)\right]\right]$$

where Φ is a N*N matrix with the (i,j)th element estimated by:

$$\left(\textstyle\sum_t = 1\,\hat{e}_{i,t}\hat{e}_{j,t}\right)\big/T$$

When computing the standard errors and the variance-covariance estimates with that method, the disturbances were, by default, assumed to be heteroscedastic and contemporaneously correlated across panels. As such, the only problem that still needed correction was the possible presence of serial correlation, which was solved by including the lagged dependent variable on the right-hand side of each equation.

Therefore, although the use of panel-corrected standard errors usually produces rather conservative results (since it tends to increase the standard errors of the estimates), it also increases our confidence that results which emerged as significant in Chapter 4 are not the consequence of unsound statistical assumptions or inappropriate econometric methods.

Appendix 4: The Effect of the Budget Process on Fiscal Policy

Chapters 3 and 4 analysed empirically the dynamic determinants of fiscal adjustments' duration and composition. Among those determinants, a set of different economic and political variables was included, and fragmentation of decision-making turned out to be one of the most important aspects influencing the fiscal adjustment strategy. The decision to include fragmentation of decision-making among the explanatory variables arose from the set of hypotheses adopted, according to which the lower the degree of internalization of the costs associated to excessive expenditures the higher the probability of running fiscal deficits. As was mentioned then, there are two basic determinants of the degree of internalization of these costs: (i) the number of decision-makers; and (ii) the structure of the process in which they interact. The first aspect was instrumented by two time-variant variables such as coalition size (number of parties in government) and cabinet size (number of spending ministers). These variables were included as regressors in all the dynamic models used in the analysis of the duration (chapter 3) and the composition (chapter 4) dimensions of fiscal consolidations, and proved to be very significant explanatory variables.

The omission of any variable attempting to control for (ii) the structure of the budgetary process in which policy-makers interact, was justified in those chapters on the grounds of two factors: (1) the impossibility of including in a dynamic panel analysis time-invariant variables (such as the ones needed to describe the structure of the budgetary process); and (2) the lack of statistical significance of such variables as demonstrated in isolated experiments ran with the same data set.

Since the second point was only suggested in Chapters 3 and 4, this appendix presents the mentioned evidence of the empirical irrelevance of those structural variables, and therefore justifies why these variables where excluded from the analyses made in those chapters.

In order to do this, this appendix draws on the section on procedural fragmentation written by Perotti and Kontopoulos (2002) since it is the most complete and recent in the related literature.

The existence of spending limits, imposed either by the finance minister or by small committees, is supposed to diminish the tendency of big coalitions and cabinets with many spending ministers (Hallerberg and Von Hagen, 1997; Hallerberg, 2005). A second notion of procedural fragmentation concerns how ministers interact with one another when making bids on the budget: fragmentation is at a maximum when aggregate expenditure is determined by multilateral negotiations among all spending ministers involved.

In order to test the influence of these two factors on the budget, I first borrow two variables from Perotti and Kontopoulos (2002): TARGET and NEGOT. TARGET takes value 0 if the spending limits or targets are set by the finance minister, the prime minister or both, 1 if they are set by a committee or the whole cabinet, and 2 otherwise. NEGOT is a variable meant to capture the negotiations among ministers. It assigns government a score of 1 if the negotiations are conducted by the finance minister or the prime minister or both (bilateral negotiations), and 0 if they are conducted by a committee or the entire cabinet (multilateral negotiations).

Then, I run a panel regression on all the time-varying variables plus the country dummies, followed by a cross-sectional regression of the estimated country dummies on TARGET and NEGOT. In the regression for TARGET one would expect positive coefficients in the deficit, the expenditure and maybe also in the revenue regression. The opposite signs are expected for NEGOT.

Despite the fact that the expected positive and negative coefficients actually appear in the results reported in Table A.3, they are not statistically significant at any confidence level.

Therefore, results above show that 'one should not expect the reform of the budget process to be the panacea for all fiscal ills. Contrary to subnational governments, which are often limited in their ability to borrow anyway, there is nothing to prevent the government of a sovereign country to disregard, in practice, stringent budget rules' (Perotti and Kontopoulos, 2002: 28). If this *freedom from institutions* exists, one should focus, as in Chapters 3 and 4, on the analysis of the economic and political variables that affect policy-makers' decisions regarding the public budget – namely ideological orientation and proximity of elections, and not time-invariant institutional factors.

Table A.3 The role of spending targets and top-down negotiations in the budget process

	Var. deficit	*Var. P. exp.*	*Var. P. rev.*
TARGET	0.051	0.121	0.066
	(0.99)	(0.87)	(0.23)
R-squared	−0.05	−0.06	−0.06
N.Obs	15	15	15
NEGOT	−0.001	−0.004	−0.002
	(0.21)	(1.01)	(0.12)
R-squared	0.01	0.01	0.03
N.Obs	15	15	15

Absolute value of *t*-statistics in parentheses: *significant at 10 per cent; **significant at 5 per cent; ***significant at 1 per cent.

Appendix 5: The Economic Impact of Consolidations

5.1 The empirical literature on the economic impact of fiscal adjustments

As can be observed in the literature review presented in Table A.4, all studies from the 1990s identified expansionary fiscal adjustments. Growth rates tended to respond more favourably to episodes of successful fiscal consolidation[7] than did episodes of unsuccessful consolidation. The same was true of unemployment rates.

However, the quantitative impact of fiscal consolidations (that is, the size of the associated – negative – multipliers) varied markedly across successful and unsuccessful consolidations.

The characteristics of expansionary fiscal consolidations were not completely clear. Such studies as Cour, Dubois, Mahfouz, and Pisani-Ferry (1996), Giavazzi and Pagano (1996), and Giavazzi, Japelli, and Pagano (2000) found that large consolidations are most effective. While Alesina and Perotti (1997) and subsequent studies by the same authors emphasized instead the composition of adjustment, and, in particular, the gains from cutting transfers and other forms of unproductive spending, McDermott and Wescott (1996) concluded that both the size and composition of fiscal consolidation are important (which is precisely what was discovered in Chapter 6 of this book). Initial fiscal conditions and the other economic policies that accompany fiscal consolidation may also play a role. While some studies found no evidence that these were important, OECD (1996), Alesina and Ardagna (1998) and Perotti (1999) suggested that the initial level of debt, an exchange rate depreciation preceding consolidation, wage restraint, and/or fiscal consolidation in the context of broader structural reform influenced whether a fiscal consolidation was expansionary or contractionary.

Finally, the investment response to fiscal consolidation was highlighted by some studies. Although the theoretical literature emphasized the role of private consumption, Alesina and Ardagna (1998) and Alesina, Perotti and Tavares (1998) found that the behaviour of investment prior to, during, and after fiscal consolidations was also a significant, and in some cases more important, determinant of growth. Further evidence supporting this thesis was also provided in Chapter 6 of this book.

Table A.4 Cross-section studies of expansionary fiscal contractions (Part A)

Authors	*Sample*	*Definition of contraction*	*Number of episodes*	*Type of analysis*
1) McDermott and Wescott (1996)	20 OECD countries, 1970–95	–Primary structural balance improves by at least 1.5 per cent of GDP in two years.	74	–Correlations of averages across groups of episodes.
2) Giavazzi and Pagano (1996)	19 OECD countries, 1970–92	–Any period when the primary structural balance moved in a consistent direction; a cumulative 5 percentage point of GDP change marks a 'large' consolidation.	223	–Panel regressions of consumption functions (error correction specification).
3) OECD (1996)	All OECD countries, 1975–95	–Primary structural balance imporoves by 3 per cent of GDP in consecutive years.	15	–Correlations of averages across groups of episodes.
4) Cour, Dubois, Mahfouz, and Pisani Ferry (1996)	17 OECD countries, 1970–94	–Continuous improvement in primary structural balance, including an 'intense' subperiod.	19	–Correlations of averages across groups of episodes, consumption functions estimated across countries.
5) Alesina and Perotti (1997)	20 OECD countries, 1960–94	–Primary structural balance improves by at least 1.5 per cent of GDP in one year or 1.25 per cent of GDP in two consecutive years.	62 years of tight fiscal policy	–Correlations of averages across groups of episodes.

6) Alesina and Ardagna (1998)	All OECD countries, 1960–95	–Primary structural balance improves by at least 1.5 per cent of GDP in two consecutive years.	51, of which 23 expansionary	–Correlations of averages across groups of episodes.
7) Alesina, Perotti, and Tavares (1998)	19 OECD countries, 1960–95	–Primary structural balance improves by at least 1.5 per cent of GDP in one year.	69, of which 19 successful	–Correlations of averages across groups of . episodes.
8) Alesina, Ardagna, Perotti and Schiantarelli (1999)	18 OECD countries, 1960–96	–Primary structural balance improves by at least 2 per cent of GDP in one year or 1.25 per cent of GDP in two consecutive years.	Not given	–Correlations of averages across groups of episodes, investment equations from pooled regression.
9) Perotti (1999)	19 OECD countries, 1965–94	–Not given.	Not given	–Panel regressions of consumption functions (Euler equation specification).
10) Giavazzi, Jappelli and Pagano (2000)	18 OECD countries, 1970–96	–Not given.	38 expansions, 65 contractions.	–Panel regressions of national saving rates.

Source: IMF (2000: 20).

Table A.4 Cross-section studies of expansionary fiscal contractions (Part B)

Authors	*Main Evidence of Expansionary Contractions*	*Channels*	*Characteristics of Expansionary Contraction*
1) McDermott and Wescott (1996)	–For successful consolidations, GDP growth rate relative to OECD average: −0.2 per cent (before), 0.1 per cent (during) and 0.7 per cent (after).	–For expansionary contractions, mostly through investment; for debt-increasing expansions, crowding-out of investment; for stable-debt expansions,growth via consumption.	–Size is important, as composition; expenditure cuts (specially transfers and government wages) more likely to be successful; timing with respect to world business cycle also important.
2) Giavazzi and Pagano (1996)	–For large/persistent consolidations, $1 increase in taxes (cuts in transfers) raises private consumption by 15–20 per cent in long run.	–Private sector consumption (other channels not tested).	–Size and persistence most important; clearer effects for government spending but also for taxes and transfers.
3) OECD (1996)	–Four of 15 consolidations had growth above potential and six were within 1 per cent point of potential.	–Not addressed.	–Supportive monetary policy helps avoid adverse activity consequences.
4) Cour, Dubois, Mahfouz, and Pisani-Ferry (1996)	–Large retrenchments on average led to 0.1 per cent reduction in G-7 corrected growth, but small retrenchments led to 0.4 per cent reduction. Non- Keynesian retrenchments had higher growth rate of private consumption than predicted by a standard consumption function.	–Consumption most important.	–Size most important; other factors not clear.
5) Alesina and Perotti (1997)	–For successful consolidations, GDP growth rate relative to OECD average: −0.2 per cent (before), 1.1 per cent (during), and 0.3 per cent (after).	–Emphasizes impact of unit labour costs and competitiveness, and hence on investment and exports.	–Composition is crucial.

6) Alesina and Ardagna (1998)	–For expansionary contractions, GDP growth rate relative to G-7 average: 0.2 per cent (before), 1.3 per cent (during), and 0.9 per cent (after).	–Emphasizes impact on unit labour costs and competitiveness, and hence on investment and exports.	–Composition more important than size; income policy and exchange rate depreciation are important preconditions.
7) Alesina, Perotti, and Tavares (1998)	–For successful consolidations, GDP growth rate relative to OECD average: −0.3 per cent (before), 0.1 per cent (during), and 0.2 per cent (after).	–Investment more important than consumption; labour market also important.	–Composition more important than size; labour market structure also important.
8) Alesina, Ardagna, Perotti, and Schiantarelli (1999)	–1 per cent cut in primary spending leads to 0.2 percent increase in investment after impact, and 0.8 per cent increase after 5 years, similar effects for 1 per cent increase in labour taxes; larger effects for cuts in government wages.	–Tax and spending affect labour costs, and hence profits and investment.	–Composition is crucial.
9) Perotti (1999)	–Expenditure shocks have Keynesian effects with low debt or deficits, but non-Keynesian effects with high debt or deficits; evidence on similar switch with tax shocks is less strong.	–Private sector consumption (other channels not tested).	–Initial fiscal conditions are crucial; composition is also important.
10) Giavazzi, Jappelli,and Pagano (2000)	–Non-Keynesian responses by private sector more likely when fiscal impulses are large and persistent.	–Private sector consumption/saving (other channels not tested).	–Size and persistence most important; but not initial fiscal conditions. Non-Keynesian effects larger for changes in taxes than spending, and for contractions rather than expansions.

Source: IMF (2000: 20–1).

5.2 The Lorenz Curve and the Gini coefficient[8]

The following gives a brief graphical explanation of the Gini coefficient and the construction of equivalence scales. For further reference on these and other issues related to the design and analysis of household surveys, see Deaton (1997).

A straightforward graphical interpretation of the Gini coefficient is the Lorenz curve, which is the thick curve in the figure below.

The horizontal axis plots the cumulative percentage of the population whose inequality is under consideration, starting from the poorest and ending with the richest. The vertical axis plots the cumulative percentage of income associated with the units on the horizontal axis.

In the case of a completely egalitarian income distribution in which the whole population has equal incomes, the Lorenz curve would be the dashed straight 45-degree line. When inequality exists, the poor population has a proportionately lower share of income compared with the rich population, and the Lorenz curve may look like the thick curve below the 45-degree line. As inequality rises, so the thick curve moves towards the bottom right-hand corner.

The Gini coefficient can be defined as: $G = A/A + B$. The Gini coefficient may be given as a proportion or percentage. From this it is clear that the Gini coefficient will be equal to 0 when the distribution is completely egalitarian. If the society's total income accrues to only one person/household unit, leaving the rest with no income at all, then the Gini coefficient will be equal to 1, or 100 per cent.

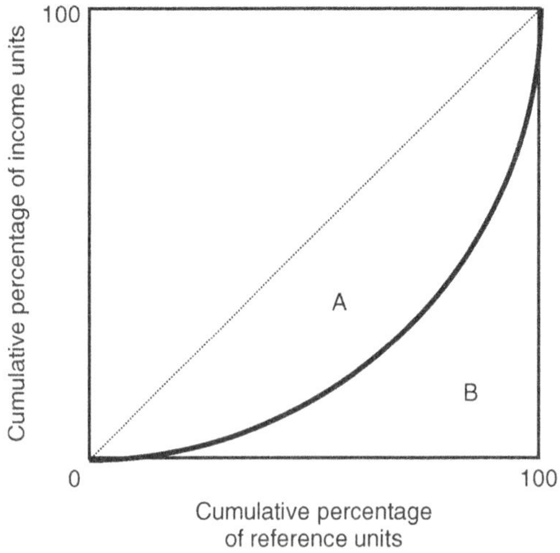

Figure A.1 The Lorenz Curve and the Gini coefficient

5.3 The economic impact of fiscal adjustments during the 1990s: complementary data

Table A.5 Initial fiscal conditions, budget composition and strategies of fiscal adjustments, 1990–2000

	Non-adjustment	Adjustment					
		Revenue-based			*Expenditure-based*		
Fiscal policy		*Before*	*During*	*After*	*Before*	*During*	*After*
Debt ratio	66.64	75.80	81.80	86.65	68.85	65.68	68.07
Δ Debt ratio	0.30	2.09	1.90	−0.49	2.42	0.39	−2.31
Budget balance	−2.84	−5.18	−4.72	−3.50	−5.56	−3.40	−1.76
Δ Budget balance	0.26	−0.81	1.11	0.75	−0.59	1.41	0.81
Total revenues	46.87	45.92	45.76	47.17	46.81	48.30	46.53
Δ Total revenues	0.31	0.08	1.26	−0.08	−0.01	0.76	−0.21
Total direct taxes	14.38	14.74	14.51	15.38	15.08	15.87	14.21
Δ T. direct taxes	−0.04	0.04	0.78	−0.03	−0.15	0.37	−0.08
Total expenditures	50.31	51.18	50.15	50.53	54.45	52.44	49.35
Δ Total expenditures	0.13	0.48	0.03	−0.12	0.74	−0.67	−0.74
Total transfers	12.23	11.87	11.06	11.74	13.11	12.30	11.52
Δ T. transfers	−0.02	−0.09	−0.05	−0.01	0.03	−0.26	−0.24
Total public wages	18.89	19.18	18.81	17.61	18.91	17.47	11.52
Δ T. public wages	−0.05	−0.09	0.20	−0.01	0.30	−0.80	−0.64
Total pub. investment	2.82	2.51	2.54	2.70	2.78	2.46	2.33
Δ T. p. investment	0.01	−0.01	0.01	0.05	−0.03	−0.07	−0.04

Source: Own elaboration.

Table A.6 Monetary policy and fiscal adjustments, 1990–2000

	Non-adjustment	Adjustment					
		Revenue-based			*Expenditure-based*		
Monetary policy		*Before*	*During*	*After*	*Before*	*During*	*After*
Real interest rate (S-term)	4.13	5.71	5.17	4.90	4.71	3.75	3.22
Δ Real interest rate	−0.24	−0.13	−0.23	−0.22	−1.13	−0.36	−0.40
Real interest rate (G4)	0.04	0.86	0.99	1.00	0.47	−0.30	0.31
Real exchange rate	100.46	100.87	101.79	101.69	99.65	106.60	100.63
Δ Real exchange rate	−0.44	0.67	0.28	−0.14	−2.66	0.96	0.40

Source: Own elaboration.

Table A.7 Microeconomic outcomes, trade policy outcomes and fiscal adjustments, 1990–2000

	Non-adjustment	Adjustment					
		Revenue-based			*Expenditure-based*		
Microeconomic outcomes		*Before*	*During*	*After*	*Before*	*During*	*After*
Private consumption	56.59	56.44	57.82	56.77	56.22	57.63	58.71
Δ Private consumption	56.59	56.44	57.82	56.77	56.22	57.63	58.71
Private investment	−0.09	−0.07	0.11	0.02	−0.04	0.43	0.69
Δ Private investment	17.83	16.82	17.37	16.71	16.74	17.41	18.44
Labour costs index	−0.09	0.11	0.27	−0.21	0.05	0.30	0.62
		102.2					
Δ Labour costs	100.65	0	102.05	100.25	102.41	100.07	99.60
Profits share	−0.63	−0.12	−0.15	−0.29	−1.20	−1.34	−1.63
Δ Profits share	0.04	0.05	0.02	0.09	0.03	0.72	0.31
Trade policy outcomes							
Imports	40.81	41.29	39.70	40.35	35.76	36.74	39.63
Δ Imports	1.33	0.97	0.43	0.97	1.67	1.54	1.76
Exports	31.19	29.60	27.50	28.37	29.46	30.47	36.14
Δ Exports	1.17	0.54	0.46	1.02	1.55	1.66	1.43
Trade balance	2.04	1.33	0.88	1.72	1.41	2.07	2.86
Δ Trade balance	0.27	0.10	0.70	0.11	0.41	0.83	0.33

Source: Own elaboration.

Statistical Annex 1: Dependent and Independent Variables; Descriptive Statistics

Table A.8 Descriptive statistics: variables used in Chapter 3 (timing analysis)

Variables (EU-15: 1970–2000)	*Obs.*	*Mean*	*Std. dev.*	*Min.*	*Max.*
Output gap	465	.105	2.334	−7.58	8.85
Output gap ($t-1$)	450	.090	2.364	−7.58	8.85
Output gap EU-15	467	.110	2.542	−3.45	6.68
Monetary conditions index	457	6.98	1.412	2.86	11.61
Debt-to-GDP ratio	449	51.675	30.335	3.97	134.55
Election year	451	.292	.455	0	1
Coalition size (no. of parties)	448	2.315	1.337	1	8
Cabinet size (no. of ministers)	448	10.746	2.176	5	17

Source: AMECO (2001) and Armingeon, Beyeler and Menegale (2000).

Table A.9 Descriptive statistics: variables used in Chapter 3 (duration analysis)

Variables (EU-15: 1970–2000)	*Obs.*	*Mean*	*Std. dev.*	*Min.*	*Max.*
Failure	441	.768	.422	0	1
Duration	441	1.315	.669	0	5
Number of failures	441	125.147	94.997	0	308
Quality of adjustment	441	−.950	3.387	−21.736	15.753
Strength of adjustment	429	1.441	1.177	.0082	6.595
Months to next election	449	17.291	14.638	0	48
Socialist control of cabinet	447	39.241	36.592	0	100

Note: The first five variables correspond to the duration analysis in chapter 3 under the strong definition of fiscal adjustment.

Source: AMECO (2001) and Armingeon, Beyeler and Menegale (2000).

Table A.10 Descriptive statistics: variables used in Chapter 4 (composition analysis, all years)

Variable (EU-15: 1970–2000) *All years*	*Obs.*	*Mean*	*Std. dev.*	*Min.*	*Max.*
Budget primary bal. cycl. adj.	463	1.312	3.245	−8.48	9.59
Total revenues cycl. adj.	462	42.869	9.176	20.62	64.37
Total prim. expend. cyc. adj	462	41.561	7.904	19.41	63.28
Direct taxes	463	13.230	5.879	3.01	30.62
Indirect taxes	465	13.439	2.469	6.08	19.07
Social contributions	463	11.877	4.918	1.32	21.06
Subsidies	465	2.738	1.370	.14	8.71
Interest payments	463	4.120	2.861	.26	13.92
Final consumption	465	17.856	4.291	9.01	28.55
Collective consumption	219	8.357	1.228	4.17	11.56
Social benefits in kind	219	12.624	2.885	5.88	22.73
Social benefits other-in kind	463	15.936	4.704	3.65	28.3
Compensation of employees	463	11.905	2.788	6.14	20.04
Public investment (GFCF)	463	3.227	1.025	1.03	6.37
Δ Total revenues cycl. adj.	454	.444	1.660	−4.3	10.12
Δ T. prim. expend. cyc.adj	454	.374	1.639	−5.06	9.31
Δ Direct taxes	454	.165	.826	−3.41	4.39
Δ Indirect taxes	457	.045	.645	−3.65	2.93
Δ Social contributions	454	.158	.554	−2.46	4.05
Δ Subsidies	457	−.019	.558	−3.74	2.82
Δ Final consumption	457	.189	.944	−1.99	10.27
Δ Collective consumption	203	−.024	.306	−.91	1.32
Δ Social benefits in kind	203	.067	.448	−1.16	1.87
Δ Social benefits oth kind	454	.161	1.088	−10.44	5.83
Δ Compensat. employees	454	.061	.481	−1.6	2.4
Δ Public invest. (GFCF)	454	−.040	.343	−1.59	1.83
Budget prim. bal. cycl. ad ($t-1$)	456	1.233	3.212	−8.477	9.591
Δ Unemployment	455	.140	1.040	−2.9	5.1
Δ Prices	464	5.296	5.694	−.41	44.43

Source: AMECO (2001).

Table A.11 Descriptive statistics: variables used in Chapter 4 (composition analysis, adjustment episodes)

Variables (EU-15: 1960–2000) *Adjustment episodes*	*Obs.*	*Mean*	*Std. dev.*	*Min.*	*Max.*
Δ Total revenues cycl. adj.	53	1.234	1.166	−1.74	4.05
Δ T. prim. expend. cyc. adj	53	−.409	1.434	−4.49	2.15
Δ Strategy type	53	.649	2.185	−5.54	4.8
Δ Direct taxes	53	.344	.479	−.69	1.95
Δ Indirect taxes	53	.367	.623	−1.9	1.9
Δ Social contributions	53	.225	.490	−.8	2.03
Δ Subsidies	53	−.222	.724	−3.74	.76
Δ Final consumption	51	−.056	.837	−1.33	4.68
Δ Compensation employees	53	−.091	.376	−1.02	.73
Δ Social benefits in kind	53	.041	.989	−5.5	1.85
Δ Public invest. (GFCF)	53	−.213	.280	−.93	.59
Budget PcAB balance ($t-1$)	53	−.339	3.901	−8.48	6.69
Δ Unemployment	53	.309	1.046	−2.2	3
Δ Prices	53	6.640	7.315	.66	42.74
Coalition size (of parties)	53	2.207	1.261	1	5
Cabinet size (of ministers)	53	10.408	2.186	6	16.5
Socialist control of cabinet	53	37.686	35.396	0	100
Election year	53	.509	.504	0	1

Source: AMECO (2001).

Table A.12 Descriptive statistics: variables used in Chapter 6

Variables (EU-15: 1960–2000)	*Obs.*	*Mean*	*Std. dev.*	*Min.*	*Max.*
Debt-to-GDP ratio	450	51.706	30.308	3.974	134.551
Δ Debt-to-GDP ratio	435	1.071	4.111	−10.131	18.022
Budget deficit (Maastricht. dfn)	593	−1.934	3.922	−15.907	6.983
Δ Budg. def. (Maastricht. dfn)	577	−.0008	1.611	−6.769	5.304
Real GDP growth	600	3.436	2.704	−6.571	13.204
Δ Real GDP growth	585	−.0475	2.850	−14.53	12.805
Inequality (Gini index)	365	34.163	6.870	23.2	54.3
Δ Inequality	336	−.0891	1.321	−4.432	7.926
Real GDP growth. (G4 countries)	600	2.951	1.639	−1.093	6.018
Δ Unemployment (G4 countries)	600	.154	.501	−.8	1.475
Δ Prices (G4 Countries)	600	3.508	2.184	.37	8.439
Short-term real interest rates	474	2.108	3.678	−12.864	12.284
Δ Short-term real interest rates	460	.062	2.596	−15.663	10.608
Short-term real interest rates (G4)	600	1.946	2.644	−5.87	6.721
Real exchange rate	574	99.342	15.312	64.331	160.764
Δ Real exchange rate	560	−.0911	5.373	−24.338	21.638
Private consumption	615	57.814	6.288	40.48	78.738
Δ Private consumption	600	−.0976	1.157	−6.072	6.764
Private investment	523	19.234	3.183	11.572	30.374
Δ Private investment	507	−.0423	1.354	−6.688	4.064
Labour costs	615	106.945	8.058	85.784	152.690
Δ Labour costs	600	−.309	2.921	−12.532	22.853
Profits share	615	31.98	3.867	23.556	48.765
Δ Profits share	600	−.14	1.123	−5.323	9.554
Imports (per cent GDP)	615	30.714	22.461	2.920	120.025
Exports (per cent GDP)	537	22.452	14.532	2.449	84.799
Trade balance	615	−.202	5.078	−19.253	24.013

Source: AMECO (2001), G4 = Germany, France, USA, Japan.

Table A.13 Descriptive statistics: variables used in Chapter 7 (all years)

Variables (EU-15: 1960–2000) *All years*	*Obs.*	*Mean*	*Std. dev.*	*Min.*	*Max.*
Government duration	573	1.900	1.057	1	5
Government termination	266	.463	.499	0	1
Change in gov't ideology	100	.573	.781	0	2
Change in prime minister	117	.443	.497	0	1
Re-election	129	.496	.501	0	1
Majority in parliament	572	.706	.455	0	1
Social mobilization	445	955.176	1577.351	0	9891

Source: AMECO (2001) and Armingeon, Beyeler and Menegale (2000).

Table A.14 Descriptive statistics: variables used in Chapter 7 (adjustment episodes)

Variables (EU-15: 1960–2000) *Adjustment episodes*	*Obs.*	*Mean*	*Std. dev.*	*Min.*	*Max.*
Re-election	51	.490	.504	0	1
Real GDP growth	51	2.222	1.934	−1.16	9.82
Δ Prices	53	6.640	7.315	.66	42.74
Δ Unemployment	53	.309	1.046	−2.2	3
Δ Inequality	49	.0007	.745	−2.05	1.8
Adjustment duration	53	−2.037	.979	−5	−1
Majority in parliament	53	.698	.463	0	1
Coalition size	53	2.207	1.261	1	5
Social mobilization	51	2250.76	4092.077	22.3	20972
Expenditure-based adjust.	53	.528	.503	0	1

Source: AMECO (2001) and Armingeon, Beyeler and Menegale (2000).

Statistical Annex 2: Data on General Government Balances and Cyclical Corrections: Definitions and Tables[9]

General Government: The general government sector covers central government, state governments, local governments and social security funds. The sector is not defined on an institutional basis but on a functional one. It includes all institutional units which are non-market producers whose output is intended for individual and collective consumption, and mainly financed by compulsory payments made by the units belonging to other sectors, and all institutional units principally engaged in the redistribution of national income and wealth. Publicly owned units dealing with commercial operations, such as public enterprises, are excluded.

Public Resources

Taxes Linked to Imports and Production (Indirect Taxes): consist of compulsory, unrequited payments, in cash or in kind, which are levied by the general government, in respect of the production and importation of goods and services, the employment of labour, the ownership or the use of land, buildings and other assets used in production. These taxes are payable whether or not profits are made.

Current Taxes on Income and Wealth (Direct Taxes): cover all compulsory, unrequited payments, in cash or in kind, levied periodically by the general government on the income and wealth of institutional units, and some periodic taxes which are assessed neither on the income nor the wealth.

Social Contributions: include actual social contributions paid by employers, employees, self-employed and non-employed people to social security funds. They also include the imputed social contributions recorded in the general government accounts

Actual Social Contributions: Do not include imputed social contributions.

Other Current Receipts: cover property income (interest received, dividends paid by public enterprises to governments, rents, etc.), other current transfers received (insurance claims, international cooperation, etc.) and gross operation surplus (which corresponds to the gross income which government obtains from its market production activities).

Total Current Receipts: total of current taxes, social contributions and other current receipts received by general government.

Capital Transfers Received: covers capital taxes (inheritance taxes, etc.), investment grants received and other capital transfers received.

Total Resources: covers current resources plus capital transfers received.

Public expenditures

Final Consumption Expenditure: consists of expenditure incurred by government on goods and services that are used for the direct satisfaction of individual or collective needs of the community. Final expenditure corresponds to expenditure on collective consumption plus expenditure on individual consumption.

Collective Consumption: covers the services for collective consumption (public services) which are provided simultaneously to all members of the community. The provision of the collective service to the individual does not reduce the amount available for other individuals.

Compensation of Employees: is defined as the total remuneration, in cash or in kind, payable by government to its employees in return for their work during the accounting period.

Social Transfers in Kind: also known as government expenditure on individual consumption, consists of individual goods and services provided as transfers in kind to individual households by government units. They include the reimbursement by social security funds of approved expenditures incurred by households, the medical treatments, social housing, dwelling allowances, day nurseries, professional training, reduction in transport prices, etc.

Social Transfers Other than in Kind: covers transfers to households, in cash, intended to relieve them from the financial burden of a number of risks or needs, made through collectively organized schemes. Examples include wages during absences of work due to ill health, accident, maternity; the payment of education or other allowances in respect of dependants; the payments of retirement or survivors' pensions to employees or their survivors.

Interest: is the amount that the government becomes liable to pay to its creditors over a given period of time without reducing the amount of principal outstanding. Interests are recorded on an accrual basis.

Subsidies: are current unrequited payments by general government to resident producers with the objective of influencing their levels of production, their prices or the remuneration of the factors of production.

Other Current Expenditure: covers rents, direct taxes and other current transfers (insurance premia, current international cooperation, voluntary payments to non-profit institutions, etc.).

Total Current Expenditure: covers final consumption expenditure, transfers and other transfers than in kind, interests, subsidies, and other current expenditure.

Gross Fixed Capital Formation: includes net acquisitions of fixed assets (dwellings, buildings, machinery and equipment), plus certain additions to the value of non-produced assets.

Other Capital Expenditures: includes changes in inventories, capital transfers paid, net acquisition of valuables, and net acquisition of non-produced and non-financial assets.

Total Expenditure: total of current expenditure, gross capital formation and other capital expenditure.

Gross Savings: balance of current resources minus current expenditure.

Net Lending (+) or Net Borrowing (−): shows the net amount of resources which the government places at the disposal of other sectors or which other sectors provide to the government sector. It corresponds to the difference between total resources and total expenditure, and it is also known as the public budget balance.

Table S.A.1 Resources and expenditure of general government (per cent GDP)

	Former definitions									*ESA 95 definitions* (¹)				
Austria	*1980*	*1985*	*1990*	*1991*	*1992*	*1993*	*1994*	*1995*	*1995*	*1996*	*1997*	*1998*	*1999*	*2000*
1. Taxes on production and imports	15.8	16.3	15.7	15.5	15.6	15.7	15.7	15.5	14.2	14.5	15.0	15.0	15.1	14.6
2. Current taxes on income and wealth	12.5	14.0	11.6	12.2	12.7	12.8	11.3	11.9	12.0	13.1	13.5	13.7	13.4	13.2
3. Social contributions	14.4	14.7	15.5	15.6	16.2	16.8	17.2	17.3	17.4	17.5	17.3	17.2	17.3	17.0
4. *Of which* actual social contributions	:	:	:	:	:	:	:	:	15.2	15.3	15.3	15.2	15.2	14.9
5. Other current resources	2.8	2.9	4.4	4.4	4.8	4.6	4.4	4.5	5.8	5.2	3.8	3.5	3.1	3.1
6. Total current resources	45.6	47.9	47.1	47.7	49.2	49.9	48.6	49.2	49.5	50.3	49.6	49.5	48.9	48.0
7. Government consumption expenditure	17.4	18.4	18.4	18.7	19.1	19.9	20.0	19.8	20.4	20.3	19.7	19.6	19.6	19.3
8. *Of which* compensation of employees	11.6	12.4	11.7	11.8	12.0	12.5	12.4	12.4	12.6	12.4	11.5	11.3	11.4	11.2
9. Collective consumption	:	:	:	:	:	:	:	:	8.1	8.0	7.8	7.8	7.7	7.5
10. Social benefits in kind	:	:	:	:	:	:	:	:	12.4	12.3	11.9	11.9	11.9	11.8
11. Social transfers other than in kind	18.4	19.8	19.5	19.7	19.9	21.5	21.7	21.6	19.5	19.5	18.9	18.6	18.7	18.7
12. Interest payments	2.4	3.5	4.0	4.2	4.2	4.3	4.0	4.3	4.4	4.2	3.9	3.8	3.5	3.6
13. Subsidies	2.9	2.8	2.8	3.1	3.0	3.1	2.5	2.9	2.9	2.6	2.6	2.8	2.6	2.5
14. Other current expenditure	:	:	:	:	:	:	:	:	2.5	2.6	2.5	2.7	2.6	2.3
15. Total current expenditure	41.3	44.7	44.9	45.9	46.5	49.1	48.6	49.6	49.7	49.3	47.5	47.4	47.0	46.3
16. Gross savings	4.2	3.1	2.2	1.8	2.7	0.8	0.0	−0.4	−0.3	1.0	2.1	2.0	1.8	1.7
17. Capital transfers received	:	:	:	:	:	:	:	:	0.2	0.2	0.3	0.1	0.1	0.1
18. Total resources	45.6	47.9	47.1	47.7	49.2	49.9	48.6	49.2	52.1	52.8	52.2	52.0	51.6	50.6
19. Gross fixed capital formation	4.3	3.6	3.2	3.2	3.2	3.2	3.3	2.8	3.1	2.8	2.0	1.9	1.8	1.7
20. Other capital expenditure	:	:	:	:	:	:	:	:	2.0	2.2	2.1	2.5	2.2	1.2
21. Total expenditure	47.2	50.3	49.6	50.6	51.2	54.1	53.5	54.2	57.2	56.6	53.9	54.3	53.7	51.8
22. Tax burden	42.7	44.9	42.6	43.2	44.4	45.3	44.0	44.7	44.9	45.9	46.9	46.7	46.5	45.6
23. Net lending (+) or net borrowing (−)	−1.7	−2.4	−2.4	−3.0	−1.9	−4.2	−4.9	−5.0	−5.2	−3.8	−1.7	−2.2	−2.1	−1.1

(¹) The table is based on ESA95 definitions which do not necessarily correspond with the former definitions: The Totals are obtained in ESA 95 as follows:
Line 6 = line 1 + line 2 + line 3 + line 5.
Line 7 = line 9 + line 10.
Line 15 = total of lines 9 to 14.
Line 16 = line 6 − line 15.
Line 18 = line 6 + line 17.
Line 21 = line 15 + line 19 + line 20.
Line 23 = line 18 − line 21.

Source: Commission services.

Table S.A.2 Resources and expenditure of general government (per cent GDP)

	Former definitions								*ESA 95 definitions* ([1])					
Belgium	*1980*	*1985*	*1990*	*1991*	*1992*	*1993*	*1994*	*1995*	*1995*	*1996*	*1997*	*1998*	*1999*	*2000*
1. Taxes on production and imports	12.2	12.0	12.2	12.1	12.0	12.4	12.7	12.2	12.2	12.7	12.9	12.9	13.3	13.2
2. Current taxes on income and wealth	18.0	19.2	16.7	16.3	16.2	16.3	17.5	17.9	16.7	16.7	17.1	17.6	17.2	17.4
3. Social contributions	14.9	17.1	16.8	17.4	17.7	18.2	17.7	17.4	16.8	16.8	16.7	16.5	16.5	16.2
4. *Of which* actual social contributions	:	:	:	:	:	:	:	:	14.8	14.7	14.6	14.5	14.5	14.2
5. Other current resources	2.6	2.3	1.8	1.9	1.8	1.8	1.5	1.5	3.1	3.2	3.0	2.9	2.8	3.0
6. Total current resources	47.7	50.6	47.4	47.7	47.7	48.6	49.4	49.0	48.9	49.4	49.7	50.0	49.9	49.8
7. Government consumption expenditure	17.3	16.7	13.9	14.3	14.1	14.6	14.6	14.5	21.5	21.8	21.3	21.2	21.4	21.1
8. *Of which* compensation of employees	13.4	13.0	11.2	11.5	11.5	12.0	12.1	12.1	12.0	11.9	11.8	11.7	11.6	11.4
9. Collective consumption	:	:	:	:	:	:	:	:	7.8	7.7	7.6	7.6	7.7	7.6
10. Social benefits in kind	:	:	:	:	:	:	:	:	13.7	14.1	13.7	13.6	13.7	13.5
11. Social transfers other than in kind	23.6	24.9	23.1	24.0	24.3	24.7	24.3	24.3	16.6	16.6	16.3	16.0	15.7	15.5
12. Interest payments	5.9	10.3	10.4	10.0	10.6	10.7	10.0	8.8	9.3	8.9	8.0	7.7	7.2	6.9
13. Subsidies	3.6	3.7	2.8	2.9	2.6	2.6	2.4	2.4	1.5	1.6	1.4	1.5	1.5	1.5
14. Other current expenditure	:	:	:	:	:	:	:	:	2.0	2.1	2.2	2.2	2.2	2.1
15. Total current expenditure	51.4	56.3	51.1	52.1	52.7	53.7	52.4	51.0	50.9	50.9	49.2	48.5	48.0	47.2
16. Gross savings	−3.7	−5.8	−3.6	−4.4	−5.0	−5.1	−3.0	−2.0	−2.0	−1.5	0.5	1.5	1.9	2.7
17. Capital transfers received	:	:	:	:	:	:	:	:	0.4	0.4	0.6	0.5	0.6	0.5
18. Total resources	47.7	50.6	47.4	47.7	47.7	48.6	49.4	49.0	48.6	49.3	49.7	50.0	50.0	49.9
19. Gross fixed capital formation	4.4	2.5	1.3	1.3	1.4	1.6	1.6	1.4	1.8	1.6	1.6	1.5	1.8	1.8
20. Other capital expenditure	:	:	:	:	:	:	:	:	1.0	1.1	1.5	1.3	1.4	1.3
21. Total expenditure	56.2	59.5	52.8	53.9	54.6	55.8	54.2	52.9	53.0	53.0	51.6	50.9	50.7	49.9
22. Tax burden	46.2	49.4	46.8	46.8	47.0	47.9	49.1	48.6	46.9	47.2	47.8	48.1	48.0	47.9
23. Net lending (+) or net borrowing (−)	−8.6	−8.9	−5.4	−6.2	−6.9	−7.2	−4.8	−3.9	−4.3	−3.8	−1.9	−0.9	−0.7	0.0

([1]) The table is based on ESA 95 definitions which do not necessarily correspond with the former definitions: The totals are obtained in ESA 95 as follows:
Line 6 = line 1 + line 2 + line 3 + line 5.
Line 7 = line 9 + line 10.
Line 15 = total of lines 9 to 14.
Line 16 = line 6 − line 15.
Line 18 = line 6 + line 17.
Line 21 = line 15 + line 19 + line 20.
Line 23 = line 18 − line 21.

Source: Commission services.

Table S.A.3 Resources and expenditure of general government (per cent GDP)

Denmark	Former definitions								ESA 95 definitions ([1])					
	1980	*1985*	*1990*	*1991*	*1992*	*1993*	*1994*	*1995*	*1995*	*1996*	*1997*	*1998*	*1999*	*2000*
1. Taxes on production and imports	18.0	17.8	17.0	16.7	16.6	16.9	17.3	17.2	16.9	17.3	17.5	18.0	17.8	17.0
2. Current taxes on income and wealth	25.1	27.8	28.3	28.5	29.0	30.1	30.6	30.3	30.4	30.6	30.3	29.6	30.1	28.7
3. Social contributions	1.6	2.5	2.3	2.3	2.4	2.5	2.8	2.6	2.6	2.6	2.6	2.6	3.1	3.2
4. *Of which* actual social contributions	:	:	:	:	:	:	:	:	1.6	1.6	1.6	1.6	2.1	2.2
5. Other current resourses	6.0	7.1	7.5	7.2	8.0	8.4	7.5	6.8	6.8	7.1	6.7	6.6	6.0	5.5
6. Total current resources	50.8	55.2	55.1	54.7	56.0	57.9	58.1	56.9	56.8	57.7	57.1	56.7	57.0	54.4
7. Government consumption expenditure	27.0	25.6	25.6	25.7	25.8	26.8	25.9	25.7	25.8	25.9	25.5	25.7	25.5	24.7
8. *Of which* compensation of employees	18.0	17.4	17.7	17.7	17.8	18.1	17.5	17.3	17.3	17.3	17.1	17.3	17.1	16.6
9. Collective consumption	:	:	:	:	:	:	:	:	8.5	8.5	8.3	8.1	8.0	7.7
10. Social benefits in kind	:	:	:	:	:	:	:	:	17.3	17.4	17.1	17.6	17.5	17.0
11. Social transfers other than in kind	16.3	15.9	18.0	18.7	19.2	20.3	21.7	20.8	20.4	19.8	18.8	18.1	17.5	16.8
12. Interest payments	3.7	9.3	7.3	7.3	6.6	7.3	6.7	6.4	6.4	6.1	5.7	5.3	4.6	4.1
13. Subsidies	3.0	2.8	3.3	3.2	3.8	3.9	3.7	3.6	2.5	2.6	2.4	2.3	2.3	2.2
14. Other current expenditure	:	:	:	:	:	:	:	:	2.2	2.4	2.4	2.5	2.5	2.5
15. Total current expenditure	50.0	54.4	54.9	56.7	56.3	58.9	58.8	57.4	57.3	56.8	54.9	53.9	52.4	50.3
16. Gross savings	0.7	0.8	0.2	−1.0	−0.4	−1.0	−0.7	−0.5	−0.5	0.9	2.2	2.9	4.6	4.1
17. Capital transfers received	:	:	:	:	:	:	:	:	0.5	0.4	0.5	0.5	0.5	0.5
18. Total resources	50.8	55.2	55.1	54.7	56.0	57.9	58.1	56.9	58.0	58.8	58.4	58.0	58.5	55.7
19. Gross fixed capital formation	3.3	2.1	1.6	1.5	1.9	1.8	1.8	1.8	1.8	1.9	1.9	1.7	1.7	1.8
20. Other capital expenditure	:	:	:	:	:	:	:	:	0.5	0.4	0.4	0.5	0.4	0.4
21. Total expenditure	53.1	56.4	56.1	57.1	58.2	60.7	60.7	59.2	60.3	59.8	58.0	56.9	55.4	53.3
22. Tax burden	44.7	48.0	47.6	47.5	48.0	49.5	50.7	50.1	50.2	50.7	50.7	50.4	51.2	49.1
23. Net lending (+) or net borrowing (−)	−3.2	−2.0	−1.0	−2.4	−2.2	−2.8	−2.6	−2.2	−2.3	−1.0	0.4	1.1	3.1	2.4

([1]) The table is based on ESA 95 definitions which do not necessarily correspond with the former definitions: The Totals are obtained in ESA 95 as follows:
Line 6 = line 1 + line 2 + line 3 + line 5.
Line 7 = line 9 + line 10.
Line 15 = total of lines 9 to 14.
Line 16 = line 6 − line 15.
Line 18 = line 6 + line 17.
Line 21 = line 15 + line 19 + line 20.
Line 23 = line 18 − line 21.

Source: Commission services.

Table S.A.4 Resources and expenditure of general government (per cent GDP)

	Former definitions								*ESA 95 definitions* ([1])					
Finland	*1980*	*1985*	*1990*	*1991*	*1992*	*1993*	*1994*	*1995*	*1995*	*1996*	*1997*	*1998*	*1999*	*2000*
1. Taxes on production and imports	13.1	14.1	14.9	15.0	14.7	14.5	14.2	13.6	13.7	13.5	14.3	14.1	14.0	13.3
2. Current taxes on income and wealth	14.2	16.5	17.7	17.6	16.9	15.2	16.8	16.7	17.4	18.9	18.4	18.8	18.6	21.0
3. Social contributions	10.9	11.4	12.9	13.6	14.6	15.0	15.8	14.8	14.9	14.3	13.4	13.0	13.0	12.1
4. *Of which* actual social contributions	:	:	:	:	:	:	:	:	14.6	14.0	13.2	12.9	12.9	12.1
5. Other current resources	3.8	5.1	5.9	6.8	7.6	8.0	6.7	7.0	7.3	6.7	6.3	5.9	5.4	6.2
6. Total current resources	42.0	47.0	51.4	53.1	53.7	52.7	53.5	52.0	53.2	53.5	52.3	51.8	51.0	52.7
7. Government consumption expenditure	17.6	19.8	20.8	23.8	24.3	22.8	21.8	21.2	22.8	23.2	22.4	21.7	21.5	20.6
8. *Of which* compensation of employees	12.0	13.9	14.4	16.8	17.3	16.2	15.2	14.8	15.4	15.6	14.6	13.9	13.6	13.0
9. Collective consumption	:	:	:	:	:	:	:	:	8.3	8.4	8.4	8.1	8.1	7.6
10. Social benefits in kind	:	:	:	:	:	:	:	:	14.5	14.8	14.1	13.6	13.5	12.9
11. Social transfers other hand in kind	12.5	15.3	15.5	19.3	23.2	24.7	24.5	22.9	22.2	21.5	19.9	18.4	17.9	16.5
12. Interest payments	1.0	1.8	1.4	1.9	2.6	4.5	5.0	5.2	4.0	4.3	4.3	3.6	3.1	2.8
13. Subsidies	3.2	3.1	2.8	3.4	3.5	3.3	3.0	3.2	2.8	2.1	1.9	1.7	1.6	1.5
14. Other current expenditure	:	:	:	:	:	:	:	:	1.9	2.1	2.3	2.2	2.3	2.2
15. Total current expenditure	34.6	40.5	42.2	50.5	55.8	57.7	56.4	54.3	53.7	53.0	50.7	47.6	46.4	43.6
16. Gross savings	7.4	6.5	9.1	2.6	−2.1	−5.0	−2.9	−2.2	−0.5	0.4	1.6	4.2	4.6	9.1
17. Capital transfers received	:	:	:	:	:	:	:	:	0.2	0.2	0.3	0.3	0.4	0.3
18. Total resources	42.0	47.0	51.4	53.1	53.7	52.7	53.5	52.0	56.2	56.8	55.3	54.5	53.6	55.1
19. Gross fixed capital formation	3.8	3.6	3.7	3.8	3.5	2.8	2.9	2.7	2.8	2.9	3.2	2.9	2.8	2.6
20. Other capital expenditure	:	:	:	:	:	:	:	:	0.6	0.9	0.3	0.3	0.3	0.1
21. Total expenditure	38.6	44.2	46.1	54.5	59.5	60.6	59.5	57.1	59.9	59.9	56.8	53.2	51.8	48.4
22. Tax burden	38.3	42.3	45.8	46.6	46.5	44.9	47.2	45.9	46.6	47.4	46.7	46.5	46.1	47.0
23. Net lending (+) or net borrowing (−)	3.3	2.8	5.3	−1.5	−5.7	−7.9	−6.0	−5.0	−3.7	−3.2	−1.5	1.3	1.8	6.7

([1]) The table is based on ESA 95 definitions which do not necessarily correspond with the former definitions: The totals are obtained in EAS 95 as follows:
Line 6 = line 1 + line 2 + line 3 + line 5.
Line 7 = line 9 + line 10.
Line 15 = total of lines 9 to 14.
Line 16 = line 6 − line 15.
Line 18 = line 6 + line 17.
Line 21 = line 15 + line 19 + line 20.
Line 23 = line 18 − line 21.

Source: Commission services.

Table S.A.5 Resources and expenditure of general government (per cent GDP)

	Former definitions								*ESA 95 definitions* [1]					
France	*1980*	*1985*	*1990*	*1991*	*1992*	*1993*	*1994*	*1995*	*1995*	*1996*	*1997*	*1998*	*1999*	*2000*
1. Taxes on production and imports	14.9	15.6	14.9	14.5	14.3	14.3	14.7	14.9	15.4	16.1	16.0	16.0	16.1	15.7
2. Current taxes on income and wealth	8.1	8.9	8.7	9.2	8.8	9.0	9.2	9.4	8.5	8.9	9.5	11.7	12.2	12.3
3. Social contributions	19.1	20.8	20.6	20.7	20.9	21.1	20.7	21.0	20.5	20.7	20.3	18.2	18.4	18.5
4. *Of which* actual social contributions	:	:	:	:	:	:	:	:	18.7	18.9	18.4	16.4	16.6	16.7
5. Other current resources	3.2	3.8	4.0	3.9	4.1	4.1	3.7	3.8	3.7	4.0	3.9	3.7	3.6	3.7
6. Total current resources	45.3	49.1	48.2	48.2	48.0	48.4	48.3	49.0	48.1	49.7	49.7	49.6	50.4	50.2
7. Government consumption expenditure	17.7	19.1	17.7	17.9	18.5	19.4	19.2	19.0	23.9	24.2	24.2	23.5	23.7	23.5
8. *Of which* compensation of employees	13.4	14.4	13.0	13.1	13.4	14.0	14.0	14.1	13.7	13.9	13.8	13.7	13.7	13.5
9. Collective consumption	:	:	:	:	:	:	:	:	9.8	9.9	10.0	9.5	9.5	9.4
10. Social benefits in kind	:	:	:	:	:	:	:	:	14.1	14.2	14.2	14.1	14.1	14.1
11. Social transfers other than in kind	18.6	21.7	20.9	21.4	22.0	23.1	22.9	23.0	18.5	18.7	18.8	18.4	18.3	18.1
12. Interest payments	1.4	2.8	2.9	2.9	3.2	3.3	3.5	3.7	3.8	3.9	3.7	3.6	3.4	3.3
13. Subsidies	2.5	3.0	2.1	2.2	2.2	2.4	2.3	2.3	1.5	1.5	1.5	1.4	1.3	1.3
14. Other current expenditure	:	:	:	:	:	:	:	:	1.6	1.7	1.6	1.7	1.7	1.7
15. Total current expenditure	41.7	48.6	45.7	46.7	48.4	50.7	50.4	50.4	49.2	50.0	49.8	48.6	48.3	47.9
16. Gross savings	3.7	0.5	2.4	1.4	−0.4	−2.2	−2.1	−1.4	−1.1	−0.3	0.0	1.1	2.1	2.3
17. Capital transfers received	:	:	:	:	:	:	:	:	0.4	0.3	0.8	1.2	1.4	1.5
18. Total resources	45.3	49.1	48.2	48.2	48.0	48.4	48.3	49.0	49.7	51.4	51.9	51.3	52.1	51.9
19. Gross fixed capital formation	3.3	3.2	3.5	3.5	3.5	3.1	3.1	3.2	3.3	3.2	3.0	2.9	2.9	3.0
20. Other capital expenditure	:	:	:	:	:	:	:	:	1.5	0.9	0.8	2.1	2.2	2.1
21. Total expenditure	45.4	52.0	49.7	50.1	51.8	54.1	54.0	53.8	55.2	55.5	55.0	54.0	53.7	53.2
22. Tax burden	42.9	46.3	45.1	45.4	45.0	45.6	45.9	46.6	45.2	46.4	46.5	46.5	47.3	47.0
23. Net lending (+) or net borrowing (−)	0.0	−2.8	−1.5	−2.0	−3.9	−5.6	−5.6	−4.8	−5.5	−4.1	−3.0	−2.7	−1.6	−1.3

(1) The table is based on ESA 95 definitions which do not necessarily correspond with the former definitions: The totals are obtained in ESA 95 as follows:
Line 6 = line 1 + line 2 + line 3 + line 5.
Line 7 = line 9 + line 10.
Line 15 = total of lines 9 to 14.
Line 16 = line 6 − line 15.
Line 18 = line 6 + line 17.
Line 21 = line 15 + line 19 + line 20.
Line 23 = line 18 − line 21.

Source: Commission services.

Table S.A.6 Resources and expenditure of general government (per cent GDP)

Germany (¹)	Former definitions								ESA 95 definitions (²)					
	1980	1985	1990	1991	1992	1993	1994	1995	1995	1996	1997	1998	1999	2000
1. Taxes on production and imports	13.1	12.6	12.5	12.2	12.4	12.7	13.1	12.7	11.4	11.4	11.4	11.6	12.2	12.0
2. Current taxes on income and wealth	12.8	12.6	11.2	11.3	11.6	11.2	10.8	11.1	11.1	11.5	11.2	11.5	12.0	12.5
3. Social contributions	16.9	17.6	16.9	17.5	17.8	18.4	18.9	19.1	18.8	19.4	19.6	19.2	18.9	18.7
4. *Of which* actual social contributions	:	:	:	:	:	:	:	:	17.7	18.3	18.5	18.1	17.9	17.6
5. Other current resources	2.3	3.2	2.7	2.6	3.1	3.0	3.0	2.7	3.5	3.4	3.2	3.2	3.1	2.9
6. Total current resources	45.1	46.0	43.3	43.5	44.9	45.3	45.9	45.6	44.8	45.7	45.4	45.5	46.1	46.0
7. Government consumption expenditure	20.2	20.1	18.3	18.9	19.5	19.6	19.4	19.5	19.8	19.9	19.5	19.1	19.0	18.9
8. *Of which* compensation of employees	11.0	10.6	9.7	10.1	10.4	10.6	10.3	10.2	9.0	8.9	8.7	8.4	8.3	8.1
9. Collective consumption	:	:	:	:	:	:	:	:	8.4	8.4	8.1	8.0	7.9	7.8
10. Social benefits in kind	:	:	:	:	:	:	:	:	11.4	11.6	11.3	11.1	11.1	11.0
11. Social transfers other than in kind	17.2	16.8	15.8	16.6	17.3	18.4	18.6	19.0	18.1	19.3	19.3	18.9	18.9	18.7
12. Interest payments	1.9	3.0	2.6	2.6	3.2	3.2	3.3	3.7	3.7	3.7	3.6	3.6	3.5	3.3
13. Subsidies	2.3	2.3	2.2	2.4	2.1	2.1	2.1	2.1	2.1	2.0	1.8	1.8	1.7	1.7
14. Other current expenditure	:	:	:	:	:	:	:	:	1.2	1.3	1.4	1.4	1.6	1.7
15. Total current expenditure	42.7	43.4	42.0	42.3	43.4	44.8	44.9	45.6	44.9	46.2	45.5	44.8	44.8	44.3
16. Gross savings	2.4	2.6	1.3	1.2	1.4	0.5	1.0	0.0	−0.1	−0.5	−0.1	0.6	1.3	1.8
17. Capital transfers received	:	:	:	:	:	:	:	:	0.5	0.4	0.4	0.5	0.4	0.4
18. Total resources	45.1	46.0	43.3	43.5	44.9	45.3	45.9	45.6	46.1	46.8	46.5	46.6	47.2	47.0
19. Gross fixed capital formation	3.6	2.4	2.3	2.6	2.8	2.7	2.5	2.3	2.3	2.1	1.9	1.8	1.8	1.8
20. Other capital expenditure	:	:	:	:	:	:	:	:	1.6	1.2	1.2	1.3	1.3	−1.1
21. Total expenditure	48.0	47.2	45.3	46.8	47.6	48.8	48.4	49.0	49.6	50.3	49.2	48.6	48.6	45.6
22. Tax burden	42.8	42.8	40.5	40.8	41.5	42.0	42.5	42.5	42.2	43.1	43.0	42.9	43.7	43.8
23. Net lending (+) or net borrowing (−)	−2.9	−1.2	−2.1	−3.2	−2.8	−3.5	−2.6	−3.4	−3.5	−3.4	−2.7	−2.1	−1.4	1.5

(¹) From 1991 including former East Germany.
(²) System is based on ESA 95 definitions which does not necessarily correspond with the former definitions:
Line 6 = line 1 + line 2 + line 3 + line 5.
Line 7 = line 9 + line 10.
Line 15 = total of lines 9 to 14.
Line 16 = line 6 − line 15.
Line 18 = line 6 + line 17.
Line 21 = line 15 + line 19 + line 20.
Line 23 = line 18 − line 21.

Source: Commission services.

Table S.A.7 Resources and expenditure of general government (per cent GDP)

Greece	Former definitions								ESA 95 definitions ([1])					
	1980	*1985*	*1990*	*1991*	*1992*	*1993*	*1994*	*1995*	*1995*	*1996*	*1997*	*1998*	*1999*	*2000*
1. Taxes on production and imports	10.4	12.5	13.9	14.6	15.3	14.7	14.3	14.2	13.5	14.0	14.3	14.4	15.2	15.3
2. Current taxes on income and Wealth	4.5	4.6	5.4	5.5	5.4	5.7	6.8	7.2	7.4	7.1	7.8	9.5	10.5	10.8
3. Social contributions	9.3	11.6	11.5	11.1	11.0	11.9	12.1	12.4	12.6	12.9	13.3	13.5	13.7	13.8
4. *Of which* actual social contributions	:	:	:	:	:	:	:	:	10.5	10.8	11.2	11.4	11.7	11.8
5. Other current resources	1.9	1.7	1.7	2.2	2.5	3.1	3.8	4.2	2.9	2.9	3.4	2.7	2.7	2.7
6. Total current resources	26.2	30.3	32.5	33.4	34.2	35.4	36.9	38.0	36.4	36.9	38.8	40.1	42.0	42.6
7. Government consumption expenditure	13.4	16.1	15.1	14.2	13.7	14.3	13.8	15.3	15.3	14.5	15.2	15.3	15.0	15.2
8. *Of which* compensation of employees	9.3	11.4	12.5	11.5	10.9	10.9	10.6	11.3	11.3	10.7	11.6	11.7	11.5	11.6
9. Collective consumption	:	:	:	:	:	:	:	:	9.4	8.5	8.9	9.1	8.9	8.8
10. Social benefits in kind	:	:	:	:	:	:	:	:	5.9	6.0	6.3	6.2	6.1	6.3
11. Social transfers other than in kind	9.3	14.1	15.0	14.9	14.8	15.1	15.2	15.5	15.1	15.4	15.6	15.6	15.8	15.9
12. Interest payments	2.0	4.9	10.0	9.3	11.5	12.6	13.9	12.7	11.1	10.5	8.2	7.8	7.6	7.2
13. Subsidies	2.2	5.2	4.0	3.5	3.6	3.9	3.6	3.3	0.4	0.5	0.2	0.1	0.2	0.2
14. Other current expenditure	:	:	:	:	:	:	:	:	1.3	1.2	1.1	1.2	1.6	1.2
15. Total current expenditure	26.2	37.7	41.9	39.8	41.2	43.4	44.0	45.1	43.3	42.2	40.3	40.1	40.1	39.7
16. Gross savings	−0.1	−7.4	−9.4	−6.4	−7.0	−7.9	−7.1	−7.1	−6.8	−5.2	−1.5	0.0	1.9	2.9
17. Capital transfers received	:	:	:	:	:	:	:	:	0.0	0.0	0.0	0.0	0.0	:
18. Total resources	26.2	30.3	32.5	33.4	34.2	35.4	36.9	38.0	37.7	38.1	40.0	41.4	43.3	43.8
19. Gross fixed capital formation	2.1	3.6	2.8	3.1	3.5	3.3	3.1	3.3	3.2	3.2	3.4	3.6	4.1	4.3
20. Other capital expenditure	:	:	:	:	:	:	:	:	0.2	−0.6	−0.2	−0.5	−0.3	−0.5
21. Total expenditure	28.8	41.9	48.4	44.7	46.8	49.0	46.8	48.5	47.8	45.9	44.7	44.6	45.2	44.7
22. Tax burden	24.4	28.8	31.0	31.4	31.9	32.6	33.4	34.0	34.4	34.8	36.0	38.2	40.1	40.6
23. Net lending (+) or net borrowing (−)	−2.6	−11.6	−15.9	−11.4	−12.6	−13.6	−9.9	−10.5	−10.2	−7.8	−4.7	−3.1	−1.8	−0.9

([1]) The table is based on ESA 95 definitions which do not necessarily correspond with the former definitions: The totals are obtained in ESA 95 as follows:
Line 6 = line 1 + line 2 + line 3 + line 5.
Line 7 = line 9 + line 10.
Line 15 = total of lines 9 to 14.
Line 16 = line 6 − line 15.
Line 18 = line 6 + line 17.
Line 21 = line 15 + line 19 + line 20.
Line 23 = line 18 − line 21.

Source: Commission services.

Table S.A.8 Resources and expenditure of general government (per cent GDP)

	Former definitions								*ESA 95 definitions* ([1])					
Ireland	*1980*	*1985*	*1990*	*1991*	*1992*	*1993*	*1994*	*1995*	*1995*	*1996*	*1997*	*1998*	*1999*	*2000*
1. Taxes on production and imports	15.3	16.7	15.5	15.2	15.2	14.4	15.3	14.6	13.5	13.7	13.5	13.2	13.4	13.4
2. Current taxes on income and wealth	11.5	13.1	13.1	13.7	14.1	14.8	15.2	13.5	13.6	14.1	14.0	13.9	13.5	13.0
3. Social contributions	4.4	5.1	5.0	5.2	5.3	5.3	5.1	4.7	6.8	6.3	6.0	5.8	5.8	5.8
4. *Of which* actual social contributions	:	:	:	:	:	:	:	:	5.0	4.6	4.4	4.3	4.5	4.5
5. Other current resources	3.3	3.8	2.2	2.5	2.5	2.4	2.1	1.8	2.8	2.9	2.7	2.5	2.8	2.7
6. Total current resources	34.5	38.8	35.9	36.6	37.0	36.9	37.6	34.7	36.7	37.0	36.2	35.4	35.5	34.9
7. Government consumption expenditure	18.1	16.9	14.2	15.1	15.4	15.3	15.2	14.2	16.4	15.8	15.2	14.5	14.0	13.3
8. *Of which* compensation of employees	11.8	11.5	9.8	10.5	10.6	10.8	10.4	9.6	10.2	9.7	9.2	8.8	8.2	7.8
9. Collective consumption	:	:	:	:	:	:	:	:	6.1	5.8	5.5	5.2	5.0	4.8
10. Social benefits in kind	:	:	:	:	:	:	:	:	10.4	10.0	9.6	9.3	8.9	8.5
11. Social transfers other than in kind	11.6	15.1	13.4	14.1	14.6	14.5	14.4	13.7	11.8	11.6	10.9	10.3	9.9	9.2
12. Interest payments	6.0	9.3	7.4	7.2	6.7	6.3	5.6	5.0	5.4	4.6	4.2	3.4	2.4	2.1
13. Subsidies	7.2	7.4	5.6	5.5	4.7	4.9	4.4	4.1	1.0	1.0	1.0	0.8	1.0	1.0
14. Other current expenditure	:	:	:	:	:	:	:	:	2.1	2.4	2.2	2.2	2.1	1.9
15. Total current expenditure	39.5	45.1	36.7	37.8	38.2	38.0	37.0	34.8	36.8	35.3	33.6	31.2	29.5	27.6
16. Gross savings	−4.9	−6.2	−0.8	−1.2	−1.2	−1.0	0.6	−0.2	−0.1	1.7	2.6	4.1	6.0	7.3
17. Capital transfers received	:	:	:	:	:	:	:	:	1.8	1.7	1.7	1.6	2.2	2.2
18. Total resources	34.5	38.8	35.9	36.6	37.0	36.9	37.6	34.7	39.4	39.5	38.6	37.7	38.4	37.8
19. Gross fixed capital formation	5.4	3.7	2.0	2.1	2.0	2.2	2.3	2.4	2.3	2.4	2.5	2.7	3.1	3.8
20. Other capital expenditure	:	:	:	:	:	:	:	:	1.6	1.2	1.1	1.0	3.0	1.2
21. Total expenditure	46.1	49.0	38.0	38.9	39.4	39.2	39.2	36.8	41.6	39.7	37.8	35.7	36.3	33.3
22. Tax burden	31.1	34.9	33.5	34.0	34.4	34.4	35.4	32.9	35.1	35.0	34.2	33.7	33.2	32.4
23. Net lending (+) or net borrowing (−)	−11.6	−10.2	−2.2	−2.3	−2.4	−2.3	−1.6	−2.1	−2.2	−0.2	0.7	2.1	2.1	4.5

([1]) The table is based on ESA 95 definitions which do not necessarily correspond with the former definitions: The totals are obtained in ESA 95 as follows:
Line 6 = line 1 + line 2 + line 3 + line 5.
Line 7 = line 9 + line 10.
Line 15 = total of lines 9 to 14.
Line 16 = line 6 − line 15.
Line 18 = line 6 + line 17.
Line 21 = line 15 + line 19 + line 20.
Line 23 = line 18 − line 21.

Source: Commission services.

Table S.A.9 Resources and expenditure of general government (per cent GDP)

	Former definitions								ESA 95 definitions (¹)					
Italy	*1980*	*1985*	*1990*	*1991*	*1992*	*1993*	*1994*	*1995*	*1995*	*1996*	*1997*	*1998*	*1999*	*2000*
1. Taxes on production and imports	9.3	9.5	11.3	11.8	11.8	12.7	12.3	12.4	12.1	11.8	12.4	15.3	15.2	15.1
2. Current taxes on income and wealth	9.7	13.0	14.3	14.4	14.6	16.0	14.8	14.5	14.8	15.4	16.1	14.4	15.1	14.6
3. Social contributions	12.9	13.5	14.3	14.6	14.9	15.4	14.8	14.6	14.8	15.0	15.3	12.8	12.8	12.7
4. *Of which* actual social contributions	:	:	:	:	:	:	:	:	13.0	14.6	14.9	12.5	12.4	12.4
5. Other current resources	2.4	2.9	2.9	3.0	3.3	3.6	3.6	3.7	3.1	3.2	3.2	3.2	3.3	3.0
6. Total current resources	34.4	38.9	42.8	43.8	44.5	47.7	45.5	45.3	44.8	45.5	47.2	45.8	46.3	45.5
7. Government consumption expenditure	15.0	16.6	17.4	17.4	17.5	17.5	17.0	15.9	17.9	18.1	18.2	17.9	18.1	18.0
8. *Of which* compensation of employees	11.1	11.8	12.6	12.6	12.5	12.4	11.9	11.3	11.2	11.5	11.6	10.7	10.7	10.5
9. Collective consumption	:	:	:	:	:	:	:	:	7.3	7.3	7.2	7.2	7.2	7.2
10. Social benefits in kind	:	:	:	:	:	:	:	:	10.6	10.8	11.0	10.8	10.8	10.8
11. Social transfers other than in kind	14.5	17.3	18.3	18.4	19.5	19.7	19.7	19.1	16.7	16.9	17.3	17.0	17.2	16.7
12. Interest payments	5.5	8.0	9.4	10.1	11.4	12.0	10.9	11.3	11.5	11.5	9.4	8.0	6.7	6.5
13. Subsidies	3.5	3.4	2.5	2.6	2.3	2.7	2.4	1.9	1.5	1.5	1.2	1.3	1.2	1.2
14. Other current expenditure	:	:	:	:	:	:	:	:	1.1	1.3	1.3	1.3	1.4	1.4
15. Total current expenditure	39.0	45.9	48.5	49.5	51.6	53.1	51.0	49.1	48.6	49.2	47.4	45.6	44.7	43.8
16. Gross savings	−4.6	−6.9	−5.7	−5.7	−7.1	−5.4	−5.4	−3.8	−3.8	−3.7	−0.2	0.2	1.6	1.8
17. Capital transfers received	:	:	:	:	:	:	:	:	0.9	0.4	1.0	0.7	0.5	0.4
18. Total resources	34.4	38.9	42.8	43.8	44.5	47.7	45.5	45.3	45.8	46.1	48.4	46.8	47.1	46.1
19. Gross fixed capital formation	3.2	3.7	3.3	3.2	3.0	2.6	2.3	2.2	2.1	2.2	2.2	2.4	2.5	2.4
20. Other capital expenditure	:	:	:	:	:	:	:	:	2.5	1.6	1.3	1.4	1.4	0.1
21. Total expenditure	43.0	51.5	53.8	53.8	54.0	57.1	54.6	52.9	53.4	53.2	51.1	49.6	48.9	46.5
22. Tax burden	31.7	36.1	40.0	40.9	41.5	44.2	42.1	41.9	42.3	42.9	44.4	43.2	43.5	43.0
23. Net lending (+) or net borrowing (−)	−8.7	−12.5	−11.0	−10.0	−9.5	−9.4	−9.1	−7.6	−7.6	−7.1	−2.7	−2.8	−1.8	−0.3

(¹) The table is based on ESA 95 definitions which do not necessarily correspond with the former definitions: The totals are obtained in ESA 95 as follows:
Line 6 = line 1 + line 2 + line 3 + line 5.
Line 7 = line 9 + line 10.
Line 15 = total of lines 9 to 14.
Line 16 = line 6 − line 15.
Line 18 = line 6 + line 17.
Line 21 = line 15 + line 19 + line 20.
Line 23 = line 18 − line 21.

Source: Commission services.

Table S.A.10 Resources and expenditure of general government (per cent GDP)

	Former definitions								*ESA 95 definitions* ([1])					
Luxembourg	*1980*	*1985*	*1990*	*1991*	*1992*	*1993*	*1994*	*1995*	*1995*	*1996*	*1997*	*1998*	*1999*	*2000*
1. Taxes on production and imports	12.3	14.7	15.1	15.3	15.5	16.1	16.1	16.0	12.5	12.6	12.9	13.4	14.2	14.9
2. Current taxes on income and wealth	15.5	17.3	:	:	:	:	:	:	18.4	18.3	17.5	16.5	16.9	16.1
3. Social contributions	13.2	12.2	:	:	:	:	:	:	12.4	12.3	11.8	11.6	11.9	11.6
4. *Of which* actual social contributions	:	:	:	:	:	:	:	:	11.2	11.1	10.7	10.6	10.9	10.7
5. Other current resources	6.2	5.6	:	:	:	:	:	:	5.5	5.4	5.3	5.3	4.8	4.3
6. Total current resources	47.2	49.9	:	:	:	:	:	:	48.9	48.6	47.4	46.8	47.7	46.9
7. Government consumption expenditure	14.3	13.5	12.7	12.6	12.4	12.3	11.8	12.5	18.2	18.8	17.9	17.2	17.3	16.6
8. *Of which* compensation of employees	10.0	9.6	:	:	:	:	:	:	9.6	9.6	9.3	9.1	8.7	8.1
9. Collective consumption	:	:	:	:	:	:	:	:	8.5	8.5	8.3	7.7	7.4	7.2
10. Social benefit in kind	:	:	:	:	:	:	:	:	9.7	10.3	9.6	9.5	9.9	9.4
11. Social transfers other than in kind	21.4	20.5	:	:	:	:	:	:	16.5	16.4	15.7	15.3	15.1	14.3
12. Interest payments	1.1	1.0	0.4	0.4	0.3	0.3	0.3	0.3	0.3	0.3	0.3	0.4	0.3	0.3
13. Subsidies	2.9	3.0	3.0	3.1	2.9	2.8	2.8	2.0	1.8	2.0	1.8	1.9	1.6	1.6
14. Other current expenditure	:	:	:	:	:	:	:	:	3.1	2.6	2.9	3.3	3.5	3.1
15. Total current expenditure	40.2	38.9	:	:	:	:	:	:	39.8	40.2	38.6	38.1	37.8	35.8
16. Gross savings	7.0	11.0	:	:	:	:	:	:	9.0	8.4	8.8	8.8	9.9	11.1
17. Capital transfers received	:	:	:	:	:	:	:	:	0.2	0.2	0.3	0.2	0.2	0.2
18. Total resources	47.2	49.9	:	:	:	:	:	:	48.3	47.9	47.0	46.4	47.3	46.5
19. Gross fixed capital formation	6.4	3.9	4.5	4.7	5.1	5.1	4.2	4.4	4.5	4.7	4.2	4.6	4.3	4.4
20. Other capital expenditure	:	:	:	:	:	:	:	:	1.5	1.3	1.2	1.1	1.2	1.6
21. Total expenditure	47.7	43.7	:	:	:	:	:	:	45.1	45.4	43.4	43.2	42.6	41.2
22. Tax burden	39.7	42.7	:	:	:	:	:	:	44.7	44.5	43.5	42.3	46.1	45.9
23. Net lending (+) or net borrowing (−)	−0.4	6.2	4.7	1.8	0.7	1.6	2.6	1.8	3.3	2.5	3.6	3.2	4.7	5.3

([1]) The table is based on ESA 95 definitions which do not necessarily correspond with the former definitions: The totals are obtained in ESA 95 as follows:
Line 6 = line 1 + line 2 + line 3 + line 5.
Line 7 = line 9 + line 10.
Line 15 = total of lines 9 to 14.
Line 16 = line 6 − line 15.
Line 18 = line 6 + line 17.
Line 21 = line 15 + line 19 + line 20.
Line 23 = line 18 − line 21.

Source: Commission services.

Table S.A.11 Resources and expenditure of general government (per cent GDP)

	Former definitions								ESA 95 definitions [1]					
The Netherlands	*1980*	*1985*	*1990*	*1991*	*1992*	*1993*	*1994*	*1995*	*1995*	*1996*	*1997*	*1998*	*1999*	*2000*
1. Taxes on production and imports	11.6	11.7	11.8	11.9	12.2	12.4	12.3	12.3	10.7	11.2	11.4	11.6	12.2	12.1
2. Current taxes on income and wealth	15.1	12.2	14.9	16.2	15.3	16.1	13.4	12.5	12.4	12.9	12.4	12.1	12.2	12.1
3. Social contributions	17.4	19.6	16.3	17.3	17.8	17.8	18.2	18.2	17.2	16.6	16.6	16.5	17.1	17.1
4. *Of which* actual social contributions	:	:	:	:	:	:	:	:	16.0	15.5	15.5	15.4	16.0	16.0
5. Other current resources	6.3	8.7	4.9	5.2	4.8	4.6	4.0	3.7	6.0	5.8	5.5	5.0	4.7	4.7
6. Total current resources	50.4	52.2	47.9	50.6	50.1	50.8	48.0	46.6	46.3	46.5	45.9	45.2	46.2	46.0
7. Government consumption expenditure	16.7	15.1	14.0	13.9	14.1	14.2	13.8	13.8	24.0	23.1	22.9	22.8	22.8	22.6
8. *Of which* compensation of employees	12.3	10.6	9.3	9.2	9.4	9.6	9.2	9.2	10.8	10.4	10.2	10.2	10.2	10.0
9. Collective consumption	:	:	:	:	:	:	:	:	11.6	11.3	11.0	10.8	10.8	10.7
10. Social benefits in kind	:	:	:	:	:	:	:	:	12.5	11.9	11.9	11.9	12.0	11.9
11. Social transfers other than in kind	25.3	26.3	26.1	26.3	26.7	26.9	25.8	25.1	15.3	14.8	13.9	13.0	12.5	12.0
12. Interest payments	3.7	6.1	5.7	5.9	6.0	6.0	5.6	5.7	5.9	5.6	5.2	4.8	4.4	4.0
13. Subsidies	2.9	3.4	2.9	3.1	3.1	2.9	2.5	1.8	1.1	1.2	1.5	1.5	1.6	1.5
14. Other current expenditure	:	:	:	:	:	:	:	:	1.1	1.2	1.2	1.4	1.4	1.9
15. Total current expenditure	49.1	51.4	49.5	50.3	51.0	51.2	49.0	47.7	47.4	45.9	44.7	43.4	42.7	42.0
16. Gross savings	1.3	0.9	−1.5	0.3	−0.9	−0.3	−1.0	−1.1	−1.1	−0.6	1.3	1.8	3.5	4.1
17. Capital transfers received	:	:	:	:	:	:	:	:	0.3	0.6	0.4	0.4	0.5	0.4
18. Total resources	50.4	52.2	47.9	50.6	50.1	50.8	48.0	46.6	47.3	47.8	47.1	46.4	47.5	47.2
19. Gross fixed capital formation	3.2	2.2	1.9	2.1	2.0	2.0	2.0	1.9	3.0	3.1	2.9	3.0	3.0	3.2
20. Other capital expenditure	:	:	:	:	:	:	:	:	0.4	−0.1	−0.2	−0.1	0.0	−0.7
21. Total expenditure	54.4	55.7	52.8	53.4	53.8	53.9	51.6	50.4	51.4	49.6	48.2	47.1	46.5	45.2
22. Tax burden	43.6	43.1	42.7	45.0	44.8	45.8	43.5	42.5	41.5	41.7	41.5	41.2	42.4	42.3
23. Net lending (+) or net borrowing (−)	−4.1	−3.5	−4.9	−2.8	−3.8	−3.1	−3.6	−3.8	−4.2	−1.8	−1.1	−0.7	1.0	2.0

[1] The table is based on ESA 95 definitions which do not necessarily correspond with the former definitions: The totals are obtained in ESA 95 as follows:
Line 6 = line 1 + line 2 + line 3 + line 5.
Line 7 = line 9 + line 10.
Line 15 = total of lines 9 to 14.
Line 16 = line 6 − line 15.
Line 18 = line 6 + line 17.
Line 21 = line 15 + line 19 + line 20.
Line 23 = line 18 − line 21.

Source: Commission services.

Table S.A.12 Resources and expenditure of general government (per cent GDP)

Portugal	*Former definitions*								*ESA 95 definitions* ([1])					
	1980	*1985*	*1990*	*1991*	*1992*	*1993*	*1994*	*1995*	*1995*	*1996*	*1997*	*1998*	*1999*	*2000*
1. Taxes on production and imports	12.4	13.8	13.1	13.0	13.8	13.0	13.4	13.6	14.3	14.4	14.2	14.6	15.0	14.8
2. Current taxes on income and wealth	5.7	7.9	8.0	8.9	9.9	9.0	8.8	9.1	9.3	9.9	10.1	9.9	10.3	10.8
3. Social contributions	8.1	8.7	10.2	10.6	11.2	11.8	11.5	11.7	11.0	11.0	11.1	11.4	11.5	11.9
4. *Of which* actual social contributions	:	:	:	:	:	:	:	:	10.1	10.3	10.4	10.7	10.8	11.1
5. Other current resources	2.0	2.7	2.9	3.1	3.6	3.1	2.6	2.8	3.9	4.1	3.8	3.8	3.5	4.3
6. Total current resources	28.2	33.1	34.2	35.5	38.4	36.9	36.3	37.1	38.4	39.3	39.1	39.6	40.3	41.8
7. Government consumption expenditure	13.5	14.2	15.2	16.8	16.9	17.5	17.2	17.2	18.7	19.0	19.1	19.1	19.7	20.6
8. *Of which* compensation of employees	10.3	10.4	11.9	13.0	13.9	14.2	13.7	13.7	13.7	13.7	13.8	14.0	14.4	14.9
9. Collective consumption	:	:	:	:	:	:	:	:	8.0	7.6	7.8	7.8	8.0	8.4
10. Social benefits in kind	:	:	:	:	:	:	:	:	10.7	11.4	11.3	11.3	11.6	12.2
11. Social transfers other than in kind	9.5	10.5	11.5	12.6	13.5	15.1	14.8	15.1	11.8	11.8	11.7	11.7	11.8	12.3
12. Interest payments	2.6	7.5	7.9	7.7	7.0	6.1	6.1	6.2	6.2	5.4	4.2	3.5	3.2	3.2
13. Subsidies	6.1	6.9	1.5	1.3	1.2	1.3	1.2	1.1	1.4	1.5	1.2	1.5	1.0	0.9
14. Other current expenditure	:	:	:	:	:	:	:	:	1.6	1.9	2.0	2.1	2.3	2.5
15. Total current expenditure	31.7	39.2	35.6	38.1	37.6	39.0	39.1	39.4	39.7	39.6	38.2	37.8	38.1	39.5
16. Gross savings	−3.5	−6.1	−1.4	−2.5	0.8	−2.1	−2.8	−2.3	−1.3	−0.2	0.9	1.8	2.2	2.3
17. Capital transfers received	:	:	:	:	:	:	:	:	1.9	2.1	2.3	1.6	2.2	1.6
18. Total resources	28.2	33.1	34.2	35.5	38.4	36.9	36.3	37.1	40.4	41.6	41.7	41.8	42.7	43.4
19. Gross fixed capital formation	4.2	3.3	3.2	3.3	3.7	3.9	3.5	3.6	3.7	4.2	4.4	4.0	4.1	3.8
20. Other capital expenditure	:	:	:	:	:	:	:	:	1.4	1.7	1.6	1.8	2.4	1.4
21. Total expenditure	36.7	43.4	39.1	41.4	41.3	42.9	42.2	42.7	44.9	45.6	44.4	44.1	44.8	44.8
22. Tax burden	25.2	28.9	31.9	33.1	35.6	34.5	34.7	35.0	34.5	35.3	35.4	35.8	36.8	37.5
23. Net lending (+) or net borrowing (−)	−8.5	−10.3	−5.0	−5.9	−2.9	−6.0	−5.9	−5.6	−4.6	−4.0	−2.7	−2.3	−2.1	−1.4

([1]) The table is based on ESA 95 definitions which do not necessarily correspond with the former definitions: The totals are obtained in ESA 95 as follows:
Line 6 = line 1 + line 2 + line 3 + line 5.
Line 7 = line 9 + line 10.
Line 15 = total of lines 9 to 14.
Line 16 = line 6 − line 15.
Line 18 = line 6 + line 17.
Line 21 = line 15 + line 19 + line 20.
Line 23 = line 18 − line 21.

Source: Commission services.

Table S.A.13 Resources and expenditure of general government (per cent GDP)

Spain	*Former definitions*								*ESA 95 definitions* ([1])					
	1980	*1985*	*1990*	*1991*	*1992*	*1993*	*1994*	*1995*	*1995*	*1996*	*1997*	*1998*	*1999*	*2000*
1. Taxes on production and imports	6.3	9.1	10.3	10.3	10.8	10.1	10.6	10.3	10.2	10.2	10.5	11.1	11.7	11.6
2. Current taxes on income and wealth	6.7	8.2	11.6	11.6	12.0	11.5	11.0	11.0	10.1	10.3	10.5	10.2	10.3	10.5
3. Social contributions	12.7	12.7	12.9	13.2	14.0	14.3	14.0	13.1	13.0	13.2	13.1	13.1	13.1	13.4
4. *Of which* actual social contributions	:	:	:	:	:	:	:	:	12.0	12.2	12.2	12.2	12.3	12.5
5. Other current resources	3.9	4.2	3.7	4.1	4.0	5.0	4.2	3.6	4.1	4.2	4.0	3.7	3.6	3.1
6. Total current resources	29.6	34.2	38.4	39.2	40.9	40.9	39.8	38.0	37.4	37.8	38.1	38.2	38.6	38.6
7. Government consumption expenditure	12.9	14.2	15.0	15.6	16.4	16.8	16.2	16.0	18.1	17.9	17.6	17.5	17.3	17.1
8. *Of which* compensation of employees	9.4	10.2	10.7	11.1	11.8	11.8	11.3	11.2	11.3	11.3	10.9	10.7	10.5	10.4
9. Collective consumption	:	:	:	:	:	:	:	:	8.0	7.8	7.7	7.6	7.5	7.4
10. Social benefits in kind	:	:	:	:	:	:	:	:	10.1	10.1	9.9	9.9	9.8	9.7
11. Social transfers other than in kind	11.8	13.8	13.9	14.7	15.5	16.2	15.8	15.1	13.9	13.8	13.3	12.8	12.4	12.4
12. Interest payments	0.4	1.9	3.9	3.7	4.3	5.0	4.7	5.3	5.2	5.3	4.8	4.3	3.6	3.3
13. Subsidies	1.8	2.4	2.4	2.5	2.5	3.1	2.9	3.0	1.1	1.0	0.9	1.1	1.2	1.3
14. Other current expenditure	:	:	:	:	:	:	:	:	0.9	1.0	0.9	1.1	1.2	1.1
15. Total current expenditure	27.7	33.9	36.7	38.0	40.2	42.6	41.3	40.3	39.2	39.0	37.6	37.0	35.9	35.2
16. Gross savings	0.5	0.3	1.7	1.2	0.7	−1.7	−1.5	−2.3	−1.8	1.2	0.4	1.2	2.8	3.4
17. Capital transfers received	:	:	:	:	:	:	:	:	1.4	1.4	1.3	1.3	1.4	1.2
18. Total resources	29.6	34.2	38.4	39.2	40.9	40.9	39.8	38.0	38.4	38.8	39.1	39.1	39.6	39.5
19. Gross fixed capital formation	1.8	3.6	4.9	4.7	4.0	4.1	3.9	3.7	3.7	3.1	3.1	3.3	3.3	3.3
20. Other capital expenditure	:	:	:	:	:	:	:	:	2.5	2.0	1.9	1.8	2.0	1.7
21. Total expenditure	31.6	40.4	42.6	43.5	44.9	47.6	45.9	45.0	45.0	43.7	42.2	41.7	40.8	39.9
22. Tax burden	26.1	30.6	35.4	35.7	37.5	36.5	36.1	35.0	34.0	34.4	34.8	35.1	35.7	36.2
23. Net lending (+) or net borrowing (−)	−2.5	−6.2	−4.2	−4.3	−4.0	−6.7	−6.1	−7.0	−6.6	−4.9	−3.2	−2.6	−1.2	−0.3

([1]) The table is based on ESA 95 definitions which do not necessarily correspond with the former definitions: The totals are obtained in EAS 95 as follows:
Line 6 = line 1 + line 2 + line 3 + line 5.
Line 7 = line 9 + line 10.
Line 15 = total of lines 9 to 14.
Line 16 = line 6 − line 15.
Line 18 = line 6 + line 17.
Line 21 = line 15 + line 19 + line 20.
Line 23 = line 18 − line 21.

Source: Commission services.

Table S.A.14 Resources and expenditure of general government (per cent GDP)

	Former definitions								ESA 95 definitions [1]					
Sweden	*1980*	*1985*	*1990*	*1991*	*1992*	*1993*	*1994*	*1995*	*1995*	*1996*	*1997*	*1998*	*1999*	*2000*
1. Taxes on production and imports	13.0	15.9	16.6	17.1	15.7	15.1	14.3	13.8	13.7	14.3	14.8	15.3	16.9	14.7
2. Current taxes on income and wealth	20.7	20.2	22.6	19.2	19.8	20.1	20.3	20.8	20.2	21.6	21.7	22.4	22.2	22.5
3. Social contributions	14.7	13.5	15.0	14.9	14.3	13.9	13.8	14.2	14.2	15.2	15.0	15.0	13.7	16.4
4. *Of which* actual social contributions	:	:	:	:	:	:	:	:	13.6	14.6	14.5	14.5	13.2	15.6
5. Other current resources	7.2	9.3	8.4	8.2	9.0	9.2	8.5	8.1	8.3	8.0	7.2	7.1	6.2	6.0
6. Total current resources	55.6	59.0	62.7	59.5	58.8	58.2	57.0	56.9	56.5	59.1	58.7	59.9	59.1	59.5
7. Government consumption expenditure	28.3	26.9	26.4	26.3	27.0	27.1	26.1	24.8	26.3	27.1	26.5	26.7	26.9	26.3
8. *Of which* compensation of employees	20.0	18.2	18.1	18.3	18.7	18.5	17.6	16.7	17.3	17.8	17.4	16.8	16.5	16.7
9. Collective consumption	:	:	:	:	:	:	:	:	:	:	:	:	:	:
10. Social benefits in kind	:	:	:	:	:	:	:	:	:	:	:	:	:	:
11. Social transfers other than in kind	17.4	18.1	19.2	20.6	22.7	24.4	24.1	22.5	21.3	20.3	19.6	19.3	18.9	18.4
12. Interest payments	3.9	8.1	4.8	5.0	5.2	6.0	6.6	6.8	6.9	6.8	6.4	5.8	4.8	4.3
13. Subsidies	4.2	4.9	4.6	4.9	5.3	5.7	5.1	4.9	3.8	3.3	2.7	2.2	2.0	1.9
14. Other current expenditure	:	:	:	:	:	:	:	:	2.1	1.8	1.8	2.1	1.9	2.1
15. Total current expenditure	54.9	59.0	56.3	58.1	62.0	65.1	63.6	61.4	60.3	59.3	57.1	56.2	54.5	53.1
16. Gross savings	0.7	−0.1	6.3	1.4	−3.3	−6.9	−6.6	−4.5	−3.9	−0.2	1.6	3.7	4.6	6.5
17. Capital transfers received	:	:	:	:	:	:	:	:	0.2	0.2	0.2	0.2	0.2	0.2
18. Total resources	55.6	59.0	62.7	59.5	58.8	58.2	57.0	56.9	60.0	62.2	61.6	62.9	62.1	62.4
19. Gross fixed capital formation	4.1	3.0	23	22	26	1.0	29	28	3.4	3.0	27	27	28	2.5
20. Other capital expenditure	:	:	:	:	:	:	:	:	0.6	0.0	0.6	−0.7	0.1	0.1
21. Total expenditure	59.5	62.7	58.6	60.6	66.3	70.1	66.9	64.4	67.6	65.3	63.1	61.0	60.3	58.4
22. Tax burden	48.4	49.6	54.2	51.3	49.8	49.0	48.5	49.4	48.8	51.8	52.2	53.5	53.5	54.2
23. Net lending (+) or net borrowing (−)	−3.9	−3.7	4.0	−1.1	−7.5	−11.9	−9.9	−7.5	−7.7	−3.1	−1.5	1.9	1.8	4.0

[1] The table is based on ESA 95 definitions which do not necessarily correspond with the former definitions: The totals are obtained in EAS 95 as follows:
Line 6 = line 1 + line 2 + line 3 + line 5.
Line 7 = line 9 + line 10.
Line 15 = total of lines 9 to 14.
Line 16 = line 6 − line 15.
Line 18 = line 6 + line 17.
Line 21 = line 15 + line 19 + line 20.
Line 23 = line 18 − line 21.

Source: Commission services.

Table S.A.15 Resources and expenditure of general government (per cent GDP)

	Former definitions								*ESA 95 definitions* ([1])					
United Kingdom	*1980*	*1985*	*1990*	*1991*	*1992*	*1993*	*1994*	*1995*	*1995*	*1996*	*1997*	*1998*	*1999*	*2000*
1. Taxes on production and imports	15.8	15.9	15.6	16.0	15.7	15.4	15.5	15.8	13.2	13.3	13.6	13.5	14.0	14.1
2. Current taxes on income and wealth	13.4	14.5	13.8	12.9	12.1	11.5	11.9	12.7	15.0	14.8	15.0	16.5	16.3	16.9
3. Social contributions	6.0	6.8	6.2	6.2	6.1	6.1	6.2	6.2	7.6	7.5	7.5	7.6	7.5	7.6
4. *Of which* actual social contributions	:	:	:	:	:	:	:	:	6.8	6.8	6.9	6.9	6.9	7.0
5. Other current resources	4.5	4.1	2.7	2.5	2.3	2.2	2.2	2.2	2.9	3.0	2.7	2.6	2.6	2.4
6. Total current resources	39.8	41.4	38.3	37.5	36.2	35.2	35.8	36.9	38.6	38.6	38.9	40.2	40.5	41.1
7. Government consumption expenditure	21.7	21.2	20.3	21.2	21.7	21.6	21.3	21.0	19.8	19.4	18.4	18.2	18.5	18.7
8. *Of which* compensation of employees	12.8	12.2	11.5	11.7	11.8	10.7	9.1	8.5	8.8	8.3	7.8	7.4	7.5	7.5
9. Collective consumption	:	:	:	:	:	:	:	:	8.2	8.1	7.4	7.4	7.6	7.7
10. Social benefits in kind	:	:	:	:	:	:	:	:	11.5	11.3	11.0	10.8	10.9	11.1
11. Social transfers other than in kind	10.6	12.8	10.6	11.9	13.2	13.8	13.7	13.5	15.4	14.9	14.4	13.7	13.5	13.3
12. Interest payments	4.7	5.0	3.1	2.7	2.7	2.8	3.2	3.4	3.7	3.7	3.7	3.6	3.0	2.7
13. Subsidies	2.5	2.0	1.1	1.0	1.1	1.1	1.1	1.1	0.7	0.8	0.6	0.5	0.6	0.6
14. Other current expenditure	:	:	:	:	:	:	:	:	1.9	2.0	2.0	2.2	2.2	2.5
15. Total current expenditure	40.3	41.9	35.9	37.0	39.5	40.2	40.0	40.0	41.5	40.8	39.2	38.2	37.8	37.8
16. Gross savings	−0.5	−0.5	2.4	0.5	−3.3	−5.0	−4.2	−3.1	−2.9	−2.2	−0.3	2.0	2.7	3.3
17. Capital transfers received	:	:	:	:	:	:	:	:	0.3	0.3	0.3	0.3	0.3	0.4
18. Total resources	39.8	41.4	38.3	37.5	36.2	35.2	35.8	36.9	40.1	39.8	40.0	41.2	41.4	42.1
19. Gross fixed capital formation	2.5	2.1	2.3	2.1	2.0	1.8	1.8	1.7	2.0	1.5	1.2	1.2	1.1	1.2
20. Other capital expenditure	:	:	:	:	:	:	:	:	1.2	0.9	0.7	0.6	0.6	−1.9
21. Total expenditure	43.2	44.2	39.2	39.8	42.3	43.0	42.5	42.4	45.8	44.2	42.0	40.7	40.1	37.7
22. Tax burden	33.5	35.2	33.4	33.2	32.1	31.4	32.0	33.1	36.8	36.5	36.9	38.3	38.5	39.3
23. Net lending (+) or net borrowing (−)	−3.4	−2.9	−0.9	−2.3	−6.1	−7.8	−6.7	−5.4	−5.8	−4.4	−2.0	0.4	1.3	4.3

([1]) The table is based on ESA 95 definitions which do not necessarily correspond with the former definitions: The totals are obtained in ESA 95 as follows:
Line 6 = line 1 + line 2 + line 3 + line 5.
Line 7 = line 9 + line 10.
Line 15 = total of lines 9 to 14.
Line 16 = line 6 − line 15.
Line 18 = line 6 + line 17.
Line 21 = line 15 + line 19 + line 20.
Line 23 = line 18 − line 21.

Source: Commission services.

Table S.A.16 Resources and expenditure of general government (per cent GDP)

	Former definitions								ESA 95 definitions ([2])					
Euro area ([1])	*1980*	*1985*	*1990*	*1991*	*1992*	*1993*	*1994*	*1995*	*1995*	*1996*	*1997*	*1998*	*1999*	*2000*
1. Taxes on production and imports	12.3	12.6	12.7	12.6	12.7	12.9	13.2	13.0	12.5	12.6	12.8	13.5	13.8	13.6
2. Current taxes on income and wealth	10.9	11.7	11.9	12.1	12.1	12.2	11.7	11.7	11.5	12.0	12.2	12.4	12.8	13.0
3. Social contributions	16.0	16.8	16.5	16.8	17.2	17.8	17.8	17.8	17.5	17.7	17.6	16.5	16.5	16.3
4. *Of which* actual social contributions	:	:	:	:	:	:	:	:	16.1	16.5	16.4	15.4	15.3	15.2
5. Other current resources	3.0	3.7	3.3	3.4	3.6	3.7	3.5	3.3	3.8	3.8	3.6	3.5	3.4	3.3
6. Total current resources	42.2	44.9	44.4	44.9	45.6	46.6	46.1	45.9	45.3	46.1	46.3	46.0	46.5	46.2
7. Government consumption expenditure	17.5	18.1	17.2	17.7	18.1	18.4	18.1	17.9	20.6	20.7	20.4	20.0	20.1	19.9
8. *Of which* compensation of employees	11.8	12.0	11.4	11.6	11.8	12.0	11.7	11.6	11.1	11.2	11.0	10.8	10.7	10.5
9. Collective consumption	:	:	:	:	:	:	:	:	8.6	8.6	8.4	8.2	8.2	8.1
10. Social benefits in kind	:	:	:	:	:	:	:	:	12.0	12.1	11.9	11.8	11.8	11.7
11. Social transfers other than in kind	17.3	18.8	18.2	18.7	19.4	20.3	20.3	20.2	17.3	17.7	17.6	17.2	17.1	16.7
12. Interest payments	2.6	4.5	4.8	4.9	5.4	5.5	5.3	5.5	5.5	5.6	5.1	4.7	4.2	4.0
13. Subsidies	2.7	3.0	2.4	2.5	2.3	2.5	2.3	2.2	1.7	1.7	1.5	1.5	1.5	1.4
14. Other current expenditure	:	:	:	:	:	:	:	:	1.4	1.4	1.5	1.5	1.6	1.7
15. Total current expenditure	41.0	45.4	44.4	45.3	46.7	48.3	47.5	47.2	46.5	47.1	46.1	45.0	44.5	43.8
16. Gross savings	1.1	−0.5	−0.1	−0.4	−1.1	−1.7	−1.4	−1.4	−1.2	−0.8	0.2	1.0	2.0	2.5
17. Capital transfers received	:	:	:	:	:	:	:	:	0.6	0.5	0.7	0.8	0.8	0.8
18. Total resources	42.2	44.9	44.4	44.9	45.6	46.6	46.1	45.9	46.6	47.4	47.7	47.2	47.8	47.4
19. Gross fixed capital formation	3.3	3.0	3.0	3.1	3.0	2.9	2.7	2.6	2.7	2.6	2.4	2.4	2.5	2.5
20. Other capital expenditure	:	:	:	:	:	:	:	:	1.7	1.2	1.1	1.5	1.6	0.4
21. Total expenditure	45.6	49.7	48.6	49.4	50.3	52.1	51.1	50.7	51.6	51.6	50.3	49.4	49.0	47.0
22. Tax burden	39.4	41.5	41.4	41.8	42.3	43.1	42.9	42.9	42.3	43.1	43.4	43.1	43.7	43.5
23. Net lending (+) or net borrowing (−)	−3.4	−4.8	−4.2	−4.5	−4.7	−5.5	−5.0	−4.8	−5.0	−4.2	−2.6	−2.1	−1.2	0.4

([1]) Due to problem with availability of the data, Luxembourg data are not included.
From 1991 including former East Germany.
([2]) System is based on ESA 95 definitions which does not necessarily correspond with the former definitions:
Line 6 = line 1 + line 2 + line 3 + line 5.
Line 7 = line 9 + line 10.
Line 15 = total of lines 9 to 14.
Line 16 = line 6 − line 15.
Line 18 = line 6 + line 17.
Line 21 = line 15 + line 19 + line 20.
Line 23 = line 18 − line 21.

Source: Commission services.

Table S.A.17 Resources and expenditure of general government (per cent GDP)

EU-15 ([1])	Former definitions 1980	1985	1990	1991	1992	1993	1994	1995	ESA 95 definitions ([2]) 1995	1996	1997	1998	1999	2000
1. Taxes on production and imports	13.0	13.4	13.4	13.4	13.3	13.4	13.6	13.5	12.7	12.9	13.1	13.6	14.0	13.8
2. Current taxes on income and wealth	11.8	12.7	12.8	12.7	12.6	12.6	12.3	12.4	12.5	13.0	13.2	13.7	14.0	14.3
3. Social contributions	14.0	14.7	14.5	14.8	15.2	15.7	15.7	15.8	15.7	15.9	15.6	14.7	14.6	14.5
4. *Of which* actual social contributions	:	:	:	:	:	:	:	:	14.5	14.7	14.5	13.6	13.6	13.4
5. Other current resources	3.5	4.0	3.5	3.5	3.7	3.7	3.5	3.4	3.9	3.9	3.6	3.5	3.4	3.3
6. Total current resources	42.3	44.8	44.2	44.4	44.8	45.4	45.1	45.1	44.8	45.6	45.6	45.5	46.0	45.8
7. Government consumption expenditure	18.7	19.0	18.2	18.6	19.0	19.2	18.9	18.7	20.7	20.7	20.3	20.0	20.0	19.9
8. *Of which* compensation of employees	12.3	12.4	11.8	12.0	12.2	12.1	11.6	11.4	11.1	11.1	10.9	10.5	10.4	10.3
9. Collective consumption	:	:	:	:	:	:	:	:	:	:	:	:	:	:
10. Social benefits in kind	:	:	:	:	:	:	:	:	:	:	:	:	:	:
11. Social transfers other than in kind	16.1	17.6	17.1	17.7	18.6	19.5	19.4	19.3	17.2	17.4	17.2	16.7	16.5	16.2
12. Interest payments	3.0	4.8	4.7	4.7	5.2	5.3	5.2	5.4	5.4	5.5	5.0	4.6	4.1	3.9
13. Subsidies	2.8	2.9	2.3	2.4	2.3	2.4	2.3	2.2	1.6	1.6	1.4	1.4	1.4	1.3
14. Other current expenditure	:	:	:	:	:	:	:	:	1.5	1.6	1.6	1.7	1.8	1.9
15. Total current expenditure	41.4	45.4	43.8	44.7	46.4	47.8	47.1	46.9	46.4	46.8	45.4	44.3	43.7	43.0
16. Gross savings	0.8	−0.6	0.4	−0.3	−1.6	−2.4	−2.0	−1.7	−1.6	−1.0	0.2	1.3	2.2	2.8
17. Capital transfers received	:	:	:	:	:	:	:	:	0.6	0.5	0.6	0.6	0.7	—
18. Total resources	42.3	44.8	44.2	44.4	44.8	45.4	45.1	45.1	46.3	46.9	47.0	46.8	47.2	47.0
19. Gross fixed capital formation	3.2	2.9	2.9	2.9	2.9	2.7	2.6	2.5	2.6	2.4	2.2	2.2	2.3	2.3
20. Other capital expenditure	:	:	:	:	:	:	:	:	1.6	1.1	1.0	1.2	1.3	−0.1
21. Total expenditure	45.6	49.3	47.7	48.5	49.8	51.5	50.5	50.1	51.4	51.1	49.4	48.4	47.9	45.8
22. Tax burden	38.7	40.7	40.6	40.9	41.1	41.7	41.6	41.8	41.8	42.5	42.6	42.7	43.2	43.1
23. Net lending (+) or net borrowing (−)	−3.4	−4.5	−3.5	−4.1	−5.0	−6.0	−5.4	−5.0	−5.2	−4.2	−2.4	−1.5	−0.6	1.2

([1]) Due to problem with availability of the data, Luxembourg data are not included.
From 1991 including former East Germany.
([2]) System is based on ESA 95 definitions which does not necessarily correspond with the former definitions:
Line 6 = line 1 + line 2 + line 3 + line 5.
Line 7 = line 9 + line 10
Line 15 = total of lines 9 to 14.
Line 16 = line 6 − line 15.
Line 18 = line 6 + line 17.
Line 21 = line 15 + line 19 + line 20.
Line 23 = line 18 − line 21.

Source: Commission services.

Notes and References

1 Introduction

1 From this point forward the expressions 'fiscal adjustment' and 'fiscal consolidation' will be used to refer to the same process of reducing the public budget deficit or increasing the public budget surplus.

2 The public deficit reduction in the rest of EU member states was as follows: Belgium 5 percentage, Spain 4.7 percentage, Portugal 3.6 percentage, France 2.8 percentage, The Netherlands 2.6 percentage, Austria 2.7 percentage, and Germany 0.7 percentage. Among the countries that already fulfilled the deficit criteria in 1993, because they consolidated their budgets in the 1980s, Denmark improved its budget balance by 3.5 per cent, and Ireland by 3.6 per cent. Luxembourg maintained its superavit during the whole period (EC, 1998: 93).

3 This objective was postponed by the European Commission to 2006 for those countries such as Germany, France and Portugal that in 2002 were subject of the warnings associated to the *excessive deficit procedure* mechanisms envisaged in the Stability and Growth Pact (SGP) for those countries with budget deficits above the 3 per cent GDP limit.

4 See EC (1998: 108).

5 'The Public Choice theory abandons the assumption of benevolent exercise of economic policy-making (as formulated by Wicksell), and substitutes it by the principle of individual utility maximisation by politicians and bureaucrats' (Casares Ripol, 2002: 88).

6 See Frey and Schneider (1978), and Nordhaus (1989).

7 See Grilli, Masciandaro and Tabellini (1991), Halleberg and Von Hagen (1997) and Milesi-Ferretti, Perotti and Rostagno (2001).

8 See Boix (1996, 1997), Garrett (1998) and Perotti and Kontopoulos (2002).

9 See the classical work by Roubini and Sachs (1989). For a literature review on the political economy of budget deficits, see Alesina and Perotti (1995a) and Persson and Tabellini (1999). See also the very interesting work by Franzese (2002) on the political management of public debt in advanced economies.

10 See McDermott and Wescott (1996); Alesina and Perotti (1996b).

11 See Alesina, Perotti and Tavares (1998).

12 If the reader is interested in a political economy analysis of the fiscal consolidation experiences in Central and Eastern European countries during the 1990s, see Gleich (2003), Yläoutinen (2004) and Mulas-Granados *et al.* (2006).

13 Note that the size of the adjustment is sometimes treated as an additional dimension of fiscal consolidations. However, this dimension is not directly dealt with in this book, because it enters the decision-making process through the duration dimension: i.e. given a certain level of initial budget deficit and given the final target of balanced budgets introduced by EMV, it is obvious that smaller adjustments will imply longer consolidation episodes to reach the objective while more sizeable adjustments will require a shorter duration of these consolidation experiences.

14 See Hallerberg and Von Hagen (1997) and Hallerberg (2004) for these types of institutional constraints. Although they argued that spending limits have a

remarkable effect in fiscal output, Perotti and Kontopoulos (2002) demonstrated that these limits may affect aggregate figures, but not the specific composition of the budget.

15 See Franzese (2002) for an extensive review of theories related to public debt management and the strategic use of public debt.

16 Downs (1957).

17 For some, left and right only defend different mechanisms to achieve common goals of economic growth and social welfare. However, left and right have traditionally been differentiated by their attitude towards equality. This is the case of Bobbio who defines the 'egalitarian politician' as the one whose 'attitudes are born in the conviction that most inequalities that he cannot stand, are social inequalities, and as such, they can be suppressed. [While the non-egalitarian] is convinced that these inequalities are natural, and as such, they cannot be suppressed' (Bobbio, 1995: 144).

18 See Hibbs (1977, 1987); Hall (1986): Alesina and Summers (1993); Boix (1996, 1997, 2000); Maravall (1997); Garrett (1998); and Notermans (2000).

19 See Quine (1963) and Harding (1976).

20 According to Przeworski (1986), Keynesianism was once embraced by social democracy as the economic doctrine that solved the contradiction between growth and redistribution to which classical economics had relegated state intervention. By depicting unemployment and slow growth as a problem of lack of demand, Keynesianism gave public spending (traditionally thought to be as distortionary if used to redistribute income) the main role in boosting aggregate demand and generating economic growth. Boix (1996, 1997) argues that, once Keynesian policies of demand management were abandoned, social democratic parties in Western Europe embraced supply-side policies of human and physical capital formation, as the means to affect the economy in the long run, and make compatible their growth and redistributive concerns. Even the most centrist 'new labour' theorists recognize today that the Left of the next century has to promote 'equality as inclusion', and transform the state into a 'social investor', that plays a leading role in the provision of human capital, research and technologies, and infrastructures (Giddens, 1999).

2 Economics, Politics and Fiscal Policy

1 For a review of the literature on the effect of fiscal policy on growth, via supply-side effects, see Gerson (1998) and Tanzi and Zee (1997). According to Gerson (1998: 3): 'the empirical evidence suggests that tax policy may have its main impact on growth through the location of investment and labour costs across sectors, rather than through the aggregate supply of labour and capital'.

2 The very simple formulation of Keynesian macroeconomics assumes that nominal wages, and thus prices, are fixed in the short run. The keystone of Keynesian theory is that autonomous growth in demand has an income effect, which will be a multiple of the initial impulse (the multiplier). The degree of openness of the economy reduces the expansionary effects of an increase in demand because it spreads them to other countries. For example, in a small open economy where imports amount to about 50 per cent and where the marginal consumption rate is 60 per cent, the multiplier will be around 1.1. This means that an increase in government spending of 2 million euros, would increase the total output by 2.2 million euros.

3 'The traditional business-cycle theory argues that there are built-in forces within the economy that give rise to fluctuations. The real business-cycle theory argues that the fluctuations are nothing more than the result of random and

unpredictable shocks. Monetarists and new classical economists see the fluctuations as largely the consequence of misguided monetary policy. And new Keynesians see the fluctuations as originating from a variety of sources both inside and outside the economy, but believe that built-in characteristics of modern economies amplify some of the disturbances and make their effects persist' (Stiglitz and Boadway, 1994: 1988).

4 'The way of relating business cycles to the internal working of the economy is called the multiplier-accelerator model, first developed by the Nobel Paul Samuelson' (Stiglitz and Boadway, 1994: 1090).

5 'Public goods are those goods that it costs nothing extra for an individual to enjoy (their consumption is nonrivalrous), and that it costs a great deal to exclude any individual from enjoying them (they are nonexcludable). The standard example of a public good is defence' (Stiglitz and Boadway, 1994: 181). Because of their characteristics, the private sector would not supply most of those public goods, and it is the public sector which has to provide them, and finance their provision through public taxation. The theory of public goods, in fact, provided a new justification for government intervention in the production process of capitalist systems, because those goods were needed by the society but not provided by the market.

6 For a more detailed description of consolidation experiences in Europe during the 1990s, see Briotti (2004).

7 In fact, the anti-globalization movement postulates, among other things, the cancellation of the developing countries' foreign debt, because the size of their debts prevents them from launching any domestic public initiative to generate growth and alleviate poverty.

8 Taxes can be lump-sum taxes or proportional taxes. In fact, most taxes in real life are proportional taxes. These taxes are distortionary from the efficiency point of view, because they affect the efficient consumption decision and generate a loss of consumer utility, but they are preferred to lump-sum taxes because they are superior from an equity perspective. Barro's starting point for his research was his observation that 'proponents of the Ricardian view that the choice between debt and taxes (to finance the budget deficit) does not matter are left with an embarrassing absence of a theory of public debt creation' (Barro, 1979: 940). In fact, the Ricardian equivalence between taxes and debt was based on the assumption that governments raise lump-sum taxes.

9 In De Wolff (1998: 14).

10 For a detailed formal presentation of the tax smoothing theory, see Roubini and Sachs (1989a).

11 The tax-smoothing hypothesis has been empirically rejected several times, at least for the period since 1973. For a review of these empirical tests see Roubini and Sachs (1989a).

12 See Table 2.1 in the previous section.

13 See the classical work by Roubini and Sachs (1989a, 1989b) that related instability of the government associated to its relative fragmentation, and the proclivity of some types of electoral systems to generate coalition governments. For a literature review on the political economy of budget deficits, see Alesina and Perotti (1995a), and Persson and Tabellini (1999). See also Franzese (2002).

14 For the effects of electoral systems on fiscal policy, see Grilli, Masciandaro and Tabellini (1991), Halleberg and Von Hagen (1997), and Milesi-Ferretti, Perotti and Rostagno (1999).

15 For models on intergenerational distribution see the very first work of Musgrave (1959), and that by Cukierman and Meltzer (1989). And for models on intragenerational geographical distribution see Weingast, Shepsle and Johnson (1981).

16 For the effects of different budgetary rules related to spending limits see Halleberg and Von Hagen (1997), Perotti (1998) and Halleberg (2004).
17 For a detailed analysis of the theoretical contributions of these different new political economy models, see De Wolff (1998).
18 See McDermott and Wescott (1996), Giavazzi and Pagano (1990) and Alesina and Perotti (1996a).
19 Von Hagen, Hallett and Strauch (2001) find evidence that 'governments are more likely to undertake consolidation efforts when the domestic economy is doing well ... and [these adjustments] are more likely to be successful if started from high debt-GDP ratios' (pp. 12–14). Also, accompanying tax reforms and labour market reforms will increase the chances of success of the fiscal adjustment. In general, gradual implementation of reforms can enhance their political support, even when these reforms are complementary (see Lindbeck, 1994).
20 See Alesina and Ardagna (1998).
21 Alesina, Perotti and Tavares (1998) show that large consolidations, and those mostly based on public wages and transfers, are not conducive to electoral defeat or a change in the government more frequently than average.
22 A war of attrition model consists of a group of players locked in a battle, in which all make and accumulate losses as long as the battle lasts. The one who stays longest wins the prize. This model was first formalized by Riley (1980).
23 See Nordhaus (1975), McRae (1977), and Alesina, Cohen and Roubini (1992). See also Brender and Drazen (2005) for a wider testing of this hypothesis.
24 See Buchanan and Wagner (1976) for fiscal illusion.
25 See Persson and Svensson (1989) for this concrete example. And, for a more general overview of the models that analyse the strategic use of debt, see De Wolff (1998) and Franzese (2002).
26 More concretely, the three factors that speak against the policy convergence hypothesis are: '(1) In order to be elected as the party's candidate a politician has to take the party's median position. For credibility and reputation reasons he cannot change his position later; (2) If parties can choose their ideology, new parties may form to suit a group that is currently not represented and political fragmentation will ensue; (3) Unhappy voters can abstain from voting' (De Wolff, 1998: 29).
27 For this argument, see Lipset (1961) and Klingemann, Hofferbert and Budge (1994).
28 The literature on the impact of labour market institutions on the economy is vast. For a brief overview, see the original theoretical work by Olson (1982), and the later empirical studies by Calmfors and Driffill (1988) and Golden (1993). See also Boix (1996, 1997, 2000), and Garrett (1998). Notermans (2000) has lately expanded the analysis of the impact of labour market institutions to study their effect not only on the success of interventionist economic policies, but also in the success of social democratic or liberal policy regimes. He affirms that while social democratic policy regimes need labour market institutions that contain wages to prevent inflation, liberal regimes need labour market institutions that maintain nominal wages, to prevent the price level from falling. These regimes end when their required institutions change.
29 For example, Alesina and Rodrik (1994) present empirical results that show that 'inequality in land and income ownership is negatively associated with subsequent economic growth' (p. 465).
30 Alesina (1989), Alesina and Roubini (1992).
31 Cameron (1984), Álvarez, Garrett and Lange (1991) and Scharpf (1987).

32 Alesina and Summers (1993), Hall (1986).

33 Alt (1985); Garrett (1993, 1998); Frieden and Rogowski (1994). This review of the literature on partisan economic policy management is based on the review made by Boix (1997: 817).

34 According to Glyn (1998: 2), the common aspirations of social democracy in Western Europe 'can be divided into three broad categories: full employment, the welfare state and redistribution, and, finally, supply-side interventions aimed at guiding and controlling capital'.

35 To date, the only studies that have directly addressed the question of how political factors such as the ideology of the party in government affect the composition of the budget are those of Perotti and Kontopoulus (2002) and Tavares (2004). On a panel of OECD countries in the period 1960–95 they find that both ideology of the cabinet, and its fragmentation (measured as number of spending ministers and number of parties in the coalition) are significant factors. The problem is that these articles do not cover entirely the most recent period of strong fiscal adjustments in the European Union (1993–99), and they focus on fiscal decisions in general, rather than those directly designed to achieve a fiscal adjustment within a more comprehensive strategy.

3 Timing and Duration of Fiscal Adjustments

1 Some parts of this chapter have been extracted from two different works (FEDEA Working Paper, 2001/19 and EEG Working Paper 18/2002), both co-authored with Reyes Maroto, whom I thank for her cooperation and for authorizing me to reproduce these parts here. The first work was later awarded the II Jean Monnet-UCM-Uni2 Research Award in European Economy 2002.

2 Because the whole book uses data from AMECO, the Macroeconomic Database of the European Commission, I follow the Commission's method for estimating the cyclically adjusted budget balances. This method involves three steps. In the first step, the output gap is computed as the difference between the actual output and an estimated output trend, applying the Hodrick–Prescott (HP) filter. In the second step, the budget sensitivity to the output gap is computed. This allows the cyclical component of the budget to be computed. Finally, the cyclically adjusted budget balance is obtained by deducting the cyclical component from the actual government budget balance. For further details on this issue, see Appendix 1.

3 The *Fiscal Stance* is a measure of the discretionary fiscal policy component, usually defined as the change in the *primary structural budget balance* relative to the preceding period. When the change is positive (negative) the fiscal stance is said to be expansionary (contractionary).

4 See 'Covergence Report 1998' (EC, 1998). And see also Table 2.3.

5 In the literature on fiscal adjustments the threshold that authors use to classify a certain year as a fiscal adjustment year varies, but it ranges between an annual change in the cyclically adjusted budget balance of 1per cent–1.25per cent (Von Hagen, Hallett and Strauch, 2001), to an annual change of 1.5per cent–2.0 per cent in the cyclically adjusted primary balance (excluding interest payments) (Alesina and Perotti, 1997). Since the section on duration will offer a discussion on the sensitivity of results to different definitions of fiscal adjustment, I prefer to start here with the lowest threshold used in the literature.

6 For descriptive statistics of all dependent and independent variables used in this book, see Statistical annex 1.

7 Note that no politico-institutional variable accounting for the budget process or the relative majority in Parliament are included in any of the empirical analyses of Chapters 3 and 4. A detailed explanation of the reasons for this exclusion is given in the second section of Chapter 4 and in Appendix 4.

8 In the literature of fiscal adjustments there are many articles that prefer to use as a proxy for degree of decision-making fragmentation an explanatory variable called 'type of government' that was used for the first time by Roubini and Sachs (1989a, 1989b). I prefer, however, to use the simplest measure of all and the least subjective one, which is the number of parties in the government. I follow here Perotti and Kontopoulos (2002). Data on the number of parties in government until 1995 has been borrowed from Prof. Roberto Perotti, whom I thank for his generosity. His source is Woldendorp, Keman and Budge (1993) and I have completed the series using data from *The Europa World Yearbook* for Greece, Portugal and Spain (the whole period), and all countries from 1995–2000.

9 I have considered spending ministers to be the following: 1) Industry or Trade and/or ministers with related and/or subdivided competences like Foreign Trade, Commerce, and State Industries (if not attributed to Public Works-see next); 2) Public Works and/or Infrastructure and/or ministers with related and/or subdivided competences like (Public) Transportation, Energy, Post, Telecommunications, Merchant Marine, Civil Aviation, National Resources, Construction (if not specifically attributed to Housing-see below), Urban Development, etc; 3) Defence, 4) Justice; 5) Labour; 6) Education; 7) Health; 8) Housing; 9) Agriculture. Also all ministers with economic portfolio are added to this group: 10) Finance and/or ministers with related and/or subdivided competences like First Lord of the Treasury, Budget, Taxation, etc.; 11) Economic Affairs and/or ministers with related and/or subdivided competences like (Regional) Economic Planning or Development, Small Businesses. As with the previous variable, I have borrowed this variable from Prof. Perotti until 1995, and I have reproduced the rest of data until 2000 following the same criteria. The sources were again: Woldendorp, F. Keman and Budge (1993), and *The Europa World Yearbook* for Greece, Portugal and Spain (the whole period), and all countries from 1995–2000.

10 Data on election dates has been extracted from Armingeon, Beyeler, and Menegale (2000).

11 'A consolidation is deemed successful, if, two years after the initial adjustment, the government budget balance is at least 75 per cent of the balance in the first year of the consolidation episode. A consolidation is called unsuccessful, if this condition is not met' (Von Hagen, Hallett and Strauch, 2001: 6). This is the standard definition in the literature, started by Alesina and Perotti (1995, 1996b). In those two articles they discuss the robustness of their results with regard to this arbitrary definition.

12 Duration models have been also used in the field of industrial organization, to analyse, for example, the life duration of multinational subsidiaries in the UK manufacturing industry (McCloughan and Stone, 1998), or to analyze investment decisions (Licandro, Goicolea and Maroto, 1999).

13 See also Sosvilla-Rivero and Maroto (2001) for a detailed study of the duration of exchange rates regimes in the European Monetary System (EMS).

14 Note that in this case I do not subtract interest payments, in order to show during the parametric analysis how important is the level of accumulated debt in the duration of fiscal adjustment episodes. I will subtract interest payments during the composition analysis in Chapter 4, in order to follow the traditional method

used in the literature on fiscal adjustments, and to make my results comparable with previous works on the subject.

15 Note also that I start the section on duration analysis using the lowest threshold possible to identify years of fiscal adjustment. This is so because it will allow me at the end of the chapter to test the sensitivity of results to stronger definitions of adjustment that imply higher thresholds.

16 The three countries that ended their consolidation episodes in 2000 are Denmark, Germany and the Netherlands.

17 T is the discrete random variable that measures the time that passes between the beginning of a fiscal consolidation until its transition to a non-consolidation period. For further details on these functions and the related estimation techniques, see Appendix 2.

18 Mathematically, the baseline hazard function, $h_0(t)$, is defined for all time t in which a change has taken place, and it is not defined for other moments of time. But the survivor function $S_0(t)$ is defined for all values of t.

19 Again, for descriptive statistics of all dependent and independent variables used in this book, see Statistical annex 1.

20 In this concrete definition of the variable I follow Von Hagen, Hallett and Strauch (2001: 10).

21 'In the most extreme form of proportional representation, in the Netherlands, the country is treated as one single constituency, so that anyone who can amass 1/150th of the national vote gets a seat in the 15-member Second Chamber, the principal legislative body ... [But] some [other] countries try to limit the number of parties represented in parliament. Germany, for example, insists that a party must get at least five per cent of the vote to qualify (a provision that has effectively created a three-party system), and Spain has a three per cent threshold. Ireland has a complicated system of transferable votes, allowing voters to list candidates in order of preference, which many experts believe most accurately reflects the electorate's wishes' (Dale, 1993: 2).

22 *The Economist*, London, 7 June 1997.

23 *The New York Times*, New York, 25 March 1997. This article described the strikes against plant closings and job losses in Belgium, France and Spain; a march by German coal miners afraid of subsidies cuts; protests by French medical interns 'angered by budget cutbacks'; and a demonstration by 300,000 Italian workers demanding more jobs. The article also links all this social discontent to the pressures that politicians felt at the time to combine the fulfilment of the Maastricht criteria, and the partial satisfaction of these protestors by means of targeted public outlays, in a crucial electoral year.

24 See Buchanan and Wagner (1977) on fiscal illusion, and see Alesina, Cohen and Roubini (1992) on electoral business cycles, and all the discussion presented in chapter 2. More recently, Philippopoulus and Tzavalis (2001), with data on Greece between 1960 and 1997, have found evidence of pre-election cycles, but no partisan differences in fiscal laxity.

25 See Appendix 2 for further details on these tests.

26 These results for Europe are similar to those found by Poterba (1994) for the US, where he found that: 'When a single party controls the state house and the governorship, deficit adjustment is much faster than when party control is divided. In gubernatorial election years, tax increases and spending cuts are both significantly smaller than at other times' (p. 799).

27 *Dow Jones Euronomics*. London, 27 June 2001. A similar situation was also recently described by *Business Europe*, in an article about the political situation in Greece,

and the social tensions created by the still-pending economic reforms that were needed to secure the entry ticket for EMU in 2001, when the author of that article affirmed that: 'These pressures make PASOK victory in the next general election which must be held by October 2000, seem less assured'. *Business Europe*, New York, 19 May 1999.

4 The Composition of Fiscal Adjustments

* Some parts of this chapter were originally published in *European Political Economy Review*, 1(1): 25–39.

1 See also the more recent empirical work by Giavazzi, Jappelli and Pagano (1999).

2 See in this respect Bergström (1997), especially the chapter dedicated to 'Income Distribution, Fiscal Policy and Growth' by Alesina and Perotti. See also the compilation of articles by Tanzi and Chu (1998) on income redistribution and high-quality growth.

3 For example, Przeworski perfectly exemplified the differences that Keynesians established between productive government spending and redistribution spending (that increases equality but not necessarily output growth). In his words: 'Keynesian economics favors government spending over redistribution of income: the multiplier for government spending is greater than unity. Hence, at least in principle, government spending more than pays for itself in increased production, while distribution of income partially hurts other components of demand' (Przeworski, 1986: 210).

4 'Fiscal policy-taxation and spending is a government's most direct tool for redistributing income, both in the short and the long-run' (Tanzi, Chu and Gupta, 1999: 23).

5 Ford (1998: 37).

6 Only the IMF and the World Bank have systematically studied the effect of stabilization policies (that include serious fiscal adjustments) in developing countries on both growth and equality. Their studies have almost always concluded that successful stabilization experiences have increased economic growth and decreased inequalities, normally as a 'collateral effect' of general economic stabilization, and sometimes also helped by World Bank's poverty reduction programmes (see Nelson, 1993; and Tanzi, Chu, and Gupta, 1999). For industrial countries, among the very few studies that have addressed the equity dimension of fiscal adjustments is the work by Ford (1998), who affirms that fiscal consolidations among OECD countries have run parallel to widening distribution of incomes and poverty increases.

7 The effects of economic performance in both retrospective an prospective voting decisions by the electorate is a large field in political science. Some of the most prominent works in this literature are: Lewis-Beck (1988), Markus (1992), Harrington (1993), Maravall and Przeworski (1998) and Cheibub and Przeworski (1999). Further discussion on this subject is presented in chapter 7.

8 Some examples are the presidential elections that Ronald Reagan (in 1982) and George W. Bush (in 2000) won with the promise of future tax cuts. In Europe, some of the most recent examples are those of Blair's victory in 1997, Aznar's electoral triumph in 1996 and 2000, and Berlusconi's victory in 2001, all campaigning for a rationalization of public expenditures that would eventually allow them to reduce income taxes.

9 The period is reduced to 1970–2000 compared to the broader period covered by the timing and duration analysis performed in Chapter 3 (1960–2000), because

the lack of sub-aggregate data for many countries in the 1960s did not allow me to extend the composition analysis to that decade.

10 These variables are the same that were used in the duration analysis of Chapter 3. Refer to that chapter for specific definitions of these variables. Also see Appendix 5 for further specification of all variables used in this book.

11 Note that in the duration analysis the Cox regression-based tests showed that there was temporal heterogeneity but not spatial heterogeneity in the sample. Recall however that the sample used in Chapter 3 was a sample of exclusively adjustment episodes, whereas now the sample covers all years and all countries, including both adjustment and non-adjustment years. In this case there also exists spatial heterogeneity, and the country dummies included in the model used in this chapter attempt to capture this effect.

12 This type of control is especially important for some sub-items of the budget, where the European Commission does not perform cyclical adjustments.

13 That variable was first used in this context by Roubini and Sachs (1989a) to study the relationship between 'type of governments' and deficit, which they found positively associated. As already mentioned in previous chapters, this variable is a multinomial variable with six levels that decrease from single party government to caretaker government.

14 See Halleberg and Von Hagen (1997) and Halleberg (2004).

15 The effect of parliamentary majorities on the duration and composition of fiscal adjustments has been tested separately from the models of Chapters 3 and 4 that include coalition and cabinet size as regressors, and the corresponding coefficients were not statistically significant. These results seem to confirm the decisive role that those variables affecting the cabinet have in determining fiscal policy outcomes. One cannot forget in this respect that in all European parliamentary democracies it is the cabinet the governmental body who designs the budget, the Parliament discusses and votes it, but it is the cabinet again who finally implements it (with a wide margin to depart from the initial budget) (González-Páramo, 2001: 24–6).

16 In any case, I have replicated with this book's database their analysis on the effect of spending limits (targets) and top-down negotiations in fiscal outcomes. Results of this replication are reported in Appendix 4, and looking at them one can arrive at the same conclusion that the impact of procedural fragmentation variables is rather insignificant.

17 To test the importance of the Maastricht Treaty, as a possible better criterion to split up the sample in two periods, all regressions have been run also for periods 1970–92 and 1993–2000 (excluding 1995), and results are basically the same as those for the periods 1970–94 and 1996–2000.

18 According to Kaufman and Segura-Ubiergo (2001: 18), 'the use of panel-corrected standard errors usually produces rather conservative results, since it tends to increase the standard errors of the estimates. Moreover, the inclusion of dummy variables tends to deflate the statistical significance of the other regressors (Sayrs 1989) ... this carries some risk that causal hypotheses will be rejected prematurely. On the other hand, it also increases our confidence that results which do emerge as significant are not the consequence of unsound statistical assumptions or inappropriate econometric methods.' For further details on this technique, see Appendix 3.

19 These results are consistent with those obtained by Perotti and Kontopoulos (2002) for the same period, but surveying a larger sample of OECD countries.

20 Significant only at the 80 per cent confidence level.

21 Because the last section of Chapter 3 demonstrated that results on duration of consolidations were sensitive to the definition of adjustment, in the sense that

political variables were more relevant than economic variables to explain the strongest fiscal adjustments, then I will stick to the strongest definition of adjustment. This *stronger* definition also has the advantage that it is the most commonly used in the literature (see Alesina and Perotti, 1995a and 1996b). To be consistent with this literature and to make my findings comparable, I have followed the same criteria to select the periods of fiscal adjustment from my sample. Therefore in this chapter I define episodes of fiscal consolidations as those in which the cyclically adjusted primary budget balance increased by at least 1.25 per cent of GDP in two consecutive years, or if the change in the cyclically adjusted budget balance exceeded 1.5 per cent of GDP in one year and was less than 1.25 per cent of GDP in the following or the precedent year. The only innovation that I have introduced is that if, for example, a period of fiscal adjustment lasts for 4 years and there is a change in the government's ideology in the middle, I split the episode into two consecutive but different episodes. This facilitates the comparison between leftist and rightist strategies of adjustment.

22 Centre-right governments are classified as those where at least 51 per cent of cabinet posts are held by right-wing parties alone or in combination with centre parties. Centre-left governments are those where at least 51 per cent of cabinet posts are held by left-wing parties alone or in combination with centre parties.

23 If a different definition of fiscal adjustment were used, for example considering periods of fiscal adjustment as every case in which the variation of the cyclically adjusted primary budget balance is > 0, the total number of adjustment episodes would increase from 12 to 34, out of which 17 were held under leftist governments and 17 under rightist governments.

24 In fact, some politicians even ran their campaigns during the second half of the 1990s on their capability to fulfil the Maastricht criteria better that the opponent.

25 Also if I had introduced time dummies, I would have encountered a problem of insufficient degrees of freedom, since the sample is small ($N = 53$).

26 These results are in line with those obtained by Tavares (2004), who also found that left-wing governments were associated with revenue-based adjustments and right-wing governments with expenditure-based ones, using a sample of OECD countries from 1960 to 1995.

27 See the already mentioned article in the *New York Times* (25 March 1997) for a description of this calendars' overlapping.

28 Alesina and Perotti (1996b).

5 Fiscal Adjustments in the 1990s: Case Studies

1 'The IGC on EMU met at different levels: on eleven occasions as a ministerial IGC, but twice as regularly at the level of officials ("Permanent Representatives"). Alongside the IGC negotiations, three "informal" meetings of ECOFIN (ministers of finance) were important for the progress of the negotiations. The Dutch Presidency also instituted a third technical level to agree texts, involving central bank and finance ministry officials. In addition, the IGC asked the Committee of EC Central Bank governors to make various technical submissions; its papers on the statutes of the ECB and of the European Monetary Institute (EMI) determined much of the final content' (Dyson and Featherstone, 2000: 5).

2 See *The Economist* (1991a, 1991b), Giordano and Persaud (1998), and Levitt and Lord (2000).

3 For a detailed account of the reasons that motivated each country to join the EMS, see Oatley (1997).
4 'Two hotly debated topics included (1) the degree of convergence in economic criteria (inflation, interest rates, public budgets) that should be required before moving to EMU and (2) the possibility of delayed entrance for some members. Germany, the Netherlands, and the United Kingdom favoured strong conditions that there would be no move to EMU until a sufficient number of states have met strict and explicit economic conditions. France, Greece, Italy and Spain favoured looser criteria, arguing that EMU would produce full convergence' (Sandholtz, 1993: 16–17). A similar split emerged over the delayed participation of countries, where Germany and the Netherlands supported a plan whereby a core of strong-currency countries (5 or 6) would move first to monetary union, and the other would follow later. This notion of a two-speed EMU was opposed by most other states, especially by Greece, Ireland, and Italy.
5 Note that the final push towards monetary union came from the decisive impulse given by a series of Franco-German bilateral meetings. In 1991 these two countries celebrated two presidential summits on monetary union, two Economic Council meetings, and six top-secret bilaterals of French and German negotiators. In addition to this Franco-German leading dynamic, various delegations submitted papers to the IGC. 'Draft treaties on EMU were presented by the EC Commission (10 December 1990), the French (28 January 1991), and the Germans (26 February 1991). The Spanish presented a more limited text (25 September 1990); whilst the British tabled an updated version of its 'hard' ECU plan [alternative to monetary union] (8 January 1991). The two presidencies were obliged to present composite draft treaties to signal the progress made in the IGC. The Luxembourg text (18 June 1991) proved much more consensual than the various submissions of the Dutch (29 August, 24 September, 28 October, 8 November), and served as the basis for the final version of the Treaty' (Dyson and Featherstone, 2000: 5).
6 On the discussion of whether Europe is or not an optimal currency area see Eichengreen (1990); and Wihlborg and Willett (1993). With respect to the more technical discussion that took place at the beginning of the 1990s regarding the economic pros and cons of the Maastricht criteria, the literature is abundant. However, some articles can be selected from all of them. For example, a critique of the arbitrariness and inutility of the Maastricht criteria was made, among others, by Eichengreen and Von Hagen (1996); Eichengreen and Wyplosz (1998); and Dailey (1999). Additional critiques regarding the economic contraction that these criteria would create in Europe was made by Barrell and Sefton (1997). Nevertheless, there were also strong supporters of the EMU design. Among the most important works in favour of the Maastricht criteria and the Stability and Growth Pact were those by Buti, Franco, and Ongena (1998); and Thygesen (1999).
7 Here, I follow Sandholtz (1993: 18–35).
8 Theoretical debates concerning the European Union often frame the central issue as a contest between 'intergovernmentalist' and 'institutionalist' (or 'neorealist' and 'neofunctionalist') perspectives. Intergovernmentalists hold that nation-states dominate European politics and that outcomes directly reflect the interests and relative powers of the member states (see, for example, Grieco, 1988; and Moravcsik, 1991). Institutionalists argue, in contrast, that the supranational institutions of the EU can exercise an independent effect on European politics and help shape their outcomes (see, for example, Keohane and Hoffmann, 1991; and Cameron, 1992). These theoretically opposed approaches meet at a central point due to the fact that

European institutions have both intergovernmental bodies and procedures (the Council), and supranational ones (the Parliament, the Court of Justice, and the Commission). Both types of institutions are interconnected, and influence each other, in defining their interest, their projects and their ideas. For some of the classical arguments on the impact of international institutions on national interests, see Keohane (1984) and Nye (1988).

9 After this contribution, Frieden, Gros and Jones (1998) arrive at an interesting perspective of understanding EMU at the intersection of Europe as a whole, the member states, and the socioeconomic groups within them.

10 'A Gallup poll of 1,428 EC company presidents in July 1989 found that 83 per cent were in favor of a common European currency and that only 10 per cent were against it ... A separate poll conducted by Ernst & Young for the Commission found similar results. EC businesspersons were asked their opinion on the prospects for the business climate with the 1992 program, and with 1992 plus a single currency. The total positive response rate rose just over 80 per cent for 1992 alone to almost 90 per cent for 1992 plus a single currency; within that the "very positive" response increased from about 16 per cent to over 45 per cent.' (Sandholtz, 1993: 24–5).

11 These reforms implied the strengthening of the mutual credit mechanism in order to improve the defence of the weak EMS currencies in light of the approaching liberalization of capital flows. Without restrictions to capital mobility, further speculative attacks against weak currencies were expected. 'The Bundesbank, however, worried that the commitment it had already assumed in support of the weaker currencies in the system would interfere with its constitutional commitment to price stability' (Thiel and Schroeder, 1998: 110).

12 For an interesting overview of the process that led from the EMS to EMU, see Cobham and Zis (1999).

13 For a detailed explanation of the importance of the Genscher's leadership during the German presidency of the EU in the second semester of 1988, see Dyson and Featherstone (2000: 370–451).

14 For a complete review of the challenges that EMU presented to small member states in Europe, see Jones, Frieden and Torres (1998).

15 In fact, it was the socialist González government which was widely recognized as the 'creator' of the European structural and cohesion funds in order to compensate the poorer countries for the efforts needed to achieve economic convergence before joining the single currency.

16 For a comparative analysis of the economic policy choices faced by Scandinavian social democracy during the 1990s, see Iversen (1998).

17 See Gamble and Kelly (2001).

18 As a consequence of these extraordinary measures, some countries that qualified for the third stage of EMU and that joined the euro in 1999 were unable to keep their public finances within the limits. In fact, between 2001 and 2005 the European Commission was forced to launch early warnings and start 'excessive deficit' procedures against at least six countries (Ireland, The Netherlands, France, Germany, Italy and Portugal).

By March 2005 only three member states remained below the 3 per cent threshold. As a consequence, the Stability and Growth Pact was relaxed during the Spring Council of the Luxembourg Presidency, opening up the chance to take into consideration the cycle, the debt burden and public investment prospects within the 3 per cent limit.

19 The reduction of the public deficit was even higher once the cycle is taken into account. The cyclically adjusted budget balance improved from −7.3 to −4.0.
20 Antonio Guterres, quoted in EIU-Portugal Country Report (1996: 11)
21 The two crucial budgets of 1996 and 1997 were passed by the socialist government with the abstention of the two main opposition parties (right-wing PSD and PP), and the rejection vote of the Communist party. The abstention vote of the PSD was agreed as a policy of national interest, while the abstention vote from the PP was negotiated in exchange for some political concessions and the abolition of the stamp tax. This bilateral negotiation between the cabinet and the leader of the PP, Manuel Monteiro, originated internal critiques to the cabinet from some members of the Socialist parliamentary group.
22 Up to 22 public enterprises where projected to be partly sold to private investors during 1996 and 1997.
23 This clearly contrasts with the freezing of public wages imposed by the conservative PP government in Spain, the same year.
24 In March 1996, José María Aznar, 20 seats short of the majority needed to govern, formed a minority government with the parliamentary support of the Catalan nationalists (CiU), the Basque nationalists (PNV), and the Canarian Coalition. Previously, Felipe González governed between 1993 and 1996 with the parliamentary support of the 17 seats of CiU.
25 Note, however, that the last González government already took some measures to restrain public spending under the leadership of the new independent minister of finance, Pedro Solbes, and with the support of the right-wing nationalists of CiU. Basically, they tightened unemployment benefits, reached an agreement on wage moderation in 1995, and sealed a pact with regional governments to share the financing of health services for the period 1994–97 (Banco de España Annual Report, 1995). In spite of these measures, the consolidated government deficit at the end of 1995 reached 6.6 per cent of GDP.
26 'So far, José María Aznar has defined himself as a classic liberal' (Frain and Wiarda, 1998: 210).
27 While Felipe González lost the 1996 elections to José María Aznar by a razor-thin margin of 1.4 per cent of the vote (around 400,000 votes), Aznar obtained an absolute majority in 2000 with a much wider margin (2,900,000 votes) over PSOE. These results caused the immediate resignation of the socialist candidate, Joaquín Almunia, and led to a profound renewal of the party that started after the 35th extraordinary congress that chose José Luís Rodríguez Zapatero as the new Secretary General.
28 The index is a weighted average of: 1) the relative strength of the prime minister or the finance minister in the government to establish spending targets early in the negotiation process; 2) the relative presence of amendments or item-by-item votes in the parliamentary process; 3) the degree of transparency of the budget; 4) the relative strength of the finance minister over the rest of spending ministers. A high score of the index signals that a country's budget conforms to the above strategies, and therefore is centralized, while the opposite signals strong fragmentation in decision-making (Von Hagen and Harden, 1995; Von Hagen, Hallett and Strauch, 2001).
29 The UK's 'reductions only' powers of the Parliament are unique and have evolved from a peculiar historical situation. 'The explanation of this provision can be traced to the early days of the House of Commons, to the time when it met to consider demands for subsidies made by the Crown. Its task was to decide

whether to comply with the demand and, if so, within what limits and by what means. This explains the prohibition on proposals to increase expenditure and consequently on proposals to increase taxation. The British parliament still respects this long-standing custom and practice and, as a result, it may not vote sums in excess of government's estimates. Consequently, the only amendments that are in order are those which aim to reduce the sums requested and have as their purpose the chance for Members to raise explanations before the sums in question are approved' (IPU, 1986: 1093). Cited in Krafchik and Wehner (1999).

30 See also EC (1993) and OECD Economic Survey (1993: 58, 1995: 118).

31 It is important to note that some complementary measures were also taken on the spending side. 'In 1998 the government continued its rather restrictive policy concerning social transfers, and health care expenditures, which could be cut due to an increase in the contribution rates for the self-employed, and transfers to local governments (OECD Economic Survey, 1999: 52–3). An expansionary initiative was also taken with the introduction of a minimum income scheme aiming to help low earners and families to find employment' (Von Hagen, Hallett and Strauch, 2001: 103).

32 Note that these four countries were the most indebted countries in terms of GDP of the EU, at the beginning of the 1990s. Only Ireland started to modify its budgetary process and reduce its debt in the mid 1980s. The rest followed similar processes at the beginning of the 1990s.

33 For more information on the role of international constraints on domestic decisions regarding the budget deficit in the European Union, see Freitag and Scianni (2001). For the system of incentives that the Maastricht Treaty created among member states to implement difficult convergence policies, see Winkler (1995).

34 In the 1995 presidential elections Chirac campaigned giving the vague impression that faster progress could be made in reducing unemployment by the government opting for the pursuit of more growth-oriented policies. When Juppé addressed the Assembly after succeeding Balladur, he also promised job creation without mentioning any painful economic medicine (EIU France Country Report, 1996, $^1/_4$: 14).

35 Education spending increased in nominal terms by 3.5 per cent in 1996 and 1.3 per cent in 1996, but this implied a cut in real terms that was unprecedented in France (EIU France Country Report, 1996, $^3/_4$).

36 In February and March 1997, Sofres, an important French opinion pollster, predicted a comfortable majority of the RPR-UDF alliance if elections were to take place in the following Spring. (EIU-France Country Report, $^1/_4$, 1997).

37 The first two *cohabitations* occurred under the presidency of François Mitterrand, during the periods 1986–88 and 1993–95.

38 See, for example, 'Losing Bet' in *Time Europe*, 16 June 1997.

39 According to the European Commission, at the end of 2002 the budget deficit of Germany reached 3.8 per cent of its GDP.

40 Note also that these labour market measures coincided with an economic downturn provoked in all Europe by the tight monetary policy with which the Bundesbank accommodated the fiscal expansion associated to the German reunification. This tight monetary policy rose German interest rates and appreciated the DM vis-à-vis the rest of European currencies. As a consequence the economic deceleration of the early 1990s worsened. See Giordano and Persaud (1998).

41 The solidarity surcharge on personal and corporate income was introduced in 1991. The surcharge of 7.5 per cent of the tax liability was implemented until June 1992, and then was reintroduced in 1995.

42 Together with these revenue raising measures, the government took some fiscal initiatives from 1994 onwards to reduce the tax burden on firms and to improve business conditions. The *Investment Location Law* envisaged a reduction of corporate taxes on retained profits from 50 per cent to 45 per cent, and on dividends from 36 per cent to 30 per cent. In addition, the top rate of taxes on business income was reduced from 53 per cent to 47 per cent. These reductions were 'to be financed through the replacement of the declining-balance depreciation by the linear depreciation on company buildings and the closure of several tax loopholes and tax simplifications reducing tax evasion' (OECD Economic Survey, 1995: 158).

43 Von Hagen and Strauch describe perfectly the importance of the Treuhand: '*De jure*, it was an independent federal agency under the supervision of the Ministry of Finance and subject to the scrutiny of a special parliamentary committee. *De facto*, the Ministry of Finance exercised special control, at best, over its activities (...) Requests of the Ministry concerning the usage of funds the Treuhand borrowed in the capital markets or received from other sources were not necessarily answered. For example, the Treuhand's president Birgit Breuel flatly refused to produce information on the credit commitments which the Treuhand had made to firms taking over ex-socialist enterprises, commitments that reached an amount of Deutsche Mark 20 billion' (Czada, 1994: 40; in Von Hagen and Strauch, 1999: 88).

6 The Economic Consequences of Fiscal Adjustments

* Some parts of this chapter have been used for an article of mine published in *Hacienda Pública Española*, 172-(1/2005), pp. 61–92.

1 Section 6.3 offers a detailed formulation of the null and alternative hypotheses tested in this chapter.

2 In this respect, the article that I take as the main reference for the first sections of this chapter is Alesina and Ardagna (1998).

3 For example, OECD (1996), Alesina and Ardagna (1998) and Perotti (1999).

4 Lately, there has been an effort to evaluate the effect that tax and expenditure policies have in the distribution of income. For example, Ayala *et al.* (1999), and Chu *et al.* (2000) find that social spending has a strong and significant impact in reducing inequalities (especially public health spending, pensions and primary-secondary education spending). Taxes, however, have an indirect and limited impact in reducing inequalities. These findings have been confirmed by Oliver *et al.* (2001) for the Spanish case.

5 This is the most popular approach in the literature. See, for example, Alesina and Perotti (1997), Alesina and Ardagna (1998), and Alesina, Perotti and Tavares (1998). These authors compare the average values of the main variables two or three years before the adjustment takes place with those from two or three years after the adjustment. None of them has, however, looked at the evolution of income distribution.

6 This literature is enormous, ranging from the original theoretical works of Kuznets (1955) to the most recent empirical works of Alesina and Rodrik (1994), Persson and Tabellini (1994) or Perotti (1996). Some works include very informative revisions of the literature in this field: see, for example, Aghion, Caroli and García-Peñalosa (1999).

7 This is the same criteria used for the selection of adjustment episodes in the most important chapters in this field. See for example, Alesina and Ardagna (1997, 1998), Perotti and Kontopoulos (2002) and Maroto and Mulas-Granados (2002) for a discussion on the sensitivity of results to different fiscal adjustment definitions.

8 An episode of fiscal adjustment is considered to be revenue-based when more than half of the contribution to average deficit reduction during the adjustment episode comes from an increase in the average total revenues during the episode. The opposite is the case with expenditure-based adjustments.
9 This confirms the findings of Von Hagen, Hallett and Strauch (2001) who showed that the probability of starting a fiscal adjustment rose when public debt increased.
10 Data on inequality comes from the World Income Inequality Database of the United Nations (2000), and has been completed for some years and some countries with the database from the Luxembourg Income Study Group (2001). Overlapping three-year moving averages have been used to fill in the gaps in the series. The Gini and Theil coefficients as expressed in these databases run from 0 to 100. They equal 0 when the distribution of income is completely egalitarian, and they equal 100 when it is completely inegalitarian and one person holds all the income in a society. Besides the Gini and Theil coefficients, calculations also include the ratio between the highest and the lowest deciles. Both databases (WIID and LIS) contain comparable data in terms of *equivalent disposable household income*, which includes all income obtained by families from any source (work, property, capital, private transfers, social security benefits, etc.), applying an equivalent scale of a parameter of 0.5 to family income figures, to take account of differences in household sizes. Although other, and possibly better, indicators may exist on the economic situation of households than disposable monetary income, it is this variable that provides an adequate basis for comparison.

Definition of the Gini coefficient: $$G(x) = \left[\frac{\sum_{i=1}^{n}\sum_{j=1}^{n} \left| x_i - x_j \right|}{2\mu_x} \right]$$

Definition of the Theil index (c=1): $$T(x) = \left[\frac{1}{n}\right]\sum_{i=1}^{n}\left[\frac{x_i}{\mu}\right]\ln\left[\frac{x_i}{\mu}\right], c = 1$$

11 See for example, Gottschalk, Gustaffson and Palmer (1997); Danzinger and Reid (1999); Ford (1998); Atkinson (2000); Smeeding (2000); Freeman (2000), Álvarez, Prieto and Salas (2002).
12 Note that these results are very similar to those reported by Alesina and Ardagna (1998), and all other similar studies collected in Appendix 5. Note also that the importance of bad initial fiscal conditions in generating expansionary fiscal adjustments, while very much stressed in studies dealing with advanced economies (Perotti, 1999; Giavazzi, Jappelli and Pagano, 2000), has been also corroborated in studies dealing with low-income countries (Gupta, Clements, Baldacci and Mulas-Granados 2005).
13 Giavazzi and Pagano (1996) argue that a large adjustment, by inducing a permanent change of fiscal regime, may be expansionary because expectations are less susceptible to the effects of smaller adjustments.
14 See Argimón, González-Páramo and Roldán (1997) for similar evidence on crowding-in after fiscal adjustments.
15 According to Alesina and Perotti (1997b), in such cases where trade unions are not weak nor strong enough, a 1 per cent income tax increase raises labour costs by 2 per cent.
16 Note that the size of the increase in private consumption depends on the absence of liquidity-constrained consumers (Alesina and Ardagna, 1998), and therefore, as

noted by Perotti (1999), the result hinges on the efficiency of financial markets, and should be stronger when fiscal consolidation occurs in bad times when the debt-to-GDP ratio is growing rapidly. For similar previous arguments in this respect, see also Blanchard (1990) and Bertola and Drazen (1993).

17 These conclusions are based on the calculations that replicate Tables 6.1, 6.3 and 6.4, now estimated only for the sub-sample of adjustment episodes occurring during the 1990s. These tables are not included in the text, following the editor's indications, due to space constraints. Nonetheless, they are available from the author.

18 Budget quality is a variable that measures the contribution of primary expenditures to the total amelioration of the budget balance.

19 See, for example, Barro (1990, 1991), Easterly, Rodríguez and Schmidt-Hebbel (1994), Tanzi and Zee (1996), Barro and Sala-I-Martin (1995) and Mendoza, Milesi-Ferretti and Asea (1997).

20 The model replicates the baseline specification of the one proposed by Von Hagen *et al.* (2001). Note, however, that they used a sample of 19 OECD countries for the period 1965–95, while this chapter uses a sample of 15 EU member states for the period 1960–2000, with data from the AMECO database.

21 Measured as the difference between aggregate demand and potential output, as defined by the European Commission in the AMECO database.

22 The monetary policy stance is measured by the Monetary Conditions Index built specifically for this purpose. The index is the sum of the short-term real interest rate and the real exchange rate, each weighted by its sample standard deviation.

23 For a more detailed review of the potential factors affecting income distribution, see Chu *et al.* (2000).

24 See for example Garrett (1998) or Kaufman and Segura-Ubiergo (2001).

25 For details on this technique, see Beck and Katz (1995, 1996). According to Kaufman and Segura-Ubiergo (2001: 18), 'the use of panel-corrected standard errors usually produces rather conservative results, since it tends to increase the standard errors of the estimates. Moreover, the inclusion of dummy variables tends to deflate the statistical significance of the other regressors . . . this carries some risk that causal hypotheses will be rejected prematurely. On the other hand, it also increases our confidence that results which do emerge as significant are not the consequence of unsound statistical assumptions or inappropriate econometric methods.'

7 The Political Consequences of Fiscal Adjustments

* Some parts of this chapter have been used for an article of mine published in *European Union Politics*, 5(4)-2004: 467–93.

1 As will become clear during this chapter, I claim that assessing the political consequences of fiscal adjustments looking at the probability of government termination implies an indirect approach to this question. A much direct approach is to look at the probability of re-election, which excludes from the sample the reshuffling of cabinets that are the result of coalition rearrangements, but are totally independent of the public reaction to fiscal adjustments.

2 Peltzman (1992) and Kraemer (1997) have reached similar conclusions for Latin America and the US States, respectively.

3 In the same vein Alesina, Perotti, and Tavares (1998), Lowry, Alt, and Ferree (1998) analysed the electoral response of American voters to the fiscal policy implemented by American State-level governments and found that: 'the incumbent governor's party is punished in legislative elections for failing to maintain fiscal balance.' (p. 759). Nevertheless, Obstfeld and Eichengreen (1998) reject the idea of fiscally

conservatist voters at the national level pointed out by Alesina, Perotti and Tavares (1998), and affirm that they find fiscal conservatism 'much more plausible at the local level (because) at the national level, there are too many "other" onto whom the burden of public spending can be shifted.' (p. 253).

4 Some authors advocate institutional approaches to explain these differences (Pacek and Radcliff, 1995), but others emphasize the role of monitoring difficulties that may prevent the electorate from attributing correctly the responsibility for bad economic outcomes (Powell and Whitten, 1993; Chappell and Veiga, 2000; and Anderson, 2000). This monitoring problem could have an institutional origin or be the result of intended disinformation strategies implemented by political party elites and government authorities not interested in making the process of attributing responsibility for economic outcomes easier (Maravall, 1998).

5 Government terminations can occur for a variety of reasons: elections, voluntary resignation of the prime minister, resignation of the prime minister due to health reasons, dissension within government, lack of parliamentary support, intervention of the Head of State, or broadening of the coalition. The source of data to build this variable is Woldendorp, Keman and Budge (2000).

6 Alesina *et al.* (1998: 220) say, 'we have examined whether our results vary substantially when we use only changes following elections but we find that they do not'. Unfortunately, they do not show the results of this sensitivity analysis in their article.

7 The total number of data points is 615 (the 15 EU member states for the period 1960–2000), but for this analysis, years under non-democratic governments in Spain, Portugal and Greece have been excluded from the sample.

8 Cited in Cheibub and Przeworski (1998: 234).

9 Recall from previous chapters that $\Delta BBAL$ is a continuous variable. If the annual change in the budget balance has been positive between year t-1 and t, then year t can be considered a fiscal adjustment year. The rest can be considered non-adjustment years. As already done in Chapters 3 and 4, the analysis starts here with all years included together in the same sample, since the isolation of adjustment years would generate a problem of selection bias. Again, the results will be tested later in a sub-sample that only includes adjustment years.

10 Note, however, that for the regressions on government termination, positive variations in the price index are associated with higher probabilities of government termination. This is the same finding reported by Alesina, Perotti and Tavares (1998).

11 Note that Brender and Drazen (2005) tested this 'economic voting hypothesis' in a large cross section of countries from developed and developing democracies. They have found that economic growth increases the chances of being re-elected, while budget deficits do not increase the likelihood of re-election. Their findings confirm the 'economic voting hypothesis', but do not find anything related to our 'fiscal voting hypothesis'. The fact that voters dislike budget deficits (as they find) is perfectly compatible with the hypothesis of this chapter according to which voters dislike expenditure-based adjustments (whenever the deficit has to be reduced and governments undertake fiscal consolidations).

12 'Quality of the budget' is a variable that measures the contribution of cyclically adjusted primary expenditures to the total amelioration of the budget balance. Most prominent studies in the literature affirm that only 'good quality' adjustments are sustainable which implies that sustainability is increased when

the relative contribution of primary spending (mainly transfers and wage bill) to the total budget decreases.

13 Recall that this sub-sample uses the most standard definition in the related literature, according to which episodes of fiscal adjustment would include every year in which the amelioration of the cyclically-adjusted primary balance was higher than at least 1.25 per cent of GDP, and when there was a positive variation in the budget balance in the next or the previous year as well.

Appendices

1 From EC (2000b: 121–4).

2 Baxter and King (1995) show that close to the end points the HP filter has a tendency to already dampen the influence of cycles with a period larger than four years.

3 From Maroto and Mulas-Granados (2001: 8–13).

4 T is the discrete random variable that measures the time that passes between the beginning of a fiscal consolidation until its transition to a non-consolidation period.

5 Mathematically, the baseline hazard function, $h_0(t)$, is defined for all time t in which a change has taken place, and it is not defined for other moments of time. But the survivor function $S_0(t)$ is defined for all values of t.

6 I am specially grateful to Alex Segura-Ubiergo for his expert advice on the writing of this appendix and for his feedback during the process of choosing the best regression models and estimation procedures in Chapter 4.

7 Successful consolidations are larger, of longer duration, or have a significant impact on the debt ratio.

8 World Income Inequality Database (2000: 21).

Statistical Annex 2: Data on General Government Balances and Cyclical Corrections: Definitions and Tables

9 From Statistical Annex in *Public Finances in EMU-2001* (EC, 2001b).

Bibliography

Aalen, O. 1978. 'Nonparametric Inference for Family of Counting Processes', *Annals of Statistics*, 6, 701–26.

Aghion, P., Caroli. E. and García-Peñalosa, C. 1999. 'Inequality and Economic Growth: The Perspective from New Growth Theories'. *Journal of Economic Literature*, 37(4): 1615–60.

Ahrendt, D. 1999. *European Public Opinion on the Single Currency*. Europinion. Special Edition. European Commission. Luxembourg: Office for Official Publications of the EC.

Akaike, H. 1974. 'A New Look at the Statistical Model Identification', *IEEE Transactions on Automatic Control*, AC-19, 716–23.

Alesina, A. 1989. 'Politics and Business Cycles in Industrial Democracies', *Economic Policy*, 8: 57–98.

Alesina, A. and Ardagna, S. 1998. 'Tales of Fiscal Contractions: Fiscal Adjustments. Why They Can be Expansionary', *Economic Policy*, 27: 489–543.

Alesina, A., Ardagna, S. Perotti, R. and Schiantarelli, F. 1999. 'Fiscal Policy, Profits, and Investment'. NBER Working Paper, No. 7207.

Alesina, A., Cohen, G.D., Roubini, N. 1992. 'Macroeconomic Policies and Elections in OECD Democracies', *Economics and Politics*, 4: 1–30.

Alesina, A. and Drazen, A. 1991. 'Why are Stabilizations Delayed?', *American Economic Review*, 82(5): 1179–88.

Alesina, A. and Perotti, R. 1995a. 'The Political Economy of Budget Deficits', *IMF Staff Papers*, 42(1): 1–31.

Alesina, A. and Perotti, R. 1995b. 'Fiscal Expansion and Fiscal Adjustments in OECD Countries', *Economic Policy*, 21: 205–48.

Alesina, A. and Perotti, R. 1996a. 'Budget Deficits and Budget Institutions', *NBER Working Papers*, No. 5556.

Alesina, A. and Perotti, R. 1996b. 'Fiscal Adjustments in OECD Countries: Composition and Macroeconomic Effects', *IMF Working Paper*, WP/96/70.

Alesina, A. and Perotti, R. 1997a. 'Fiscal Adjustments in OECD Countries: Composition and Macroeconomic Effects', *IMF Staff Papers*.

Alesina, A. and Perotti, R. 1997b. 'The Welfare State and Competitiveness', *American Economic Review*, 87: 920–39.

Alesina, A., Perotti, R. and Tavares, J. 1998. 'The Political Economy of Fiscal Adjustments', *Brookings Papers on Economic Activity*, 0(1): 197–248.

Alesina, A and Rodrik, D. 1994. 'Distributive Politics and Economic Growth', *Journal of Economics*, 109(2): 465–90.

Alesina, A. and Rosenthal, H. 1994. *Partisan Politics, Divided Government and the Economy*. New York: Cambridge University Press.

Alesina, A. and Roubini, N. 1992. 'Political Cycles: Evidence from OECD Economies', *Review of Economic Studies*, 59: 663–88.

Alesina, A. and Summers, L. 1993. 'Central Bank Independence and Macroeconomic Performance: Some Comparative Evidence'.

Alt, J. 1985. 'Political Parties, World Demand, and Unemployment: Domestic and International Sources of Economic Activity', *American Political Science Review*, 85: 539–56.

Álvarez, R.M, Garrett, G. and Lange, P. 1991. 'Government Partisanship, Labor Organization and Macroeconomic Performance', *American Political Science Review*, 85: 541–56.

Álvarez, S., Prieto, J. and Salas, R. 2002. 'The Evolution of Income Inequality in the European Union', Instituto de Estudios Fiscales (Ministerio de Hacienda). Documento de Trabajó, 10.02.

Anderson, C.J. 2000. 'Economic Voting and Political Context: A Comparative Perspective', *Electoral Studies*, 19: 151–70.

Argimón, I., González-Páramo, J.M. and Roldán, J.M. 1997. 'Evidence of Public Spending Crowding-out from a Panel of OECD Countries', *Applied Economics*, 29: 1001–10.

Armingeon, K., Beyeler, M. and Menegale, S. 2000. 'Comparative Political Data Set 1960–98'. Institute of Political Science, University of Berne.

Artis, M. and Winkler, B. 1998. 'The Stability Pact: Safeguarding the Credibility of the European Central Bank', *National Institute Economic Review*, 183: 87–98.

Aschauer, D. 1989. 'Is Public Expenditure Productive?', *Journal of Monetary Economics*, 23: 177–200.

Atkinson, A.B. 2000. 'Is Rising Income Inequality Inevitable? A Critique of the Transatlantic Consensus', WIDER Annual Lecture no. 3. Helsinki and Japan: United Nations World Institute for Development Economics Research, mimeo.

Auerbach, A. and Kotlikoff, L. 1987. *Dynamic Fiscal Policy*. Cambridge: Cambridge University Press.

Ayala, L., Martinez, R. and Ruiz-Huerta, J. 1999. 'Inequality, Growth and Welfare: An International Comparison', Luxembourg Income Study (LIS) Working Papers, 215.

Aylott, N. 2001. 'The Swedish Social Democratic Party'. In T. Notermans (ed.), *Social Democracy and Monetary Union*. New York: Berghahn Books, pp. 149–74.

Banca d'Italia. 1995, 1996, 1998. *Economic Bulletin. (Bolletino Economico)*. Rome: Banca d'Italia. No. 28, No. 30, No. 34.

Banco de España. 1992, 1995, 1996, 1997, 1998. *Annual Report (Informe Anual)*. Madrid: Banco de España.

Banco de Portugal. 1996, 1997, 1998, 1999. *Annual Report (Relatório anual)*. Lisbon: Banco de Portugal.

Banque de France. 1995, 1996. *Bulletin Digest (Bulletin de la Banque de France)*. Paris: Banque de France. No. 2/95, No. 11/96.

Barrell, R. and Sefton, J. 1997. 'Fiscal Policy and the Maastricht Solvency Criteria', *The Manchester School*, 65(3): 259–79.

Barro, R. 1979. 'On the Determination of Public Debt', *Journal of Political Economy*, 87: 940–71.

Barro, R.J. 1990. 'Government Spending in a Simple Model of Endogenous Growth', *Journal of Political Economy*, 98(1): 103–17.

Barro, R.J. 1991. 'Economic Growth in a Cross Section of Countries', *Quarterly Journal of Economics*, 106: 407–43.

Barro, R.J. and Sala-i-Martin, X. 1995. *Economic Growth*. New York: McGraw-Hill.

Baxter, M. and King, G. 1995. 'Measuring Business Cycles: Approximate Band-Pass Filters for Economic Time Series', *NBER Working Paper*, No. 5022.

Beck, N. and Katz, J. 1995. 'What to Do (and Not to Do) with Time-Series Cross-Section Data', *American Political Science Review*, 89(3): 634–47.

Beck, N. and Katz, J. 1996. 'Nuisance versus Substance: Specifying and Estimating Time-Series Cross-Section Models', *Political Analysis*, 6 (July): 1–37.

Bergström, V. (ed.). 1997. *Government and Growth*. Oxford: Clarendon Press.

Bertola, G. and Drazen, A. 1993. 'Trigger Points and Budget Cuts: Explaining the Effects of Fiscal Austerity', *American Economic Review*, 83: 11–26.

Blanchard, O.J. 1990. 'Comment on "Can Severe Fiscal Contractions be Expansionary?" '. In O.J. Blanchard and S. Fisher (eds), *Macroeconomics Annual 1990*. Cambridge, MA: National Bureau of Economic Research.

Blundell, R. and MacCurdy, T. 1999. 'Labor Supply: A Review of Alternative Approaches'. In O. Ashenfelter and D. Card (eds), *Handbook of Labor Economics, Vol. 3*. Amsterdam: Elsevier.

Bobbio, N. 1995. *Derecha e Izquierda*. Madrid: Taurus.

Bohrer, R.E. and Tan, A.C. 2000. 'Left Turn in Europe? Reactions to Austerity and EMU', *Political Research Quarterly*, 53(3): 575–95.

Boix, C. 1996. *Partidos Políticos: Crecimiento e Igualdad. Estrategias Económicas Conservadoras y Socialdemócratas en la Economía Mundial*. Alianza Universidad.

Boix, C. 1997. 'Political Parties and the Supply Side of the Economy: The Provision of Physical and Human Capital in Advance Economies, 1960–90', *American Journal of Political Science*, 41(3): 814–45.

Boix, C. 2000. 'Partisan Governments, The International Economy and Macroeconomic Policies in Advanced Nations, 1960–93', *World Politics*, 53: 38–43.

Bordignon, 2000. 'Problems of Soft Budget Constraints in Intergovernmental Relationships: The Case of Italy'. Milano: Istituto di economia e finanza, Quaderno No. 30.

Brender, A. and Drazen, A. 2005. 'How Do Budget Deficits and Economic Growth Affect Re-election Prospects? Evidence from a Large Cross-Section of Countries, NBER Working Paper, no. 11862.

Briotti, M.G. 2004. 'Fiscal Adjustment Between 1991 and 2002: Stylised Facts and Policy Implications', ECB Occasional Paper Series, no. 9.

Brittan, S. 1975. 'The Economic Contradictions of Democracy', *British Journal of Political Science*, 5: 129–59.

Buchanan, J.M. 1960. *Fiscal Theory and Political Economy*. Chapel Hill, NC: University of North Carolina Press.

Buchanan, J.M. and Wagner, R.E. 1976. 'Revenue Structure, Fiscal illusion and Budgetary Choice'. *Public Choice*, 25: 45–61.

Buti, M, 2003. 'Discretionary Fiscal Policy and Elections: The Experience of Early Years in EMU', European Commission Group of Policy Advisors, mimeo.

Buti, M., Franco, D. and Ongena, H. 1998. 'Fiscal Discipline and Flexibility in EMU: The Implementation of the Stability and Growth Pact', *Oxford Review of Economic Policy*, 14: 81–97.

Buti, M. and Sapir, A. 1998. *Economic Policy in EMU*. Oxford: Oxford University Press.

Calmfors, L. and Driffill, J. 1988. 'Bargaining Structure, Corporatism and Macroeconomic Performance', *Economic Policy*, 6: 13–61.

Cameron, D.R. 1984. 'Social Democracy, Corporatism, Labor Quiescence, and the Representation of Economic Interest in Advance Capitalist Society'. In J. Golthorpe (ed.), *Order and Conflict in Contemporary Capitalism*. Oxford: Oxford University Press.

Cameron, D.R. 1992. 'The 1992 Initiative: Causes and Consequences'. In A.M. Sbragia (ed.), *Europolitics: Institutions and Policymaking in the 'New' European Community*. Washington, DC: Brookings Institution, pp. 25–30.

Casares Ripol, J. 2002. *El Pensamiento en la Política Económica*. Madrid: ESIC.

Chamley, C. 1986. 'Optimal Taxation of Capital Income Equilibrium with Infinite Lives'. *Econometrica*, 54(3): 607–22.

Chappell, H.W. Jr., and Gonçalves Veiga, L. 2000. 'Economics and Elections in Western Europe: 1960–1997'. *Electoral Studies*, 19: 183–97.

Chari, V.V. and Kehoe, P.J. 1998. 'Optimal Fiscal and Monetary Policy'. *Research Department Staff Report.* Minneapolis: Federal Reserve Bank of Minneapolis.

Cheibub, J.A. and Przeworski, A. 1999. 'Democracy, Elections and Accountability for Economic Outcomes'. In B. Manin, A. Przeworski and S. Stokes (eds), *Democracy, Accountability, and Representation.* New York: Cambridge University Press.

Chiorazzo, V. and Spaventa, L. 1999. 'The Prodigal Son or a Confidence Trickster? How Italy got into EMU'. In D. Cobham and G. Zis (eds), *From EMS to EMU: 1979 to 1999 and Beyond.* New York: St Martin's Press, pp. 129–55.

Chu. K., Davoodi. M. and Gupta, S. 2000. 'Income Distribution and Tax and Government Social Spending Policies in Developing Countries', International Monetary Fund Working Papers, WP/00/62.

Cobham, D. and Zis, G. 1999. *From EMS to EMU: 1979 to 1999 and Beyond.* New York: St Martin's Press.

Cour, P., Dubois, E., Mahfouz, S., and Pisani-Ferry, J. 1996. 'The Cost of Fiscal Retrenshment Revisited: How Strong is the Evidence?'. *Institut National de la Statistique et des Études Économiques. Série des Documents de Travail 9612.* Paris. INSEE.

Cox, D.R. 1972. 'Regression Models and Life Tables'. *Journal of the Royal Statistical Society,* Series B, 34: 187–202.

Cox, D.R. and Snell, E.J. 1968. 'A General Definition of Residuals (with Discussion)'. *Journal of the Royal Statistical Society,* Series B, 39: 248–75.

Crawford, M. 1996. *One Money for Europe? The Economics and Politics of EMU.* New York: St Martin's Press.

Cukierman, A. and Meltzer, A. 1989. 'A Positive Theory of Government Debt and Deficits in a Neo-Ricardian Framework'. *American Economic Review,* 79(4): 713–32.

Dailey, C. 1999. 'Fiscal Policy in the Eurozone'. *University of Dublin-Student Economic Review,* 10: 1–4.

Dale, R. 1993. 'European Politics: A Country by Country Look at Europe's Government Systems'. *Europe*: Washington. Dec 92/Jan93.

Danzinger, S. and Reed, D. 1999. 'Winners and Losers: The Era of Inequality Continues'. *Brookings Review* (Fall): 14–17.

De Beus, J. 2001. 'Dutch Social Democracy and EMU'. In T. Notermans (ed.), *Social Democracy and Monetary Union.* New York: Berghahn Books, pp. 225–52.

De Haan, J., Moessen, W. and Volkerink, B. 1999. 'Budgetary Procedures-Aspects and Changes: New Evidence for Some European Countries'. In J.M., Poterba and J. Von Hagen (eds), *Fiscal Institutions and Fiscal Performance.* Chicago: The University of Chicago Press, pp. 265–300.

Deaton, Angus. 1997. *The Analysis of Household Surveys: A Microeconometric Approach to Development Policy.* Baltimore and Lodon: John Hopkins Press and World Bank.

Deutsche Bundesbank. March 1990, April 1998. *Monthly Report.* Frankfurt am Main: Deutsche Bundesbank.

Deutsches Institut Für Wirstchaforschung (DIW). 1998. 'The State of the State's Deficit in January 1997'. *Working Paper,* 25/98.

De Wolff, J. 1998. *The Political Economy of Fiscal Decisions: The Strategic Role of Public Debt.* Heidelberg: Physica-Verlag.

Dornbusch, Rudi. 1996. 'Euro Fantasies', *Foreign Affairs,* 75(5): 110–24.

Downs, A. 1957. *An Economic Theory of Democracy.* New York: Harper.

Dyson, K. and Featherstone, K. 2000. *The Road to Maastricht.* Oxford: Oxford University Press.

Easterly, W. and Rebelo, S. 1993. 'Fiscal Policy and Economic Growth: an Empirical Investigation'. NBER Working Paper No. 4499.

Easterly, W., Rodríguez, C.A. and Schmidt-Hebbel, K. 1994. *Public Sector Deficits and Macroeconomic Performance*. Washington: The World Bank.

Economist Intelligence Unit. *France-Country Report*. London: The Economist Intelligence Unit. Various numbers: 1996, 1st, 2nd quarter; 1997, 1st, 2nd, 3rd, 4th quarter; 1998, 3rd quarter.

Economist Intelligence Unit. *Ireland-Country Report*. London: The Economist Intelligence Unit. Various numbers: 1998, 1999, always 1st quarter.

Economist Intelligence Unit. *Portugal-Country Report*. London: The Economist Intelligence Unit. Various numbers: 1996, 1997, 1998, 1999, 2000, 2001, always 1st quarter.

Economist Intelligence Unit. *Spain-Country Report*. London: The Economist Intelligence Unit. Various numbers: 1996, 1997, 1998, 1999, 2000, 2001, always 1st quarter.

Economist, The. 1991a. 'Seven Stops to Maastricht'. 321: 47–48. 9–15 November.

Economist, The. 1991b. 'History of the Maastricht Summit'. 321: 47–9. 30 November–6 December.

Eichenberg, R.C. and Dalton, R.J. 1993. 'Europeans and the European Community: The Dynamics of Public Support for European Integration', *International Organization*, 47: 507–34.

Eichengreen, B. 1990. 'Currency Union: One Money for Europe? Lessons from the U.S. Currency Union'. *Economic Policy*, 10: 117–87.

Eichengreen, B. and Von Hagen, J. 1996. 'Fiscal Restrictions and Monetary Union: Rationales, Repercussions, Reforms', *Empirica*, 23: 3–23.

Eichengreen, B. and Wyplosz, C. 1998. 'Stability Pact. More that a Minor Nuisance?', *Economic Policy*, 26: 67–113.

Erikson, R.S. 1989. 'Economic Conditions and the Presidential Vote', *American Political Science Review*, 34(2): 373–99.

Esping-Andersen, G. 1995. *Politics Against Markets: The Social Democratic Road to Power*. Princeton, NJ: Princeton University Press.

Esping-Andersen, G. (ed.). 1996. *Welfare States in Transition: National Adaptations in Global Economies*. London: Sage Publications.

Esping-Andersen, G. 1999. *Social Foundations of Postindustrial Economies*. Oxford: Oxford University Press.

European Commission. 1989. 'Report on Economic and Monetary Union [Delors Report]'. Brussels: Committee for the Study of Economic and Monetary Union, European Council.

European Commission. 1990. 'One Market, One Money'. *European Economy*, No. 46. Luxembourg: Office for Official Publications of the EC.

European Commission. 1993a. *Eurobarometer*. Nos 39–56. Luxembourg: Office for Official Publications of the EC.

European Commission. 1993b. 'The Economics of Community Public Finances'. *European Economy*, No. 51. Luxembourg: Office for Official Publications of the EC.

European Commission. 1996. 'Economic Trend – 1996'. *European Economy-Supplement A*, No. 9. Luxembourg: Office for Official Publications of the EC.

European Commission. 1998a. 'Commission's Recommendation Concerning the Third Stage of Economic and Monetary Union. Convergence Report 1998'. *European Economy*, No. 65. Luxembourg: Office for Official Publications of the EC.

European Commission. 1998b. 'The Commission's Autumn 1998 Forecasts for 1998–2000'. *European-Economy. Supplement A. Economic Trends*, No. 10. Luxembourg: Office for Official Publications of the EC.

European Commission. 1999. *Annual Economic Report*. Luxembourg: Office for Official Publications of the EC.

European Commission. 2000a. DG ECFIN. AMECO-Macroeconomic Database: 1960–2001. Brussels.
European Commission. 2000b. 'Public Finances in EMU-2000'. *European Economy – Report and Studies*. No. 3. Luxembourg: Office for Official Publications of the EC.
European Commission. 2000c. 'The EU Economy: 2000 Review'. *European Economy*, No. 71. Luxembourg: Office for Official Publications of the EC.
European Commission. 2001. 'The Contribution of Public Finances to Growth and Employment: Improving Quality and Sustainability'. *Commission's Communication to the Council*. COM (2000) 846 final. Brussels. Partially published in *European Economy – Reports and Studies*, No. 1. Supplement A.
European Commission. 2001b. 'Public Finances in EMU-2001'. *European Economy – Report and Studies*. No. 3. Luxembourg: Office for Official Publications of the EC.
European Commission. 2001c. 'EMU: the First To Years'. *Euro Papers*. No. 42. Luxembourg: Office for Official Publications of the EC.
European Commission 2003. 'Public Finances in EMU-2003'. *European Economy Report and Studies*, no. 3.
El País. 2002. 'Tony Blair sube impuestos para mejorar la sanidad pública'. Economics section, Thursday 18 April.
Ferejohn, J. 1986. 'Incumbent Performance and Electoral Control'. *Public Choice*, 50: 5–25.
Fiorina, M. 1981. *Retrospective Voting in American National Elections*. New Haven: Yale University Press.
Ford, R. 1998. 'Fiscal Consolidation, Growth and Equity'. *The OECD Observer*, 210: 37–44.
Frain, M.T. and Viarda, H. 1998. 'Conservative Parties in Democratic Transitions: The Center Right in Spain and Portugal'. In F.L. Wilson (ed.), *The European Center-Right at the End of the Twentieth Century*. New York: St Martin's Press, pp. 199–224.
Franzese, R.J. 2003. *Macroeconomic Policies of Developed Democracies*. Cambridge: Cambridge University Press.
Freeman, R. 2000. 'Single Peaked vs. Diversified Capitalism: The Relation Between Economic Institutions and Outcomes'. NBER Working Paper, No. 7556. Cambridge, MA: National Bureau of Economic Research.
Freitag, M. and Scianni, P. 2001. 'The Political Economy of Budget Deficits in the European Union. The Role of International Constraints and Domestic Structure'. *EUP Issues*, 2(2).
Frey, B. and Schneider, F. 1978. 'A Politico-Economic model of the U.K', *Economic Journal*, 88: 243–53.
Frieden, J. 1991. 'Invested Interests: The Politics of National Economic Policies in a World of Global Finance'. *International Organization*, 45: 425–51.
Frieden, J. and Rogowski, R. 1994. 'The Impact of the International Economy on National: An Analytical Overview'. Harvard University. Mimeo.
Frieden, J., Gros, D. and Jones, E. (eds) 1998. *The New Political Economy of EMU*. New York: Rowman & Littlefield.
Gamble, A. and Kelly, G. 2001. 'The British Labour Party and Monetary Union'. In T. Notermans (ed.), *Social Democracy and Monetary Union*. New York: Berghahn Books, pp. 47–70.
García, S. and Hénin, P.-Y. 1999. 'Balancing Budget Through Tax Increases or Expenditure Cuts: Is it Neutral?' *Economic Modelling*, 16: 591–612.
Garrett, G. 1998. *Partisan Politics in the Global Economy*. Cambridge: Cambridge University Press.
Gemmell, N. and Kneller, R. 2001. 'The Impact of Fiscal Policy on Long-Run Growth'. *European Economy*, 1: 101–29.

Gerson, P. 1998. 'The Impact of Fiscal Policy Variables on Output Growth'. *Working Papers*. International Monetary Fund. WP/98/1.

Giavazzi, F., Jappelli, T. and Pagano, M. 1999. 'Searching for Non-Keynesian Effects of Fiscal Policy: Evidence from Industrial and Developing Countries'. Mimeo. *IGIER*.

Giavazzi, F., Jappelli T. and Pagano, M. 2000. 'Searching for Non-Linear Effects of Fiscal Policy: Evidence from Industrial and Developing Countries'. *National Bureau of Economic Research*. Working Paper Series, No. 7460: 1–36.

Giavazzi, F. and Pagano, M. 1990. 'Can Severe Fiscal Contractions be Expansionary?' *NBER Macroeconomics Annual*: 75–116.

Giavazzi, F. and Pagano, M. 1996. 'Non-Keynesian Effects of Fiscal Policy Changes: International Evidence and the Swedish Experience'. *Swedish Economic Policy Review*, 3: 67–103.

Giddens, A. 1999. *La Tercera Via: La Renovación de la Social Democracia*. Madrid: Taurus.

Giordano, F. and Persaud, S. 1998. *The Political Economy of Monetary Union*. London and New York: Routledge.

Gleich, H. 2003. 'Budget Institutions and Fiscal Performance in Central and Eastern European Countries', ECB Working Paper, no. 215.

Glyn, A. 1998. 'The Assessment: Economic Policy and Social Democracy'. *Oxford Review of Economic Policy*, 14.

Golden, M. 1993. 'The Dynamics of Trade Unionism and National Economic Performance', *American Political Science Review*, 89: 439–54.

González-Páramo, J.M. 1994. 'Tax and Spend or Spend and Tax? Causality Between Revenues and Expenditures and the Size of the Public Budget in Spain, 1955–1991'. *European Economy (Reports and Studies)*, 3: 166–70.

González-Páramo, J.M. 1997. 'Política fiscal y convergencia macroeconómica: ¿Quién teme la disciplina presupuestaria?' In J.A. Nieto (ed.), *La economía española ante la Unión Económica y Monetaria*. Madrid: Síntesis, pp. 69–86.

González-Páramo, J.M. 1998. 'Disciplina fiscal e instituciones presupuestarias ante la Unión Económica y Monetaria', *Revista de Estudios Europea*, 19: 13–18.

González-Páramo, J.M. 2001. 'Costes y Beneficios de la Disciplina Fiscal: La Ley de Estabilidad Presupuestaria en Perspectiva'. *Estudios de Hacienda Pública*. Madrid: Instituto de Estudios Fiscales.

Gordo and Hernándes de Cos, 2000. 'The Financing Arrangements for the Regional (Autonomus) Governments for the Period 1997–2001'. Universidad de Alicante, Dept. Análisis Económico: Documento de Trabajo, No. 2000–3.

Gottschalk, P., Gustaffson, B. and Palmer, E. (eds) 1997. *The Distribution of Economic Welfare in the 1980s: An Economic Perspective*. Cambridge: Cambridge University Press.

Grieco, J. 1988. 'Anarchy and the Limits of Cooperation: A Realist Critique of the Newest Liberal Institutionalism', *International Organization*, 42: 485–507.

Grilli, V., Masciandaro, D. and Tabellini, G. 1991. 'Institutions and Policies: Political and Monetary Institutions and Public Financial Policies in the Industrial Countries'. *Economic Policy*, 13: 341–92.

Gupta, S., Clements, B., Baldacci, E. and Mulas-Granados, C. 2005. 'Fiscal Policy Expenditure Composition, and Growth in Low Income Countries'. *Journal of International Money and Finance*, 24: 441–63.

Haar, J.H. 2001. 'Pleasing the Voters or Maximizing Influence? The Danish SDP and European Monetary Integration'. In T. Notermans (ed.), *Social Democracy and Monetary Union*. New York: Berghahn Books, pp. 175–202.

Haas, E.B. 1958. *The Uniting of Europe*. Stanford, CA: Stanford University Press.

Hall, P. 1986. *Governing the Economy: The Politics of State Intervention in Britain and France*. Oxford: Oxford University Press.

Halleberg, M. 2000a. 'The Role of Parliamentary Committees in the Budgetary Process within Europe'. In R. Strauch and J. Von Hagen (eds), *Institutions, Politics and Fiscal Policy*. Boston: Kluwer Academic Publishers, pp. 87–106.

Halleberg, M. 2000b. 'The Importance of Domestic Political Institutions: Why and How Belgium and Italy Qualified to EMU'. *ZEI Working Paper*, B10-2000. Bonn: ZEI.

Halleberg, M. 2004. '*Domestic Budgets in a United Europe. Fiscal Governance from the End of Bretton Woods to EMU*', Ithaca, NY: Cornell University Press.

Halleberg, M. and Von Hagen, J. 1997. 'Electoral Institutions, Cabinet Negotiations and Budget Deficits in the European Union'. *CEPR WP*, 1555.

Halleberg, M. and Von Hagen, J. 1999. 'Electoral Institutions, Cabinet Negotiations, and Budget Deficits in the European Union'. In J.M. Poterba and J. Von Hagen (eds), *Fiscal Institutions and Fiscal Performance*. Chicago: The University of Chicago Press, pp. 209–32.

Hannon, P. 2001. 'EU Deficits Widening, But May Be Temporary'. *Dow Jones Euronomics*. London, 27 June.

Harding, S.G. 1976. *Can Theories Be Refuted?: Essays on the Duhem-Quine Thesis*. Boston: D. Reidel Publication Company.

Harrington, J.E., Jr. 1993. 'Economic Policy, Economic Performance, and Elections', *American Economic Review*, 83: 27–42.

Hellwig, M. and Neumann, M.J.M. 1987. 'Economic Policy in Germany: Was There a Turn-Around', *Economic Policy*, 5: 103–46.

Herce, J.A., Sosvilla-Rivero, S. and de Lucio, J.J. 2001. 'Growth and the Welfare State in the EU: A Causality Analysis', *Public Choice*, 109: 55–68.

Hibbs, D. 1977. 'Political Parties and Macroeconomic Policies', *American Political Science Review*, 71: 1467–87.

Hibbs, D. 1987. *The American Political Economy*. Harvard University Press.

Howarth, D. 2000. *The French Road to Monetary Union*. London: Palgrave.

Huttner, 1999. 'Reforms in the Budget Process: the Austrian Case'. The University of Innsbruck. Economics Department: Working Paper, 99/12.

International Monetary Fund. 2000. 'The Effectiveness of Fiscal Policy in Stimulating Economic Activity: A Review of the Literature'. Internal Document. Prepared by the Fiscal Affairs Department, Washington.

Iversen, T. 1998. 'The Choices for Scandinavian Social Democracy in Comparative Perspective'. *Oxford Review of Economic Policy*, 14(1): 59–75.

Jacobs, L.R. and Shapiro, R.Y. 2000. *Politicians Don't Pander: Political Manipulation and the Loss of Democratic Responsiveness*. Chicago: Chicago University Press.

Jones, E. Frieden, J. A. and Torres, F. S. 1998. *Joining Europe's Monetary Club*. New York: St. Martin's Press.

Jones, L.E., Manuelli, R.E. and Rossi, P.E. 1993. 'On the Optimal Taxation of Capital Income'. NBER Working Paper, No. 4525.

Judd, K. 1995. 'On the Performance of Patents', *Econometrica*, 53(3): 567–85.

Judt, T. 1997. 'Continental Rift'. *The New York Times*, New York, 5 June.

Kaplan, E.L. and Meier, P. 1958. 'Nonparametric Estimation for Incomplete Observations'. *Journal of American Statistical Association*, 53: 457–81.

Kaufman, R. and Segura-Ubiergo, A. 2001. 'Globalization, Domestic Politics and Social Spending in Latin America: A Time-Series Cross Section Analysis', *World Politics*, 53(4): 53–587.

Keohane, R.O. 1984. *After Hegemony*. Princeton, NJ: Princeton University Press.

Keohane, R.O. and Hoffmann, S. 1991. 'Institutional Change in Europe in the 1980s'. In Keohane and Hoffmann (eds), *The New European Community: Decision-making and Institutional Change*. Boulder, CO: Westview Press.

Key, V.O. Jr. 1966. *The Responsible Electorate*. New York: Vintage.

Kiefer, N.M. 1988. 'Economic Duration Data and Hazard Functions', *Journal of Economic Literature*, 26: 646–79.

King, G., Keohane, R.O. and Verba, S. 1994. *Designing Social Inquiry: Scientific Inference in Qualitative Research*. Princeton, NJ: Princeton University Press.

King, R.G. and Rebelo, S. 1990. 'Public Policy and Economic Growth: Developing Neoclassical Implications'. NBER Working Paper, No. 3338.

Klingemann, H.D., Hofferbert, R. and Budge, I. 1994. *Parties, Politics and Democracy*. Boulder, CO: Westview Press.

Kmenta, J. 1986. *Elements of Econometrics* New York, NY: Macmillan.

Kneller, R., Bleaney, M. and Gemmell, N. 1999 'Fiscal Policy and Growth: Evidence from OECD Countries' *Journal of Public Economics*, 74: 171–90.

Kraemer, M. 1997. 'Electoral Budget Cycles in Latin America and the Caribbean: Incidence, Causes and Political Futility'. *Inter American Development Bank*, Working Paper No. 354. Washington, DC.

Krafchik, W. and Wehner, J. 1999. 'The Role of Parliament in the Budget Process'. Budget Information Service: Institute for Democracy in South Africa.

Kramer, G.H. 1983. 'The Ecological Fallacy Revisited: Aggregated versus Individual Level Findings on Economics and Elections and Sociotropic Voting', *American Political Science Review*, 77(1): 92–111.

Krugman, P. 2001. 'The Levitating Dollar'. *The New York Times*, New York; 1 April.

Kuznets, S. 1955. 'Economic Growth and Income Inequality', *American Economic Review*, 45(1): 1–28.

Lancaster, T.D. and Lewis-Beck, M.S. 1986. 'The Spanish Voter: Tradition, Economics, and Ideology'. *Journal of Politics*, 48(3): 648–74.

Lane, T.D. and Perotti, R. 1996. 'Profitability, Fiscal Policy, and Exchange Rate Regimes'. *CEPR Discussion Paper*, No. 1449. London: Centre for Economic Policy Research.

Laswell, H. 1936. *Politics: Who Gets What, When, and How*. New York: McGraw-Hill.

Levitt, M. and Lord, C. 2000. *The Political Economy of Monetary Union* Basingstoke: Palgrave. Oatley, T.H. 1998. *Monetary Politics: Exchange Rate Cooperation in the European Union*. Ann Arbor: The University of Michigan Press.

Lewis-Beck, M.S. 1988. *Economics and Elections: The Major Western Democracies*. Ann Arbor: University of Michigan Press.

Lewis-Beck, M.S. and Mitchell, G. 1990. 'Transnational Models of Economic Voting: Tests from a Western European Pool'. *Revista del Instituto de Estudios Economicos*, 4: 65–81.

Licandro O., Goicolea, A. and Maroto, R. 1999. 'Inversión y progreso técnico en el sector industrial de la Comunidad de Madrid'. *Papeles de Economía Española, Economía de las Comunidades Autónomas*. 18: 212–24.

Lindbeck, A. 1994. 'Overshooting, Reform and Retreat of the Welfare State'. *De Economist*, 142(1): 1–19.

Lindblom, C. 1977. *Politics and Markets*. New York: Basic Books.

Lipset, S.M. 1961. *Political Man*. Baltimore: Johns Hopkins University Press.

Lowry, R.C., Alt, J.E. and Ferree, K.E. 1998. 'Fiscal Policy Outcomes and Electoral Accountability in American States', *The American Political Science Review*, 92(4): 759–74.

Lucas, R.E. 1975. 'An Equilibrium Model of Business Cycle', *Journal of Political Economy*, 83: 1113–44.

Lucas, R.E. 1988. 'on the Mechanisms of Economic Development: W.A. Mackintosh Lecture, 1985', *Journal of Monetary Economics*, 22: 3–42.
Lucas, R.E. and Stokey, N.L. 1983. 'Optimal Fiscal and Monetary Policy in an Economy Without Capital'. *Journal of Monetary Economics*, 12: 55–94.
Maravall, J.M. 1997. *Regimes, Politics and Markets*. Oxford: Oxford University Press.
Maravall, J.M. 1998. 'Accountability and Manipulation'. In A. Przeworski, S.C. Stokes and B. Manin (eds), *Democracy, Accountability and Representation*. Cambridge: Cambridge University Press.
Maravall, J.M. and Przeworski, A. 1998. 'Political Reactions to the Economy: The Spanish Experience'. Instituto Juan March. Working Paper 1998/127.
Markus, G.B. 1988. 'The Impact of Personal and National Income Conditions on the Presidential Voting: 1956–88'. *American Journal of Political Science*, 36: 829–34.
Markus, G.B. 1992. 'The Influence of Personal and National Conditions on Presidential Voting, 1956–88'. *American Journal of Political Science*, 36(3): 829–35.
Maroto, R. and Mulas-Granados, C. 2001. 'Duration of Fiscal Consolidations in the European Union'. *FEDEA–Documento de Trabajo*. No. 19/2001.
Maroto, R. and Mulas-Granados, C. 2002. 'The Duration of Budgetary Consolidations in the European Union'. *European Economy Group Working Paper*, No. 18/2002. Universidad Complutense de Madrid. (forthcoming in *Public Choice* 2007).
Mauro, P. and Spilimbergo, A. 2001. 'Physical Capital Adjustment within Spain: Long-Run and Short-Run Analysis'. *IMF Working Paper*. WP/01/17. Washington, DC: International Monetary Fund.
McCloughan, P. and Stone, I. 1998. 'Life Duration of Foreign Multinational Subsidiaries: Evidence from UK Northern Manufacturing Industry 1970–93'. *International Journal of Industrial Organization*, 16: 719–47.
McDermott, C. and Wescott, J.R.F. 1996. 'An Empirical Analysis of Fiscal Adjustments'. *IMF Staff Papers*, 43: 725–53.
McRae, D. 1977., 'A Political Model of the Business Cycle', *Journal of Political Economy*, 85: 239–63.
Mélitz, J. 1997. 'The Cost an Benefits of a Common Monetary Policy in France and Germany and Possible Lessons for Monetary Union'. *European University Institute*, Working Paper, No. 37.
Mendoza, E., Milesi-Ferretti, G.M. and Asea, P. 1997. 'On The Ineffectiveness of Tax Policy in Altering Long-run Growth: Harberger's Superneutrality Conjecture'. *Journal of Public Economics*, 66: 99–126.
Merkel, W. 1995. *Final de la socialdemocracia? Recursos de poder y política de gobierno de los partidos socialdemócratas en Europa occidental*. Valencia: Alfons el Magnánim.
Merkel, W. 2001. 'The Third Ways of Social Democracy'. In A. Giddens (ed.), *The Global Third Way Debate*. Cambridge: Cambridge University Press, pp. 50–73.
Milesi-Ferretti, G.M., Perotti, R. and Rostagno, M. 2001. 'Electoral Systems and the Composition of Government Spending'. *CEPR Discussion Papers*, 2742: 1–49.
Ministério da Economia de Portugal. 1997. *Convergence Report*. Lisbon: Ministério da Economia de Portugal.
Molander, P. 2001. 'Budgeting Procedures and Democratic Ideals: An Evaluation of Swedish Reforms'. *Journal of Public Policy*, 21: 1–23.
Moravcsik, A. 1991. 'Negotiating the Single European Act: National Interests and Conventional Statecraft in the European Community'. *International Organization*, 45: 19–56.
Mueller, J. 1970. 'Presidential Popularity from Truman to Johnson'. *American Political Science Review*, 64: 18–34.

Mulas-Granados, C. 2002a. 'The Political Economy of Fiscal Adjustments in the European Union'. *Institute Juan March, Working Paper Series*. No. 2002/174.

Mulas-Granados, C. 2002b. 'Elecciones, partidos políticos y política fiscal'. *Firmas, Diario Expansión*. 8 November.

Mulas-Granados, C. 2003a. 'The Political and Economic Determinants of Budgetary Consolidations in Europe'. *European Political Economy Review*, 1(1): 25–39.

Mulas-Granados, C. 2003b. 'The Trade-Off between Growth and Equality and the Economic Impact of Alternative Fiscal Adjustment Strategies'. *European Economy Group Working Paper*, No. 23/2003. Universidad Complutense de Madrid.

Mulas-Ganados, C. 2004. 'Voting Against Spending Cuts. The Electoral Costs of Fiscal Adjustments in Europe'. *Europe Union Politics*, 5(4): 467–493.

Mulas-Ganados, C. 2005. 'Fiscal Adjustments and the Short-Term Trade-of-Between Economic Growth and Equality'. *Hacienda Pública Española*, 172-(I/2005): 61–92.

Mulas-Ganados, C., Onzubia, J. and Salinas, J. 2006. 'An Enlarged EMU? The Procedural Sources of Fiscal Policy in the New Member States'. *International Journal of Public Policy* 1(3): 279–96.

Mundell, R. 1962. 'A Theory of Optimum Currency Areas', *American Economic Review*, 51: 657–65.

Murphy, K.M., Shleifer, A. and Vishny, R.W. 1989. 'Industralization and the Big Push', *Journal of Political Economy*, 97: 1003–26.

Musgrave, R.A. 1959. *The Theory of Public Finance: a Study in Public Economy*. New York: McGraw-Hill.

Nelson, J.M 1993. 'Stabilization, Growth and Equity: The Narrowing Parameters of Debate'. In V.P. Nanda, G.W. Shepherd and E. McCarthy-Arnolds (eds), *World Development and the Human Condition: Structural Adjustment and the Right to Development*. London: Greenwood Press.

Nelson, W. 1972. 'Theory and Applications of Hazard Plotting for Censored Failure Data', *Technometrics*, 14: 945–65.

Nordhaus, W.D. 1975. 'The Political Business Cycle', *Review of Economic Studies*, 43(2): 169–90.

Nordhaus, W.D. 1989. 'Alternative Approaches to the Political Business Cycle'. *Brookings Papers on Economic Activity*, 2: 1–68.

Norpoth, H., Lewis-Beck, M.S. and Lafay, J. (eds) 1991. *Economics and Politics: the Calculus of Support*. Ann Arbor: University of Michigan Press.

Notermans, T. 2000. *Money, Markets and the State. Social Democratic Policies Since 1918*. Cambridge: Cambridge University Press.

Notermans, T. (ed.) 2001a. *Social Democracy and Monetary Union*. New York: Berghahn Books.

Notermans, T. 2001b. 'The German Social Democrats and Monetary Union'. In T. Notermans (ed.), *Social Democracy and Monetary Union*. New York: Berghahn Books, pp. 71–96.

Nye, J. 1988. 'Neorealism and Neoliberalism', *World Politics*, 40: 131–46.

Oatley, T. 1997. *Monetary Politics: Exchange Rate Cooperation in the European Union*. Ann Arbor: University of Michigan Press.

Obstfeld, M. and Eichengreen, B. 1998. 'The Political Economy of Fiscal Adjustments: Comments and Discussion', *Brookings Papers on Economic Activity*, 1: 249–66.

Oliver, J., Ramos. X. and Raymond, J.L. 2001. 'Recent Trends in Spanish Income Distribution: A Robert Picture of Falling Income Inequality'. Universidad Autonoma de Barcelona Working Papers, 01.07.

Olson, M. 1982. *The rise and decline of nations*. New Haven, Connecticut: Yale University Press.

Organization for Economic Cooperation and Development. 1992, 1993, 1995, 1998, 1999. *Economic Survey*. Paris: OECD.

Organization for Economic Cooperation and Development. 1996. 'The Experience with Fiscal Consolidations in OECD Countries'. *Economic Outlook* (June): 33–41. Paris: OECD.

Organization for Economic Cooperation and Development. 1999. *Economic Outlook*. December. Paris.

Pacek, A. and Radcliff, B. 1995. 'Economic Voting and the Welfare State: A Cross-National Analysis'. *Journal of Politics*, 57: 44–61.

Padoa-Schioppa, 1988. 'The European Monetary System: A Long-Term View'. In F. Giavazzi, S. Micossi and M. Miller (eds), *The European Monetary System*. Cambridge: Cambridge University Press, pp. 373–6.

Paldam, M. 1986. 'The Distribution of Electoral Results and the Two Explanations of the Cost of Ruling'. *European Journal of Political Economy*, 2: 5–24.

Paldam, M. 1991. 'How Robust is the Vote Function?: A Study of Seventeen Nations over Four Decades'. In H. Norpoth, M.S. Lewis-Beck and J. Lafay (eds), *Economics and Politics: The Calculus of Support*. Ann Arbor: University of Michigan Press.

Parks, R. 1967. 'Efficient Estimation of a Series of Equations When Disturbances are Both Serially and Contemporaneously Correlated'. *Journal of the American Statistical Association*, 62: 500–9.

Pasquino, G. 1994. 'Shaping a Better Republic? The Italian Case in a Comparative Perspective', *Working Paper*, 62. Madrid: Instituto Juan March de Estudios e Investigaciones.

Pekkarinen, J. 2001. 'Finnish Social Democrats and EMU'. In T. Notermans (ed.), *Social Democracy and Monetary Union*. New York: Berghahn Books, pp. 123–48.

Peltzman, S. 1992. 'Voters as Fiscal Conservatives'. *Quarterly Journal of Economics*, 107: 327–61.

Perotti, R. 1996. 'Democracy, Income Distribution and Growth: What the Data Say?" *Journal of Economic Growth*, 1: 149–87.

Perotti, R. 1998. 'The Political Economy of Fiscal Consolidations'. *Scandinavian Journal of Economics*, 100(1): 367–94.

Perotti, R. 1999. 'Fiscal Policy in Good Times and Bad'. *Quarterly Journal of Economics*, 114(4): 1399–436.

Perotti, R. and Kontopoulos, Y. 2002. 'Fragmented Fiscal Policy'. *Journal of Public Economics*, 82(2): 191–222.

Persson, T. and Svensson, L.E. 1989. 'Why a Stubborn Conservative would Run a Deficit: Policy with Time-Inconsistent Preferences'. *Quarterly Journal of Economics*, May: 325–45.

Persson, T. and Tabellini, G. 1999. 'Political Economics and Public Finance'. In A. Auesrbach and M. Feldstein (eds), *Handbook of Public Economics. Vol III*. Amsterdam: North Holland.

Philippopoulus, A. and Tzavalis, E. 2001. 'Fiscal Policy and Politics: Theory and Evidence from Greece 1960–1997', *Economic Modelling*, 18(2): 253–68.

Poterba, J.M. 1994. 'State Responses to Fiscal Crises: The Effects of Budgetary Institutions and Politics'. *The Journal of Political Economy*, 102(4): 799–821.

Powell, G.B. Jr. and Whitten, G. 1993. 'A Cross-National Analysis of Economic Voting: Taking Account of the Political Context'. *American Journal of Political Science*, 37: 391–414.

Przeworski, A. 1986. *Capitalism and Social Democracy*. Cambridge: Cambridge University Press.

Przeworski, A. and Sprague, J. 1986. *Paper Stones: a History on Electoral Socialism.* Chicago: Chicago University Press.
Quine, W.V.O. 1963. *Set Theory and its Logic.* Cambridge: Belknap Press of Harvard University.
Rasmussen, 1997. "What Kind of Vision is That?" British Public Attitudes Towards the European Community During the Thatcher Era'. *British Journal of Political Science,* 27(1): 111–36.
Rattinger, H. 1991. 'Unemployment and Elections in West Germany'. In H. Norpoth M.S. Lewis-Beck and J. Lafay (eds), *Economics and Politics: The Calculus of Support.* Ann Arbor: University of Michigan Press.
Rees, A. 2000. 'One fits all in the EMU? One Monetary Policy for Eleven Countries', *Intereconomics,* 35 (4): 162–9.
Reland, J. 1998. 'France'. In J. Forder and A. Menon (eds), *The European Union and National Macroeconomic Policy.* New York: Routledge, pp. 85–104.
Riley, J. 1980. 'Strong Revolutionary Equilibrium and the War of Attrition'. *Journal of Theoretical Biology,* 82: 383–400.
Rogoff, K. 1990. 'Equilibrium Political Budget Cycles'. *American Economic Review,* 80(1): 21–36.
Rose, R. and Mackie, T. 1983. 'Incumbency in Government: Asset of Liability'. In H. Daalder and P. Maier (eds), *Western European Party Systems: Continuity and Change.* Beverly Hills: Sage.
Ross, G. 2001. 'French Social Democracy and EMU: Presidential Prose and Its Pitfalls'. In T. Notermans (ed.), *Social Democracy and Monetary Union.* New York: Berghahn Books, pp. 21–46.
Roubini, N. and Sachs, J.D. 1989a. 'Fiscal Policy: Government Spending and Budget Deficits in the Industrial Countries'. *Economic Policy,* 8: 99–132.
Roubini, N. and Sachs, J.D. 1989b. 'Political and Economic Determinants of Budget Deficits in the Industrial Democracies'. *European Economic Review,* 33: 903–38.
Ruíz-Huerta, J. 2001. 'Comparaciones internacionales de bienestar: Una aplicación con datos LIS'. *Papeles de Economía Española,* 88: 44–66.
Ruíz-Huerta, J. and Jiménez, A. (eds) 1993. 'Estructura institucional y gestión del gasto público en algunos países de la OCDE'. Madrid: Instituto de Estudios Fiscales.
Sanders, D., Ward, H. and Marsh, D. 1991. 'Macroeconomics, the Falklands War, and the Popularity of the Thatcher Government: A Contrary View'. In H. Norpoth, M.S. Lewis-Beck and J. Lafay (eds), *Economics and Politics: The Calculus of Support.* Ann Arbor: University of Michigan Press.
Sandholtz, W. 1993. 'Choosing Union: Monetary Politics and Maastricht', *International Organization* 47(10): 1–39.
Sargent, T. and Wallace, N. 1975. 'Rational Expectations, the Optimal Monetary Instrument, and the Optimal Money Supply Rule', *Journal of Political Economy,* 83: 241–54.
Scharpf, F.W. 'A Game-Theoretical Interpretation of Inflation and Unemployment in Western Europe', *Journal of Public Policy,* 7: 227–57.
Schmitter, P. 1970. 'A Revised Theory of Regional Integration', *International Organization,* 24(4): 836–68.
Schwim, O. 1997. *Die Finanzierung der deutchen Einheit.* Opladen: Leske and Budrich.
Smeeding, T. 1997. U.S. Income Inequality in a Cross-National Perspective: Why Are We So Different?. In J. Auerbach and R. Belous (eds), *The Inequality Paradox: Growth of Income Disparity.* Washington, DC: National Policy Association, pp. 194–217.

Smeeding, T. 2000. 'Changing Income Inequality in OECD Countries: Updated Results from the Luxembourg Income Study (LIS)'. *Luxembourg Income Study Working Paper*, No. 252.

Solow, R. 1956. 'A Contribution to the Theory of Economic Growth'. *Quarterly Journal of Economics*, 71(1): 65–94.

Sosvilla-Rivero, S. and Maroto, R. 2001. 'Duración de los Regímenes del SME'. *Fedea. Documento de Trabajo*, 2001–05.

Stienlet. 2000. 'Institutional Reforms and Belgian Fiscal Policy in the 90s'. In R. Strauch and J. Von Hagen (eds), *Institutions, Politics and Fiscal Policy*. Boston: Kluwer Academic Publishers.

Stiglitz, J.E. and Boadway, R.W. 1994. *Economics and the Canadian Economy*. New York: W.W. Norton & Company.

Stimson, J. 1985. 'Regression in Space and Time: A Statistical Essay'. *American Journal of Political Science*, 29: 914–47.

Strauch, R. 1999. 'Monitoring Fiscal Adjustments in the European Union and EMU'. Deutsches Bundesbank Discussion Paper, No. 1999/4

Sturm, R. 1998. 'Finanzpolitik am Endeoder vor der Wahl? Akteure, Instrumente und Blockaden in der Finanypolitik'. In U. Andersen (ed.), *Der Deutsche Steuerstaat in der Finazkrise*. Schwalbach: Wochenschau Verlag.

Swan, T.W. 1956. 'Economic Growth and Capital Accumulation'. *Economic Record*, 32(3): 334–61.

Tanzi, V. and Chu, K.Y. (eds) 1998. *Income Distribution and High-Quality Growth*. Cambridge: MIT Press.

Tanzi, V., Chu, K.Y. and Gupta, S. (eds) 1999. *Economic Policy and Equity*. Washington, DC: International Monetary Fund.

Tanzi, V. and Zee, H.H. 1997. 'Fiscal Policy and Long-Run Growth'. *IMF Staff Papers*, 44: 3–15.

Tavares, J. 2004. 'Does Right or Left Matter? Cabinets, Credibility and Fiscal Adjustments', *Journal of Public Economics*, 88(12): 2447–68.

The Economist. 1997. 'Kicking and Screaming into 1999', London, 7 June, 19–21.

The Europa World Yearbook. London: Europa Publications.

The New York Times. 1997. 'Insecure or Jobless. Europeans Renew Protests'. New York, 25 March, 4.

Thiel, E. and Shroeder, I. 1998. 'Germany'. In J. Forder and A. Menon (eds), *The European Union and National Macroeconomic Policy*. London and New York: Routledge, pp. 105–18.

Thygesen, Niels. 1999. 'Fiscal institutions in EMU and the Stability Pact'. In Hallett., A.H. Hutchison, M.M. and Jensen, S. (eds.) *Fiscal Aspects of European Monetary Integration*. New York: Cambridge University Press.

Time Europe. 1997. 'Losing Bet', 16 June.

Tufte, E.R. 1978. *Political Control of the Economy*. Princeton: Princeton University Press.

Von Hagen, J. 1992. 'Budgeting Institutions and Fiscal Performance', *Economic Papers Series*. Brussels: European Commission.

Von Hagen, J., Hallett, A.H. and Strauch, R. 2001. 'Budgetary Consolidation in EMU' *Economics Papers*, 148 Brussels: European Commission.

Von Hagen, J. and Harden, I.J. 1995. 'Budget Processes and Commitment to Fiscal Discipline', *European Economic Review*, 39: 771–9.

Von Hagen, J. and Lutz, S. 1996. 'Fiscal and Monetary Policy on the Way to EMU', *Open Economies Review*, 7: 299–325.

Von Hagen, J. and Strauch, R. 1999. 'Tumbling Giant: Germany's Experience with the Maastricht Fiscal Criteria'. In D. Cobham and G. Zis (eds), *From EMS to EMU: 1979 to 1999 and Beyond*. New York: St Martin's Press, pp. 70–94.

Weingast, B., Shepsle, K. and Johnson, C. 1981. 'The Political Economy of Benefits and Costs: A Neoclassical Approach to Redistributive Politics'. *Journal of Political Economy*, 89: 642–64.

Wihlborg, C. and Willett, T.D. 1993. 'Optimal Currency Areas Revisited'. In C. Wihlborg, M. Fratianni and T. Willett (eds), *Financial Regulations and Monetary Arrangements After 1992*. Amsterdam: North Holland.

Winkler, B. 1995. 'Reputation for EMU: An Economic Defence of the Maastricht Criteria'. *European University Institute Working Paper*, No. 95/18.

Woldendorp, J., Keman, H. and Budge, I. 1998. 'Party Government in 20 Democracies since 1945: an Update (1990–1995)'. *European Journal of Political Research*, 33(1): 1–16.

Woldendorp, J., Keman, H. and Budge, I. 2000. *Party Government in 48 Democracies (1945–1998): Composition–Duration–Personnel*. London: Kluwer Academic Publishers.

World Income Inequality Database (WIID). 2000. By the World Institute for Economic and Development Research at the United Nations University.

Wyplosz, C. 1999. 'EMU: Why and How It Might Happen', *CEPR Discussion Papers*, 1685.

Yläoutinen, S. 2004. 'Fiscal Frameworks in the Central and Eastern European Countries', Ministry of Finance of Finland, Discussion Paper, no.72.

Index

Notes: f = figure; n = note; t = table; **bold** = extended discussion or heading emphasized in main text.

The manufacturer's authorised representative in the EU is Springer Nature Customer Service Centre GmbH, Europaplatz 3, 69115 Heidelberg, Germany. If you have any concerns regarding our products, please contact ProductSafety@springernature.com

Printed and bound by CPI Group (UK) Ltd, Croydon, CR0 4YY

10/10/2026

02231228-0011